CIVIL WAR AUTOGRAPHS

& MANUSCRIPTS

PRICES CURRENT

**Listing every Confederate and Union General,
Confederate and Union Cabinet members.
Plus many Marine Corps & Naval Officers, Artists,
Photographers, Nurses and others relevant to
the "War between the States."**

by
Ronald Roy Seagrave

ISBN 0-9632137-2-5

Manufactured in the United States of America

2nd Edition

While supplies last, the price of this volume is \$32.95 postpaid within the United States. Foreign purchasers are requested to write for shipping charges. Requests for information and all other correspondence should be sent to:

Sgt. Kirkland's Museum & Historical Society
912 Lafayette Blvd.
Fredericksburg, Virginia 22401
703-899-5565

This volume is dedicated
to my father, LeRoy K. Seagrave
with a profound sense of sorrow and loss.

He passed into God's hands
on Dec., 13, 1993.[1]

My father always brought joy and comfort to his family and friends, from the battlefields of Europe during World War II to his very last day. His warmth and kindness could always be felt. His lost leaves an enormous void that will never be filled.

Ronald Roy Seagrave

---

[1]. Sgt. Richard R. Kirkland, 2nd S.C.I., brought aid and comfort to his enemy on this day 131 years ago, on that very same day, Dec., 13, 1862, at Fredericksburg, Va. It was in his name we formed the Sgt. Kirkland's Musuem & Historical Society of Fredericksburg, Va.

And to my family ancestors who fought on both sides of the War between the States. Wanted any material related to any of these individuals or regiments:

Rebels...

Calvin Seagrave, Pvt., Co. G., 1st North Carolina Infantry.
Wounded at Sharpsburg. Captured in Hospital at Richmond, Va., April 3, 1865 and transferred to Newport News, Va. as POW released June 30, 1865.

James Seagrave, Pvt., Co. G., 1st North Carolina Infantry.
Captured, paroled Sharpsburg, Md. Sept. 1862; Captured Spotsylvania Court House May 12, 1864 - POW (1) Point Lookout, Md., then Elmira, NY from Aug. 1864 - June 12, 1865.

Thomas Seagrave, Pvt., Co. G., 1st North Carolina Infantry.
Wounded at Chancellorsville, Va., Captured at Farmville, Va. April 6, 1865 - June 19,1865 POW at Point Lookout, Md.

William H. Seagrave, Pvt., Co. G., 1st North Carolina Infantry.
Captured at Sharpsburg Sept. 28, 1862 - Aug. 1863 POW at Fort McHenry, Baltimore, Md. Died Aug. 1863 while a POW of the Yankee's.

Yankees...

Alpheus Mason Seagrave, Pvt., Co. H., 4th Reg't R. I. Vols.

Charles Stowe Seagrave, Pvt., Co. H., 25th Reg't Mass. Vols.,
In May 14, 1865 With 27 men took charge of the rebel archives in Charlotte, N. C. and delivered them to Maj. Gen. Schofield.

David Walker Seagrave, Pvt., 2nd Kansas Regiment of Infantry.
Wounded at Wilson's Creek.

Edward Fletcher Seagrave, of California, Pvt., 2nd Mass. Cavalry
Wounded at Cedar Creek.

Henry Merritt Seagrave, Pvt., Co. G, 42nd Reg't Mass. Vols. Inf.

James Ross Seagrave, Corp'l, 42nd Reg't Mass Vols. Inf.

Gilbert Henry Seagrave, Pvt., Co. C, 43rd Reg't Mass. Vols. Inf.

George Legard Seagrave, 1st Lt., 36th Reg't U. S. Colored Troops.
[Prior Pv't Co.A, 25th Reg't Mass. Vols.]

John Newton Seagrave, Pvt., Co. D, 62nd Reg't Mass. Vols. Inf.

Joseph William Seagrave, Pvt., 9th R. I. Reg't of Infantry 1862 & U.S. Signal Corps 64/65

Lawson Augustus Seagrave, Corp'l, Co. H., 15th Reg't Mass. Vols.
Wounded in the leg at Antietam.

Clinton Seagrave, Pvt., Co. G, Mass. Vet. Reserve Corps.

Wellington Seagrave, Pvt., Co. H, 25th Reg't Conn. Vols.

William Henry Seagrave, Capt., Co. K, 30th U.S. Colored Troops.
Died 3 Nov. 1865, Uxbridge, Ma., of wounds received 30 July 64 at the Battle of the Crater, Petersburg, VA. taken prisoner & sent to the Poplar Lawn Hospital, Petersburg, Va., Transferred to prison on Sept. 18, 1864, paroled Oct. 8,1864. [Prior Pv't Co. H., 25th Reg't Mass. Vols. till Feb. 1864.]

Orville Barton Seagrave, Paymaster in the U.S. Navy 1863-6

ACKNOWLEDGMENTS

It would be an impossible task for me to name all the generous friends and associates who helped me in the creation of this book. But I should like to express my appreciation to some of those who contributed to this edition an the earlier edition: the staffs of the National Archives and the Virginia Historical Society, Dr. Francis Lord, Berry Smith, K. C. Owings, Jr., David Zullo, Dug Sanders, Jim Hayes, Lewis Leigh, Jr., Joe Rubinfine, Don Nidiffer, Brian Green and many others.

In writing the present revision, I received enthusiastic cooperation from many dealers and auctioneers whose superb, illustrated catalogs provided me with a huge source of scarce or unusual signatures. My book is now, and will always be, at their disposal.

Finally, I must fondly recognize the love and support of Pat, who listen perceptively to my ideas, and endured this project too long.

INTRODUCTION

In the 1815 - 1914 period, nothing else in the world compared to the War between the States. The North-South conflict was the biggest thing that had ever touched the lives of Americans. Naturally, those participants with the ability to do so wrote about it, usually to a copious degree; since American armies of the 1860s contained the most literate soldiers in history to that point, a flood of letters, diaries, and reminiscences gushed forth. The home folk were as responsive as conditions would allow.

Censorship was non-existent in during the War between the States. Northerners and Southerners alike wrote what they felt. Their opinions, for the most part, were many and strong; they encompassed every facet of life. That is why Civil War literature provides perhaps the keenest, most honest insights of any era in American social history. Certainly no other war was blessed with anything akin to the volume of personal narratives.

Many changes have occurred since the last edition of this reference guide. I have average signatures, signatures with rank, pre. & post war documents, war dated documents, pre. & post war autographed letters signed and those that are war dated.

Many factors determine what a document or autograph is worth; date, content, condition, daily market demand, personalities of those involved, etc. Most important is the actual content of any letter or document, which has a relative value scale all it's own.

The prices averaged herein have been compiled through April 1994. This updated edition includes virtually hundreds of additional military and civilian personalities, plus several signature examples. The previous edition of this text published in May 1992 should continue to serve as a valuable reference.

Yearly price averages are statistical averages based on the selling price alone. Averages are based on at least four references each and serve merely as a basic reference point. Data is often not available to average all of the names herein recorded. Blank spaces are offered so that you may insert a future price or make your own notations. A few of these figures quoted herein were at 'wholesale.' A few dealers still turn their stock over in hours or within a few days. Their figures are simply history, usually the day their catalogs or lists hit the streets.

War dated material has become even harder to locate and purchase in today's market. Rarer manuscripts are often sold through a well-established network of individuals and fax machines. Generally signatures offered on today's market are generally post or prewar. I have attempted to give some interesting examples of extreme rarity offered either at auction or through private sales.

Do not assume the material averaged was war dated material with great content, specially if the averages seem low for that signer.

Lastly, as Mr. Lewis Leigh, Jr., often states "content can be everything!"

WRITING IT UP.

WAR BETWEEN THE STATES

"The Congressional Record of March 2, 1928, reports Senate joint resolution No. 41 wherein Congress recognized the title "War between the States as proper.""

A war was waged from 1861 to 1865 between two organized governments; the United States of America, and the Confederate States of America. These were the official titles of the contending parties. It was not a "Civil War," as it fought between two parties within the same government. It was not a "War of Secession," for the Southern States seceded without a thought of war. The right of a State to secede had never been questioned. It was not a "War of Rebellion" for sovereign, independent State co-equal, cannot rebel against each other. It was a War between the States, because twenty-two non-seceding States made war upon eleven seceding States to force them back into the Union of States. It was not until after the surrender of 1865 that secession was decided to be unconstitutional.

Contributed by Jim Hayes.

WARNING!

Users of this work are warned that minor typographical errors may be present, and that prices for some items may not reflect the price that would be set by a majority of dealers. The author and publisher disclaims responsibility for any consequences of such errors or omissions.

Price information is offered as an approximate guide to current market values.

Chapter One

"War between the States" Ephemera.

American Colonization Society

Founded by anti-slave supporters including Henry Clay and John Randolph of Roanoke, Va., its purpose was to return blacks to Liberia, Africa. Any records of this society are collectible and uncommon. The American Colonization Society operated from 1816 until the early 1860's.

Broadsides $200 - $1,000.
Booklets $25 - $100.
Related manuscript material: ALS $25- $500; DS $25 - 250

Items signed or related to Lincoln and the IL. chapter would bring a premium

Confederate Imprints, Questioned

Broadsides:
Broadside, appox. 9.5 x 4 inches. Parrish & Willingham 1529.

To the people of Western Virginia. (Text begins): The Army of the Confederate States has come among you to expel the enemy, to rescue the people from the despotism of the counterfeit State Government imposed on you by /northern bayonets, and to restore to country once more to its natural allegiance to the state. (Signed in type): Maj. Gen. Lorning. Charleston, Va., September 14, 1862.

<u>Reprint Issued in 1900:</u>

Confederate Partially Imprinted & Manuscript Documents

		AVERAGES
1.	**Confederate Cabinet departments**	$115
	Signed by secretary of department	$425
2.	**Confederate State Navy**	$275
	Signed by secretary of Navy	$500
3.	**Confederate State Marine Corps:**	
	Orders	$350
	Letters	$1500
4.	**Confederate military prison:**	
	Documents	$300
5.	**Confederate muster rolls:**	
	CSA, depends on Reg. & date	$235
	Naval	$500+

6.	**Confederate quartermaster:**	
	Reports, receipts, etc.	$50
	Naval	$100+
7.	**Oaths of amnesty or allegiance**	$50 - 100
8.	**Imprinted documents,** with high-ranking signers:	
	Brigadier General	$400
	Lieutenant General	$300
	Major General	$250
	(Add actual signer's signature value to document)	
9.	**Confederate Military discharges:**	
	Enlisted	$150
	Officer's	$200
10.	**Confederate military prison documents**	$250
	Libby & Andersonville	$350
11.	**Confederate military railroad**	
	tickets for soldier	$50
12.	**Confederate Adjutant General orders**	$28 - 58
13.	**Confederate Military enlistment broadsides:**	
	full-sheet size	$1,200+
	halve sheet size	$750+
14.	**Confederate Field imprints**	$125 - 500
15.	**Public notices / broadside, c. 1861-April 65**	$187 - 275

Confederate Newspapers

Confederate newspaper are highly collectible and generally range from $75. to $150. depending on content and condition. A few editions of Confederate newspapers were actually printed on wall paper stock, they are most desired. However, there are a number of late wall paper editions and novices should used great care and ask for written guarantees.

May 30, 1862. THE PEOPLES PRESS. Ft. pg. "The Fall of New Orleans, A report of the Battle of Williamsburg. ("Only known issue.") J 1993 $265.

October 1, 1862 THE TRI-WEEKLY TELEGRAPH. A single sheet issue. Ft. pg. "The Glorious Victory at Harper's Ferry," "The Battle of Sharpsburg." includes a report of the unconditional surrender of 11,000 Yankees at Harpers Ferry. TH August 1993 $390.

November 21, 1862. TRI-WEEKLY TELEGRAPH, Houston, Texas, A complete account of the Texas Rangers and Confederates at Tennessee and Kentucky. J 1993 $375.

December 30, 1862. THE CHARLESTON MERCURY, the positioning and skirmishing of the two armies near Murfreesboro, TN. J 1993 $125.

March 24, 1863. SOUTHERN CONFEDERACY, Atlanta, Georgia, 4 page paper. Masthead "Confederacy." Pg. 2 "Engagement on the Upper Rappahannock" has 3 dispatches signed in type: J. E. B. Stuart. TH August 1993 $155.

August 1, 1863. OPELOUSAS COURIER, Opelousas, Louisiana., 4pp. published in English on recto and in French on verso. Features war news, including a list of exchanged officers and men of the Confederate army and a casualty list. J 1993 $380.

August 15, 1863. The DAILY RICHMOND INQUIRER, Richmond, VA., Two front page proclamations signed in type by Jefferson Davis. VCS Feb. 1994 $175.

March 1, 1864. STAUNTON SPECTATOR, Staunton, VA., 1 Sheet paper. An Address of Congress to the people of the Confederate States running the full front page. VCS Feb. 1994 $275.

June 3, 1864. RICHMOND EXAMINER. A single sheet issue. Ft. pg. contains a letter to the sec. of War signed: R. E. Lee, General. "The Negro Troops on the Southside." TH August 1993 $165.

June 10, 1864. The DAILY INQUIRER. Fr. pg. Proceedings of the Confederate States Congress - the Battle in Virginia. tears. RWS October 1992 $75.

Newspaper Imprints, Questioned

The Daily Citizen, Vicksburg, Mississippi, July 4, 1863, wall paper editions. A great number of later copies of this paper exist, they have small monetary value. The Library of Congress has four copies of the original of this issue, and originals are reported to be held in at least nine other American libraries.

OVER THIRTY REPRINTS OF THIS ISSUE EXISTS.

The genuine originals can be distinguished by the following tests:
Single type page, 91/8 inches in width by 167/8 inches in length.
Column 1, line 1, title, THE DAILY CITIZEN, in capitals, not capitals and lower case, or capitals and small capitals.
Column 1, line 2, " J.M.Swords, ... Proprietor". Notice the comma (or imperfect dot) and six periods.
Column 1, Last line, reads: "them as they would the portals of hell itself."
Column 3, line 1, reads: "Yankee News From All Points."
Column 4, line 1, reads: tremity of the city. These will be defended."
Column 4, paragraph 3, line 7, first word is misspelled "Secossion."
Column 4, article 2, line 2, word 4 is spelled "whistle."
Column 4, last article before Note, final word is printed with the question mark misplaced, 'dead' instead of dead".
Column 4, Note, line 1, comma following the word "changes" rather than a period.
(Source Information Circular 3, rev. 1955, Library of Congress.)
And is very rare.

Confederate Music Sheets

1.	Large & bold type texts	$ 50 - $150.
	Illustrated cover	$100 - $250.
	Colored illustrated cover	$125.- $350.

THE CONFEDERATE FLAG, By Blackmar & Co., 1861, New Orleans, written by E.D. Eider, music by G. George. Colored 1st National Flag on cover. HS July $200.

Only a few serious collectors of these very rare sheets are active in the market place. This is one area that will see a mark increase in value and interest in the near future.

Confederate Manuscript & Documents

1. Soldier's letter with camp life or personal content	$30+
2. Soldier's letter describing battles, casualties, historic events	$75+
POW letters	$95+

1862 Dec. 16. 2.5pp., legal folio, Jackson, Ms., firsthand account of the Battle of Shiloh (April 6-7, 1862), a report by Colonel Bankhead on the role of his battery at the "Hornet's Nest". Written to "Captain R. M. Hooe A. A. Gen'l, Jackson Miss. JM Oct. 1992 $9,500.

May 14, 1864. 1p. from W.W. Hubert 1st Lt. 4th GA Vols. one of the IMMORTAL 600. On Board the Steamer Swan, on way to Fort Delaware. DZ Dec. 1991 $225.

1864 June 29. 1p w/envelope. from H.T. Walker, Co. C., 39th Ala., to his dad in Greensboro, Ala., says he was in the battle yesterday and has come out without a scratch...we lost very heavily too... " KO August 1992 $85.

3. Soldier's letter with battle content from:	
Florida & Missouri	$200 - 400
Kentucky, Arkansas & Indian	$150 - 350
4. War dated civilian ltr. desc. historic events	$75.
5. War dated civilian ltr. containing personal news	$30.

Misc.

April 10, 1865. 1pg. General Order No. 9, a foot soldier's copy in unknown hand. GH June 1990 $750.

Nov. 1, 1863. 1pg. Imprinted discharge for Private E. L. Cornwell, Co.G 2nd GA., Capt. Maddox's Co., discharged on a surgeons certificate. LR Dec. 1991 $225.

Lot: A. ALS 21 Aug. 1863. From John S. Preston on the failure of the Confederate effort and incompetence of P. G. T. Beauregard. B. Signatures of Wade Hampton I, II, & III.

C. Signature of Jefferson Davis. D. Application for membership in DAR. E. Handwritten Biographies of the S.C. soldiers. & misc.. SG October 1991 $1,100.

Twenty Letters dated 1863-65 written by Clarence Caulkins of Massachusetts 58th Regiment who fought at Petersburg and was held prisoner at Libby and Danville prisons. S Nov. 1994 $880.

****

With all letters, covers can be a very important addition., cancellation marks can be very valuable and should be checked in Confederate States of America Stampless Cover Catalog. David G. Phillips Publishing Co. P.O. Box 611388 N. Miami, Fl. 33261-1388.

Slavery

1.	Confederate slave action notices, war dated	$650.
	Imprinted with bold & larger text lettering	$750.
	Non-war date or n.d.	$300.
2.	Slave bills of sale, imprinted, war dated	$350.
	Manuscript	$295.
	Non-war date or n.d.	$250.

July 3, 1863. 1p., Bill and endorsements for Hire of Negro Slave Agnus for one year for $86. BJP Feb. 1994 $250.

Colonial Slavery Document (1768) - Capt. Wm. Pinniger's account with C. Farant, Dealer, rendered in English Pounds. BJP Feb. 1994 $145.

3.	Slave inventory, for taxes	$165.
4.	Documents of 'Freed' blacks owing slaves	$350.
5.	Slaves impressed as laborers by Confederate forces	$250.
6.	Anti-Slavery Broadsides, pre-war	$750.
	War dated	$950.
7.	Slave reward Broadside - Printed	$750.
	Manuscript	$450.
8.	Tax documents paid to local governments	$75.
	" " " to school districts	$95.
9.	Letters referring to Slaves	$50 - 350
10.	Pension applications	$65.
	Confederate Servant to a CSA Officer	$125.
11.	Estate Appraisal	$95-275

Union Imprinted Documents

		AVERAGES
1.	Broadsides	$250 - $1,800.

-, 21x26", "RALLY FOR THE UNION/ Down with Traitors/ GUM TREE INN, Highland/ .../ Buckeye Blacksmith." Printed in West Chester, PA., Sept. 1864. SK Dec. 1993 $850.

2.	Executive Department Plus value of signature	$125.
3.	Signed by President Lincoln	$5,465.
4.	Signed by Vice President Hannibal Hamlin	$1,150.
5.	Cabinet Departments Plus value of signature	$150.
6.	Naval Departments Plus value of signature	$175.
7.	Military subdepartments Identifying a corps, battalion, regt., battery.	$35. $45.
8.	Field Imprints	$45 - $150.
9.	Military Commissions	$175.
10.	Military Discharges, Officers Enlisted U.S.C.T.'s add $75. Naval add $35.	$115. $65.
11.	Testimonials For soldiers in Major Battles or POW's	$200. $250.
12.	Union military prison documents	$150.
13.	Union military passes	$45.
14.	Union military railroad tickets for soldiers	$35.
15	Union muster rolls with prisoners, battle losses, killed and wounded.	$100. $175.

Muster roll, July 1863, 1.5p., Indian Legion, "called into service by O.P. Morton, Governor of Indiana...in consequence of the invasion of the State by the Rebel Forces under Gen. John Morgan, C.S.A." HCS Feb. 1994 $395.

16.	Union quartermaster reports, receipts	$35.
17.	Union sutler receipts	$35.

Union Manuscript Documents

AVERAGES

1. Soldier's letter w/camp life or personal content $30. - $95.

2. Soldier's letter describing battles or historic events $75. - $350.

3. Letters from Union POWs $50. - $175.
   Andersonville & Libby prison Letters $95. - $350.
   With cover add $75. - $150.

4. War dated civilian ltrs. describing historic events $35. - $75.

5. War dated civilian ltrs. containing personal news $25.

Union Newspapers

Frank Leslie's Illustrated Newspaper:

March 22, 1862. Text on the Naval Battle in Hampton Roads, center has two page engraving of this naval battle. VCS Feb. 1994 $22.

June 7, 1862. Front two scenes and text on "Recruiting" for the 1st SC Contraband Brigade. VCS Feb. 1994 $75.

New York Herald:

March 5, 1861. Fr. Pg. devoted to Lincoln's inauguration as President. SR Dec. 1993 $450.

Sept. 16, 1861. Fr. Pg. The Confiscation of Slave Property. HIH Dec. 1993 $45.

Oct. 8, 1861. Fr. Pg. Map of the Seat of War in Kentucky. HIH Sept. 1993 $35.

Feb. 17, 1862. Fr. Pg. Map Showing the Strategic Points Captured in the Recent Victories in Kentucky and Tennessee. HIH Sept. $45.

July 2, 1862. Fr. Pg. A Call for Three Hundred Thousand Additional Troops to be Issued. HIH Dec. 1993 $20.

July 3, 1863. This paper , with large maps on the front page, reports the desperate battle taking place at Gettysburg, the death of General Reynolds, and the events of the first & second day's battles. SR Nov. 1993 $295.

April 15, 1865. Fr. Pg. Important. Assassination of President Lincoln. (An original., most issues on the market are reprints.) SR Nov. 1993 $1,095.

New York Times:

Jan. 28, 1865. Fr. Pg. The appointment of General-In-Chief, Robert E. Lee, Jeff. Davis' Views on the matter, signed in type. HIH Dec. 1993 $45.

Apr. 5, 1865. Fr. Pg. THE END - Our Details on of the Decisive Contest of Sunday - The Destruction of Lee's Army. HIH Dec. 1993 $145.

8

New York Tribune:

April 17, 1862. Fr. Pg., Emancipation in the District / The President's Message / The Bill Signed. LS Dec. 1993 $450.

April 19, 1862. Fr. Pg., 9x10.5" Map of the Field of Operations in the Cotton States. HIH Dec. 1993 $35.

Philadelphia Public Ledger:

Jan. 2, 1863. Reports Lincoln's Emancipation Proclamation. SR Nov. 1993 $195.

ARRIVAL OF THE NEWS-BOY.

If You Think All Autograph Buyers Are The Same, Look More Closely.

We are one of the top buyers of Civil War autographs in the country.

At a glance, all dealers of Civil War autographs and documents look alike. Look more closely, however, and you'll discover major differences.

University Archives stakes it's reputation on treating each client with the utmost integrity – your merchandise is "handled with care," fully insured during shipment, you can be assured of receiving top dollar for your merchandise, and you'll always receive your payment in the most timely fashion.

University Archives buys clipped signatures, signed books and photographs, letters, documents, manuscripts and family correspondence from not only the Civil War, but all fields from 1400 A.D. to the present.

Whether your individual items or collection is valued at one hundred dollars or one million dollars, you can contact us by writing **University Archives, 600 Summer Street, Stamford, CT 06901, by calling (800) 237-5692, or by faxing (203)348-3560.**

And, as you can see from "our" fifty dollar bill, either Grant or Lee is fine with us; we purchase Union and Confederacy!

University Archives. If there's one signature collectors recognize, it's ours.

Member: Antiquarian Booksellers Association of America, Manuscript Society, UACC, Ephemera Society of America, Collectors Club of NY, U.S. Classics Society, ASDA, APS, PF & PRA.

University Archives

A division of UNIVERSITY STAMP CO., INC.
Serving collectors since 1979

Thomas H. Martin, Photographer, New York City

Henry Deeks

dealer   nistorian

Civil War Photographs Books and Objects of the Period

Post Office Box 2260, Acton, Mass. 01720
Call First: 468 Main Street, Acton

508-263-1861

Image Catalogs Issued Twice Yearly

Chapter Two

Autographs

ABBREVIATIONS AND TERMS

As is usual for any trade, those dealing in autographs use certain terms that are baffling & unintelligible to others. Adding further chaos to the situation is the fact that individual dealers sometimes invent their own codes.

ALS Autograph Letter Signed, all in the hand of the writer. A letter is greater than a simple sentence, or it should be noted as ANS.

AQS Autograph Quotation Signed

AES Autograph Endorsement Signed, an endorsement on another person's document, entirely in the hand of the endorser.

ANS Autograph Note Signed. Generally a very brief message, usually a sentence but not greater than a single paragraph.

LS Letter Signed. Body of the letter in the hand of a secretary, with one signature in the hand of the author.

TLS Typed Letter Signed. Body of the letter typewritten, with one signature in the hand of the author.

DS Document Signed. Text in the hand of another person; signature in the hand of the author.

S Signature

Frank The signature of a sender on an envelope, wrapper or folded letter indicating the right of the sender to free mailing.

FFC Free Franked Cover

P Photo

PS Photo Signed, in the hand of the subject.

IPS Inscribed Photograph Signed, dedication and signature in hand of the subject.

CDV Carte-de-Visite

b/m Back Marked

Brig. Brigadier

Brvt. Brevet

Gen'l General

p Page - a single side of a leaf or one of the leaves of a book.

pp Pages

Page sizes:

Folio	11" by 14" or larger
Quarto 4to	8" by 10"
Octavo/ 8vo	5" by 7"
12mo	3" by 5"
16mo	2" by 4"

Broadside Generally folio size, unface imprinted poster.

verso Back of, the side that has to read second.

recto The side of a page that has to be read first.

typescript Typewritten manuscript.

n.d. No Date

n.p. No Place

n.y. No Year

silken Backing or lamination of a manuscript leaf with fine semi-transparent silk mesh.

foxing Brown spots due to acidity of paper.

LOC Library of Congress, Washington, D. C.

A

Abbot, Henry Larcon, 1831-1927   Union Brevet General

1854 WP Graduate. 1st Conn. Heavy Artillery; Commander of Siege Artillery, Army of the Potomac; Bvt. Brig. Gen., USV, Aug. 1, 1864, for gallant and distinguished services in the operations before Richmond and especially in the lines before Petersburg, Va.

Signature	Signature with rank	Pre & post War DS	War Dated DS	Pre & post War ALS	War Dated ALS
$25	$35	$	$	$	$

TLS, Dec., 16, 1910, Cambridge, Ma., 1p., 4x6.25", a summation of Abbott's military career. Signed in full with rank. MS Nov. 1993 $95.

Abbott, Henry Livermore, 1842-64   Union Brevet General

Harvard University, Law student. Pvt., 4th Battalion, Mass. Militia., Major, 20th Mass. Infantry, Bvt. Brig. Gen., USV, March 13, 1865, for gallant and meritorious services in the battle of the Wilderness. Killed May 6, 1864, Wilderness, Va.

Signature	Signature with rank	Pre War DS	War Dated DS	Pre War ALS	War Dated ALS
$65	$95	$	$	$	$

Abbott, Ira Corney, 1824-1908   Union Brevet General

Colonel, 1st Mich. Infantry. Bvt. Brig. Gen., USV, March 13, 1865, for gallant and meritorious services during the war.

Signature	Signature with rank	Pre & post War DS	War Dated DS	Pre & post War ALS	War Dated ALS
$20	$25	$	$	$	$

Abbott Joseph Carter, 1825-81   Union Brevet General

Colonel, 7th N. H. Infantry, Bvt. Brig Gen., USV, Jan. 15, 1865, for gallant services in the capture of Fort Fisher.

Signature	Signature with rank	Pre & post War DS	War Dated DS	Pre & post War ALS	War Dated ALS
$25	$35	$	$	$	$

Abercrombie, John Joseph, 1798-1877   Union Brigadier General
Graduated from West Point 1822; he had seen action in the Blackhawk & Seminole wars. He served in the 2nd, 4th, and 5th Corps. then again in the regular Army after the War.

Signature	Signature with rank	Pre & post War DS	War Dated DS	Pre & post War ALS	War Dated ALS
$35	$45	$50	$85	$90	$150

DS, 1841. 1p. in ink. To Capt. Tompkins, requesting transportation for troops. 1991 $70.

Abert, William Stretch, 1836-67   Union Brevet General
Captain, ADC, Staff of Major Gen. George B. McClellan, Lt. Col., AIG, Staff of Major Gen. Nathaniel P. Banks, Colonel, 3rd Mass. Heavy Artillery. Bvt. Brig. Gen., USV, March 13, 1865.

Signature	Signature with rank	Pre & post War DS	War Dated DS	Pre & post War ALS	War Dated ALS
$25	$35	$	$	$	$

Acker, George Sigourney, 1835-79   Union Brevet General
Major, 1st. Mich. Cavalry, Colonel, 9th Mich. Cavalry, Bvt. Brig. Gen., USV, March 13, 1865, fought at Morristown, TN., wounded at Bean's Station in 1863.

Signature	Signature with rank	Pre & post War DS	War Dated DS	Pre & post War ALS	War Dated ALS
$35	$45	$	$	$	$

Adams, Daniel Weisiger, 1821-72   Confederate Brigadier General
Brother of William Adams. Lawyer before and after the war. Killed a man in a prewar duel. 1st Louisiana, he lost his right eye at the Battle of Shiloh, wounded at Stone River and Chickamauga and was in command of the District of Central Alabama.

Signature	Signature with rank	Pre & post War DS	War Dated DS	Pre & post War ALS	War Dated ALS
$145	$200	$250	$350	$900	$

Adams, John, 1825-64   Confederate Brigadier General

Graduated from West Point 1846 and served in the army before the war. Killed Nov. 30, 1864 at the battle of Franklin, TN. with five other CSA Generals.

Signature	Signature with rank	Pre War DS	War Dated DS	Pre War ALS	War Dated ALS
$275	$375	$600	$2,500	$	$

S, Clip signed as Capt. CSA/ Comdg at Memphis. KO July 1993 $375.
An extremely rare signature.

Adams, William Wirt, 1819-88   Confederate Brigadier General

Brother of Daniel Adams. Farmer and banker before the war and Postmaster after. 1st Mississippi Cavalry; he turned down the Postmaster's job on Davis' Cabinet. Killed in street argument with a newspaper editor May 1, 1888 at Jackson, Mississippi.

Signature	Signature with rank	Pre & post War DS	War Dated DS	Pre & post War ALS	War Dated ALS
$200	$350	$	$	$600	$1,400

ALS, 1864 June 26. 2.25p. 4to.: Jackson, Miss., To Jefferson Davis notes concentrating enemy forces at Natches, Vicksburg and Memphis and infers suspension of active operations west of the Mississippi River. Nov. 1992 $1,350.
A scarce signature.

Akin, Warren, 1811-77   Member Confederate Congress

He ran as a Whig for Governor of Georgia in 1859.

Signature	Signature with rank	Pre & post War DS	War Dated DS	Pre & post War ALS	War Dated ALS
$50	$	$75	$	$95	$

Agnus, Felix, 1839-1925   Union Brevet General

1st Lt., 5th NY Infantry, Major, 165th NY Infantry, Bvt., Brig. Gen., USV, March 13, 1865. Baltimore newspaper publisher after the War.

Signature	Signature with rank	Pre & post War DS	War Dated DS	Pre & post War ALS	War Dated ALS
$20	$35	$25	$	$	$238

DS, December, 1886. Check signed. JH June 1992 $20.

Alcorn, James Lusk, 1816-94   Confederate Militia General

Mississippi Militia, signer of his states Secession; postwar Gov. of Mississippi and U.S. Senator.

Signature	Signature with rank	Pre & post War DS	War Dated DS	Pre & post War ALS	War Dated ALS
$45	$110	$	$278	$289	$

S, Clipped signature. SK Feb. 1994 $50.

Alcott, Louisa May, 1832-88   Union Nurse & Author

She was a Union Nurse in a Georgetown Hospital.

Signature	Signature with rank	Pre & post War DS	War Dated DS	Pre & post War ALS	War Dated ALS
$145	$	$	$575	$750	$1200

S, Closely-clipped signature. Private sale, August 1992 $125.
-, 1872 - Album page signed, in ink bold. SK Feb. 1994 $150.
Misc.
Books Authored:
Hospital Sketches and Camp and Fireside Stories (1863)1869 Boston ed. $ 75; 1886 ed. $ 65; 1890 ed. $ 50; 1957 ed. $ 20; 1960 ed. $ 30
Little Women, 1st. edtion rare.

Alden, Alonzo, 1834-1900   Union Brevet General

1st Lt., Adjutant, 30th NY Infantry Colonel, 169th NY Infantry. Bvt. Brig. Gen., USV, Jan. 15, 1865. Real estate agent after the War.

Signature	Signature with rank	Pre & post War DS	War Dated DS	Pre & post War ALS	War Dated ALS
$75	$110	$	$178	$	$

S, Clipped signature, with rank. SK March 1994 $100.

Alden, James, 1810-77   Union Naval Captain of the Ship Brooklyn

Signature	Signature with rank	Pre & post War DS	War Dated DS	Pre & post War ALS	War Dated ALS
$75	$110	$	$178	$	$

Misc.
Books Authored:
Official Memoir of Lt. Com. A. Boyd Cummings, U.S.N., Wraps (1862) $45.

Alexander, Andrew Jonathan, 1833-87   Union Brevet General
Captain, 3rd U.S. Cavalry, Lt. Col., A.A.G., Staff of Major Gen. George Stoneman, Frank P. Blair, Jr., James H. Wilson. Bvt. Brig. Gen., USA, April 16, 1865. Fought at Ebenezer Church, Ala., and Columbus, Ga. Retired regular army, Lt. Col., 1885.

Signature	Signature with rank	Pre & post War DS	War Dated DS	Pre & post War ALS	War Dated ALS
$30	$56	$	$78	$	$

Alexander, Barton Stone, 1819-78   Union Brevet General
Major, Corps of Engineers, Chief Engineer, Defenses of Washington, DC, He was Chief Engineer for Sheriden in the Shenandoah. Bvt. Brig. Gen., USA, March 13, 1865.

Signature	Signature with rank	Pre & post War DS	War Dated DS	Pre & post War ALS	War Dated ALS
$45	$80	$	$118	$	$

Alexander, Edward Porter, 1835-1910   Confederate Brigadier General
Graduated West Point 1857 and served in the army before the war. He was Chief of Ordnance for the Army of Northern Virginia, and was severely wounded at Petersburg. College professor of engineering after the war. LOC. papers, 1854-65. 15 items.

Signature	Signature with rank	Pre & post War DS	War Dated DS	Pre & post War ALS	War Dated ALS
$275	$500	$	$878	$1850	$3500

ALS, September 20, 1889. 1p. 4to: Savannah, Ga.. To Mr. Johnson acknowledges a check for some items which were too late for your 'war book'. Nov. 1992 $875.
---, May, 1863. 2p. 4to to his father concerning the Battle of Chancellorsville. Sept. 1993 $6,500.
Books Authored:
Military Memoirs of a Confederate, Critical Narrative, 1907 ed. $125; 1908 ed. $ 80.
The American Civil War, 1908 ed. $100.

Alexander, Peter Wellington, 1824-86   Confederate Reporter
With the Savannah Republican, Atlanta Confederacy, Columbus Sun, Mobile Advertiser
and Mobile Register. As a Whig he had voted against Georgia's Secession. He served on
General Tomb's Staff and postwar was Gov. J. M. Smith's private secretary.

Signature	Pre & post War DS	War Dated DS	Pre & post War ALS	War Dated ALS
$75	$	$178	$	$

Alger, Russell Alexander, 1836-1907   Brevet Brigadier General
5th Michigan Cavalry; captured and escaped at Boonville. He was badly wounded at
Boonsboro, Maryland. Pres. McKinley Secretary of War.

Signature	Signature with rank	Pre & post War DS	War Dated DS	Pre & post War ALS	War Dated ALS
$28	$46	$	$	$	$

Allaire, Anthony Johnson, 1829-1903   Brevet Brigadier General
Lt. Col., 133rd NY Infantry, Bvt. Brig. Gen., USV, March 13, 1865.

Signature	Signature with rank	Pre & post War DS	War Dated DS	Pre & post War ALS	War Dated ALS
$18	$27	$	$	$	$

Allcock, Thomas, 1815-91   Brevet Brigadier General
Lt. Col., 4th NY Heavy Artillery, Bvt. Brig. Gen., USV, March 13, 1865, fought at
Richmond in 1864, and in battles before Petersburg, Va.

Signature	Signature with rank	Pre & post War DS	War Dated DS	Pre & post War ALS	War Dated ALS
$24	$35	$	$87	$	$

Allen, Harrison, 1835-1904   Brevet Brigadier General
Major, 10th Pa. Reserves, Colonel, 151st Pa. Infantry. Bvt. Brig. Gen., USV, March 13,
1865. Lawyer & U.S. Post Office Dept. auditor.

Signature	Signature with rank	Pre & post War DS	War Dated DS	Pre & post War ALS	War Dated ALS
$18	$28	$	$	$	$

Allen, Henry Watkins, 1820-66   Confederate Brigadier General

Attended Marion College, and a school teacher and lawyer before the war. Enlisted as a Private; he was soon elected Colonel of the 4th Louisiana Infantry. He was wounded at Baton Rouge and Shiloh and later resigned commission and became Gov. of LA Jan 25, 1864 - June 1865; following the war he was a Mexico newspaper editor.   LOC. Letter, 1865. 1 item.

Signature	Signature with rank	Pre & post War DS	War Dated DS	Pre & post War ALS	War Dated ALS
$140	$250	$	$356	$	$878

Allen, Robert, 1811-86   Union Brigadier General

Quartermaster

Signature	Signature with rank	Pre & post War DS	War Dated DS	Pre & post War ALS	War Dated ALS
$18	$35	$	$58	$	$

Allen, Thomas Scott, 1825-1905   Brevet Brigadier General

Lt. Col., 2nd Wis. Infantry, Colonel, 5th Wis. Infantry. Bvt. Brig. Gen., USV, March 13, 1865.

Signature	Signature with rank	Pre & post War DS	War Dated DS	Pre & post War ALS	War Dated ALS
$18	$35	$	$	$	$

Allen, William Wirt, 1835-94   Confederate Brigadier General

A graduate of Princeton. 1st Alabama Cavalry, he was wounded at Murfreesboro and Perryville.   During the Atlanta Campaign, he commanded a brigade of Wheeler's Cavalry.

Signature	Signature with rank	Pre & post War DS	War Dated DS	Pre & post War ALS	War Dated ALS
$150	$225	$	$485	$	$825

DS, 2pp. 7.25 x 12.75," HQ Allen's Div. 10/24/64 signed endorsement pert. to having officers sent to rear to bring up stragglers from Crew's Brig. (2nd Ga. Cav.) near Gadsden, Ala. BG Nov. 1993 $550.

Allison, Alexander, (?-?)   Artist / Publisher / Chromolithographer

Signature	Pre & post War DS	War Dated DS	Pre & post War ALS	War Dated ALS
$50	$	$	$	$

Allison, Richard Taylor, 1823-1909 Confederate Major, Marine Corps

Signature	Signature with rank	Pre & post War DS	War Dated DS	Pre & post War ALS	War Dated ALS
$	$	$	$	$	$

Alvord, Benjamin, 1813-84   Union Brigadier General

1833 WP Graduate; this Mexican war veteran spent the war in charge of the Oregon Territory. His problem was the Nez Perces rather than the Confederacy.

Signature	Signature with rank	Pre & post War DS	War Dated DS	Pre & post War ALS	War Dated ALS
$22	$30	$	$	$	$

Ames, Adelbert, 1835-1933   Union Brigadier General

Graduated from West Point 1861. Medal of Honor winner for 1st Manassas, Ft. Fisher hero. A carpetbag Governor of Mississippi following the war. He was the last surviving General on either side, April 13, 1933.

Signature	Signature with rank	Pre & post War DS	War Dated DS	Pre & post War ALS	War Dated ALS
$50	$68	$78	$	$120	$

S, Clip w/rank. BG Nov. 1993 $65
-, On card. SAR Oct. 1993 $39.
-, Clip. HS July 1993 $45.
Misc.
Books Authored:
Capture of Fort Fisher, North Carolina January 15, 1865. Wraps. 1897 ed. $65.

24

Ames, John Worthington, 1833-78   Union Brevet General

Captain, 11th U.S. Infantry, Colonel, 6th USCT, Bvt. Brig. Gen., USV, Jan. 15, 1865.

Signature	Signature with rank	Pre & post War DS	War Dated DS	Pre & post War ALS	War Dated ALS
$50	$75	$	$	$	$

S, Clip signature. JH May 1993 $50.

Ames, William, 1842-1914   Brevet Brigadier General

Capt., 2nd RI Infantry, Lt. Col., 3rd RI Heavy Artillery, Lt. Col., Chief of Artillery, Staff of Major Gen. Quincy A Gillmore. Bvt. Brig. Gen., USV, March 13, 1865.

Signature	Signature with rank	Pre & post War DS	War Dated DS	Pre & post War ALS	War Dated ALS
$	$48	$	$	$	$

Ammen, Daniel, 1820-?   Union Naval Officer

Signature	Signature with rank	Pre & post War DS	War Dated DS	Pre & post War ALS	War Dated ALS
$35	$55	$65	$	$87	$

Misc.
Books Authored:
The Old Navy and the New. 1891 ed. $ 65.

Ammen, Jacob, 1806-94   Union Brigadier General

1831 WP graduate. After fighting at Shiloh and Corinth he served mostly on Garrison duty in Tenn. & Ky.

Signature	Signature with rank	Pre & post War DS	War Dated DS	Pre & post War ALS	War Dated ALS
$20	$35	$	$	$	$

Anderson, _____, ? - ?   Photographer

Richmond, VA

Signature	Pre & post War DS	War Dated DS	Pre & post War ALS	War Dated ALS
$	$	$	$	$

Misc.
Stereoviews Published - Anderson Gallery @ 915 Main St., Richmond

African Church	$ 65
The Crater & Blanford Church	$ 85
Libby Prison	$ 85
Castle Thunder - Confederate Prison	$ 85

Belle's Isle - Prisoner's Camp	$ 85
Drury's Bluff	$ 50
Jeff Davis' Mansion	$ 75
General Lee's Residence	$ 75
Monument to Confederate Dead	$ 50
Monumental Church	$ 40
Ruins of Confederate Arsenal	$ 85
State Capitol (VA)	$ 45
Stonewall Jackson Statue	$ 65
Tredegar Iron Works	$ 85
View of Main Street (Richmond, Va.)	$ 50
Views of the James River	$ 50

Anderson, Clifford, 1833-99 — Member Confederate Congress

Georgia Attorney General - he served briefly in the CSA Army.

Signature	Signature with rank	Pre & post War DS	War Dated DS	Pre & post War ALS	War Dated ALS
$60	$	$	$	$	$

Anderson, Frank Maloy, 1871-1961 — Historian

LOC. papers, 1899-1954. ca. 40,000 items.

Signature	DS	ALS
$	$	$76

Misc.
Books Authored:
The Mystery of "A Public Man." 1948 ed. $30.

Anderson, George Burgwyn, 1831-62 — Confederate Brigadier General

4th NC, a fierce fighter, he saw action at Williamsburg, Va., led to his promotion by Pres. Davis to Brig. Genl. He died October 16, 1862 of wounds rec'd at Antietam, Md. on September 17, 1862.

Signature	Signature with rank	Pre War DS	War Dated DS	Pre War ALS	War Dated ALS
$225	$345	$435	$	$	$

Anderson, George Thomas, 1824-1901   Confederate Brigadier General
Fought in the Mexican War. With the 11th Georgia; he was with Longstreet's Corps in the Suffolk Expedition Manassas, Sharpsburg, Fredericksburg, and was wounded at Gettysburg. Also at Chickamauga, Knoxville, Wilderness, Spotsylvania, Petersburg and Appomattox. After the war, he was Chief of Police in Atlanta.

Signature	Signature with rank	Pre & post War DS	War Dated DS	Pre & post War ALS	War Dated ALS
$110	$365	$	$	$	$

A rare signature.

Anderson, James Patton, 1822-72   Confederate Major General
Physician. With the 1st Florida, he served with Genl. Bragg in Penascola, Florida. Fought bravely at Shiloh, and was severely wounded at Jonesboro. He lived in Memphis after the war.

Signature	Signature with rank	Pre & post War DS	War Dated DS	Pre & post War ALS	War Dated ALS
$95	$150	$278	$	$378	$

Anderson, Joseph Reid, 1813-92   Confederate Brigadier General
1836 WP Graduate. He was wounded in the Battles of the Seven Days, he was in charge of the famous Tredegar Iron Works before, during, and after the war. Resigned his commission in 1862 to devote all his time to the Iron Works. Family papers 1850-66 held by the VA State Lib., Richmond, Va.

Signature	Signature with rank	Pre & post War DS	War Dated DS	Pre & post War ALS	War Dated ALS
$78	$385	$	$650	$	$

DS, 1863. Richmond, VA., req. for supplies. SK Feb. 1994 $650.

Anderson, Richard Heron, 1821-79   Confederate Lieutenant General
1842 WP Graduate. Fought in the Mexican War; was present at the bombardment of Fort Sumter, with the first South Carolina. In command of Charleston after Genl. Beauregard went to Virginia. Lived in poverty after the war.

Signature	Signature with rank	Pre & post War DS	War Dated DS	Pre & post War ALS	War Dated ALS
$85	$225	$	$485	$	$

Anderson, Robert, 1805-71   Union Brigadier General
1825 WP graduate. He was a veteran of the Blackhawk, Seminole and Mexican wars. Ft. Sumter hero. LOC. papers, 1819-1919. ca 5,000 items.

Signature	Signature with rank	Pre & post War DS	War Dated DS	Pre & post War ALS	War Dated ALS
$110	$185	$245	$325	$	$

ALS, 1863 Sept. 18, 1p 12mo, Newport, RI, to Mrs. Robetson, concerning Fort Sumter's flag, enclosing a piece of the Flag staff and two pieces of the "dear old Sumter flag"., Relics not present. W October 1992 $880
---, 1866 Oct. 28. 1p, 8vo, New York., To C. S. Andrews, Roxbury, Mass, regret that ill health prevented sending sooner the autograph requested. AL Nov. 1992 $225
S, Clip, "Fort Sumter, S.C./Feby. 17, 1861/ Yours Sincerely/ Robert Anderson/ Major U.S.A.," mtd on card. BG Nov. 1993 $750.
Misc.
Relic & signature, "E.B. Anderson to Mr. Edward David, I send you with pleasure, the autograph and piece of the Sumter Flag which you so earnestly ask for. Very truely E.B. Anderson." Comes with Robert Anderson signature and fragment of the Fort Sumter Flag. S AG Feb. 1994 $7,000.

Anderson, Robert Houston, 1835-88   Confederate Brigadier General
He graduated from West Point, 1857. Severed in the 5th Georgia Cavalry. In 1864, as part of Genl. Wheeler's Corps, he fought in all engagements until he surrendered in North Carolina. He was Police of Savannah after the war.

Signature	Signature with rank	Pre & post War DS	War Dated DS	Pre & post War ALS	War Dated ALS
$100	$175	$	$325	$	$

28

DS, February 1865. 1p. Wheelers Cavalry near Graham, SC. Morning Report. JH May 1992 $275

Anderson, Samuel Read, 1804-83   Confederate Brigadier General
Fought in the Mexican War. 1st Tenn., he was with R. E. Lee in the Virginia Campaign. Anderson resigned in 1862 because of poor health, but was reappointed by Pres. Davis in 1864.

$$\mathcal{S}\ \mathcal{R}\ Anderson$$

Signature	Signature with rank	Pre & post War DS	War Dated DS	Pre & post War ALS	War Dated ALS
$90	$165	$265	$	$650	$1,455

Anderson, William Black, 1830-1901   Union Brevet General
60th Illinois.

Signature	Signature with rank	Pre & post War DS	War Dated DS	Pre & post War ALS	War Dated ALS
$18	$	$	$	$	$

Andrew, John A., 1818-83   Gov. of Mass.

Signature	Pre & post War DS	War Dated DS	Pre & post War ALS	War Dated ALS
$20	$	$	$45	$

ALS, 1857. 3pp, pert. to the Danvers R.R. OP Jan. 1994 $30.

Andrews, Christopher Columbus, 1829-1922   Union Brigadier General
Captured by Forrest near Murfreesboro in mid 1862, he spent 3 months as a POW. After his exchange, he served in the 7th and 13th Corps. After the war he was Minister to Sweden & Norway, then Consul General to Brazil.

Signature	Signature with rank	Pre & post War DS	War Dated DS	Pre & post War ALS	War Dated ALS
$20	$35	$45	$	$	$

Andrews, George Leonard, 1828-99   Union Brigadier General
1851 WP graduate. He organized and trained the "Corps de Afrique" for General Banks.

Signature	Signature with rank	Pre & post War DS	War Dated DS	Pre & post War ALS	War Dated ALS
$25	$35	$	$78	$	$

S, On Card, "Geo. L. Andrews/ Brig. Gen. & Bvt. Gen./ U.S.V." RAS Oct. 1993 $33.

Andrews, Timothy Patrick, 1794-1868 — Union Brevet General

Signature	Signature with rank	Pre & post War DS	War Dated DS	Pre & post War ALS	War Dated ALS
$18	$	$45	$	$	$

Ankeny, Rollin Valentine, 1830-1901 — Union Brevet General

Signature	Signature with rank	Pre & post War DS	War Dated DS	Pre & post War ALS	War Dated ALS
$	$35	$	$	$	$

Anthony, Edward ?-? — Photographer

Signature	Pre & post War DS	War Dated DS	Pre & post War ALS	War Dated ALS
$	$	$	$	$

Misc.
E & H.T. Anthony & Co. (1863 - 87) Stereoviews, $50-$175.

Anthony, DeWitt Clinton, 1828-91 — Union Brevet General
66th Indiana.

Signature	Signature with rank	Pre & post War DS	War Dated DS	Pre & post War ALS	War Dated ALS
$20	$	$	$48	$	$

Anthony, Susan Brownell, 1820-1906 — Women's Suffrage

Signature	Pre & post War DS	War Dated DS	Pre & post War ALS	War Dated ALS
$200	$387	$	$675	$

ALS, 1887 April 11. 2 pp., 8.5x5.5", on special National Suffrage letterhead, Rochester, NY. Addressing a friend promotes her History of Women Suffrage. CB December 1992 $750.
---, 1898 April 25. 2pp, 5.5x8.5". To Alexander Hill concerning the autograph of B. Gratz Brown and attesting that he was a staunch champion of women's enfranchisement when in the U.S. Senate in 1866". HD June 1992 $700.
AQS, 1881 September 25, Rochester, NY.. On 4x2.5" gilt-edged card. "The right to vote underlies & is the safeguard of all other rights - religious, social, industrial, educational, legal and political. HD June 1992 $650
S, Clip. NA July 1992 $200.

Appleton, John Francis, 1838-70   Union Brevet General
81st U.S. Colored Infantry.

Signature	Signature with rank	Pre & post War DS	War Dated DS	Pre & post War ALS	War Dated ALS
$	$	$	$	$	$

Archer, Edward Richard, 1834-1918 Tredegar Co., Army of TN, C.S.A.

Signature	Signature with rank	Pre & post War DS	War Dated DS	Pre & post War ALS	War Dated ALS
$	$	$	$	$	$

Archer, James Jay, 1817-64   Confederate Brigadier General
5th Texas, he fought with great distinction with the Army of Northern Virginia in every battle, from the Seven Days to Gettysburg. A POW at Johnson's Island for one year, he died in Richmond a few months after his release. Captured 1-7 Gettysburg, exchanged summer 64; d. Oct. 24, 1864 of ill health.

Signature	Signature with rank	Pre War DS	War Dated DS	Pre War ALS	War Dated ALS
$350	$500	$675	$2850	$	$

DS, 1859. 1p. folio, abstract of provision issued to troops in Oregon Ter. Signed as Capt., 9th, Inf. Cmdg. BG Nov. 1993 $450.
--, 1859. 1p. Texas. [no desc]. JH May 1992 $550.
S, Clip. JH Nov. 1992 $300.
A scarce signature, extremely rare as a war date.

Armistead, Lewis Addison, 1817-63   Confederate Brigadier General
He was dismissed at West Point for breaking a plate on Jubal Early's head. Led the 57th Virginia. Died 5 July 1863 of wounds rec'd 3 July at Gettysburg, Pa. leading his brigade in Pickett's Charge.. Served in the U.S. Army before the War.

Signature	Signature with rank	Pre War DS	War Dated DS	Pre War ALS	War Dated ALS
$2,500	$	$	$	$	$

An extremely rare signature in any form.

Armstrong, Frank Crawford, 1835-1909 Confederate Brigadier General
Attended Holy Cross Academy. A Union Officer at 1st Manassas. The only CSA
General to have served on both sides. He commanded units under Forrest, S. D. Lee, and
Chalmers. U.S. Indian Inspector after the war.

Signature	Signature with rank	Pre & post War DS	War Dated DS	Pre & post War ALS	War Dated ALS
$145	$285	$375	$	$	$

Armstrong, James F., ? - ?   Union Naval Commander

Signature	Signature with rank	Pre & post War DS	War Dated DS	Pre & post War ALS	War Dated ALS
$	$65	$	$	$	$

Armstrong, Samuel Chapman, 1839-93   Union Brevet General
8th U.S. Colored Infantry. He founded Hampton Institute.

Signature	Signature with rank	Pre & post War DS	War Dated DS	Pre & post War ALS	War Dated ALS
$35	$90	$115	$	$	$

Arnold, Lewis Golding, 1817-71   Union Brigadier General
1837 WP graduate. He served in the Seminole war and had escorted the Cherokee to
Oklahoma.

Signature	Signature with rank	Pre & post War DS	War Dated DS	Pre & post War ALS	War Dated ALS
$24	$32	$	$90	$	$

Arnold, Richard, 1828-82   Union Brigadier General
1850 WP graduate. He led Artillery, Infantry and Cavalry.

Signature	Signature with rank	Pre & post War DS	War Dated DS	Pre & post War ALS	War Dated ALS
$30	$45	$	$110	$	$

32

Arrington, Archibald Hunter, 1809-72   Member Confederate Congress
North Carolina - both U.S. and C.S. Congress.

Signature	Signature with rank	Pre & post War DS	War Dated DS	Pre & post War ALS	War Dated ALS
$50	$	$	$165	$	$

Arthur, Chester A., 1830-86   21st U. S. President
1881-85. LOC. papers, 1843-1938 ca. 4,400 items.

Signature	Signature with rank	Pre & post War DS	War Dated DS	Pre & post War ALS	War Dated ALS
$150	$245	$	$425	$625	$

ALS, June 29, 1880. 1p, 5x5.75". NY, To George Jones concerning seeing him tomorrow. HD June 1992 $700.
LS, Nov. 18, 1862. 1p, 7.5x10. NY, To General Thomas Hillhouse, Albany, will explain everything more fully to   you when I see you. HD June 1992 $700.
DS, 1862. NY, A Military Pass - New York State Volunteers # 1338 (not filled in). Signed as Quartermaster-Gen., State of New York. HD June 1992 $275.
--, August 8, 1864. 7.25x2.75" bank check, drawn on the Nassau Bank to Thomas G. Davis for $125. HD June 1992 $600.

Asboth, Alexander Sandor, 1811-68   Union Brigadier General
A veteran of the 1848 Hungarian Revolution. He was Fremont's Chief of Staff. He was wounded at Pea Ridge and Marianna, Fl., the latter wound became malignant and was fatal.

Signature	Signature with rank	Pre & post War DS	War Dated DS	Pre & post War ALS	War Dated ALS
$45	$75	$	$	$	$365

ALS, July 22, 1861. 2pp., 7.45 x 12.75, to Dr. Cooper pert. to his apt. as Asst. Surgeon on Genl. Fremont's staff and to procure ambulances and medicines for the Western Army (Fremont). BG Nov. 1993 $350.
Misc.
-, CDV, mid-chest b/m Anthony & Brady. DZ March 1992 $55.

Ashby, Turner, 1828-62   Confederate Brigadier General

7th Virginia Cavalry; he helped to make "Stonewall Jackson" a household word. In 1862 in command of all of Stonewall Jackson's cavalry, he participated brilliantly in the Shenandoah Valley. A General for only two weeks when killed June 6, 1862 at Harrisonburg, Va.

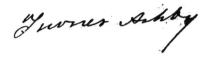

Signature	Signature with rank	Pre War DS	War Dated DS	Pre War ALS	War Dated ALS
$345	$400	$575	$725	$	$

DS, Jan. 15, 1862. 1p. 4to., Winchester, Va., requisition. SAG Feb. 1994 $500.

--, 1862. 1p. 4to., Winchester, Va. requisition for supplies. LR Nov. 1993 $750.

----, Feb. 28, 1862. 1p. 4to., Winchester, Va., requisition on blue paper. BG Nov. 1993 $695.

---, March 4, 1862. 1p. 4to., Winchester, Va., requisition. RAS Oct. 1993 $523.

----, Mar. 2, 1862. 1p. 4to., Winchester, Va. requisition for forage, approved & signed by Ashby. BG July 1993 $700.

----, 1862. 1p. Requisition for supplies. JH August 1993 $700.

----, 1862. 1p. Requisition for clothing. JH Nov. 1992 $700.

S, Signature affixed inside a diary cover; stained. Front & back covers (5.5x9") only, said to be Ashby's diary (no contents). HD June 1992 $170.

A very rare signature. A small number of war dated requisition were placed on the market appox. four years ago, but little else war period has ever been offered.

Ashe, Thomas Samuel, 1812-87   Member Confederate Congress

North Carolina CSA Senator - U.S. & C.S. Congressman.

Signature	Signature with rank	Pre & post War DS	War Dated DS	Pre & post War ALS	War Dated ALS
$45	$65	$85	$	$	$

Ashe, William Sheppard, 1813-62   Confederate Bureaucrat

Killed 14 Sept. in a railroad accident in Wilmington, NC

Signature	Signature with rank	Pre War DS	War Dated DS	Pre War ALS	War Dated ALS
$75	$	$	$	$	$

Ashley, James Mitchell, 1824-96   U.S. Congressman

Ohio Congressman proposed Constitutional Amendment abolishing slavery and led to the 13th Amendment. He was later Gov. of Montana Territory.

Signature	Signature with rank	Pre & post War DS	War Dated DS	Pre & post War ALS	War Dated ALS
$	$	$	$	$	$

ALS, June 25, 1854. 3pp. from Toledo, Ohio. [nod.]   JH June 1992 $50.

Askew, Frank, 1837-1902   Union Brevet General

15th Ohio; wounded at Stones River and Nashville.

Signature	Signature with rank	Pre & post War DS	War Dated DS	Pre & post War ALS	War Dated ALS
$	$38	$	$	$	$

Astor, John Jacob, Jr., 1822-90   Union Brevet General

Aide-de-camp to McClellan.

Signature	Signature with rank	Pre & post War DS	War Dated DS	Pre & post War ALS	War Dated ALS
$	$45	$	$105	$	$

Atkins, John DeWitt, 1825-1908   Member Confederate Congress

Lt. Colonel 5th Tennessee; under Cleveland he was an Indian Commissioner.

Signature	Signature with rank	Pre & post War DS	War Dated DS	Pre & post War ALS	War Dated ALS
$45	$	$115	$	$	$

Atkins, Smith Dykins, 1835-1913   Union Brevet General

92nd Illinois.

Signature	Signature with rank	Pre & post War DS	War Dated DS	Pre & post War ALS	War Dated ALS
$18	$28	$	$	$	$

Atzerodt, George A., 1835-65   Conspirator; Andrew Johnson attempt

Hung July 7, 1865.

Signature	Pre War DS	War Dated DS	Pre War ALS	War Dated ALS
$300	$	$	$	$

Augur, Christopher Columbus, 1821-98   Union Major General

1843 WP graduate. Superintendent of West Point when the Civil War broke out. Led the 22nd Corps and was effective against both Indians & Confederates.

Signature	Signature with rank	Pre & post War DS	War Dated DS	Pre & post War ALS	War Dated ALS
$50	$65	$	$128	$	$

S, Clip, "C. C. Auger/ Brig. Genl. U.S.A./ Comdg. Dept. of the South." JB Dec. 1993 $45.

-, Clip. JH Aug. 1993 $50.

--, Clip. HS July 1993 $35.

Augusta, Alexander T., Dr., 1825-90   Lt. Colonel 7th U.S.C.T.

Highest ranking black soldier to serve in the Union Army during the Civil War.

Signature	Signature with rank	Pre & post War DS	War Dated DS	Pre & post War ALS	War Dated ALS
$85	$150	$	$	$	$

Averell, William Woods, 1832-1900   Union Brigadier General

1855 WP graduate. He was the first Union Commander who had a victory over the superior CSA Cavalry. He defeated them at Kelly's Ford in March 1863. Postwar he was a Diplomat and inventor.

Signature	Signature with rank	Pre & post War DS	War Dated DS	Pre & post War ALS	War Dated ALS
$35	$45	$115	$	$150	$

S, On Card. RAS Oct. 1993 $38.

-, Clip. HS July 1993 $35.

Averett, Samuel Wootton, ?-?   Confederate Naval Commander

Signature	Signature with rank	Pre & post War DS	War Dated DS	Pre & post War ALS	War Dated ALS
$55	$95	$	$	$	$

Averill, John Thomas, 1825-89   Union Brevet General

6th Minnesota; he later was a Congressman from Minnesota.

Signature	Signature with rank	Pre & post War DS	War Dated DS	Pre & post War ALS	War Dated ALS
$20	$35	$	$	$	$

Avery, Matthew Henry, 1836-81
Union Brevet General

1st Provincial New York Cavalry.

Signature	Signature with rank	Pre & post War DS	War Dated DS	Pre & post War ALS	War Dated ALS
$	$38	$	$	$	$

Avery, Robert, 1839-1912
Union Brevet General

102nd New York; lost a leg at Lookout Mt.

Signature	Signature with rank	Pre & post War DS	War Dated DS	Pre & post War ALS	War Dated ALS
$20	$38	$	$98	$	$

S, Clip signature. JH Nov. 1993 $20.

Avery, William Waigstill, 1816-64
Member Confederate Congress

Signed the North Carolina Secession. He was killed 3 July 64 at Morgantown, TN., while fighting a group of Tennessee Tories/ Federalists.

Signature	Signature with rank	Pre War DS	War Dated DS	Pre War ALS	War Dated ALS
$50	$	$90	$	$	$

Ayer, Lewis Malone, Jr., 1821-95
Member Confederate Congress

South Carolina Secession signer. This former militia General was also elected to U.S. Congress, on one occasion he defected Barnwell Rhett Sr. for his seat in the C.S. Congress.

Signature	Signature with rank	Pre & post War DS	War Dated DS	Pre & post War ALS	War Dated ALS
$35	$60	$	$155	$	$

Ayres, Romeyn Beck, 1825-88
Union Brigadier General

1847 WP graduate; he had seen service in Mexico's occupation as well as on the Frontier. He was a hard fighter who led Artillery and Infantry. He was wounded at Petersburg, Va.

Signature	Signature with rank	Pre & post War DS	War Dated DS	Pre & post War ALS	War Dated ALS
$40	$65	$	$125	$	$

S, Clip. HS July 1993 $35.

B

Babbitt, Edwin Burr, 1803-81   Brevet Brigadier General
1826 WP graduate. Veteran of the Mexican war and Indian wars both in the west and in
Florida. Quartermaster District of Oregon was this senior officer's job.

Signature	Signature with rank	Pre & post War DS	War Dated DS	Pre & post War ALS	War Dated ALS
$20	$32	$	$	$	$

Babcock, Orville Elias, 1845-84   Brevet Brigadier General
1861 WP graduate. Aide de camp to General Grant

Signature	Signature with rank	Pre & post War DS	War Dated DS	Pre & post War ALS	War Dated ALS
$20	$35	$58	$165	$87	$245

Bacot, Richard H., ?-?   Confederate Naval Officer

Signature	Signature with rank	Pre & post War DS	War Dated DS	Pre & post War ALS	War Dated ALS
$	$110	$	$	$	$

Badeau, Adam, 1831-95   Brevet Brigadier General
Union Staff Officer, to both Sherman and Grant. He ghost wrote U.S. Grant's Memoirs.

Signature	Signature with rank	Pre & post War DS	War Dated DS	Pre & post War ALS	War Dated ALS
$35	$50	$76	$123	$135	$

Misc.
B, Grant in Peace. From Appomattox to Mt. McGregor. 1887 ed. $ 50; 1888 ed. $ 40;
1971 ed. $ 25

Bagby, Arthur Pendleton, 1833-1921   Confederate Major General
7th Texas Cavalry, an 1852 West Point Graduate; Assigned as brigadier general April
13, 1864., trans-mississippi department.

Signature	Signature with rank	Pre & post War DS	War Dated DS	Pre & post War ALS	War Dated ALS
$100	$175	$	$	$	$

Bagby, George William, 1828-1883   Newspaper Editor
Editor of the Southern Literary Messenger - he created "Mozis Adduma," a Cracker
Barrel philosopher. At wars end he was editing "The Richmond Whig."

Signature	Pre & post War DS	War Dated DS	Pre & post War ALS	War Dated ALS
$45	$	$	$	$

Bailey, James Edmund, 1822-95   Col. 49th Tenn. Inf.
Captured Ft. Donelson. He replaced Andrew Johnson in the U.S. Senate.

Signature	Signature with rank	Pre & post War DS	War Dated DS	Pre & post War ALS	War Dated ALS
$20	$35	$	$	$	$

S, Clip signature mounted on card with biography. BG July 1993 $15.

Bailey, Joseph, 1825-67   Union Brigadier General
He was credited with saving 33 naval vessels in Banks' Red River Campaign by using
3000 men in building 2 dams to raise the water levels. As a postwar Missouri Sheriff, he
was murdered by a pair of bushwhackers he had apprehended.

Signature	Signature with rank	Pre & post War DS	War Dated DS	Pre & post War ALS	War Dated ALS
$78	$125	$	$	$	$

Bailey, Theodorus, 1805-77   Union Naval Officer

Signature	Signature with rank	Pre & post War DS	War Dated DS	Pre & post War ALS	War Dated ALS
$35	$48	$76	$132	$145	$

Bainbridge, Absalom Ruggles, ? - ? Pvt., CSA

Aided John W. Booth in his escape.

Signature	Signature with rank	Pre & post War DS	War Dated DS	Pre & post War ALS	War Dated ALS
$	$	$	$	$	$

S, 1863. On fragment of a document. SK Feb. 1994 $1,250.

Baird, Absalom, 1824-1905 Union Brigadier General

Signature	Signature with rank	Pre & post War DS	War Dated DS	Pre & post War ALS	War Dated ALS
$20	$35	$	$	$	$

Baker, Adam Neill, Pa. ?-? Confederate Marine Officer

Signature	Signature with rank	Pre & post War DS	War Dated DS	Pre & post War ALS	War Dated ALS
$	$125	$	$	$	$

Baker, Alpheus, 1828-91 Confederate Brigadier General

54th Alabama; he captured 204 enemy at Bentonville, North Carolina. During the war he had two serious wounds. Promoted brigadier general on March 5, 1864. He participate in the Atlanta campaign.

Signature	Signature with rank	Pre & post War DS	War Dated DS	Pre & post War ALS	War Dated ALS
$110	$275	$275	$	$475	$

Baker, Edward Dickinson, 1811-61 Union Major General

Killed 21 Oct. 1861 at Ball's Bluff, Va. He was the 2nd Union General to fall in this war. An intimate friend of Lincoln. Rare.

Signature	Signature with rank	Pre War DS	War Dated DS	Pre War ALS	War Dated ALS
$158	$375	$425	$	$875	$

Baker, James McNair, 1821-92   Member Confederate Congress

Signature	Signature with rank	Pre & post War DS	War Dated DS	Pre & post War ALS	War Dated ALS
$35	$55	$	$	$	$

Baker, La Fayette Curry, 1826-68   Union General

A Jack of all Trades, a drifter and even a California claim jumper. He was a spy for W. Scott and Lincoln. He was credited with the capture of many Lincoln conspirators. Rare.

Signature	Signature with rank	Pre & post War DS	War Dated DS	Pre & post War ALS	War Dated ALS
$125	$275	$	$	$	$

Baker, Laurence Simmons, 1830-1907   Confederate Brigadier General

1st North Carolina Cavalry, an 1851 West Point Graduate; this veteran of Apache and Comanche warfare was many times wounded and lost an arm. Attached to General Wade Hampton's brigade he and his command participated in all the engagements of the Army of Northern Virginia from the Peninsular campaign until Gettysburg. Promoted to brigadier, July 23, 1863.

Signature	Signature with rank	Pre & post War DS	War Dated DS	Pre & post War ALS	War Dated ALS
$98	$185	$	$350	$	$

EDS, War dated endorsement signed. BS 1993 $250.

Baldwin, John Brown, 1820-73   Member Confederate Congress, VA.

LOC. papers, 1863, 1865. 2 items.

Signature	Signature with rank	Pre & post War DS	War Dated DS	Pre & post War ALS	War Dated ALS
$35	$48	$	$127	$	$

Baldwin, William Edwin, 1827-64   Confederate Brigadier General
Book & stationery business before the war. Surrender at Fort Donelson and imprisoned
at Fort Warren until Aug. 1862. Then commissioned brigadier general on Sept. 19,
1862. Participated in the Vicksburg campaign and again captured. Died Feb. 19, 1864
near Dog River Factory, after failing from his horse.

Signature	Signature with rank	Pre War DS	War Dated DS	Pre War ALS	War Dated ALS
$245	$375	$675	$	$	$

An extremely scarce signature.

Ball, Dabney, 1820-78   CSA Major, Stuart's Staff
Chief of commissary and chaplain.

Signature	Signature with rank	Pre & post War DS	War Dated DS	Pre & post War ALS	War Dated ALS
$	$150	$	$	$	$

Banks, Nathaniel Prentiss, 1816-94   Union Major General
Fought at Kernstown, & Cedar Mountain, Va., Port Hudson, La., & the Red River
Campaign. Commander of Dept. of the Gulf. LOC. papers, 1841-1911. ca. 50,000
items.

Signature	Signature with rank	Pre & post War DS	War Dated DS	Pre & post War ALS	War Dated ALS
$45	$145	$88	$400	$125	$475

ALS, Undated, 1pg. giving subject of speech he'll give. JH Nov. $100.
---, 1863. 1pg. in ink, 5.25x8.5," Headquarters Department of the gulf, New Orleans,
"Pass Capt. William Green to Baton Rouge or other points to which he may wish to go
on board any government transport or rail way, N. P. Banks, M.G.C. LR Sept. 1993
$425.
-----, 1876. 1pg. Recommendation letter. JH May 1993 $100.
-----, 1874. 2pgs. declining attending a Military Reunion, w/engraving. JH August
1992 $85.
ANS, Asks Major Hatch for a steamer to get the 47th Mass to N.Y. JH Feb. 1994
$150.
DS, May 30, 1864. 4pp. 4to., New Orleans, pert. to appointment of surgeon in 2nd La.
Cav. (U.S.). Provisional Commission form (signed on front). BG Nov. 1993 $350.
S, 1862 Oct. 13. Clipped Manuscript endorsement, "N. P. Banks" as Maj. General. AL
August 1992 $185.
-, Clip signature, bold. SK Feb. 1994 $48.
-, Clip. , very bold. HS July 1993 $35.
Misc.

P, CDV, 2/3 view, standing pose, wearing a double breasted frock coat of Maj. Gen., sword belt with eagle plate and sash. LR Dec., 1993 $85.
-, CDV, as noted above. SK Feb. 1994 $95.

Barksdale, Ethelbert, 1824-93   Member Confederate Congress

Signature	Signature with rank	Pre & post War DS	War Dated DS	Pre & post War ALS	War Dated ALS
$28	$45	$56	$	$78	$

S, 1863. Clipped signature. KS Feb. 1994 $48.

Barksdale, William, 1821-63   Confederate Brigadier General

Served in the Mexican war. In 1852 elected Congressman from Miss. Colonel of the 13th Miss., which he commanded at First Manassas. He distinguished himself on all the early fields of the Army of Northern Virginia. Died 3 July 1863 of wounds rec'd 2 July 1863 at Gettysburg.

Signature	Signature with rank	Pre War DS	War Dated DS	Pre War ALS	War Dated ALS
$425	$875	$	$	$750	$

ALS, August 14, 1856. 1p. accepting an invitation "to address a mass meeting of the Citizens of Baltimore opposed to the Know Nothing party and favorable to the election of James Buchanan."with envelope with free frank of Barksdale. RAS Oct. 1993 $715.
S, Clip signature with Columbus, Miss. BG July 1993 $475.
--, Clip signature. SK July 1993 $350.
A rare signature.

Barlow, Francis Channing, 1834-96   Union Brigadier General

Left for dead at Gettysburg, he later led a 2nd Corps Division.

Signature	Signature with rank	Pre & post War DS	War Dated DS	Pre & post War ALS	War Dated ALS
$	$	$	$	$	$

ALS, Undated, 4 pgs., giving travel plans through New England. JH Aug. 1993 $225.

Barnard, George N., ?-?   Civil War Photographer

Signature	Signature with rank	Pre & post War DS	War Dated DS	Pre & post War ALS	War Dated ALS
$	$	$	$	$	$

Misc.
-, Albumen print, 10 x 14" *Scene of General McPherson's Death.* est. at $550.
-, Albumen print, 10 x 14" *Battlefield of New Hope Church, Ga.,* est. at $500.
-, Albumen print, 10 x 14" *The Capital at Nashville & Chattanooga Valley from Lookout Mountain.* est. at $500.

Barnard, John Gross, 1815-82   Union Brigadier General

1833 WP graduate, deaf, he put 48 years in the Army Engineers. He was Grant's Chief of Engineers at wars end.

Signature	Signature with rank	Pre & post War DS	War Dated DS	Pre & post War ALS	War Dated ALS
$25	$35	$	$	$	$135

ALS, 22 Oct. 1864. To General ___. referring to Engineering material. JLS February 1992 $100.

Barnes, James, 1801-69   Union Brigadier General

Wounded at Gettysburg leading a Division of the 5th Corps. He was Robert E. Lee's classmate at West Point. LOC. Letter, 1865. 1 item.

Signature	Signature with rank	Pre & post War DS	War Dated DS	Pre & post War ALS	War Dated ALS
$25	$50	$	$	$	$

S, Clip, with rank. JH Aug. 1993 $50.

Barnes, Joseph K., 1817-83   Union Brigadier General/Surgeon

He was a veteran of the Seminole and Mexican wars. He replaced General Hammond as Surgeon General when the latter was court marshaled and dismissed. He war At the death beds of Lincoln and Garfield.

Signature	Signature with rank	Pre & post War DS	War Dated DS	Pre & post War ALS	War Dated ALS
$45	$65	$385	$	$525	$

LS, Feb. 12, 1877, pert. to a volume of the *Medical and Surgical History of the War*, signed "JK Barnes." Accompanied by an autograph on card. RAS Oct. 1993 $467.

Barnum, Henry Alanson, 1833-1892   Union General

He was gravely wounded and left for dead at Malvern Hill, captured and put in Libby Prison. Received the MoH for Lookout Mountain.

Signature	Signature with rank	Pre & post War DS	War Dated DS	Pre & post War ALS	War Dated ALS
$35	$55	$	$	$	$

S, On card. RAS Oct. 1993 $35.

44

Barnum, Phineas Taylor, 1810-91   Business Leader & Circus Owner

Signature	Pre & post War DS	War Dated DS	Pre & post War ALS	War Dated ALS
$175	$525	$	$670	$

ALS, Mar 18, 1876. 2.5pp. 4.75x7.75". On stationery personalized with his initials and "Waldmere," to Baswell Smith, he mentions Mark Twain and Frank Leslie. UA Feb. 1994 $950.

---, Sept. 2, 1866. 1p. New York. In part: "...Will fill any engagement you make for me 22, 24, and 25th Sept. I have heard from Mr. Bryant in Buffalo." LP Sept. 1993 $475.

---, 1878 July 13. 1p., 4to., Niagara Falls, on ornate International Hotel letterhead, declines attendance at a meeting. NS Dec. 1992 $575.

ANS, 1p. 5.5x8.75" On stationary printed Barnum on his feet again, in pencil, "Please by no means let this be seen in the city & oblige. Truly yours P.T. Barnum." UA Feb. 1994 $300.

---, Brief note signed. NAL July 1992 $225.

S, Large bold signature on a card. SK Feb. 1994 $200.

-, 1890 Feb. 20. Signature, London. ALE August 1992 $175.

-, May 11, 1876. Card signed, "Bridgeport, (date), Truly yours, P. T. Barnum." LP Sept. 1993 $150.

Misc.

Books Authored:

Struggles and Triumphs. Buffalo 1872, "Author's edition." 8vo, 880pp. Full-page plates. Gd. SP August 1992 $40.

Barnwell, Robert Woodward, 1801-82   Member Conf. Congress, S.C.
LOC. Letter, 1863. 1 item.

Signature	Signature with rank	Pre & post War DS	War Dated DS	Pre & post War ALS	War Dated ALS
$30	$	$78	$	$115	$

Barron, Washington, 1817-66   TN Representative
Arrested by Governor Andrew Johnson in 1862 because of his Southern sympathies and released by Lincoln.

Signature	Pre War DS	War Dated DS	Pre War ALS	War Dated ALS
$35	$165	$	$	$

DS, Dec. 8, 1847. 1p. 7.75x10", Request that one William D. Miller be reappointed as a Senate page, signed by several southern colleagues. MS Nov. 1993 $150.

Barringer, Rufus, 1821-95   Confederate Brigadier General

Captain 1st North Carolina Cavalry and still held this rank as late as the battle of Gettysburg, although he had served gallantly in all the engagements of the Army of Northern Virginia. On June 1, 1864 he was promoted brigadier general, in command of a brigade of W. F. Lee's division.

Signature	Signature with rank	Pre & post War DS	War Dated DS	Pre & post War ALS	War Dated ALS
$100	$165	$278	$	$	$

Barry, John Decatur, 1839-67   Confederate Brigadier General

A private in Co. I, 18th NC, then elected Capt., fought through the Seven Days, Cedar Mountain, Second Manassas, Chantilly, Harper's Ferry, and Sharpsburg. Promoted Major, after Chancellorsville, colonel, took a gallant part in Pickett's assault at Gettysburg. Appointed brigadier Aug. 3, 1864 wounded a few days later his appointment was canceled.

Signature	Signature with rank	Pre & post War DS	War Dated DS	Pre & post War ALS	War Dated ALS
$225	$	$	$	$	$

His signature is extremely rare.

Barry, William Farquhar, 1818-79   Union Brigadier General

1838 WP graduate. He was a veteran of the Seminole and Mexican wars as well as Bleeding Kansas. McDowell and Sherman had him for Chief of Artillery.

Signature	Signature with rank	Pre & post War DS	War Dated DS	Pre & post War ALS	War Dated ALS
$25	$65	$	$	$	$

S, On a card, "William F. Barry/ Bvt. Maj. Genl./ Chief of Arty:/ Sherman's Army." RAS Oct. 1993 $72.

-, Clip. JH August 1992 $25.

Barry, William Taylor, 1821-68   Member Confederate Congress

Signature	Signature with rank	Pre & post War DS	War Dated DS	Pre & post War ALS	War Dated ALS
$35	$45	$	$	$	$

Bartlett, Ezra, 1832-1886   Union Naval Officer/U.S.S. Kearsarge
LOC. Bartlett family papers, 1710-1931. ca. 10,000 items.

Signature	Signature with rank	Pre & post War DS	War Dated DS	Pre & post War ALS	War Dated ALS
$	$145	$	$	$	$

Bartlett, Joseph Jackson, 1834-93   Union Brigadier General
He served in 3 different corps all in the Army of the Potomac. He was surprised at New Baltimore, Va., by JEB Stuart and fought in his underwear.

Signature	Signature with rank	Pre & post War DS	War Dated DS	Pre & post War ALS	War Dated ALS
$	$65	$	$	$	$

Bartlett, William Francis, 1840-76   Union Brigadier General
He lost a leg at Yorktown; on at least 4 other occasions he was wounded. He was wounded and then captured at Petersburg, Va.

Signature	Signature with rank	Pre & post War DS	War Dated DS	Pre & post War ALS	War Dated ALS
$35	$	$87	$	$	$

Barton, Clara, 1821-1912   Union Nurse & Founder of Red Cross
Although not trained as a nurse, nor connected with any nursing or relief agencies, she worked throughout the War as an independent, bringing medicine and supplies to the front lines, and taking care of the wounded. LOC. papers, 1834-1918. ca. 70,000 items.

Signature	Pre & post War DS	War Dated DS	Pre & post War ALS	War Dated ALS
$275	$365	$	$485	$

S, Large album page signature. SK Dec. 1993 $295.
War dates are extremely rare.

Barton, Seth Maxwell, 1829-1900   Confederate Brigadier General

Lt. Col. 3rd Arkansas Infantry and acted as Stonewall Jackson's engineer officer in the valley during the winter of 1861-62. He participated in the Vicksburg campaign, where he was captured, paroled, and exchanged. He was taken prisoner at Saylor's Creek, April 6, 1865 and imprisoned at Fort Warren.

Signature	Signature with rank	Pre & post War DS	War Dated DS	Pre & post War ALS	War Dated ALS
$90	$165	$	$	$225	$

ALS, June 15, 1853, 1p., Fort Clark, Texas, to his sister explaining he was jilted by his sweetheart "Sue"..BJP Feb. 1994 $195.

Bartow, Francis Stebbins, 1816-61   Member Confederate Congress

Colonel Ga.

Signature	Signature with rank	Pre & post War DS	War Dated DS	Pre & post War ALS	War Dated ALS
$	$	$	$	$	$

DS, 1861. Receipt for arms for Ga. Troops, signed as Colonel. BS Aug. 1993 $700.

Bass, Nathan, 1808-90   Member Confederate Congress

Signature	Signature with rank	Pre & post War DS	War Dated DS	Pre & post War ALS	War Dated ALS
$35	$	$	$	$	$

Bate, William Brimage, 1826-1905   Confederate Major General

He entered the C.S. Army as a Private, wounded at Shiloh; he also fought with great distinction in all battles with the Army of Tennessee. He was wounded three times and surrendered at Greensboro, N.C. Newspaper editor before the war, Governor of Tennessee after.

Signature	Signature with rank	Pre & post War DS	War Dated DS	Pre & post War ALS	War Dated ALS
$50	$105	$110	$	$	$

48

TLS, March 15, 1899. 3pp., 4to. To Capt. Thos. B. Yancy regarding the efforts of Nate attempting to have Yancy's son remain in the Army. JSA January 1993 $150.
DS, 1905 check signed. BS 1993 $100.

Bates, Edward, 1793-1869   Lincoln's Attorney General
He served until 24 Nov. 1864, when he resigned to return to Missouri.

Signature	Signature with rank	Pre & post War DS	War Dated DS	Pre & post War ALS	War Dated ALS
$250	$	$	$	$	$

Quite Scarce, the rarest of all of Lincoln's cabinet members.

Batson, Felix Ives, 1819-71   Member Confederate Congress

Signature	Signature with rank	Pre & post War DS	War Dated DS	Pre & post War ALS	War Dated ALS
$45	$	$	$	$	$

Battle, Cullen Andrews, 1829-1905   Confederate Brigadier General
He was promoted to Colonel after the Battle of Seven Pines, and was injured when his horse fell before the Battle of Chancellorsville. He saw no future action after the battle of Cedar Creek, in which he was badly wounded.

Signature	Signature with rank	Pre & post War DS	War Dated DS	Pre & post War ALS	War Dated ALS
$125	$185	$	$	$	$

S, Album page signed. BS June 1993 $100.

Baxter, Henry, 1821-73   Union Brigadier General
He spent 3 yr. in California during the gold rush. His horse was shot through his leg at the Wilderness. In all he was wounded 3 times.

Signature	Signature with rank	Pre & post War DS	War Dated DS	Pre & post War ALS	War Dated ALS
$	$40	$	$	$	$

Bayard, George Dashiell, 1835-62   Union Brigadier General

1856 WP graduate. His killing of Chief Big Pawnee caused a Kiowa - Comanche uprising in the late 1850's. He was MWIA by an artillery shell on Dec. 12, 1862 died Dec. 14, 1862 at Fredericksburg, Va.

Signature	Signature with rank	Pre & post War DS	War Dated DS	Pre & post War ALS	War Dated ALS
$145	$287	$	$	$535	$

Baylor, John Robert, 1822-94   Member Confederate Congress

Signature	Signature with rank	Pre & post War DS	War Dated DS	Pre & post War ALS	War Dated ALS
$30	$48	$	$	$	$

Beal, George Lafayette, 1825-96   Union Brigadier General

Said to be the first man in Maine to enlist.

Signature	Signature with rank	Pre & post War DS	War Dated DS	Pre & post War ALS	War Dated ALS
$30	$45	$76	$	$87	$

Beale, Richard Lee Turberville, 1819-93   Confederate Brig. General

1st Lt. of Cavalry in Lee's Legion. He served with distinction in the Cavalry Corps in the Army of Northern Virginia. Resigned three times during 1862 & 63, but it was never accepted.

Signature	Signature with rank	Pre & post War DS	War Dated DS	Pre & post War ALS	War Dated ALS
$80	$145	$	$	$	$

Beal, John Yates, 1835-65   Confederate Spy

Signature	Signature with rank	Pre & post War DS	War Dated DS	Pre & post War ALS	War Dated ALS
$	$	$	$	$	$

Beall, Lloyd James, 1808-87   Confederate Marine Officer

Signature	Signature with rank	Pre & post War DS	War Dated DS	Pre & post War ALS	War Dated ALS
$	$	$	$378	$	$

Beall, William Nelson Rector, 1825-8   Confederate Brig. General
Brig. Genl. at Port Hudson, Louisiana, and surrendered with Genl. Gardner in 1863. He was released from prison at Johnson's Island, and by agreement between C.S. and Union authorities, he was appointed C.S. Agent to supply prisoners-of-war. He was finally paroled in August, 1865.

Signature	Signature with rank	Pre & post War DS	War Dated DS	Pre & post War ALS	War Dated ALS
$100	$178	$	$	$	$650

ALS, August 21, 1862. 2pp., "Confederate States of America" to General Daniel Ruggles, "I will be at your post To-morrow with my command - I am Genl Very Respectfully Your Obedt Servt, W.N.R. Beall Brig. Genl." SAG Feb. 1994 $575.

Beatty, John, 1828-1914   Union Brigadier General
He had two horses killed under him at Murfreesboro. Postwar he was a Congressman and candidate for Governor of Ohio.

Signature	Signature with rank	Pre & post War DS	War Dated DS	Pre & post War ALS	War Dated ALS
$25	$45	$57	$	$76	$

Beatty, Samuel, 1820-85   Union Brigadier General
A Mexican war veteran, he was one of the best. He served in the 2nd, 14th, 21st and 4th Corps in such places as: Shiloh, Corinth, Perryville, Murfreesboro, Chickamauga, Atlanta, Missionary Ridge and Nashville.

Signature	Signature with rank	Pre & post War DS	War Dated DS	Pre & post War ALS	War Dated ALS
$18	$	$38	$	$	$

Beauregard, Pierre Gustave Toutant, 1818-93   Confederate General
Commanded the Southern forces at Charleston, S.C. that bombarded Fort Sumter, also
fought at 1st Manassas, Shiloh, was in charge of defense of S.C. & Ga. in 1863-64, &
served with Lee in Petersburg campaign. LOC. papers, 1844-83. ca. 6,500 items.

Signature	Signature with rank	Pre & post War DS	War Dated DS	Pre & post War ALS	War Dated ALS
$295	$350	$650	$2275	$785	$3875

ALS, May 2, 1861. 2pp., to congress, " Finding that the cars start at 5 3/4h. A.M.
which might be unfavorable to my state of health & having still something here to
attend to, I have concluded not to start until 2 h. P.M..." SAG Feb. 1994 $2,200.
---, Jan. 20, 1881. 1p., 8to., New Orleans, to F.F. Beauregard in Maine pert. to origin of
the Beauregard family (Rochelle, France) with one branch settling in Canada. BG Nov.
1993 $825.
---, Sept. 19, 1881, 1pp. 8vo., Warm Spring, NC, to Frederick Ward Putnam, pert. to
being elected to the 'Am. Soc. for the advance of Science.' UA Sept. 1993 $650.
---, Nov. 17, 1882, 1pp. 8vo., New Orleans, to Marcus J. Wright, "I have ordered Genl.
Hagood's Report, copies & the original copy ... sent to you. I don't think I have a copy of
it among my files ... G.T. Beauregard." UA Sept. 1993 $750.
AES, 28 February 1862. 1pp. 5.5"x8.5", "Send company to Gen. Polk at Columbus.
Send no troops if possible without 3 days cooked rations & 40 rounds ammunition. G. T.
B" On lower portion of a S-W Telegraph Co. telegram sent to him the previous day by
General Lovell from New Orleans. UA May 1993 $2,200.
DS, 26 April 1866. signed check. To the Widow Peters for six thousand dollars for
Beauregard's lease on her land. GH July 1992 $45.
PS, CDV, in civilian dress, signed "G.T. Beauregard/ 1868." UA Feb. 1994 $1,600.
--, CDV, in civilian attire, standing 3/4 view. "G.T. Beauregard/ 1867." UA Feb. 1994
$1,500.
S, Clipped leaf, "G. T. Beauregard," JB Dec. 1993 $350.
-, Card Sign. LR Sept. 1993 $250.
-, Card Sign. JH Nov. 1992 $200.
-, Card Sign. 2 by 3.5". RS October 1992 $165.
Misc.
P, CDV, 2/3 standing view with name imprinted on mount, in civilian attire. LR Sept.
1993 $125.

Beaver, James Addams, 1837-1914   Union Brevet General
148th Pennsylvania; at Chancellorsville and Reams' Station he sustained wounds.
Postwar Governor of Penn.

Signature	Signature with rank	Pre & post War DS	War Dated DS	Pre & post War ALS	War Dated ALS
$20	$28	$	$45	$	$

DS, [n.d.] A requisition as Colonel commanding 45th PA.. JH August 1992 $40.

Beckham, Robert Franklin, 1837-64   Major CSA, Stuart Staff
Commander of the Stuart Horse Artillery.

Signature	Signature with rank	Pre War DS	War Dated DS	Pre War ALS	War Dated ALS
$	$225	$	$378	$	$

Bee, Barnard Elliott, 1824-61   Confederate Brigadier General
At 1st Bull Run, he commanded two regiments: the 2nd Mississippi and 4th Alabama. Bell fell mortally wounded and died 22 July 1861 of wounds rec'd 21 July 1861 at Bull Run, Va.

Signature	Signature with rank	Pre War DS	War Dated DS	Pre War ALS	War Dated ALS
$500	$1,250	$	$	$	$

S, Small clip signature. SK Sept. 1993 $500.
One of the rarest war dates of all Confederate signatures.

Bee, Hamilton Prioleau, 1822-97   Confederate Brigadier General
He was in command of the Brownsville District. He handled the importation of arms from Europe through Mexico, and exported cotton to pay for these arms.

Signature	Signature with rank	Pre & post War DS	War Dated DS	Pre & post War ALS	War Dated ALS
$65	$225	$78	$	$	$

DS, Pre-war tax document, signed. BS Spring 1993 $75.

Bell, Caspar Wistar, 1819-98   Member Confederate Congress

Signature	Signature with rank	Pre & post War DS	War Dated DS	Pre & post War ALS	War Dated ALS
$35	$	$	$	$	$

Bell, Charles H., ?-?   Union Naval Captain

Signature	Signature with rank	Pre & post War DS	War Dated DS	Pre & post War ALS	War Dated ALS
$40	$67	$	$	$	$

Bell, Hiram Parks, 1827-1907   Member Confederate Congress

Signature	Signature with rank	Pre & post War DS	War Dated DS	Pre & post War ALS	War Dated ALS
$40	$	$	$	$	$

Bell, John, 1797-1869   Politician

He ran for president in 1860 on the Constitutional Union Ticket, and was a moderate who hoped to keep the Union together by drawing both sides to compromise. He ran on a platform of upholding the Constitution, the Union and the laws, and carried three states.

Signature	Signature with rank	Pre & post War DS	War Dated DS	Pre & post War ALS	War Dated ALS
$100	$	$275	$	$	$

S, Cut signature dated Sept. 7, 1860. SR Nov. 1993 $95.

Bell, Tyree Harris, 1815-1902   Confederate Brigadier General

He had command at the Battles of Belmont and Shiloh. He was in charge of a cavalry brigade under Genl. Forrest, a prosition he held until the end of the war.

Signature	Signature with rank	Pre & post War DS	War Dated DS	Pre & post War ALS	War Dated ALS
$78	$175	$	$	$	$

Belknap, William Worth, 1829-90   Union Brigadier General

He led Iowa troops in Sherman's March. Signed as Sec. of War for Grant.

Signature	Signature with rank	Pre & post War DS	War Dated DS	Pre & post War ALS	War Dated ALS
$45	$78	$67	$	$165	$

ALS, Jan. 3, 1867. 1.5pp., 8to., Col. Wm. Allen, Davenport, IA. pert. to 600 officers thought to be off duty. With franked War Dept. imprint envelope & Wash., DC 1/3/67 CDS. BG Nov. 1993 $150.
LS, 1873. 1.5pps, [no desc.] JH May 1992 $50.

54

S, Signature as Sec. of War. JH Nov. 1993 $35.

Benham, Henry Washington, 1813-84   Union Brigadier General
Led his West Point class of 1837. Captured Fort Pulaski.

Signature	Signature with rank	Pre & post War DS	War Dated DS	Pre & post War ALS	War Dated ALS
$50	$110	$125	$225	$	$450

ALS, December 27, 1864. 3pp, Camp at City Point, To Gen. M.R. Patrick, regarding "Smiths goods" not being removed and in fact being used for the celebrations of Ketchums' victories. HCS January 1993 $450.

Benjamin, Judah Philip, 1811-84   Confederate Secretary of State
From Feb. 1862 to end of the war.

Signature	Signature with rank	Pre & post War DS	War Dated DS	Pre & post War ALS	War Dated ALS
$150	$350	$	$1750	$	$

Misc.
---, Clip. "Yr. Obt. Svt. J. P. Benjamin / Acting Sec. of War." On the verso, are partial lines in his hand, "greatly superior force...communicating to you...of the President...on this brilliant affair." AL August 1992 $425.

Benning, Henry Lewis, 1814-75   Confederate Brigadier General
He was attached to General Hood's 1st Corps. He took part in several battles, from Manassas to Appomattox.

Signature	Signature with rank	Pre & post War DS	War Dated DS	Pre & post War ALS	War Dated ALS
$135	$278	$278	$	$487	$

Benton, Samuel, 1820-64   Confederate Brigadier General

He fought under General Johnston at Atlanta. During the Battle of Atlanta, he was struck in the heart and foot by a shell fragment and died a week later. Died 29 July 1864.

Signature	Signature with rank	Pre War DS	War Dated DS	Pre War ALS	War Dated ALS
$350	$	$	$	$	$

Benton, William Plummer, 1828-67   Union Brigadier General

He served briefly in Missouri with Fremont, then with the 13th Corps at Vicksburg and Baton Rouge. Rare. Rare.

Signature	Signature with rank	Pre & post War DS	War Dated DS	Pre & post War ALS	War Dated ALS
$	$	$135	$	$	$

Berry, Albert Seaton, 1836-1908   Confederate Marine Officer

Signature	Signature with rank	Pre & post War DS	War Dated DS	Pre & post War ALS	War Dated ALS
$	$165	$	$	$	$

Berry, Hiram Gregory, 1824-62   Union Major General

Killed 3 May 1863 at Chancellorsville, Va., while leading a Bayonet charge. Rare.

Signature	Signature with rank	Pre War DS	War Dated DS	Pre War ALS	War Dated ALS
$300	$450	$	$	$	$

AL, 1862 April 21. Unsigned, 2p. 4to.; probably a draft of a letter never sent. Berry defends the men of the 63rd regiment of Pa. Vols. against an accusation by Gen. Samuel Heintzelman. AL August 1992 $295.

Misc.

-, CDV, Standing view, with double row of buttons, epaulets. No b/m. TM September 1992 $65.

Bidwell, Daniel Davidson, 1819-64   Union Brigadier General

He fought at South Mountain, Antietam, Fredericksburg, Chancellorsville and Gettysburg. He was killed 19 Oct. 1864 at Cedar Creek. Rare.

Signature	Signature with rank	Pre War DS	War Dated DS	Pre War ALS	War Dated ALS
$225	$	$	$	$785	$

Bigelow, John, 1854-1936   Author

Professor of military science and author of *The Campaign of Chancellorsville* and other works.

Signature	DS	ALS
$25	$	$100

ALS, Oct. 23, 1913. 1p. 6x10", Minneapolis, MN. Addressed to the well-known autograph collector, Rev. George B. Thomas. Thanks for the "Photo of Scanlans Knee," showing the scar occasioned by one of my canister at Gettysburg." MS Nov. 1993 $150.

Billings, John, 1838-1913   Union Surgeon

Signature	Signature with rank	Pre & post War DS	War Dated DS	Pre & post War ALS	War Dated ALS
$40	$75	$	$	$185	$

Birge, Henry Warner, 1825-88   Union Brigadier General

Signature	Signature with rank	Pre & post War DS	War Dated DS	Pre & post War ALS	War Dated ALS
$25	$	$	$	$85	$

Birney, David Bell, 1825-64   Union Major General

Brother of William Birney. Lawyer before the war. At Gettysburg he led the 3rd Corps after General Sickles near fatal wounding. While leading the 10th Corps he died of malaria October 18, at Philadelphia, PA.

Signature	Signature with rank	Pre War DS	War Dated DS	Pre War ALS	War Dated ALS
$200	$325	$250	$	$	$

DS, Pre-war legal document signed. BS 1993 $200.

Birney, William, 1819-1907   Union Brigadier General

He led a Negro division of the 10th Corps at Hilton Head, then a division of the 25th Corps.

Signature	Signature with rank	Pre & post War DS	War Dated DS	Pre & post War ALS	War Dated ALS
$30	$75	$75	$	$95	$

Black, John Charles, 1839-1915   Brevet Brigadier General

Union Off. 37th Illinois; for Prairie Grove, Arkansas he war Awarded the Medal of Honor.

Signature	Signature with rank	Pre & post War DS	War Dated DS	Pre & post War ALS	War Dated ALS
$18	$28	$	$	$138	$

S, Clip signature. JSA January 1993 $15.

Blackford, William Willis, 1831-1905   Captain CSA, Stuart's Staff

Engineer Officer.

Signature	Signature with rank	Pre & post War DS	War Dated DS	Pre & post War ALS	War Dated ALS
$	$135	$	$	$	$

Blair, Francis Preston Jr., 1821-75   Union Major General

He was the active leader of the pro-Union party in Missouri before and at the outbreak of the War, and organized the Wide Awakes. He was instrumental in holding Missouri for the Union. He commanded two corps on Sherman's march through Georgia.

Signature	Signature with rank	Pre & post War DS	War Dated DS	Pre & post War ALS	War Dated ALS
$45	$65	$87	$	$125	$

S, On Card. RAS Oct. 1993 $45.

Blair, Montgomery, 1813-83   Lincoln's Postmaster General

Signature	Signature with rank	Pre & post War DS	War Dated DS	Pre & post War ALS	War Dated ALS
$65	$98	$	$575	$	$850

ALS, [1862 docket]. 3pp, 4to, to Cochran, concerning a speech by "Frank", which Blair represents Lincoln's views , in regard to slavery. W October 1992 $990.

ADS, 1861 Sept. 20. 1p, 4to, Wash, telegraph draft in Blair's hand to his brother, Col. Francis Blair at St. Louis, concerning the quarrel between Col. Blair and Fremont. W October 1992 $577.

Blanchard, Albert Gallatin, 1810-91   Confederate Brigadier General

WP graduate. He was ordered to report to the Trans-Mississippi Department, but did not receive a command.

Signature	Signature with rank	Pre & post War DS	War Dated DS	Pre & post War ALS	War Dated ALS
$98	$165	$	$	$	$

A scarce signature.

Blandford, Mark Harden, 1826-1902   Member Confederate Congress

Signature	Signature with rank	Pre & post War DS	War Dated DS	Pre & post War ALS	War Dated ALS
$35	$	$87	$	$	$

Blenker, Louis (Ludwig), 1812-63   Union Brigadier General

Colonel 8th NY Inf., at 1st Bull Run his regiment effectively covered the Union retreat, commanded a division under Fremont in the Sheandoah Valley operating against Stonewall Jackson, fought at Cross Keys. Blenker died Oct. 31, 1863 as a result of injuries received in a fall from his horse earlier in the war. Rare.

Signature	Signature with rank	Pre War DS	War Dated DS	Pre War ALS	War Dated ALS
$98	$178	$	$	$	$

Misc.

P, CDV, 2/3 standing view posed with arms behind him. Wears Brig. Gen. frock coat, kepi with rain cover, sword belt & keeper with eagle plate. B/M Brady/Anthony. LR Dec. 1993 $125.

Bliss, Zenas R., 1835-80   Union Officer

Signature	Signature with rank	Pre & post War DS	War Dated DS	Pre & post War ALS	War Dated ALS
$30	$	$	$	$	$

Blunt, James Gillpatrick, 1826-81   Union Major General

His cavalry had far more victories than defeats. His foremost success was repelling Price's raid into Missouri. A Doctor before and after the war he died insane.

Signature	Signature with rank	Pre & post War DS	War Dated DS	Pre & post War ALS	War Dated ALS
$30	$48	$	$	$	$

Bocock, Thomas Stanhope, 1815-91   Member Confederate Congress

Signature	Signature with rank	Pre & post War DS	War Dated DS	Pre & post War ALS	War Dated ALS
$25	$	$	$58	$	$

Boggs, Charles S., ?-?   Union Naval Captain

Signature	Signature with rank	Pre & post War DS	War Dated DS	Pre & post War ALS	War Dated ALS
$	$50	$87	$	$115	$

Boggs, William Robertson, 1829-1911   Confederate Brigadier General
He was Ordnance Officer with Genl. Beauregard at Charleston. Chief of Engineers and Artillery for Genl. Bragg in Florida. Under Genl. Smith in the Trans-Mississippi Department, he was Chief of Staff.

Signature	Signature with rank	Pre & post War DS	War Dated DS	Pre & post War ALS	War Dated ALS
$78	$145	$175	$	$267	$

Bohlen, Henry, 1810-62   Union Brigadier General
While leading a brigade of Blenkers' Division at Freemans Ford, he was killed by Jackson's Troops when acting as rear guard for the retreat. Rare.

Signature	Signature with rank	Pre War DS	War Dated DS	Pre War ALS	War Dated ALS
$145	$	$	$	$	$

Misc.
P, CDV, in uniform, B/M Anthoney/Brady. RAS Oct. 1993 $45.

Bomford, James Vote, 1811-92   Union Brevet General
1832 WP graduate. He was at Perryville as Chief of Staff for McCook.

Signature	Signature with rank	Pre & post War DS	War Dated DS	Pre & post War ALS	War Dated ALS
$18	$	$	$	$	$

ANS, 1863. no description of content. JH August 1992 $25.

Bonham, Milledge Luke, 1813-90   Confederate Brigadier General

He was Commander of the South Carolina Army, but resigned to become a member of the First Confederate Congress, a prosition he held until 1863, when he was elected Governor of South Carolina. He was reappointed Brig. Genl., and severed with Genl. Johnston in the Carolinas until the end of the war.

Signature	Signature with rank	Pre & post War DS	War Dated DS	Pre & post War ALS	War Dated ALS
$95	$178	$190	$	$	$

AES, On a postal cover, addressed by him to Manchester, S.C., imprint at T.: "State of South Carolina, Executive Department" and franked with No. 12 tied "Sumter S.C. Aug. 23: cds. Endorsement signed as Governor, "M.L.B." RAS Oct. 1993 $132.

Booth, Edwin Gilliam, Dr., ?-?   Confederate Naval Surgeon

War Assistant surgeon on board C.S.S. Selma

Signature	Signature with rank	Pre & post War DS	War Dated DS	Pre & post War ALS	War Dated ALS
$	$265	$	$	$	$

Booth, Edwin Thomas, 1833-93   Actor, brother of John W. Booth

Signature	Pre & post War DS	War Dated DS	Pre & post War ALS	War Dated ALS
$57	$	$	$250	$

Booth, John Wilkes, 1838-65   Assassin of Lincoln

Noted actor, played the Duke of Gloster. Rare.

Signature	Pre War DS	War Dated DS	Pre War ALS	War Dated ALS
$2,100	$6,800	$	$	$

Autograph poem, Feb. 18, 1860 in ablum. BG 1992 $7,250.
Broadside,   Feb. 28, 1863, playbill, Mrs. John Drew's Arch Street Theater, Philadelphia. At the bottom reads, "Monday, John Wikes Booth will make his first appearance in Philadelphia, in his great character of the Duke of Gloster!" SR Nov. 1993 $1,995.

Boteler, Alexander Robinson, 1815-92   Member Confederate Congress

CSA Colonel and voluntary aide-de-camp to Stuart's Staff.

Signature	Signature with rank	Pre & post War DS	War Dated DS	Pre & post War ALS	War Dated ALS
$65	$	$145	$	$350	$

Boudinot, Elias Cornelius, 1835-90   Member Confederate Congress

Signature	Signature with rank	Pre & post War DS	War Dated DS	Pre & post War ALS	War Dated ALS
$45	$	$	$	$	$

Bouton, Edward, 1834-1921   Union Brevet General

59th U.S. Colored Infantry.

Signature	Signature with rank	Pre & post War DS	War Dated DS	Pre & post War ALS	War Dated ALS
$20	$	$35	$	$	$

DS, 1875. Check signed. JH August 1992 $25.

Bowen, James, 1808-86   Union Brigadier General

Railroad president before the war, retired after.

Signature	Signature with rank	Pre & post War DS	War Dated DS	Pre & post War ALS	War Dated ALS
$35	$50	$65	$	$96	$

Bowen, John Stevens, 1830-63   Confederate Major General

Graduated from West Point 1853. Worked as architect until war. He fought with distinction at Vicksburg. Died of dysentery July 13, 1863 at Raymond, Mississippi.

Signature	Signature with rank	Pre War DS	War Dated DS	Pre War ALS	War Dated ALS
$85	$165	$225	$	$425	$

An extremely rare signature.

62

Bowie, George Washington, 1835-82   Brevet Brigadier General
5th California.

Signature	Signature with rank	Pre & post War DS	War Dated DS	Pre & post War ALS	War Dated ALS
$45	$65	$275	$	$	$

Boyce, William Waters, 1818-90   Member Confederate Congress

Signature	Signature with rank	Pre & post War DS	War Dated DS	Pre & post War ALS	War Dated ALS
$25	$	$	$	$	$

Boyd, Belle, 1843-1900   Confederate Female Spy

Signature	Pre & post War DS	War Dated DS	Pre & post War ALS	War Dated ALS
$2,750	$	$	$	$

Boyd, Joseph Fulton, ?-?   Brevet Brigadier General
A Quartermaster officer.

Signature	Signature with rank	Pre & post War DS	War Dated DS	Pre & post War ALS	War Dated ALS
$18	$	$45	$	$	$

Boyle, Jeremiah Tilford, 1818-71   Union Brigadier General
Attended Princeton University. Lawyer before the war, in the railroad business after.

Signature	Signature with rank	Pre & post War DS	War Dated DS	Pre & post War ALS	War Dated ALS
$25	$	$	$	$	$

Boynton, Henry Van Ness, 1835-1905   Union Off. & MOH

Signature	Signature with rank	Pre & post War DS	War Dated DS	Pre & post War ALS	War Dated ALS
$35	$	$76	$	$138	$

S, Clip. JH May 1992 $20.

Bradford, Alexander Blackburn, 1799-1873   Member Confed. Congress

Signature	Signature with rank	Pre & post War DS	War Dated DS	Pre & post War ALS	War Dated ALS
$45	$	$87	$	$137	$

Bradford, David, 1832-1903   Confederate Marine Officer

Signature	Signature with rank	Pre & post War DS	War Dated DS	Pre & post War ALS	War Dated ALS
$	$130	$	$	$	$

Bradley, Benjamin Franklin, 1825-97   Member Confederate Congress

Signature	Signature with rank	Pre & post War DS	War Dated DS	Pre & post War ALS	War Dated ALS
$20	$	$87	$	$	$

Bradley, Luther Prentice, 1822-1910   Union Brigadier General

Signature	Signature with rank	Pre & post War DS	War Dated DS	Pre & post War ALS	War Dated ALS
$23	$	$75	$	$	$

Brady, Mathew B., 1823-96   Photographer

Signature	Signature with rank	Pre & post War DS	War Dated DS	Pre & post War ALS	War Dated ALS
$325	$	$1,250	$	$2,450	$

Bragg, Braxton, 1817-76   Confederate General
Graduated from West Point 1837. Served in the army until the war. He assumed command of Genl. A.S. Johnston's 2nd Corps at the Battle of Shioh. Bragg was called to Richmond by Pres. Davis to handle military operations for the Confederacy. He was a farmer and engineer after.

Signature	Signature with rank	Pre & post War DS	War Dated DS	Pre & post War ALS	War Dated ALS
$350	$475	$675	$	$935	$

ALS, 1868. 1p. New Orleans, [n.d.] "absolutely superb letter"... GH July 1992 $650.
PS, Large period oval uniform, signed on mat. SK Nov. 1993 $2,800.
Misc.
P, CDV, a bust view in CSA uniform showing 3 stars & wreath on his collar. B/M Vannerson & Jones, Richmond, Va., Reverse has a 2¢ orange revenue stamp. LR Sept. 1993 $400.

Bragg, Edward Stuyvesant, 1827-1912   Union Brigadier General

Attended Hobart College. Lawyer before the war. He commanded the famous Iron Brigade, and participated in almost every battle of the Army of the Potomac. After the War, he served as a member of the US Congress.

Signature	Signature with rank	Pre & post War DS	War Dated DS	Pre & post War ALS	War Dated ALS
$45	$	$	$	$	$

S, On card. RAS Oct. 1993 $38.

Bagg, Thomas, 1810-72   Att'y Gen'l of the Confederacy

From 11/1861 to 3/62.

Signature	Signature with rank	Pre & post War DS	War Dated DS	Pre & post War ALS	War Dated ALS
$145	$	$187	$	$	$

DS, Pre-war document signed as Gov. of NC BS April 1993 $175.

Branch, Anthoney Martin, 1823-67   Member Confederate Congress

Signature	Signature with rank	Pre & post War DS	War Dated DS	Pre & post War ALS	War Dated ALS
$45	$	$	$	$98	$

Branch, Lawrence O'Bryan, 1820-62   Confederate Brigadier General

He was with Stonewall Jackson in the Valley, distinguished himself at the Battles of Cedar Mountain and 2nd Bull Run. Killed 17 Sept. at Antietam, Md.

Signature	Signature with rank	Pre War DS	War Dated DS	Pre War ALS	War Dated ALS
$150	$	$350	$	$	$

DS, Pre-War Stock certificate, signed as President. BS 1993 $350.
An extremely rare war period signature.

Brand, Benjamin, ? - 1843   Official of American Colonization Society

Signature	DS	ALS
$45	$	$

Brandon, William Lindsay, 1801-90   Confederate Brigadier General
Lt. Col. of the 21st Mississippi Infantry. After losing his leg at Malvern Hill, he
commanded the Conscription Bureau in Mississippi.

Signature	Signature with rank	Pre & post War DS	War Dated DS	Pre & post War ALS	War Dated ALS
$97	$178	$243	$	$	$

Brannan, John Milton, 1819-92   Union Brigadier General

Signature	Signature with rank	Pre & post War DS	War Dated DS	Pre & post War ALS	War Dated ALS
$25	$	$58	$	$76	$

Brantley, William Felix, 1830-70   Confederate Brigadier General
Commander of the 29th Mississippi at Murfreesboro, Chattanooga, and Atlanta. With
Genl. Joe Johnston in North Carolina. He was assassinated on November 2, 1870.

Signature	Signature with rank	Pre & post War DS	War Dated DS	Pre & post War ALS	War Dated ALS
$250	$	$	$	$	$

A scarce signature.

Bratton, John, 1831-98   Confederate Brigadier General/Physician
He entered C.S. service as a Private. He was wounded and captured at Seven Pines. He
was promoted to Brig. Genl. after Genl. Jenkins was killed. He surrendered at
Appomattox Court House.

Signature	Signature with rank	Pre & post War DS	War Dated DS	Pre & post War ALS	War Dated ALS
$85	$175	$145	$	$378	$

Brayman, Mason, 1813-95   Union Brigadier General

Signature	Signature with rank	Pre & post War DS	War Dated DS	Pre & post War ALS	War Dated ALS
$18	$	$65	$	$	$

Breckinridge, John Cabell, 1821-75   Confederate Major General
Vice President USA 1856-60, ran for president against Lincoln in 1860, fought at Shiloh, Vicksburg, Murfreesboro, Chickamauga & in the Shenandoah Valley of Va.

[signature: John C Breckinridge]

Signature	Signature with rank	Pre & post War DS	War Dated DS	Pre & post War ALS	War Dated ALS
$250	$478	$	$1,450	$775	$

ALS, March 2, 1860, declining a speaking engagement. BS Summer 1993 $700.; Nov. $875.
---, March 11, 1851. 1p. 4to. Lexington, Ky., (to Congressman J. Randolph) pert. to legal matter. Mounting glue traces. BG Nov. 1993 $850.
Misc.
Breckinridge-Lane 1860 campaign token, 1" dia., w/portraits of each candidate back to back, hole for lapel ribbon. BG Nov. 1993 $250.
P, CDV, Chest up view in CSA uniform. Stars & wreath insignia is clearly visible on collar. B/M C. D. Fredericks & Co., NY, Habana & Paris., w/2¢ blue revenue stamp. LR Sept. 1993 $150.

Breckinridge, Margaret E., 1832-64   Sanitary Commission Worker
She died July 27, 1864 from Typhoid Fever

Signature	Pre War DS	War Dated DS	Pre War ALS	War Dated ALS
$150	$	$	$	$

Breckinridge, Robert Jefferson Jr., 1833-1915   Mem. Conf. Congress

Signature	Signature with rank	Pre & post War DS	War Dated DS	Pre & post War ALS	War Dated ALS
$35	$	$86	$	$	$

Breckinridge, William Campbell Preston, 1837-?   Confederate Colonel

Signature	Signature with rank	Pre & post War DS	War Dated DS	Pre & post War ALS	War Dated ALS
$	$	$157	$	$	$

Brent, Daniel Gozalez, 1842-1918   Confederate Marine Officer

Signature	Signature with rank	Pre & post War DS	War Dated DS	Pre & post War ALS	War Dated ALS
$	$110	$	$	$	$

Brent, Joseph Lancaster, 1826-?   Confederate Colonel
Not appointed Brig Genl. by President Davis or the C.S. Congress. But signs as "Brig. Gen. C.S.A.

Signature	Signature with rank	Pre & post War DS	War Dated DS	Pre & post War ALS	War Dated ALS
$87	$176	$	$	$367	$

Brevard, Theodore Washington, 1835-82   Conf. Brigadier General
He holds the distinction of being the last General Officer approved and appointed and appointed by Jefferson Davis, on March 28, 1865.

Signature	Signature with rank	Pre & post War DS	War Dated DS	Pre & post War ALS	War Dated ALS
$78	$135	$215	$	$	$

Bridgers, Robert Rufus, 1819-88   Member Confederate Congress

Signature	Signature with rank	Pre & post War DS	War Dated DS	Pre & post War ALS	War Dated ALS
$35	$	$	$	$87	$

Briggs, Henry Shaw, 1824-87   Union Brigadier General
Mass. Gen'l. badly wounded at 7 Pines.

Signature	Signature with rank	Pre & post War DS	War Dated DS	Pre & post War ALS	War Dated ALS
$48	$	$	$	$	$275

ALS, July 8, 1863. 1p. 4to. Maryland Heights, to his wife. Mentions Genl. Kenly's Brigade driving away bushwhackers in the area. BG Nov. 1993 $225.

Brisbin, James Sanks, 1837-92   Union General

Signature	Signature with rank	Pre & post War DS	War Dated DS	Pre & post War ALS	War Dated ALS
$25	$	$	$	$98	$

Brockenbrough, John White, 1806-77   Member Confederate Congress

Signature	Signature with rank	Pre & post War DS	War Dated DS	Pre & post War ALS	War Dated ALS
$45	$	$	$	$98	$

Brooke, John Rutter, 1838-1926   Union Brigadier General
Wounded in the Wheatfield at Gettysburg.

Signature	Signature with rank	Pre & post War DS	War Dated DS	Pre & post War ALS	War Dated ALS
$50	$87	$	$	$	$

S, Clip signature. JH Feb. 1994 $35.

Brooke, Richard Norris, 1847-1920   Artist
Painted *Robert E. Lee*, 1864-65 on canvas, 20x15"., National Portrait Gallery, Smithsonian Institution; *John Singleton Mosby*, 1865 oil on canvas, 29x24"., The Museum of the Confederacy, Richmond, Virginia. He fashioned a full-length painting of Lee from life that remains missing since Feb. 1865. Painted *the Furling the Flag*, 1872, Oil on canvas, 22x30"., West Point Museum, U.S. Military Academy.

Signature	DS	ALS
$65	$	$145

Brooke, Walker, 1813-69   Member Confederate Congress

Signature	Signature with rank	Pre & post War DS	War Dated DS	Pre & post War ALS	War Dated ALS
$45	$	$97	$	$	$

Brooks, William Thomas Harbaugh, 1821-70   Union Major General

Signature	Signature with rank	Pre & post War DS	War Dated DS	Pre & post War ALS	War Dated ALS
$35	$	$65	$	$	$

S, Clip sig. JH August 1992 $30.

Brough, John, 1811-65 Gov. of Ohio

A rigorous opponent of Clement Vallandigham and the Copperheads.

Signature	Signature with rank	Pre & post War DS	War Dated DS	Pre & post War ALS	War Dated ALS
$30	$	$	$	$	$

Misc.
Group, 15 manuscript documents, 58 pp., 5 printed documents, and a broadside, most are ADsS dating from Jan. of 1864 to Nov. 1864. OP Dec. 1994 $750.

Brown, Albert Gallatin, 1813-80 Member Confederate Congress

Signature	Signature with rank	Pre & post War DS	War Dated DS	Pre & post War ALS	War Dated ALS
$45	$	$	$	$	$

Brown, Egbert Benson, 1816-1902 Union Brigadier General

Signature	Signature with rank	Pre & post War DS	War Dated DS	Pre & post War ALS	War Dated ALS
$20	$	$56	$	$78	$

Brown, John, 1800-59 Abolitionist

This fanatical abolitionist was instrumental in the Underground Railroad, helping the escape of runaway slaves. Going to Kansas, he & four of his sons, murdered five proslavery men on the banks of the Pottawatamie. In 1859 he seized the U.S. Arsenal at Harpers Ferry, eventually being captured & convicted of treason. He was hung on Dec. 2, 1859 at Charleston, Va.

Signature	DS	ALS
$1,250	$1,950	$2,550

S, Clip w/ CDV., matted and frame. AL August 1992 $1,350.
Misc.
-, CDV, chest up view in large oval format, featuring the beardless John Brown. B/M Philadelphia Photographic Co. LR Dec. 1993 $175.
-, 1. Copy of a lt. from Gov. Henry A. Wise of Va., at Richmond to Mrs. Mary A. Brown, Phila. Pa.; and on the verso of the same letter a duplicate of an order from Wise to Maj. Gen. Wm. Taliaferro. 3pgs., 8vo. 2. A lock of John Brown's hair, sewn to a piece of red silk. <u>Ltrs. given to Brown while in prison and the verso bears the docketing in his hand," Gov. Wise to Mary A./ Brown"</u>. Concerns ordering his remains to his wife and those of his son....to protect from mutilation. AL August 1992 $6,500.

Brown, John Calvin, 1827-89   Confederate Major General
Lawyer before the war, Governor of Tennessee 1871-75

Signature	Signature with rank	Pre & post War DS	War Dated DS	Pre & post War ALS	War Dated ALS
$110	$200	$215	$	$278	$

S, Clip with rank, Brig. Gen'l. HS July 1993 $200.

Brown, Joseph Emerson, 1821   Governor. of GA. 1857-85

Signature	Pre & post War DS	War Dated DS	Pre & post War ALS	War Dated ALS
$25	$65	$	$	$

DS, Post war. Check signed. BS 1993 $50.

Browne, William Garl, 1823-1894   Artist
Painted *Stonewall Jackson*, 1869, Oil on canvas, 46x35", Stonewall Jackson House, Historic Lexington Foundation, Lexington, Virginia.

Signature	DS	ALS
$45	$	$

Browne, William Montague, 1823-83   Confederate General
On personal staff of President Jefferson Davis, he later commanded a brigade in Savannah against Genl. Sherman.

Signature	Signature with rank	Pre & post War DS	War Dated DS	Pre & post War ALS	War Dated ALS
$84	$	$211	$	$	$486

ALS, Oct. 3, 1862 as Colonel and A.D.C., writing on behalf of President Davis, with envelope in his hand, franked with faulty No. 2 tied by Richmond cds. RAS Oct. 1993 $440.

Brownell, Francis Edwin, ? - 1894 — Union Soldier

The Union soldier who killed James T. Jackson, who had killed Col. Elmer E. Ellsworth at the Marshall House, on May 21, 1861. Brownell was a member of Co. A, 11th NY Fire Zouaves. Rare.

Signature	Signature with rank	Pre & post War DS	War Dated DS	Pre & post War ALS	War Dated ALS
$300	$	$	$	$	$

PS - Post war in GAR uniform, wearing medal of honor. Signed. SK Dec. 1993 $500.
Misc.
CDV - 1861. b/m M. Brady, NY, a full standing view, wearing red battle shirt, Zouave jacket with red facings & trim, & arm band. Plus kepi with company numeral "A." Mint. SK Dec. 1993 $450.

Bruce, Eli Metcalfe, 1828-66 — Member Confederate Congress

Signature	Signature with rank	Pre & post War DS	War Dated DS	Pre & post War ALS	War Dated ALS
$38	$	$86	$	$	$

Bruce, Horatio Washington, 1830-1903 — Member Confederate Congress

Signature	Signature with rank	Pre & post War DS	War Dated DS	Pre & post War ALS	War Dated ALS
$35	$	$	$	$98	$

Bryan, Goode, 1811-85 — Confederate Brigadier General

WP graduate. A Major in the Mexican War. Genl. Bryan fought in the Battles of Fredericksburg, Chancellorsville, Gettysburg, and in the siege of Knoxville. Because of poor health, he resigned his commission on Sept. 20, 1864.

Signature	Signature with rank	Pre & post War DS	War Dated DS	Pre & post War ALS	War Dated ALS
$150	$275	$	$	$	$

A scarce signature.

Buchanan, Franklin, 1800-74 — Admiral Confederate Navy

Signature	Signature with rank	Pre & post War DS	War Dated DS	Pre & post War ALS	War Dated ALS
$	$	$	$1,175	$	$

S, Clipped signature as Commander. BG Nov. 1993 $375.

Buchanan, James, 1791-1868   15th President of the U.S.

Signature	Signature with rank	Pre & post War DS	War Dated DS	Pre & post War ALS	War Dated ALS
$275	$	$1,768	$	$2,780	$

ALS, 10 Sept. 1863. 2pp. 8vo. Wheatland. To Joseph C. G. Kennedy, health and business content, mentioning Jeremiah S. Black. LS October 1992 $1,500.
ANS, June 2, 1838. Six lines in his hand dealing with a land warrant and signed "J.B." with free frank. HC Feb. 1994 $895.
MDS, 27 October 1860. small 4to., oblong, Washington, appointment of Auditor of Treasury. NS December 1992 $475.
S, Signature, "Yours very respectfully, James Buchanan". UA May 1993 $250.

Buchanan, Robert Christie, 1811-78   Union General

Signature	Signature with rank	Pre & post War DS	War Dated DS	Pre & post War ALS	War Dated ALS
$20	$	$45	$	$	$

Buckingham, Catharinus Putnam, 1808-88   Union General

Signature	Signature with rank	Pre & post War DS	War Dated DS	Pre & post War ALS	War Dated ALS
$25	$	$	$	$87	$

Buckingham, William A., 1804-75   Connecticut's War Governor

Signature	Pre & post War DS	War Dated DS	Pre & post War ALS	War Dated ALS
$18	$	$	$	$

S, Clip sig. JH August 1992 $10.

Buckland, Ralph Pomeroy, 1812-92   Union General

Signature	Signature with rank	Pre & post War DS	War Dated DS	Pre & post War ALS	War Dated ALS
$25	$	$85	$	$	$

Buckner, Simon Bolivar, 1823-1914   Confederate Lt. General
Surrendered Fort Donelson, fought at Perryville, Chickamauga & Mobile. He was post war Governor of Ky.

Signature	Signature with rank	Pre & post War DS	War Dated DS	Pre & post War ALS	War Dated ALS
$150	$	$275	$	$	$

DS, March 13, 1889, 1p. 10.5 x 14" Commonwealth of Ky. appointment for Police Judge. BG Nov. 1993 $295.
S, Signature "S.B. Buckner" on Small card. JB Dec. 1993 $225.
Misc.
P, CDV, Half view in double breasted, Kentucky state coat. B/M C.D. Fredricks & Co., N.Y., Habana & Paris. LR Sept. 1993 $125.

Buell, Don Carlos, 1818-98   Union General
Although instrumental in the early victories at Shiloh and Fort Donelson, he was later ineffective in Kentucky and Tennessee. He may have had problems at home - his wife was a Southerner.

Signature	Signature with rank	Pre & post War DS	War Dated DS	Pre & post War ALS	War Dated ALS
$80	$145	$	$	$315	$

ALS, June 4, 1875. 4pp. Airdrie, to Col. John P. Nicholsen of Philadelphia pert. to Sherman's recently published Memoirs (1875) calling it "egotistical" and full of "unfounded assumptions." RAS Oct. 1993 $467.
---, 1871. 1p. 8x5, Airdie (Ky.)., expresses thanks for report on reunion of Society of the Army of the Cumberland. EB August 1992 $125.
S, Clip signature. JH Feb. 1994 $75.

Buford, Abraham, 1820-84   Confederate Brigadier General
WP graduate. He fought at the siege of Vicksburg, and was with Genl. Forrest's Cavalry Corps until the end of the war. He had two relatives who were Union Generals during the war. He committed suicide in Indiana.

Signature	Signature with rank	Pre & post War DS	War Dated DS	Pre & post War ALS	War Dated ALS
$200	$375	$550	$	$	$

A very rare signature.

Buford, John, 1826-63   Union General

At Gettysburg while commanding a division on July 1, 1863, he ordered one of his brigades, under Colonel Willliam Gamble, to dismount in order to oppose the advance of A.P. Hill's Confederate corps on the road from Cashtown. He died in Washington Dec. 16, 1863.

Signature	Signature with rank	Pre War DS	War Dated DS	Pre War ALS	War Dated ALS
$325	$450	$	$	$	$

S, Clip signature with rank, war dated. BS Sept. 1993 $400.
A very rare signature.

Buford, Napoleon Bonaparte, 1807-83   Union General

Signature	Signature with rank	Pre & post War DS	War Dated DS	Pre & post War ALS	War Dated ALS
$50	$	$	$	$	$

S, Clip. RAS Oct. 1993 $45.

Bulloch, James Dunwoody, 1823-1901   Confederate Naval Official

Signature	Signature with rank	Pre & post War DS	War Dated DS	Pre & post War ALS	War Dated ALS
$	$138	$	$	$	$

Bullock, Robert, 1828-1905   Confederate Brigadier General

He fought with distinction at Chickamauga and around Atlanta. He was severely wounded while retreating from Nashville.

Signature	Signature with rank	Pre & post War DS	War Dated DS	Pre & post War ALS	War Dated ALS
$80	$165	$	$	$	$

Burbridge, Stephen Gano, 1831-94   Union General

Signature	Signature with rank	Pre & post War DS	War Dated DS	Pre & post War ALS	War Dated ALS
$25	$40	$	$	$	$

S, Signature as Major General on a card. RAS Oct. 1993 $35.

Burnett, Henry Cornelius, 1825-66   Member Confederate Congress

Signature	Signature with rank	Pre & post War DS	War Dated DS	Pre & post War ALS	War Dated ALS
$55	$	$	$	$	$

Burnett, Theodore Legrand, 1829-1917   Member Confederate Congress

Signature	Signature with rank	Pre & post War DS	War Dated DS	Pre & post War ALS	War Dated ALS
$45	$	$	$	$	$

Burnham, Hiram, 1814-64   Union General
Killed 30 Sept. 1864 at Chapin's Farm, Va.

Signature	Signature with rank	Pre War DS	War Dated DS	Pre War ALS	War Dated ALS
$	$	$	$145	$	$

DS, March 1863. Requisition. JH May 1863 $100.

Burns, William Wallace, 1825-92   Union Brig. General

Signature	Signature with rank	Pre & post War DS	War Dated DS	Pre & post War ALS	War Dated ALS
$28	$	$65	$	$87	$

ANS, Nov. 13, 1862. 7.75x2.25", 1p., HQ 1st Div. pert. to safeguarding a citizen's property, signed as genl. comg. BG Nov. 1993 $110.
LS, 1861, no content. BS 1993 $75.

Burnside, Ambrose Everett, 1824-81   Union General
He engineered the successful taking of the North Carolina coast, and this in part led Lincoln to invest him with the command of the Army of the Potomac after relieving McClellan. His belief that he was unqualified for high command war Amply proven to be correct, leading to military disaster at Fredericksburg and frustration on the Mud March. He was later Gov. and U.S. Senator from RI

Signature	Signature with rank	Pre & post War DS	War Dated DS	Pre & post War ALS	War Dated ALS
$115	$145	$250	$387	$295	$675

ALS, May 18, 1865, 2pp., Providence, Rhode Island, To General Nathaniel P. Banks, "Will you allow me the pleasure to introduce to you Col. Nelson Viall of the 11th Heavy Arty. SAG Feb. 1994 $600.
ANS, 4.5x3.5", He has signed the back side of a black edge card with a message on both sides, sending some books off. From Edgehill Farm, Bristol, RI, Jan. 1, 1881. OP Jan. 1994 $120.
DS, Stock Cert., signed. JH Feb. 1994 $225.

76

S, Clip signature on an album leaf. RS Nov. 1993 $95.
-, Clip signature, on 3x1" sheet, with engraving. NS Nov. 1993 $125.
-, Clip. "Yours Truely A E Burnside / Gen R. I." NAL July 1992 $150.
Misc.
P, CDV, Half view, seated pose with hand inside his Maj. Gen. frock coat. B/M C.D.
Frederick's & Co., N.Y. $100.

Bussey, Cryus, 1833-1915   Union General

Signature	Signature with rank	Pre & post War DS	War Dated DS	Pre & post War ALS	War Dated ALS
$30	$	$70	$	$	$

Busteed, Richard, 1822-98   Union General

Signature	Signature with rank	Pre & post War DS	War Dated DS	Pre & post War ALS	War Dated ALS
$20	$35	$	$	$	$

Butler, Benmjamin Franklin, 1818-93   Union General
Attended Colby College and practiced law before the war. Dominated Jefferson Davis at
the 1860 Presidential convention. He was the first major general of volunteers
appointed by Lincoln, and suffered the first defeat in a major action at Big Bethel. He
made himself odious to southerners as Military Governor of New Orleans. Governor of
Massachusetts after the war.

Signature	Signature with rank	Pre & post War DS	War Dated DS	Pre & post War ALS	War Dated ALS
$35	$50	$65	$245	$115	$345

LS, May 28, 1861, 1p., To Flag Officer Pendergast, U.S.N., " I will place at your
disposal, the first Transport which reports to me for orders..." SAG Feb. 1994 $400.
--, Sept. 18, 1864, 2p. To Gov. of Pa., Andrew Curtin. recommends promotion John
Cassels, 11th Pa Cav. to Major. DZ October 1992 $185.
--, 1868, he declines the invitation. KO June 1991 $45.
PS, CDV, in civilian attire, B/M C.D. Frederick's. UA Feb. 1994 $600.
S, Signature "Benj. F. Butler/ Maj. Genl./ Com'd'g." clipped from letter. JB Dec. 1993
$45.
-, Clip sig. BG Nov. 1993 $75.
-, Clip sig. JSA January 1993 $35.
-, Clip sig. ALE August 1992 $35.
-, Clip. " Benj. F Butler / Mass". NAL July 1992 $75.
Misc.
P, CDV, Full seated view, wearing frock coat of Brig. Gen. with braided collar, and
poses with kepi on leg, with letters "MASS." within wreath insignia. B/M
Brady/Anthony. LR Dec. 1993 $75.

Butler, Matthew Calbraith, 1836-1909   Confederate Major General

Lawyer before the war, served with Hampton's Legion at 1st Manassas, appointed Colonel 2nd S.C. Cavalry, fought in Peninsula campaign, Sharpsburg & Fredericksburg. He lost his right foot in the Battle of Brandy Station, June 1863. Promoted to Major General Sept. 19, 1864. U.S. Senator after the War.

Signature	Signature with rank	Pre & post War DS	War Dated DS	Pre & post War ALS	War Dated ALS
$75	$145	$178	$350	$265	$578

S, Clip sig. SR Nov. 1993 $65.
-, Clip sig., in ink, "M.C. Butler, S.C." LR Sept. 1993 $75.

Butterfield, Daniel, 1831-1901   Union General, composer

Attended Union College. Lawyer and in business before and after the war.

Signature	Signature with rank	Pre & post War DS	War Dated DS	Pre & post War ALS	War Dated ALS
$65	$145	$	$	$155	$

ALS, Oct. 12, 1891. 1p. 8x10", Cold Spring, NY, Discusses details concerning a reception & dinner in Philadelphia. MS Nov. 1993 $160.
---, May 8, 1899 1p. To My Dear Nicholson, writes "Gnl. Sickles, Gnl Greene & myself have agreed to go to Gettysburg...". JSA Jan. 1993 $150.
---, January 1, 1891 2pp. To Dear Nicholson requests a 1/2 dozen copies... of the Count De Paris Speech...Don't forget you are to give me all their claims about Gettysburg..." JSA January 1993 $150.

Butterfield, Daniel

C

Cabell, William Lewis, 1827-1911   Confederate Brigadier General
Graduated from West Point 1850 and served in the army before the war. Served with Beauregard, Johnston, Van Dorn & Price, was wounded leading a charge on the Union breastworks at Corinth. Appointed Brigadier General Jan. 20, 1863. He was captured on Price's 1864 Missouri raid. Following the war worked as lawyer and U.S. Marshal.

Signature	Signature with rank	Pre & post War DS	War Dated DS	Pre & post War ALS	War Dated ALS
$100	$185	$450	$	$	$

DS, June 30, 1855, 1p., 10x16", requisition, for the 7th U.S. Inf. at Fort Gibson, Cherokee Nation, "W.L. Cabell, 2LT. & R.Q.M., 7th Infty." LR Oct. 1993 $395.

Cadwalader, George, 1806-79   Union General
In the Mexican war he had been Brigadier General of the Volunteers. He saw some combat although his main function was in an advisory position the Secretary of War.

Signature	Signature with rank	Pre & post War DS	War Dated DS	Pre & post War ALS	War Dated ALS
$35	$	$90	$	$145	$

Cadwallader, Sylvanus, 1825-1905   War Correspondent, N.Y. Herald
LOC. papers, 1818-1904. ca. 250 items.

Signature	Pre & post War DS	War Dated DS	Pre & post War ALS	War Dated ALS
$35	$	$	$	$

Caldwell, John Curtis, 1833-1912   Union General
He was at Gettysburg and Mine Run where he led the 2nd Corps.

Signature	Signature with rank	Pre & post War DS	War Dated DS	Pre & post War ALS	War Dated ALS
$35	$78	$	$	$	$

Callahan, Samuel Benton, 1833-1911   Member Confederate Congress

Signature	Signature with rank	Pre & post War DS	War Dated DS	Pre & post War ALS	War Dated ALS
$45	$	$	$	$	$

Cameron, Francis Hawkes, 1838-1900   Confederate Marine Officer

Signature	Signature with rank	Pre & post War DS	War Dated DS	Pre & post War ALS	War Dated ALS
$	$90	$	$	$	$

Cameron, Robert Alexander, 1828-94   Union General

He served in such places as Island #10, New Madrid, Memphis, Vicksburg and the Red River Campaign. Briefly led the 13th Corps, served the entire war.

Signature	Signature with rank	Pre & post War DS	War Dated DS	Pre & post War ALS	War Dated ALS
$30	$	$	$68	$	$

Cameron, Simon, 1700-1889   Lincoln's Secretary of War

American financier and politician, he threw his support to Lincoln in the 1860 Republican National Convention in return for a promised Cabinet post. He served as Secretary of War under Lincoln marked by corruption and military failures, he was soon replaced by Stanton.. LOC. papers, 1738-1889. ca. 7,600 items.

Signature	Signature with rank	Pre & post War DS	War Dated DS	Pre & post War ALS	War Dated ALS
$67	$	$125	$178	$165	$258

ALS, June 27, 1863. 1p. 4to, Harrisburg, to A.W. Richly "...state your inability to march to your commanding officer and through him some arrangement can be made." JB Dec. 1993 $225.

---, Oct. 8, 1840. 1p., thanking someone for sending him a check. SR Nov. 1993 $145.

---, Nov. 26, 1862, 1p., 8vo, confirming information. NS Nov. 1993 $175.

---, May 27, 1861, 1p, quarto, War Department, Washington, to A. Lankey Latty Esq., of Ohio, concerning the quota of troops allotted to the State of Ohio. JM October 1992 $ 650.

LS, Jan. 15, 1862. 1p., 6.5x6.5". one sentence to his son, "Come to Washington on Friday, the 17th." MS Nov. 1993 $125.

Campbell, Alexander William, 1828-93   Confederate Brigadier General

Colonel 33rd TN Infantry Regiment. A.I.G. to General B. F. Cheatham. Colonel, A. & I.G. to General L. Polk, appointed Brigadier General, March 1, 1865.

Signature	Signature with rank	Pre & post War DS	War Dated DS	Pre & post War ALS	War Dated ALS
$95	$187	$	$	$327	$

Campbell, Charles Thomas, 1823-95   Union General

He was wounded seven times during the war, at Fredericksburg he was shot through his liver and was expected to die. He had two horses killed under him.

Signature	Signature with rank	Pre & post War DS	War Dated DS	Pre & post War ALS	War Dated ALS
$35	$65	$	$120	$	$

Campbell, Josiah Adams P., 1830-1917   Mem. Confederate Congress

Signature	Signature with rank	Pre & post War DS	War Dated DS	Pre & post War ALS	War Dated ALS
$38	$	$	$	$	$

Campbell, William Bowen, 1807-67   Union General

He was a veteran of the Seminole and Mexican wars. He had been Tennessee's last Whig Governor. At the wars end he was a member of Congress.

Signature	Signature with rank	Pre & post War DS	War Dated DS	Pre & post War ALS	War Dated ALS
$30	$	$	$	$90	$

Canby, Edward Richard, 1817-73   Union General

1839 WP graduate. He was one of the most seasoned savage fighters in the Union army. He spent the first entire year of the war in New Mexico and Arizona area. The Modoc Indians murdered him when he was negotiating their removal to a reservation.

Signature	Signature with rank	Pre & post War DS	War Dated DS	Pre & post War ALS	War Dated ALS
$50	$78	$250	$	$	$

Cantey, James, 1818-74   Confederate Brigadier General
Colonel, 15th Alabama Infantry Regiment. Appointed Brigadier General Jan. 8, 1863.

Signature	Signature with rank	Pre & post War DS	War Dated DS	Pre & post War ALS	War Dated ALS
$85	$178	$	$	$	$

Capers, Ellison, 1837-1908   Confederate Brigadier General
Colonel 24 South Carolina Infantry. He served with Genl. Bragg during the Battle of Chickamauga. After the war, he was the Episcopal Bishop of South Carolina.

Signature	Signature with rank	Pre & post War DS	War Dated DS	Pre & post War ALS	War Dated ALS
$65	$110	$	$	$	$

Caperton, Allen Taylor, 1810-76   Member Confederate Congress

Signature	Signature with rank	Pre & post War DS	War Dated DS	Pre & post War ALS	War Dated ALS
$35	$	$	$	$	$

Carleton, James Henry, 1814-73   Union General
He led the Union's Calif. Column from the Colorado River to the Rio Grande. He relieved Canby as Commander of the New Mexico and Arizona Department. He stayed in the same area at wars end.

Signature	Signature with rank	Pre & post War DS	War Dated DS	Pre & post War ALS	War Dated ALS
$18	$35	$	$	$87	$

Carlin, William Passmore, 1829-1903   Union General

Signature	Signature with rank	Pre & post War DS	War Dated DS	Pre & post War ALS	War Dated ALS
$30	$	$40	$	$	$

Carr, EuGenerale Asa, 1830-1910   Union General

1850 WP graduate. He received the Medal of Honor for Pea Ridge. Fought with the 5th and 6th Cavalries.

Signature	Signature with rank	Pre & post War DS	War Dated DS	Pre & post War ALS	War Dated ALS
$18	$	$45	$	$	$

DS, Check. JH May 1992 $60.
--,   Check. HS July 1992 $55.

Carr, Joseph Bradford, 1828-95   Union General

Led divisions of the 3rd, 2nd, and 18th Corps. Later he was New York's Secretary of State.

Signature	Signature with rank	Pre & post War DS	War Dated DS	Pre & post War ALS	War Dated ALS
$20	$35	$	$	$87	$

ALS, 1881. As NY Sec. of State re: an appointment that he will discuss with the Governor. ML May 1992 $80.
S, Signature as Major General, on card. RAS Oct. 1993 $35.

Carrington, Henry Beebee, 1824-1912   Union General

Abolitionist. Yale 1845, His war effort was in mashing opposition in the North.

Signature	Signature with rank	Pre & post War DS	War Dated DS	Pre & post War ALS	War Dated ALS
$20	$35	$	$	$	$

Carroll, David Williamson, 1816-1905   Member Confederate Congress

Signature	Signature with rank	Pre & post War DS	War Dated DS	Pre & post War ALS	War Dated ALS
$40	$	$	$	$	$

Carroll, Samuel Sprigg, 1832-93   Union General

1856 WP graduate. He saw service in the 2nd and 3rd Corps at Cadar Mt., Chancellorsville, Gettysburg, the Wilderness and Spotsylvania.

Signature	Signature with rank	Pre & post War DS	War Dated DS	Pre & post War ALS	War Dated ALS
$28	$48	$	$	$	$

Carroll, William Henry, 1810-68   Confederate Brigadier General

He fought at the Battle of Fishing Creek. Genl. Bragg had him appear before a Military Court of Inquiry for drunkenness. He resigned his commission in 1863.

Signature	Signature with rank	Pre & post War DS	War Dated DS	Pre & post War ALS	War Dated ALS
$90	$	$172	$	$	$

Carter, John Carpenter, 1837-64   Confederate Brigadier General

Colonel of the 38th TN Infantry. He fought at Shiloh, Murfreesboro, and Chickamauga. Died 13 February 1862 of wounds rec'd at the battle of Franklin, TN.

Signature	Signature with rank	Pre & post War DS	War Dated DS	Pre & post War ALS	War Dated ALS
$325	$	$	$	$	$

A very rare signature.

Carter, Samuel Powhatan, 1819-91   Union General

1846 Annapolis graduate. The only Bvt. Major Genl. in U.S. History to also hold the rank of a Rear Admiral. He led the Cavalry Division of the 23rd Corps.

Signature	Signature with rank	Pre & post War DS	War Dated DS	Pre & post War ALS	War Dated ALS
$20	$35	$58	$	$	$

Caruthers, Robert Looney, 1800-82   Member Confederate Congress

Signature	Signature with rank	Pre & post War DS	War Dated DS	Pre & post War ALS	War Dated ALS
$35	$	$68	$	$	$

Casey, Silas, 1807-82   Union General

1826 WP Graduate. He was the author of an infantry tactics as well as an infantry tactics for colored troops. He spent 46 years in the Army.

Signature	Signature with rank	Pre & post War DS	War Dated DS	Pre & post War ALS	War Dated ALS
$45	$	$87	$	$154	$

S, On a card. RAS Oct. 1993 $55.
-, Clip, as Major General. HS July 1993 $30.

Catterson, Robert Francis, 1835-1914   Union General

He was a hard fighting, intelligent man, rose from Private to Brigadier General in 4 years. In the 15th Corps, he compiled an excellent record.

Signature	Signature with rank	Pre & post War DS	War Dated DS	Pre & post War ALS	War Dated ALS
$20	$	$45	$	$	$

Catton, Bruce, ?-?   Civil War Historian

Signature	DS	ALS
$25	$67	$

Chalmers, James Ronald, 1831-98   Confederate Brigadier General

Colonel of the 9th Mississippi. He was stationed in Pensacola, Florida. He served in the Cavalry under Genl. Forrest in Mississippi, Kentucky, and Tennessee.

Signature	Signature with rank	Pre & post War DS	War Dated DS	Pre & post War ALS	War Dated ALS
$125	$245	$345	$	$	$

Chamberlain, Joshua Lawrence, 1828-1914   Union General

On Aug. 8, 1862, he was commissioned Lt. Col. of the 20th Maine. He participated in twenty-four engagements, received the Medal of Honor for gallantry at Gettysburg.

Signature	Signature with rank	Pre & post War DS	War Dated DS	Pre & post War ALS	War Dated ALS
$625	$950	$825	$	$1,878	$

ALS, 1867 June 25. 2pp, 4to, Augusta, Me., on Maine Executive Department letterhead to the noted historian Benson J. Lossing, concerning planned 4th of July celebrations. W October 1992 $710.

ANS, Aug. 17, 1867. reads in full: "$69.62 First National Bank, Brunswick, (Date) Pay to A.J. Booker or bearer sixty-nine dollars 62/100, J. L. Chamberlain." EC August 1993 $650.

DS, 1880 1st Maine M. M., pass, imprinted, signed, as general. SK Feb. 1994 $750.

--, 1862 period Lewiston, Maine Autograph Album containing the signature of J. Chamberlain. SK Nov. $795.

--, June 29, 1869. 1p. 8.5x14" State of Maine Pension Cert. for soldier in the 31st Me. Inf., signed as Gov., mailing folds. BG Nov. $950.

--, May 15, 1869. Signed check. Signed with full first name. BG Nov. $750.

--, 1869. State of Maine Pension Certificate for Jason C. Cole, Co. B. 31st Infantry Me. Vols. Signature light. EC August 1993 $525.

--, 1876. Check signed. TM Sept. 1992 $225.

(Post War-Checks have been reported selling as high as $750, 1993.)

S, Clip "J. L. Chamberlain" w/ Maj. Genl. & Gov. of Maine 1868, in another hand. AL August 1992 $225.

Misc.

-, Framed print. 11x12.5, in color with hat in hand. TM September 1992 $35.

Hymn Book signed, 1855, signed. SK Feb. 1994 $1,200.

-, Autograph Album, Lewiston, Maine, belonged to a young lady who collected various signatures from that area, during 1862-64. SK Nov. 1994 $795.

Has become very popular & in high demand, since late 1991.

Chambers, Alexander, 1832-88   Union General

1853 WP graduate. A Frontiersman and Indian fighter spent the entire war in the 17th Corps. At Corinth and Iuka he received wounds.

Signature	Signature with rank	Pre & post War DS	War Dated DS	Pre & post War ALS	War Dated ALS
$25	$	$	$	$	$

Chambers, Henry Cousins, 1823-1871   Member Confederate Congress

Signature	Signature with rank	Pre & post War DS	War Dated DS	Pre & post War ALS	War Dated ALS
$35	$	$97	$	$	$

Chambliss, John Randolph, 1809-75   Member Confederate Congress

Signature	Signature with rank	Pre & post War DS	War Dated DS	Pre & post War ALS	War Dated ALS
$45	$	$125	$	$	$

Chambliss, John Randolph, Jr., 1833-64   Conf. Brigadier General

Colonel of the 13th Virginia Cavalry. He saw service in the Maryland Campaign. He was Killed 16 Aug. 1864 at Deep Bottom, Va.

Signature	Signature with rank	Pre War DS	War Dated DS	Pre War ALS	War Dated ALS
$365	$	$	$	$	$

An extremely rare signature.

Champlin, Stephen Gardner, 1827-64   Union General

He was wounded at Seven Pines which caused his death two years later. Rare.

Signature	Signature with rank	Pre War DS	War Dated DS	Pre War ALS	War Dated ALS
$125	$	$	$	$	$

Channing, William E., 1780-1842   Abolitionist

Signature	Pre War DS	War Dated DS	Pre War ALS	War Dated ALS
$45	$	$	$187	$

ALS, 1849 May. Boston, with postmarked integral address leaf to Toulmin Smith. ML October 1992 $135.

Chapin, Edward Payson, 1831-63   Union General

Killed 27 May 1863 at Port Hudson, La. Rare.

Signature	Signature with rank	Pre War DS	War Dated DS	Pre War ALS	War Dated ALS
$185	$	$478	$	$	$

Chapman, George Henry, 1832-82   Union General

A midshipman during the Mexican war. He published the "Indiana Republican" a Leftist Newspaper.

Signature	Signature with rank	Pre & post War DS	War Dated DS	Pre & post War ALS	War Dated ALS
$25	$35	$60	$	$	$

Chapman, Reuben, 1799-1882   CSA Rep. in France 1862-65

Signature	Signature with rank	Pre & post War DS	War Dated DS	Pre & post War ALS	War Dated ALS
$35	$	$75	$	$185	$

Chase, Salmon P., 1808-73   Lincoln's Secretary of Treasury

He lusted too openly for Lincoln's job, and his resignation war Accepted on June 30, 1864. A few months later, he war Appointed Chief Justice of the U.S. Supreme Court.

Signature	Signature with rank	Pre & post War DS	War Dated DS	Pre & post War ALS	War Dated ALS
$95	$	$176	$450	$285	$

ALS, 1868, 1p. 5x8", to Sarah Chase, sends money to this aunt with financial problems. OP Jan. 1994 $175.
LS, 1863 Aug. 22. 4pp, 4to, [Wash}, on Treasury Department letterhead, to Andrew Jamieson, detailing a protocol for seizure and declaration of commerce into and out of "any state, or part of state, heretofore declared in insurrection. W October 1992 $412.
Free Frank, April 30, 1861. SR Nov. 1993 $75.
S, Lower portion of printed document signed as Gov. of Ohio. BJ Dec. 1993 $125.

Cheatham, Benjamin Franklin, 1820-86   Confederate Major General
Served with distinction at Shiloh, Perryville, Murfreesboro, Chickamauga, Chattanooga, Atlanta, Franklin & Nashville.

Signature	Signature with rank	Pre & post War DS	War Dated DS	Pre & post War ALS	War Dated ALS
$175	$375	$425	$	$	$

Misc.
P, CDV, Engraved photo, chest up portrait of him in uniform (pre-war). B/M C. Taber & co., New Bedford, Ma. OP Jan. 1994 $80.
--, CDV, Bust view in state uniform, with Tenn. B/M with 2¢ blue revenue stamp. LR Oct. 1993 $200.

Chestnut, James Jr., 1815-85   Confederate Brigadier General

A Princeton graduate. He married Mary Boykin Miller, the daughter of a former governor of the state, on April 23, 1840. He was with Genl. Beauregard at Fort Sumter, and saw limited service on President Davis' Staff. Appointed brigadier general on April 23, 1864, in command of all reserve forces in South Carolina.

Signature	Signature with rank	Pre & post War DS	War Dated DS	Pre & post War ALS	War Dated ALS
$76	$145	$287	$	$	$1,115

Chestnut, Mary Boykin,?-?   James Chestnut, Jr.'s wife

Wrote *Diary from Dixie*.

Signature	Pre & post War DS	War Dated DS	Pre & post War ALS	War Dated ALS
$150	$	$	$287	$

Chetlain, Augustus Louis, 1824-93   Union General

He was a Captain in U.S. Grant's 12th Ill., he helped recruit and raise a Negro Regiment.

Signature	Signature with rank	Pre & post War DS	War Dated DS	Pre & post War ALS	War Dated ALS
$25	$	$65	$	$145	$

Chew, Roger Preston, 1843-1921   Major CSA, Sturats Staff

Commander of the Stuart Horse Artillery.

Signature	Signature with rank	Pre & post War DS	War Dated DS	Pre & post War ALS	War Dated ALS
$	$185	$	$575	$	$

Chilton, Robert Hall, 1815-79   Confederate Brigadier General

WP graduate. He served with distinction as Chief of Staff under Genl. R.E. Lee. Relieved from field duty, he saw service in the I.G. Department at Richmond.

Signature	Signature with rank	Pre & post War DS	War Dated DS	Pre & post War ALS	War Dated ALS
$185	$365	$	$	$	$

S, Clip. JH May 1992 $150.

Chilton, William Paris, 1810-71   Member Confederate Congress

Signature	Signature with rank	Pre & post War DS	War Dated DS	Pre & post War ALS	War Dated ALS
$35	$	$	$	$	$

Chipman, Henry Laurens, 1823-1910   Union Brevet General

102nd U.S. Colored Infantry.

Signature	Signature with rank	Pre & post War DS	War Dated DS	Pre & post War ALS	War Dated ALS
$20	$	$	$	$	$

Chipman, Norton Parker, 1836-1924   Union Brevet General

Bureau of Military Justice.

Signature	Signature with rank	Pre & post War DS	War Dated DS	Pre & post War ALS	War Dated ALS
$18	$	$	$	$45	$

ALS, 1870. `Lawyertalk'. JH August 1992 $35.

Chrisman, James Stone, 1818-81   Member Confederate Congress

Signature	Signature with rank	Pre & post War DS	War Dated DS	Pre & post War ALS	War Dated ALS
$30	$	$	$	$	$

Christ, Benjamin C., 1822-69   Union Brevet General
50th Pennsylvania.

Signature	Signature with rank	Pre & post War DS	War Dated DS	Pre & post War ALS	War Dated ALS
$20	$	$48	$	$	$

Christian, Jones Rivers, ? - 1895   2nd Lt., Sturat's Staff
Assistant aide-de-camp

Signature	Signature with rank	Pre & post War DS	War Dated DS	Pre & post War ALS	War Dated ALS
$	$	$	$485	$	$

Chrysler, Morgan Henry, 1822-90   Union General
A private who rose to the rank of General. He led a Cavalry Brigade for much of the war.

Signature	Signature with rank	Pre & post War DS	War Dated DS	Pre & post War ALS	War Dated ALS
$25	$	$75	$	$	$

Churchill, Thomas James, 1824-1905   Confederate Major General
He fought against Genl. Banks in the Red River Campaign while in the Trans-Mississippi Department.

Signature	Signature with rank	Pre & post War DS	War Dated DS	Pre & post War ALS	War Dated ALS
$75	$135	$	$	$195	$

Claiborne, James F., 1833-?   Confederate Marine Officer

Signature	Signature with rank	Pre & post War DS	War Dated DS	Pre & post War ALS	War Dated ALS
$	$175	$	$	$	$

Clanton, James Holt, 1827-71   Confederate Brigadier General
He led the 1st Alabama Cavalry at Shiloh, and was Genl. Bragg's aide-de-camp at
Farmington. He was seriously wounded, and captured at Bluff Springs, Florida. He war
Assassinatcd in a private feud in Knoxville, Tenn.

Signature	Signature with rank	Pre & post War DS	War Dated DS	Pre & post War ALS	War Dated ALS
$275	$385	$585	$	$	$

Clapp, Jeremiah Watkins, 1814-98   Member Confederate Congress

Signature	Signature with rank	Pre & post War DS	War Dated DS	Pre & post War ALS	War Dated ALS
$40	$	$	$	$	$

Clark, Charles, 1811-77   Confederate Brigadier General
He saw service in the Mexican War, and was wounded at Shiloh commanding his
division. In July, 1862, he was again wounded in Baton Rouge; captured and taken to
New Orleans, his wife war Allowed through the lines to nurse him.

Signature	Signature with rank	Pre & post War DS	War Dated DS	Pre & post War ALS	War Dated ALS
$150	$	$365	$	$	$

Clark, James C., ?-?   Civil War Song Composer

Signature	Pre & post War DS	War Dated DS	Pre & post War ALS	War Dated ALS
$35	$110	$	$	$

Clark, James Louis, 1841-1910   Captain CSA, Sturat's Staff
Aide-de-camp.

Signature	Signature with rank	Pre & post War DS	War Dated DS	Pre & post War ALS	War Dated ALS
$	$	$	$	$350	$

Clark, John Bullock Jr., 1831-1903   Confederate Brigadier General
Harvard graduate. He commanded a militia at Springfield, and a brigade at Pea Ridge.

Signature	Signature with rank	Pre & post War DS	War Dated DS	Pre & post War ALS	War Dated ALS
$90	$	$	$	$	$

Clark, John Bullock, Sr., 1802-85   Member Confederate Congress

Signature	Signature with rank	Pre & post War DS	War Dated DS	Pre & post War ALS	War Dated ALS
$35	$	$	$	$	$

Clark, William Thomas, 1831-1905   Union General
He served mainly in the 15th Corps. A carpetbagger, dismissed from Congress in 1872.

Signature	Signature with rank	Pre & post War DS	War Dated DS	Pre & post War ALS	War Dated ALS
$18	$	$	$68	$	$

DS, 1863 October . Orders Vicksburg Work Detail. JH August 1992 $50.

Clark, William White, 1819-83   Member Confederate Congress

Signature	Signature with rank	Pre & post War DS	War Dated DS	Pre & post War ALS	War Dated ALS
$45	$	$	$	$	$

Clay, Albert G., ?-?   Union Naval Commander

Signature	Signature with rank	Pre & post War DS	War Dated DS	Pre & post War ALS	War Dated ALS
$45	$75	$	$275	$	$

Clay, Cassius Marcellus, 1810-1903   Union General
American Abolitionist, who refused to fight because emancipation was not declared at
the beginning of the war. Minister to Russia.

Signature	Signature with rank	Pre & post War DS	War Dated DS	Pre & post War ALS	War Dated ALS
$75	$	$210	$	$	$

AQS, April 7, 1879, 1p., 8vo., "Liberty, Equality, Law & Justice." HCS Feb. 1994 $275.

Clay, Clement Claiborne Jr., 1816-82   Member Confederate Congress

Signature	Signature with rank	Pre & post War DS	War Dated DS	Pre & post War ALS	War Dated ALS
$40	$	$76	$	$	$

Clay, Henry, 1777-1852   American Politician

Signature	Signature with rank	Pre & post War DS	War Dated DS 1812	Pre & post War ALS	War Dated ALS 1812
$78	$	$	$	$425	$

ALS, 1851, July 14, Ashland, 1p. Request to " rectify an unintentional error" and reinstate an army officer. NS Nov. 1993 $395.

Clayton, Alexander Mosby, 1801-89   Member Confederate Congress

Signature	Signature with rank	Pre & post War DS	War Dated DS	Pre & post War ALS	War Dated ALS
$45	$	$86	$	$	$

Clayton, Henry DeLamor, 1827-89   Confederate Major General

He was with Bragg in the invasion of Kentucky, and severely wounded.

Signature	Signature with rank	Pre & post War DS	War Dated DS	Pre & post War ALS	War Dated ALS
$110	$	$	$	$	$

Clayton, Powell, 1833-1914   Union General

He led Cavalry mainly in Missouri and Arkansas. Postwar Gov. of Arkansas.

Signature	Signature with rank	Pre & post War DS	War Dated DS	Pre & post War ALS	War Dated ALS
$25	$	$65	$	$97	$

Cleburne, Patrick Roynayne, 1828-64   Confederate Major General

He planned the capture of the U.S. Arsenal in Arkansas, 1861. He was wounded at Perryville, and for his defense of Ringgold Gap, he receive the Thanks of the C.S. Congress. Killed 30 Nov. 1864 at Franklin, TN.

Signature	Signature with rank	Pre War DS	War Dated DS	Pre War ALS	War Dated ALS
$375	$575	$1,750	$	$	$

Clem, John Lincoln, "Johnny Clem" 1851-1937   Union Drummer Boy

of Chickamauga, Longest surviving Union Soldier

Signature	Signature with rank	Pre & post War DS	War Dated DS	Pre & post War ALS	War Dated ALS
$100	$165	$175	$	$275	$

ALS, 1915. 1p. Concerning his travel plans. JH August 1992 $175.

Clemens, Samuel L., "Mark Twain," 1835-1910   American Writer

Wrote "Adventures of Huckleberry Finn.", "The Adventures of Tom Sawyer."

Signature	Pre & post War DS	War Dated DS	Pre & post War ALS	War Dated ALS
$550	$1,234	$	$2,876	$

ALS, May 27, 1900. 1pp., 4x6", Albert Gate, to Wm. A. Wilcot, "I must have been too figurative, too poetical, & not quite definite enough. What I meant to convey was, that I couldn't come." UA Sept. 1993 $3,000.

---, Oct. 28/ 97. 2pp. 12mo., On black bordered stationery, to his sculptress, Mrs. Wirth pert. to a MS. UA Sept. 1993 $2,500.

DS, July 12, 1875. Check signed pay to the order of the Lotos Club, (some fading to purple paper, especially along edges, signature bold and clear). S Nov. 1993 $880.

--, 1900. Check signed, "S.L. Clemens" NS Nov. 1993 $2,000.

S, 3.5 x 2.5" Card signed "Mark Twain." LP Sept. 1993 $525.

-, July 83. Clip matted with 3x5" photograph of a seated Twain wearing a hat, framed. "Truely Yours/ Mark Twain/ July '83." HD Oct. 1993 $500.

-, April 18, 1908. "Mark Twain" on a menu of the "First Beefsteak Dinner of the Comic Artists. UA Sept. 1993 $1,200.

Clingman, Thomas Lanier, 1812-97   Confederate Brigadier General
He saw service in North Carolina, and was present at Drewry's Bluff and Cold Harbor. Wounded at Weldon Railroad.

Signature	Signature with rank	Pre & post War DS	War Dated DS	Pre & post War ALS	War Dated ALS
$90	$	$347	$	$	$

Clitz, H. B. 1824-88   Union Brevet Brigadier General
1845 WP graduate. He taught infantry tactics at WP. He was captured at Yorktown and at Gaines' Mill. After a stay at Libby Prison, he became Commandant of Cadets at WP.

Signature	Signature with rank	Pre & post War DS	War Dated DS	Pre & post War ALS	War Dated ALS
$18	$	$	$	$35	$

ALS, 1888. 1p. "Cann't make the Reunion." JH Sept. 1993 $30.

Clopton, David, 1820-92   Member Confederate Congress

Signature	Signature with rank	Pre & post War DS	War Dated DS	Pre & post War ALS	War Dated ALS
$35	$	$	$	$	$

S, Clip. JH August 1992 $20.

Cluseret, Gustave Paul, 1823-1900   Union General
He led Garibaldi's French Legion in the Crimean war. Fremont made him Chief of Staff.

Signature	Signature with rank	Pre & post War DS	War Dated DS	Pre & post War ALS	War Dated ALS
$20	$	$68	$	$	$

Cluskey, Michael Walsh, 1832-73   Mem. Confed. Congress & CS Major

Signature	Signature with rank	Pre & post War DS	War Dated DS	Pre & post War ALS	War Dated ALS
$45	$	$87	$	$	$

S, Clip. JH August 1992 $15.

Cobb, Howell 1815-68   Conf. Major General & 1st Sect'y of Conf.

Gov. of Georgia, U.S. Secretary of Treasury. Advocated immediate secession of Georgia after Lincoln's election as President. He commanded one of the largest brigades in CSA, 3,800 men. His forces defeated and received the surrender of General Stoneman.

Signature	Signature with rank	Pre & post War DS	War Dated DS	Pre & post War ALS	War Dated ALS
$95	$210	$225	$	$	$

LS, Sept. 8, 1859, 1p. 4to., Washington, To Congressman Thomas B. Florence refusing a request for information on the amount of merchandise and specie imported dutiable and fee during the last fiscal year. JB Dec. 1993 $250.
S, Clipped Signature, "Howelll Cobb." LR Dec. 1993 $75.
PS, CDV, sign Howell Cobb, shoulder view civilian w/bread. AP April 1992 $895.

Cobb, Thomas Reade Rootes, 1823-62   Confederate Brigadier General

He formed "Cobb's Legion," and served with distinction in the Battles of Seven Days and 2nd Manassas. Killed 13 Dec. 1862 at Fredericksburg, Va.

Signature	Signature with rank	Pre War DS	War Dated DS	Pre War ALS	War Dated ALS
$500	$1,500	$1,750	$	$2,500	$

ALS, pre-war legal document. SK Dec. 1993 $2,000.
S, Clip. GH 1992 $425.

Cobb, W. R. W., 1807-64   Confederate Congressman

Killed himself accidentally.

Signature	Signature with rank	Pre War DS	War Dated DS	Pre War ALS	War Dated ALS
$18	$	$	$	$	$

S. Clip. JH May 1992 $15.

Cochrane, John, 1813-98   Union General

He served with the 4th Corps. In 1864 he was Fremont's running mate against Lincoln.

Signature	Signature with rank	Pre & post War DS	War Dated DS	Pre & post War ALS	War Dated ALS
$20	$	$	$	$65	$

ALS, 1873. 1p. Granting his autograph. JH August 1992 $60.

Cocke, Phillip St. George, 1809-61   Confederate Brigadier General

WP graduate. He temporary served at the head of the 19th Virginia Infantry, and commanded the 5th Brigade at 1st Manassa. After a few months in the field, he returned home and committed suicide on Dec. 26, 1861. , in Powhatan County, VA.

Signature	Signature with rank	Pre War DS	War Dated DS	Pre War ALS	War Dated ALS
$350	$	$	$	$	$

Cockrell, Francis Marion, 1834-1915   Confederate Brigadier General

Enlisted as a private, he fought from Carthage to Vicksburg. He led a brigade under General French in the Atlanta Campaign, and ended the war at Mobile.

Signature	Signature with rank	Pre & post War DS	War Dated DS	Pre & post War ALS	War Dated ALS
$65	$	$	$	$225	$

ALS, Jan. 18, 1905, 1p., to Mr. Parkhurst, thanking him for his kind favor. LR Dec. 1993 $125.

Cody, William F., "Buffalo Bill," 1846-1917   Union Scout

Signature	Signature with rank	Pre & post War DS	War Dated DS	Pre & post War ALS	War Dated ALS
$550	$	$875	$	$1,435	$

Coffey, Titian J.,   Lincoln's Attorney General

Signature	Signature with rank	Pre & post War DS	War Dated DS	Pre & post War ALS	War Dated ALS
$	$	$	$	$	$

Extremely scarce

Colfax, Schuyler, 1823-85   American politician
VP under Grant at signing.

Signature	Signature with rank	Pre & post War DS	War Dated DS	Pre & post War ALS	War Dated ALS
$	$	$	$	$165	$

ALS, 1869, June 19, 1p., 8vo., Springfield, Mass., A reply to "one of hundreds of letters" to an unnamed correspondent. NS Nov. 1993 $130.

Colhoun, Edmund R., ?-?   Union Naval Commander

Signature	Signature with rank	Pre & post War DS	War Dated DS	Pre & post War ALS	War Dated ALS
$	$75	$	$	$	$

Collins, Napoleon, ?-?   Union Naval Commander

Signature	Signature with rank	Pre & post War DS	War Dated DS	Pre & post War ALS	War Dated ALS
$35	$85	$	$	$225	$

Colquitt, Alfred Holt, 1824-94   Confederate Brigadier General
Princeton graduate, and Colonel of the 6th Georgia Infantry during the Seven Days Battle, he fought at Sharpsburg and Chancellorsville. Gov. of Ga. in 1876 and U.S. Senator in 1882.

Signature	Signature with rank	Pre & post War DS	War Dated DS	Pre & post War ALS	War Dated ALS
$100	$175	$275	$	$458	$

Colston, Raleigh Edward, 1825-96   Confederate Brigadier General
A V.M.I. graduate, he commanded a brigade in the Peninsular Campaign, and served under Beauregard at Petersburg. After the war, he was a Colonel in the Egyptian Army.

Signature	Signature with rank	Pre & post War DS	War Dated DS	Pre & post War ALS	War Dated ALS
$87	$	$210	$	$	$

Colt, Samuel, 1814-62   Founder of Colt Firearms

Signature	Pre War DS	War Dated DS	Pre War ALS	War Dated ALS
$350	$1,785	$	$2,780	$

DS, Oct. 15, 1846, 1p., 8vo., New York, "Capt. Gilbert, Bot of Samuel Colt 5 bbls shad $12 - $60.00, 4 half blues Do $6 -$24.00 = $84.00. Received payment, Samuel Colt." HCS Feb. 1994 $2,800.

Colvororessis, George Musalas, 1816-1872   Union Naval Commander

Signature	Signature with rank	Pre & post War DS	War Dated DS	Pre & post War ALS	War Dated ALS
$35	$	$76	$	$128	$

Conner, James, 1829-83   Confederate General
He was a Captain at 1st Bull Run, was wounded at Mechanicsville, and led the 22nd North Carolina at Chancellorsville and Gettysburg. He then served on court martial duty.

Signature	Signature with rank	Pre & post War DS	War Dated DS	Pre & post War ALS	War Dated ALS
$110	$	$275	$	$345	$

Connor, Patrick Edward, 1820-91   Union General

He served in Utah and Nevada; mainly, Bannocks, Shoshones, Sioux, Cheyenne and Aprapahoe were his adversaries.

Signature	Signature with rank	Pre & post War DS	War Dated DS	Pre & post War ALS	War Dated ALS
$35	$	$	$	$	$

Connor, Selden, 1839-1917   Union General

He served in the 2nd and 3rd Corps at Antietam, Fredericksburg, Gettysburg and the Wilderness. He was twice wounded during the war.

Signature	Signature with rank	Pre & post War DS	War Dated DS	Pre & post War ALS	War Dated ALS
$18	$35	$78	$	$	$

Conrad, Charles, 1804-78   Conf. Chairman of Com. of Naval Affairs

Signature	Signature with rank	Pre & post War DS	War Dated DS	Pre & post War ALS	War Dated ALS
$65	$	$285	$	$	$

Cook, Jane, ?-?   Mother of Jefferson Davis

Signature	DS	ALS
$	$	$

Misc.

-, CDV. B/M B&G Moses, New Orleans. SK Nov. 1991 $145

Cook, John, 1825-1910   Union General

Helped with the capture of Fort Donelson, he was sent to the Northwest to fight the Sioux. By marriage he was kin to Lincoln.

Signature	Signature with rank	Pre & post War DS	War Dated DS	Pre & post War ALS	War Dated ALS
$25	$45	$	$110	$	$

Cook, Philip, 1817-94   Confederate Brigadier General

He entered as a private, and was wounded at Malvin Hill, and fought at Fredericksburg and Chancellorsville. He took a leave of absence to sit in the Georgia State Legislature.

Signature	Signature with rank	Pre & post War DS	War Dated DS	Pre & post War ALS	War Dated ALS
$145	$	$290	$	$	$

S, Clip, "Philip Cook, Americus, GA" on three lines. DZ July 1992 $110.

Cooke, John Rogers, 1833-91   Confederate Brigadier General

Harvard graduate and brother-in-law of JEB Stuart, Cooke was elected Colonel in the 27th North Carolina Infantry. He fought in almost all the major campaigns in Virginia and Maryland.

Signature	Signature with rank	Pre & post War DS	War Dated DS	Pre & post War ALS	War Dated ALS
$150	$275	$	$	$	$

S, April 22, 1864. Hd Qtrs Cook's Brigade, sgn w/rank. TC Nov. 1991 $150.

Cooke, Philip St. George, 1809-95   Union General

1827 WP graduate. He was father-in-law of JEB Stuart. He led the Regular Army Cavalry in the Army of the Potomac.

Signature	Signature with rank	Pre & post War DS	War Dated DS	Pre & post War ALS	War Dated ALS
$30	$48	$	$	$	$

S, On card dated Nov. 12, 186(?). RAS Oct. 1993 $30.

Cooper, Douglas Hancock, 1815-79   Confederate Brigadier General

A Captain in the Mexican War, he entered C.S. service as a Colonel of the 1st Choctaw and Chickasaw Mounted Rifles. He patrolled the Indian Territory, and drove the Union Indians into Kansas. He saw service under General Pike at Pea Ridge.

Signature	Signature with rank	Pre & post War DS	War Dated DS	Pre & post War ALS	War Dated ALS
$125	$235	$195	$	$	$

DS, [N.D.] Concerns clothing for the recruiting service, 2nd Regt. Artillery. DZ June 1992 $150.

Cooper, James, 1810-63   Union General

Signature	Signature with rank	Pre War DS	War Dated DS	Pre War ALS	War Dated ALS
$	$	$	$	$	$

Cooper, Joseph Alexander, 1823-1910   Union General

He served in the 12th and 23rd Corps. He saw combat at Fishing Creek, Murfreesboro, Chickamauga and Chattanooga. He then led a division in Sherman's March.

Signature	Signature with rank	Pre & post War DS	War Dated DS	Pre & post War ALS	War Dated ALS
$25	$	$	$	$	$

Cooper, Samuel, 1798-1876   Confederate Brigadier General

WP graduate. He was the adjutant and Inspector General and ranking General Officer in the Confederacy. He never saw field service.

Signature	Signature with rank	Pre & post War DS	War Dated DS	Pre & post War ALS	War Dated ALS
$75	$135	$150	$	$	$

DS, 1855. Sgn as U.S. General. JH August 1992 $125.
Free Frank, Signed as Asst. Sec. of War to an Ordinance officer, Augusta, Ga. BG Nov. 1993 $175.

S, 3x3" fragment, May 31, 1864, "Submit to the President with my recommendation JAS" SAG Feb. 1994 $325.

Copeland, Joseph Tarr, 1813-93   Union General

Custer replaced him on the eve of the Gettysburg battle. He then served on Draft Duty in Indiana and Il.

Signature	Signature with rank	Pre & post War DS	War Dated DS	Pre & post War ALS	War Dated ALS
$35	$	$85	$	$	$

Corbett, Boston, ? - ?   Sgt., 16th NY Cavalry

Shot John Wilkes Booth

Signature	Signature with rank	Pre & post War DS	War Dated DS	Pre & post War ALS	War Dated ALS
$525	$900	$	$	$	$

AQS, Card signed., on reverse a bible quote. WL Nov. 1992 $1,000.
S, Card signed, with rank and reg't. SK April 1993 $875.

Corbin, Henry Clarke, 1842-1909   Union Brevet General

14th U.S. Colored Troops

Signature	Signature with rank	Pre & post War DS	War Dated DS	Pre & post War ALS	War Dated ALS
$25	$	$65	$	$	$

ANS, 1906. St. Louis, 4 lines. ML October 1992 $40.
S, Clip as Adj. Gen'l. JH August 1992 $15.
Misc.
-, CDV in uniform. RSA Feb. 1994 $250.

Corcoran, Michael, 1827-63   Union General

He was captured at 1st Manassas and spent a year POW. He died near Fairfax when his horses fell on him. Rare.

Signature	Signature with rank	Pre War DS	War Dated DS	Pre War ALS	War Dated ALS
$	$	$	$	$	$

Corse, John Murray, 1835-93   Union General

WP dropout. He led divisions of the 25th and 16th Corps. He was the Union's hero of Allatoona Pass, Ga. during Sherman's March.

Signature	Signature with rank	Pre & post War DS	War Dated DS	Pre & post War ALS	War Dated ALS
$25	$	$	$	$75	$

ALS, 1887. 1p. Mentions Altoona to a Major. JH August 1992 $45.

Corse, Montgomery Dent, 1816-1895   Confederate Brigadier General
Colonel of the 17th Virginia Infantry, he saw service in the Battles of the Seven Pines and the Seven Days. He was captured with other generals at Sayler's Creek, April 6, 1865.

Signature	Signature with rank	Pre & post War DS	War Dated DS	Pre & post War ALS	War Dated ALS
$110	$	$	$	$	$

Cosby, George Blake, 1830-1909   Confederate Brigadier General
Graduated from West Point 1852, served in the army before the war and was a farmer after. During the War he took the famous surrender note from Buckner to Grant. He led a brigade under Van Dorn at Thompson's Station, Tenn.

Signature	Signature with rank	Pre & post War DS	War Dated DS	Pre & post War ALS	War Dated ALS
$80	$165	$	$	$	$

S, Signature with rank, CSA on card. SK Nov. 1993 $165.

Cosey, Joseph, ?-?   Noted 20th Century forgerer
Perhaps the most notorious forger of all time, Cosey made his living forging documents of Lincoln, Washington, Franklin and many others. Ironically, his forgeries, which are skillfully done, fooling many "experts," have themselves become collectible.

Signature	DS	ALS
$	$	$

ADS, 8vo, 1p., on vellum, "City Point, Va., Hon. E.M. Stranton, Sec. of War, Let this man pass over the lines into Culpepper Co., A. Lincoln. Sep. 2, 1862." LS Dec. 1993 $395.

Couch, Darius Nash, 1822-97 — Union General

Signature	Signature with rank	Pre & post War DS	War Dated DS	Pre & post War ALS	War Dated ALS
$30	$	$	$	$	$

Coulter, Richard, 1827-1908 — Union Brevet General

Signature	Signature with rank	Pre & post War DS	War Dated DS	Pre & post War ALS	War Dated ALS
$35	$	$	$	$85	$

Cowdin, Robert, 1805-74 — Union General

Signature	Signature with rank	Pre & post War DS	War Dated DS	Pre & post War ALS	War Dated ALS
$25	$	$76	$	$	$

Cowen, Benjamin Rush, 1831-1908 — Union Brevet General

Signature	Signature with rank	Pre & post War DS	War Dated DS	Pre & post War ALS	War Dated ALS
$18	$	$	$	$	$

Cox, Jacob Dolson, 1828-1900 — Union General

Signature	Signature with rank	Pre & post War DS	War Dated DS	Pre & post War ALS	War Dated ALS
$30	$	$	$	$	$

S, On card, with bold paraph. RAS Oct. 1993 $38.

Cox, John Cooke, 1817-72 — Union Brevet General

Signature	Signature with rank	Pre & post War DS	War Dated DS	Pre & post War ALS	War Dated ALS
$18	$	$48	$	$	$

Cox, Robert Corson, 1823-1901 — Union Brevet General

Signature	Signature with rank	Pre & post War DS	War Dated DS	Pre & post War ALS	War Dated ALS
$18	$	$	$	$	$

Cox, William Ruffin, 1832-1919   Confederate Brigadier General
Major with the 2nd North Carolina Infantry, Cox served most of the war with the Army of Northern Virginia, and was wounded almost a dozen times.   He surrendered at Appomattox.

Signature	Signature with rank	Pre & post War DS	War Dated DS	Pre & post War ALS	War Dated ALS
$150	$275	$	$345	$	$

Craig, Henry Knox, 1791-1869   Union Brevet General

Signature	Signature with rank	Pre & post War DS	War Dated DS	Pre & post War ALS	War Dated ALS
$28	$	$	$	$95	$

Craig, James, 1817-88   Union General

Signature	Signature with rank	Pre & post War DS	War Dated DS	Pre & post War ALS	War Dated ALS
$30	$	$	$105	$	$150

ALS, Oct. 29, 1864. 1p., 7.45x9.75", n.p.[Missouri], "Henry Brett a Detective Empoled by Gen. Fisk...has Captured two Rebels in Gentry Co. who will be in tonight...The Killig of Bill Anderson is Confirmed beyond a Doubt." MS Nov. 1993 $150.

Craven, Thomas T., ?-?   Union Naval Commander

Signature	Signature with rank	Pre & post War DS	War Dated DS	Pre & post War ALS	War Dated ALS
$45	$78	$	$	$	$

Crawford, Martin Jenkins, 1820-83   Member Confederate Congress

Signature	Signature with rank	Pre & post War DS	War Dated DS	Pre & post War ALS	War Dated ALS
$35	$	$	$	$95	$

ALS, 1858. to General. Benning, speaks of a slave auction, 1860 elections & S.A. Douglas. JH August 1991 $75.

Crenshaw, Edward, 1842-1911   Confederate Marine Officer

Signature	Signature with rank	Pre & post War DS	War Dated DS	Pre & post War ALS	War Dated ALS
$	$	$	$	$	$

Crittenden, George Bibb, 1812-80   Confederate Major General

WP graduate. He fought against Genl. Thomas at Mill Springs and was badly defeated. He resigned his commission in October 1862.

Signature	Signature with rank	Pre & post War DS	War Dated DS	Pre & post War ALS	War Dated ALS
$85	$	$210	$	$	$

Crittenden, Thomas Leonidas, 1819-93   Union General

Signature	Signature with rank	Pre & post War DS	War Dated DS	Pre & post War ALS	War Dated ALS
$40	$78	$	$	$	$

Crittenden, Thomas Turpin, 1825-1905   Union General

Signature	Signature with rank	Pre & post War DS	War Dated DS	Pre & post War ALS	War Dated ALS
$38	$	$	$	$105	$

Crocker, Marcellus Monroe, 1830-65   Union General

Signature	Signature with rank	Pre & post War DS	War Dated DS	Pre & post War ALS	War Dated ALS
$	$	$	$	$	$

Crook, George, 1828-90   Union General

Signature	Signature with rank	Pre & post War DS	War Dated DS	Pre & post War ALS	War Dated ALS
$100	$	$275	$	$	$

Croxton, John Thomas, 1836-74   Union General

Signature	Signature with rank	Pre & post War DS	War Dated DS	Pre & post War ALS	War Dated ALS
$35	$	$97	$	$	$

Cruft, Charles, 1826-83   Union General

Signature	Signature with rank	Pre & post War DS	War Dated DS	Pre & post War ALS	War Dated ALS
$35	$	$	$	$	$

Cullum, George Washington, 1809-92   Union General

Signature	Signature with rank	Pre & post War DS	War Dated DS	Pre & post War ALS	War Dated ALS
$25	$50	$	$	$	$

Cumming, Alfred, 1829-1910   Confederate Brigadier General

A WP graduate, Crittenden was captured during the Mexican War, released, and served with the cavalry in the U.S. Mounted Rifles. He fought against Genl. Thomas at Mill Springs and was badly defeated. He resigned his commission in Oct. 1862, but remained in service in various positions until the end of the War.

Signature	Signature with rank	Pre & post War DS	War Dated DS	Pre & post War ALS	War Dated ALS
$90	$	$298	$	$	$

Curtin, Andrew Gregg, 1817-94   Governor. of Pennsylvania

Signature	Signature with rank	Pre & post War DS	War Dated DS	Pre & post War ALS	War Dated ALS
$35	$	$65	$	$	$

Curtis, Newton Martin, 1835-1910   Union General

Signature	Signature with rank	Pre & post War DS	War Dated DS	Pre & post War ALS	War Dated ALS
$25	$	$76	$	$	$

Curtis, Samuel Ryan, 1805-66 — Union General

Signature	Signature with rank	Pre & post War DS	War Dated DS	Pre & post War ALS	War Dated ALS
$45	$75	$	$	$110	$

Cushing, Alonzo Hersford, 1841-62 — Union Officer

Signature	Signature with rank	Pre War DS	War Dated DS	Pre War ALS	War Dated ALS
$	$	$	$	$	$

Cushing, William B., 1842-74 — Union Naval Officer

Signature	Signature with rank	Pre & post War DS	War Dated DS	Pre & post War ALS	War Dated ALS
$35	$	$	$	$	$

Cushman, Pauline, 1835-93 — Union spy

Signature	Pre & post War DS	War Dated DS	Pre & post War ALS	War Dated ALS
$	$	$	$	$

Extremely rare.

Custer, Elizabeth B., 1842-1933 — Wife of George Custer

Signature	Signature with rank	Pre & post War DS	War Dated DS	Pre & post War ALS	War Dated ALS
$150.	$	$	$	$	$

S, Clip signature. SK Nov. 1993 $150.

Custer, George Armstong, 1839-76 — Union General
Killed 25 June 1876 at the Little Big Horn

Signature	Signature with rank	Pre & post War DS	War Dated DS	Pre & post War ALS	War Dated ALS
$2,500	$3,250	$8,000	$	$7,800	$

ALS, Sept. 24, 1865. 1p. 5x8", Mr. O. Hough is hereby authorized to take possession of my horse Roanoke now in Monroe, Mich. upon his paying to Hon. D. G. Bacon of Monroe the price agreed upon viz $250. G.A. Custer Maj. Genl." RAS Oct. 1993 $6,600.
---, June 11, 1874. 1pp. 4to., 7.75x9.75", "Please inform me whether the provisions of G.O. No. 51, War Depart. ... apply to enlisted Indian Scouts or not. Very Respectfully G

A Custer, Lieutenant Colonel 7th Cavalry Brevetted Major General U.S.A. Commanding." UA Sept. 1993 $12,000.

LS, March 2, 1865. 1pp. 8vo., 4x7.25" Head Quarters 3rd Cavalry Division, written in pencil on the morning of his victory at Waynesboro, Va., to Bvt Maj Genl Grant", describing his circumstance. UA Sept. 1993 $10,500.

---, 1863 July 26. 7 3/4 pages, quarto, Head Quarters 3rd Div. Cav. Corps Amissville Va. To Judge Isaac P. Christiancy, Custer informs him that he has been appointed Brigadier- General, then offers the position of Aide-de-Camp to the Judge's son, James., to help ensure support for his confirmation against any resistance from Michigan senators. PIH Dec. 1992 $85,000.

ANS, April 22, 1865,1p. 7.68x9.75" "Guards Pickets and Everybody else Please pass the bearer of this paper to any point except to these Headquarters and confer an everlasting favor upon the undersigned. G.A. Custer BMjGen Cav Div." RAS Oct. 1993 $5,125.

DS, Feb. 1875. 1p. Folio. appointment of William B. James as Corporal in Co. E, 7th Cavalry. UA Feb. 1994 $10,000.

S, Cover addressed by Custer to his wife., "Mrs. Genl G. A. Custer..." RAS Oct. 1993 $2,200.

-, (1865 April 15 - 1866 July 28). Album leaf sgd as Maj. Genl. U.S . Vols., unifomly toned. EB August 1992 $3,850.

Misc.

SC, Nov 11, 1868. envelope to "Mrs. Genl G A Custer Fort Leavenworth Kansas", in his hand. UA Sept. 1993 $3,750.

Cutler, Lysander, 1807-66 Union General

Signature	Signature with rank	Pre & post War DS	War Dated DS	Pre & post War ALS	War Dated ALS
$50	$78	$	$	$	$

Cutts, Richard Dominicus, 1817-83 Union Brevet General

Signature	Signature with rank	Pre & post War DS	War Dated DS	Pre & post War ALS	War Dated ALS
$18	$	$	$	$65	$

ALS, 1874. Sending his autograph. JH August 1992 $25.

D

Dahlgreen, John Adolph, 1809-70   Union Naval Rear Admiral
Inventor of the Dahlgren gun. LOC. papers, 1824-89. ca. 10,000 items.

Signature	Signature with rank	Pre & post War DS	War Dated DS	Pre & post War ALS	War Dated ALS
$125	$175	$	$	$	$

S, Signature as Rear Admiral on imprinted page, 12mo, Flag Ship, SOuth Atlantic Blockading Squadron, Charleston Roads, 4 Feb. 1864. Matted with reprint of Mathew Brady photograph of Dahlgren by his famous gun. JB Dec. 1993 $175.
-, Clip, signed as rear admiral commanding South Atlantic blockading squadron. GH July 1992 $125.

Dahlgreen, Ulric, 1842-64   Union Colonel
Raided Fredericksburg, VA., Nov. 9, 1862. Soon after Gettysburg he lost a leg. After service on Meade's and other staffs he was killed in a raid on Richmond with the design of either capturing or killing Jefferson Davis.

Signature	Signature with rank	Pre & post War DS	War Dated DS	Pre & post War ALS	War Dated ALS
$225	$275	$	$	$	$

Dana, Charles Anderson, 1819-97   Federal Asst. Secretary War
LOC. papers, 1859-82. ca. 300 items.

Signature	Signature with rank	Pre & post War DS	War Dated DS	Pre & post War ALS	War Dated ALS
$30	$	$	$75	$78	$145

ALS, 1859. 1p. 4to, New York. Concerning employment openings at the N.Y. Sun. WB September 1991 $75.
LS, 1p. 4to, War Dept., 1864. Appointment of L. Carter a 2nd Lt., in 2d. Regt. G. M. Vols. Colored. Split at the folds. WB September 1991 $50.
S, Clip signature. JH Sept. 1993 $25.

Dana, Napolean Jackson Tecumseh, 1822-1905   Union General

Signature	Signature with rank	Pre & post War DS	War Dated DS	Pre & post War ALS	War Dated ALS
$25	$	$45	$	$	$

112

Daniels, Junius, 1828-64   Confederate Brigadier General
WP graduate, he was Colonel of the 14th North Carolina Infantry, and fought at Seven Days, Malvern Hill, and Drewry's Bluff. He fought with great distinction at Gettysburg, and was killed 12 May 1864 at Spotsylvania, Va., while attemping to recapture the "Mule-Shoe."

Signature	Signature with rank	Pre & post War DS	War Dated DS	Pre & post War ALS	War Dated ALS
$250	$	$	$	$	$

A rare signature.

Davidson, Henry Brevard, 1831-99   Confederate Brigadier General
WP graduate, and effective adjutant, he war Assigned to various Generals during the early part of the war. He was captured by Genl. Pope at the Battle of Island 10, and was with Genl. Lomax in the Valley Campaign.

Signature	Signature with rank	Pre & post War DS	War Dated DS	Pre & post War ALS	War Dated ALS
$85	$	$255	$	$378	$

Davidson, John Wynn, 1824-81   Union General

Signature	Signature with rank	Pre & post War DS	War Dated DS	Pre & post War ALS	War Dated ALS
$	$	$	$	$	$

Davies, Henry EuGenerale, 1836-94   Union General

Signature	Signature with rank	Pre & post War DS	War Dated DS	Pre & post War ALS	War Dated ALS
$20	$35	$65	$	$97	$

Davies, Thomas Alfred, 1809-99 — Union General

Signature	Signature with rank	Pre & post War DS	War Dated DS	Pre & post War ALS	War Dated ALS
$	$40	$	$85	$	$

Davis, Charles Henry, 1807-77 — Union Naval Admiral

He was Chief of Staff during the Port Royal, South Carolina invasion in 1861. He was later Flag Officer for the Mississippi River Flotilla he led strikes against Fort Pillow, Memphis, Vicksburg and the Yazoo River.

Signature	Signature with rank	Pre & post War DS	War Dated DS	Pre & post War ALS	War Dated ALS
$25	$45	$75	$	$	$

Davis, David, ?-? Ill. US Senator, — Lincoln Crony, Assoc. Justice

Signature	Signature with rank	Pre & post War DS	War Dated DS	Pre & post War ALS	War Dated ALS
$30	$	$	$	$	$275

ALS, May 15, [1864]. To unnamed man, Davis has appointment with President, will report next day. EB August 1992 $250.
S, Clip. NLM Nov. 1992 $25.

Davis, Edmund Jackson, 1827-83 — Union General

He served in the 19th Corps Cavalry both in Texas and Louisiana. Postwar Governor of Texas.

Signature	Signature with rank	Pre & post War DS	War Dated DS	Pre & post War ALS	War Dated ALS
$25	$35	$76	$	$87	$

Davis, George, 1820-96 Member Confederate Congress & Atty. General

Signature	Signature with rank	Pre & post War DS	War Dated DS	Pre & post War ALS	War Dated ALS
$45	$	$	$	$145	$

Davis, Hasbrouck, 1827-1870 — Union Brevet. General

12th Illinois Cavalry; during the Antietam Battle with 1300 other Cavalrymen he cut his way out of Harpers Ferry.

Signature	Signature with rank	Pre & post War DS	War Dated DS	Pre & post War ALS	War Dated ALS
$25	$	$	$	$84	$

Davis, Jefferson, 1808-89   President of the Confederacy
LOC. papers, 1806-1913 ca. 500 items.

Signature	Signature with rank	Pre & post War DS	War Dated DS	Pre & post War ALS	War Dated ALS
$600	$	$1,650	$2,455	$1,750	$15,875

EXAMPLE OF JEFFERSON DAVIS SIGNATURE FOLLOW:

EXAMPLE OF HIS PROXY WIFE'S VARINA DAVIS SIGNATURE FOLLOW:

ALS, May 3, 1863, 1p.,Richmond, To Genl. Reuben Davis, "Your dispatch recived. Genl. J.R. Davis Brigade is now in the face of the Enemy and you will perceive by intelligence now going over the wires what our condition is Genl. Pemberton is engaged with the Enemy south of Vicksburg and you know his necessities. I have no information in refernce to the troops near Okolona. If they are Militia I cannot appoint a commander for them, if there be a Brigade of Confederate troops without a Brigadier Genl. I will readily adopt the recommendation of the people of Aberdeen in relation to appointment of Ghoson. Jeffer. Davis. Copy sent by telegraph W.P.I." SAG Feb. 1994 $20,500.
---, Mar. 21, 1888, 1p. 5x8", Beauvoir, Miss. pert. to a leagal matter, request a change in venue in the case Crozier vs. Jefferson Davis. OP Jan. 1994 $1,200.
---, July 28, 1884. 1p., "My dear Genl, in answer to a question put by the special committee of the House I gave the enclosed answer. It has not been printed and I sent it to you for your perusal and such use in your committee and in the Senate as your judgement will dictate. Very truely yrs. Jeffer: Davis" RAS Oct. 1993 $1210.
---, July 7, 1873. 2pp. 5x8", 8vo., to Mrs. A.M. Upshur, responding to her questions regarding her father's estate. UA Sept. 1993 $1,650.
---, July 5, 1875. Memphis, Tn., 1p., 8vo., to G.G.Adam, Esq. "..You did not give your sister's address and therefore I can not in complying with her wish send directly to her this evidence of my readiness to serve her." Split at fold. NS Nov. 1993 $1,200. July 3, 1860, 1pg. pert. that ltr. was recieved. KO Sept. 1993 $475.
---, April 8, 1881. 1p, 8vo, Beauvois, Miss., on lined paper to Rev H.E. Hayden, thanking him for the publication of a pamphlet that refutes charges that explosive or poisoned balls were used by the Confederate Army. W October 1992 $4,950.
---, Sept. 20, 1872. 1p, 8x5" Baltimore. To Rev. W. F. Brand welcomes a visit. SA August 1992 $1,500.
---, June 1876. 2p Memphis, Tn. To Maj. Walthall inquiring about Turnbull...strict confidentiality. GH July 1992 $1,350.
---, Oct. 25, 1867. 2pp, 4.5x7" & 4.5x6", Lennoxville, Canada. To James Robb, Esqr. concerning his help in selling land davis owns in Arkansas..."It is not for obvious

reasons well that my name should be known in the transaction." matted. HD June 1992 $1,400.

Autographed Telegram: April 10, 1865, 1p. to General J.E. Johnston, announcing Lee's surrender at Appomattox. S May 1994 $145,500.

---, war dated, 1p. to General Bragg. SK Dec. 1993 $4,000

LS, April 25, 1863. 4pp. Richmond, VA., "To the House of Representatives, after much deliberation, the result of the great deference paid to the opinion of the Congress, I return to your honorable body with my objectives an Act which orginated in the House, entitled 'An Act to Aid Committess of Congress in the investigation of matters referred to them and to punish false swearing before said Committees..." SAG Feb. 1994 $37,500.

--, March 20, 1863. 2pp. Richmond, VA., In answer to an inquiry from Thomas O. Moore, Gov. of Louisina, "Sir: Upon the receipt of your letter of January 29th, transmitting a copy of a 'Joint Resolution relative to the suspension from their respective commands of Lt. Col. V.A. Fournet and Capt. E.D. Fuller,' I directed the Adjutant General to make such a Report upon the case as the records of his office should enable him to prepare..." SAG Feb. 1994 $8,000.

--, May 10, 1855. 1p., 4to., Washington, as Secretary of War to Attorney General Caleb Cushing concerning the validity of the title to some land. HCS Feb. 1994 $875.

--, Same as follows, the result of a earlier trade. HS August 1993 $1,100.

--, Oct. 22, 1855. 1p. as Secretary of War to the U.S. To consulate in Lima, Peru, being a letter of introduction. GH July 1992 $1,500.

--, Nov. 25, 1856. 1pg. Washington. Death Certificate for a soldier killed in Texas. Also signed by Samuel Cooper. GH July 1992 $2,500.

--, August 3, 1871. 8x3" partly printed check, the Savings Bank of Memphis, Tn., payable for $500. Matted w/engraving. HD June 1992 $700.

--, Feb. 20, 1879. 1p, quarto, Beauvoir, Harrison County, Miss., promise to pay to the order of Mrs Sarah A Dorsey, the sum of two thousand and five hundred dollors ... the conveyance of a tract of land. JM October 1992 $6,500.

AQS, 1p., 5.5x2.5", Beauvoir, Miss., " Respect the rights of your neighbors and sympathize with them in their sufferings. Jefferson Davis/ Beauvoir, Misspi. 29th Oct. 1883." SAG Feb. 1994 $1,050.

Franking signature:

-, Envelope addressed by Davis to Colonel Edwards & franked Jeffn Davis, U.S.S.. NLM Nov. 1992 $750.

S, Bold signature, a free frank w/ "U.S.S." SK Jan. 1994 $550.

-, Bold signature on a card, with portrait. JB Dec. 1993 $550.

-, Clipped signature on 4x1.25" sheet. Smudge of ink. NS Nov. 1993 $450.

-, Clipped signature, free frank, "Jefferson Davis/ U.S.S." SK Nov. 1993 $550.

-, Clipped signature, mounting traces on verso. BG Nov. 1993 $550.

-, Clipped signature, signed "Jefferson Davis/ U.S.S." UA Oct. 1993 $550.

-, Bold signature, clip, "Jefferson Davis". UA Sept. 1993 $495.

P, CDV, b/m C.R. Rees, Richmond, Va. ca, 1863/64. KO Sept. 1993 $6,500.

-, Signed Cabinet card, 4.25 x 6.5", a portrait by W. W. Washburn, New Orleans, La, 1882. Signed on image "Jefferson Davis 1882". JM October 1992 $5,000.

MISC.

-, Cover in his hand addressed to Mrs. S. A. Barrow in Griffin, GA., Richmond, Va., May 28, 1863, Executive Department. RAS Oct. 1993 $525.

-, Mississippi Election Ticket. SK August 1993 $300.

-, Virginia Election Ticket. Nov 1861 Election. [Parrish 6041] GH October 1992 $250.

-, Virginia Election Ticket. SK Aug 1991 $265.

Davis, Jefferson Columbus, 1828-79   Union General

In response to a slap on the face, he shot and killed Genl. William Nelson, on Sept. 20, 1862.

Signature	Signature with rank	Pre & post War DS	War Dated DS	Pre & post War ALS	War Dated ALS
$35	$60	$	$	$	$

S, On card as Brevet Major Genl. RAS Oct. 1994 $50

Davis, Joseph Robert, 1825-96   Confederate Brigadier General

President Davis was his Uncle; he served for a time on Davis' Staff in Richmond. He fough at Gettysburg, the Wilderness Campaign, and was paroled at Appomattox Court House.

Signature	Signature with rank	Pre & post War DS	War Dated DS	Pre & post War ALS	War Dated ALS
$175	$	$	$	$	$

Davis, Nelson Henry, 1821-90   Union Brevet General

Led the 7th Mass. after several small fights friends planning a visit.

Signature	Signature with rank	Pre & post War DS	War Dated DS	Pre & post War ALS	War Dated ALS
$25	$35	$	$55	$	$150

S, Clip signature. JH Aug. 1993 $25.

Davis, Nicholas, Jr., 1825-75   Member Confederate Congress

Signature	Signature with rank	Pre & post War DS	War Dated DS	Pre & post War ALS	War Dated ALS
$45	$	$	$	$	$

Davis, Reuben, 1813-90   Member Confederate Congress

Signature	Signature with rank	Pre & post War DS	War Dated DS	Pre & post War ALS	War Dated ALS
$48	$	$	$	$	$

Davis, William George Mackey, 1812-98   Confed. Brigadier General

A Colonel in the 1st Florida Cavalry, which he financed and recruited. He resigned his commission, and until the end of the war was involved in blockade running.

Signature	Signature with rank	Pre & post War DS	War Dated DS	Pre & post War ALS	War Dated ALS
$85	$145	$	$	$	$

Davis, William Watts Hart, 1820-1910   Union Brevet General

Briefly commanded the 54th Mass. in his brigade.

Signature	Signature with rank	Pre & post War DS	War Dated DS	Pre & post War ALS	War Dated ALS
$25	$30	$	$50	$	$

DS, 1863. at Morris Island, S.C., Ornate & decorative. JH Aug. 1993 $40.

Davis, Varina Anne Banks Howell, 1826-1906   Wife of Jefferson Davis

Signed many letters in her husband behalf, would generally place a "." after Davis.

Signature	Pre & post War DS	War Dated DS	Pre & post War ALS	War Dated ALS
$225	$	$	$525	$

ALS, May 31, 1878. Beauvior, Miss., to a Mrs. Payne as a ltr. of introduction for Mr. Howard Mertin. UA Feb. 1994 $325.
---, April 19, 1886. 1p. 8to. Beauvoir, Miss., to Capt. Newell in la. pert. to business matters. BG Nov. 1993 $350.
---, May 14, 1895. 2pg. To the wife of Col. J. Reeves. GH August 1992 $550.
---, Jan. 20, 1897. 1p, 8vo, The Girard, W, 44th St., [N.Y.], with the original envelope addressed to Dr. D.S.Foster, Wash, D.C., concerning the last house she occupied. W October 1992 $154.
---, n.d. [ca.1880's], 1p. 7x4.5", n.p., to James Redpath" ...Mr. Davis has been & is too ill to do any literay work of any kind. She goes on with an account of the battle of Yorktown, "Geml Johnston retreated...& the enemy occupied the redoubts & slaughtered a good many of our troops..." SA August 1992 $1,050.

Dawkins, James Baird, 1820-83   Member Confederate Congress

Signature	Signature with rank	Pre & post War DS	War Dated DS	Pre & post War ALS	War Dated ALS
$38	$	$	$	$	$

Dearing, James, 1840-65   Confederate Brigadier General

Resigned from West Point in 1861 to join the famous New Orleans Washington Artillery. He fought at Gettysburg and in the Petersburg Campaign. While retreating to Appomattox, he was engaged in a pistol fight with Union Gen'l Theodore Read; Read was killed instantly and Dearing was severly wounded. He died 23 April 1865 of wounds rec'd 6 April 1865 at High Bridge, Va.

Signature	Signature with rank	Pre War DS	War Dated DS	Pre War ALS	War Dated ALS
$	$	$	$	$	$

A rare signature.

Deas, Zachariah Cantey, 1812-82   Confederate Brigadier General

He financed and assembled the 22nd Alabama Infantry. Wounded at Shiloh, he fought with distinction at Murfreesboro, Chattanooga, and in the Carolina Campaign.

Signature	Signature with rank	Pre & post War DS	War Dated DS	Pre & post War ALS	War Dated ALS
$85	$145	$	$	$	$

Debray, Xavier Blanchard, 1818-95   Confederate Brigadier General

A General designated by Genl. Kirby Smith, Trans-Mississippi Department., on April 13, 1864.

Signature	Signature with rank	Pre & post War DS	War Dated DS	Pre & post War ALS	War Dated ALS
$90	$	$	$	$	$

De Clouet, Alevander, 1812-90 Member Confederate Congress

Signature	Signature with rank	Pre & post War DS	War Dated DS	Pre & post War ALS	War Dated ALS
$	$45	$	$	$	$

Deitzler, George Washington, 1826-84 Union General

Signature	Signature with rank	Pre & post War DS	War Dated DS	Pre & post War ALS	War Dated ALS
$30	$48	$87	$	$	$

De Lagnel, Julius Adolphus, 1827-1912 Confederate Brigadier General
A Captain in the C.S. Army, R.S. Garnett made him his Chief of Artillery. He was wounded at Rich Mountain, and war Appointed and confirmed by the C.S. Congress as B.G., April 15, 1862, but he declined the appointment. He remaiuned 2nd in command of the Ordnance Bureau in Richmond.

Signature	Signature with rank	Pre & post War DS	War Dated DS	Pre & post War ALS	War Dated ALS
$75	$	$	$	$	$

Delafield, Richard, 1798-1873 Union Engineer/General

Signature	Signature with rank	Pre & post War DS	War Dated DS	Pre & post War ALS	War Dated ALS
$30	$45	$	$	$	$

Delany, Martin, ?-? First black officer in Union Army
Graduate of Harvard Medical School.

Signature	Signature with rank	Pre & post War DS	War Dated DS	Pre & post War ALS	War Dated ALS
$100	$250	$	$	$	$

Dennis, Elias Smith, 1812-94 Union General

Signature	Signature with rank	Pre & post War DS	War Dated DS	Pre & post War ALS	War Dated ALS
$18	$35	$	$	$96	$

Dent, Frederick Tracy, 1820-92   Union General

Signature	Signature with rank	Pre & post War DS	War Dated DS	Pre & post War ALS	War Dated ALS
$20	$	$48	$	$	$

DS, 1872. Check signed. JH April 1991 $35.

Denver, James William, 1817-92   Union General

Signature	Signature with rank	Pre & post War DS	War Dated DS	Pre & post War ALS	War Dated ALS
$35	$55	$	$	$	$300

ALS, Aug. 30, 1861, to Brig. Genl. Sumner at San Francisco, in preparation to going west. RAS Oct. 1993 $310.

De Russy, Gustavus Adolphus, 1818-91   Union General

Signature	Signature with rank	Pre & post War DS	War Dated DS	Pre & post War ALS	War Dated ALS
$20	$45	$	$	$96	$

Deshler, James, 1833-63   Confederate Brigadier General

WP graduate. He was Genl. H.R. Jackson's Adjutent, and was wounded at Allegheny Summitt in 1861. Promoted to Chief of Artillery in the Department of North Carolina under Genl. Holmes. He was killed 20 Sept 1863 at Chickamauga, Ga.

Signature	Signature with rank	Pre War DS	War Dated DS	Pre War ALS	War Dated ALS
$225	$375	$	$	$	$

A rare signature.

De Trobriand, Philippe Regis Denis de Keredern, 1816-97   Union Genl.

Signature	Signature with rank	Pre & post War DS	War Dated DS	Pre & post War ALS	War Dated ALS
$35	$45	$	$	$	$

Devens, Charles Jr., 1820-91   Union General

Signature	Signature with rank	Pre & post War DS	War Dated DS	Pre & post War ALS	War Dated ALS
$20	$45	$	$	$	$

Devin, Thomas Casimer, 1822-78   Union General

Signature	Signature with rank	Pre & post War DS	War Dated DS	Pre & post War ALS	War Dated ALS
$25	$	$	$	$	$

Dewey, Joel Allen, 1840-73   Union General

Signature	Signature with rank	Pre & post War DS	War Dated DS	Pre & post War ALS	War Dated ALS
$	$35	$	$	$87	$

DeWitt, William Henry, 1827-96   Member Confederate Congress

Signature	Signature with rank	Pre & post War DS	War Dated DS	Pre & post War ALS	War Dated ALS
$45	$	$	$	$	$

Dibrell, George Gibbs, 1822-88   Confederate Brigadier General

Enlisted as a Private, he served as Lt. Colonel in Kentucky and Tenn. under Genl Zollicoffer. He raised the 8th Tenn. Cavalry behind Federal lines to operate as independent partisan Rangers. Served with Genl. Forrest at Stones River.

Signature	Signature with rank	Pre & post War DS	War Dated DS	Pre & post War ALS	War Dated ALS
$150	$275	$	$	$	$

S, Clip. JH May 1992 $90.

Dickinson, James Shelton, 1818-82   Confederate Congressman

Signature	Signature with rank	Pre & post War DS	War Dated DS	Pre & post War ALS	War Dated ALS
$	$45	$	$	$	$

122

Dix, Dorothea Lynde, 1802-87   Union Nurse / Superintendant of

Signature	Signature with rank	Pre & post War DS	War Dated DS	Pre & post War ALS	War Dated ALS
$110	$	$175	$375	$225	$478

Dix, John Adams, 1798-1879   Union Major General

Signature	Signature with rank	Pre & post War DS	War Dated DS	Pre & post War ALS	War Dated ALS
$35	$50	$48	$	$80	$

ALS, 1870, 2p. to family friend planning a visit. JH Aug. 1993 $75.
---, 1874. West Hampton, (no description of content). ALE August 1992 $60.
S, Clip, with closing. BG Nov. 1993 $30.
-, 1835. Sgn. blank of a slip as Commissioner of the Canal Fund. RAS Oct. 1993 $45.
-, Clip. NLM Nov. 1992 $35.

Doak, Henry Melville, 1841-1928   Confederate Marine Officer

Signature	Signature with rank	Pre & post War DS	War Dated DS	Pre & post War ALS	War Dated ALS
$	$145	$	$	$	$

Dockery, Thomas Pleasant, 1833-98   Confederate Brigadier General
He commanded the 19th Arkansa Infantry at Wilson's Creek, and for a time was with Genl. Price in Arkansas. He commanded a brigade at Marks Mills and Jenkin's Ferry.

Signature	Signature with rank	Pre & post War DS	War Dated DS	Pre & post War ALS	War Dated ALS
$90	$210	$	$325	$	$

Dodge, Charles Cleveland, 1841-1910   Union General
A general before his 21st birthday, he resigned a year later. This Cavalry leader was not popular with his immediate commander, Genl. Peck.

Signature	Signature with rank	Pre & post War DS	War Dated DS	Pre & post War ALS	War Dated ALS
$25	$38	$	$	$	$

123

Dodge, Grenville Mellen, 1831-1916 — Union General
In the Atlanta Campaign he led Sherman's 16th Corps where he was badly wounded.

Signature	Signature with rank	Pre & post War DS	War Dated DS	Pre & post War ALS	War Dated ALS
$45	$76	$	$	$	$

Doherty, Edward P., ? - ? — Capt., 16th N.Y. Cavalry
Pursited John Wilkes Booth

Signature	Signature with rank	Pre & post War DS	War Dated DS	Pre & post War ALS	War Dated ALS
$	$150	$	$	$	$

Doles, George Pierce, 1830-64 — Confederate Brigadier General
A Colonel with the 4th Georgia Infantry, and an incredible military strategist, he fought gallantly at Fredericksburg, Chancellorsville, and the Wilderness. On June 2, 1864, Genl. Doles was killed 2 June 1864 at Bethesda Church, Va., by a Union Sharpshooter.

Signature	Signature with rank	Pre War DS	War Dated DS	Pre War ALS	War Dated ALS
$	$	$	$	$	$

An extremely rare autograph.

Donelson, Daniel Smith, 1801-63 — Confederate Major General
WP graduate, he chose the site for Fort Donelson which is named for him. He commanded a brigade under Loring in West Virginia. Died April 17, 1863.

Signature	Signature with rank	Pre War DS	War Dated DS	Pre War ALS	War Dated ALS
$	$	$	$	$	$

A very scarce signature.

Doolittle, Charles Camp, 1832-1903   Union General

His service was mainly in Kentucky and Tennessee.

Signature	Signature with rank	Pre & post War DS	War Dated DS	Pre & post War ALS	War Dated ALS
$30	$	$78	$135	$	$

Doolittle, James Rood, 1815-1897   US Senator, Wisconsin

Signature	Signature with rank	Pre & post War DS	War Dated DS	Pre & post War ALS	War Dated ALS
$20	$	$	$	$	$

Dortch, William Theophilus, 1824-89   Member Confederate Congress

Signature	Signature with rank	Pre & post War DS	War Dated DS	Pre & post War ALS	War Dated ALS
$38	$	$	$	$	$

Doubleday, Abner, 1819-93   Union General

At Fort Sumter, he is said to have fired the first shot at the Confederates. He assumed command of the 1st Corps at Gettysburg after John Reynolds was killed.

Signature	Signature with rank	Pre & post War DS	War Dated DS	Pre & post War ALS	War Dated ALS
$400	$750	$	$	$1,678	$3,875

ALS, May 7, 1892. 1p, 4to. To Col. John B Bachelder, regrets he   can't attend the dedication of the high water mark memorial at Gettysburg, due a spinal problem. JM October 1992 $2,500.

S, Signed card. SR Nov. 1993 $325.

Misc.

-, Original profile bust drawing of Doubleday in pencil, 4 x 7" grey sheet, signed "Kelly/ Nov. 6/ 1879., Lightly signed in brown ink Abner Doubleday / Major General. HD June 1992 $600.

Douglas, Frederick, 1817-95   Escaped slave & abolitionist

LOC. papers, 1854-1964. ca. 7,300 items.

Signature	Pre & post War DS	War Dated DS	Pre & post War ALS	War Dated ALS
$350	$478	$	$	$

LS, Nov. 4, 1867, 1p. 8vo., To Fred. W. Gunster Esq., pert to an to meeting date. JB Dec. 1993 $425.

S, 1885. Clip signature. ALE August 1992 $150.

Misc.

-, The Dividing Line between Federal and Local Authority. NY 1859. 8vo, 40pp. SP
August 1992 $60.

Dow, Neal, 1804-97   Temperence Reformer & Union General

Signature	Signature with rank	Pre & post War DS	War Dated DS	Pre & post War ALS	War Dated ALS
$45	$	$	$	$125	$

Drayton, Thomas Fenwich, 1808-1891   Confederate General
WP graduate, he served at Port Royal, lost Forts Walker and Beauregard. A poor field
commander, for the last years of the war he served on various Boards of Inquiry.

Signature	Signature with rank	Pre & post War DS	War Dated DS	Pre & post War ALS	War Dated ALS
$90	$165	$	$	$	$

Drum, Richard Coulter, 1825-1909   Brevet Brigadier General
Assistant Adjutant General.

Signature	Signature with rank	Pre & post War DS	War Dated DS	Pre & post War ALS	War Dated ALS
$20	$40	$	$87	$84	$

DuBose, Dudley McIver, 1834-83   Confederate Brigadier General
Lt. 15th Georgia, he was wounded at Chickamauga, commanded Wolford's Brigade
under Kershaw in the siege at Petersburg. Captured with Ewell at Sayler's Creek.

Signature	Signature with rank	Pre & post War DS	War Dated DS	Pre & post War ALS	War Dated ALS
$140	$285	$	$	$	$

Duffie, Alfred Napoleon Alexander, 1835-80   Union General

1854 St. Cyr graduate, France. He rose quickly in Pleasonton's Cavalry where he led a division.

Signature	Signature with rank	Pre & post War DS	War Dated DS	Pre & post War ALS	War Dated ALS
$20	$	$55	$	$78	$

Duke, Basil Wilson, 1838-1916   Confederate Brigadier General

Enlisted as a private in Morgan's Lexington Rifles. He was wounded at Shiloh and captured in the Ohio Raid of 1863. He disbanded his infantry and took his cavalry to join Johnston, escorting President Davis from Charlotte, until his capture.

Signature	Signature with rank	Pre & post War DS	War Dated DS	Pre & post War ALS	War Dated ALS
$85	$	$	$	$600	$

Duncan, Johnson Kelly, 1827-62   Confederate Brigadier General

WP graduate, stationed in New Orleans, Genl. Duncan was in charge of all coastal and river defenses of New Orleans. When New Orleans fell, he was captured and later exchanged. He died 18 Dec 1862 at Knoxville, TN., of natural causes.

Signature	Signature with rank	Pre War DS	War Dated DS	Pre War ALS	War Dated ALS
$375	$	$	$	$	$

A very rare signature.

Dunovant, John, 1825-64   Confederate Brigadier General

Major in the S.C. State Troops at Fort Sumter, commissioned Colonel of the 1st S.C. in 1862. He led his regiment at Drewry's Bluff and Cold Harbor. He was killed 1 Oct 1864 at Vaughan Road, Va., in action at Fort Harrison.

Signature	Signature with rank	Pre War DS	War Dated DS	Pre War ALS	War Dated ALS
$	$	$	$	$	$

A rare signature.

Dumont, Ebenezer, 1814-71   Union General

A Mexican war Lt. Col. who would rise to a divisional command in the 14th Corps. Grant appointed him Governor of the Idaho Territory.

Signature	Signature with rank	Pre & post War DS	War Dated DS	Pre & post War ALS	War Dated ALS
$25	$	$	$	$	$

Dupre, Lucius Jacques, 1822-69   Member Confederate Congress

Signature	Signature with rank	Pre & post War DS	War Dated DS	Pre & post War ALS	War Dated ALS
$50	$	$	$	$	$

DuPont, Samuel Franices, 1803-65   Union Rear Admiral

Signature	Signature with rank	Pre War DS	War Dated DS	Pre War ALS	War Dated ALS
$75	$150	$	$325	$	$

LS, 17 May 1863. 1pg. on board the flagship Wabash, Port Royal Harbor, S.C., ordering transfer of two sailors to the Montauk. GH July 1992 $250.

Duryee, Abram, 1815-90   Union General

He served with the 3rd Corps was 5 times wounded. He made a fortune importing and selling Mahogany.

Signature	Signature with rank	Pre & post War DS	War Dated DS	Pre & post War ALS	War Dated ALS
$35	$	$	$110	$	$

Duval, Issac Hardin, 1824-1902   Union General

He led a division of the 8th Corps.

Signature	Signature with rank	Pre & post War DS	War Dated DS	Pre & post War ALS	War Dated ALS
$20	$46	$65	$	$	$

Dwight, William, 1831-88   Union General

A WP dropout who was left on the field for dead at Williamsburg, he was briefly a POW. He led divisions of the 19th and 22nd Corps.

Signature	Signature with rank	Pre & post War DS	War Dated DS	Pre & post War ALS	War Dated ALS
$30	$	$	$	$	$

Dyer, Alexander Brydie, 1815-74   Union General

Veteran of the Florida & Mexican Wars. Chief Ordnance Officer.

Signature	Signature with rank	Pre & post War DS	War Dated DS	Pre & post War ALS	War Dated ALS
$25	$35	$50	$	$	$

DS, 1856. JH Aug. 1993 $45.

E

Eads, James Buchanan, 1820-87   Union ship builder

Signature	Pre & post War DS	War Dated DS	Pre & post War ALS	War Dated ALS
$80	$	$	$275	$

Early, Jubal Anderson, 1816-94   Confederate Lieutenant General

WP graduate.   He commanded a brigade at Bull Run, and was wounded at Williamsburg. Fought at the Wilderness and was routed by Genl. Sheridan at Cedar Creek

Signature	Signature with rank	Pre & post War DS	War Dated DS	Pre & post War ALS	War Dated ALS
$465	$750	$625	$2,450	$1,250	$

ALS, 1869 Jan 4. 2pp. 5x8" Drummondville, Ohio. To J.K. Finlay. In part, "In the year 1863 as we were moving into Pa., when I war Attack on Winchester then hold by Milroy, a Lt. Barton, whose father lived in the neighborhood, acted as a guide for me to show me the way to a position which I wished to assume...He afterwards lost a leg in battle..." Matted. HD June 1992 $1,300.

ANS, 7x2", pert to being unable to provide autograph of Genl. R.E. Lee. BG Nov. 1993 $375.

S, Large card signed with address, matted and framed. SK Feb. 1994 $500.

-, Clip, with address. BG Nov. 1993 $325.

-, Clip, "With best regards and wishes of J A Early." NLM Nov. 1992 $200.

A scarce signature.

Eaton, Amos Beebe, 1806-77   Union General

1826 WP graduate, a classmate of A.S. Johnston was aveteran of the Seminole and Mexican wars. He served in the Commissary Department and at wars end was the U.S. Commissary General.

Signature	Signature with rank	Pre & post War DS	War Dated DS	Pre & post War ALS	War Dated ALS
$20	$30	$45	$	$78	$

Echols, John, 1823-96   Confederate Brigadier General

Havard graduate. He was a Lt. Col. at 1st Bull Run in the "Stonewall" Regiment. He served with Genl. Loring, and succeeded him as commander of the Army of Southwest Virginia, Oct. 1862. Wounded at Kernstown and was with Genl. Breckinridge at New Market.

Signature	Signature with rank	Pre & post War DS	War Dated DS	Pre & post War ALS	War Dated ALS
$100	$185	$	$725	$	$

DS, Mar. 18, 1863. 2.5pp., 4to., Narrows of New River, (Va.) AE as Brig. Genl. on 30th Va. Bn. BG Nov. 1993 $695.

S, 1850 Cut AE, 3.5x3" as a lawyer. BG Nov. 1993 $95.

Echols, Joseph Hubbard, 1816-85   Member Confederate Congress

Signature	Signature with rank	Pre & post War DS	War Dated DS	Pre & post War ALS	War Dated ALS
$45	$	$	$	$	$

Ector, Matthew Duncan, 1822-79   Confederate Brigadier General

He commanded a brigade under Genl. Walker at Chickamauga, and was sent to Mississippi until the Spring of 1864, when he returned to Georgia for the Atlanta Campaign. While leading his brigade in Genl. French's Division, he lost his leg in the battle around Atlanta.

Signature	Signature with rank	Pre & post War DS	War Dated DS	Pre & post War ALS	War Dated ALS
$175	$	$385	$	$	$

Edwards, John, 1815-94   Union General

He served with the 7th Corps on the Missouri and Arkansas Frontier. He war An Arkansas carpetbagger.

Signature	Signature with rank	Pre & post War DS	War Dated DS	Pre & post War ALS	War Dated ALS
$20	$35	$	$	$76	$

Edwards, Oliver, 1835-1904   Union General

He helded "Bloody Angle" for 24 hours at Spotsylvania. He was in some of the heaviest fighting of the Army of the Potomac.

Signature	Signature with rank	Pre & post War DS	War Dated DS	Pre & post War ALS	War Dated ALS
$30	$50	$	$85	$	$

Egan, Thomas Wilberforce, 1834-87   Union General

Led a division of the 2nd Corps.

Signature	Signature with rank	Pre & post War DS	War Dated DS	Pre & post War ALS	War Dated ALS
$30	$	$	$	$85	$

Eggleston, Everard T., ?-?   Confederate Marine Officer

Signature	Signature with rank	Pre & post War DS	War Dated DS	Pre & post War ALS	War Dated ALS
$	$	$	$	$	$

Ellet, Alfred Washington, 1820-95   Union General

He commanded a Brigade of Marines. He burned Austin, Miss. for their loyalty to the Confederacy. At Vicksburg his ships acted as Grant's shuttles across the Mississippi River.

Signature	Signature with rank	Pre & post War DS	War Dated DS	Pre & post War ALS	War Dated ALS
$	$38	$	$67	$	$

Elliott, John Milton, 1820-79   Member Confederate Congress

Signature	Signature with rank	Pre & post War DS	War Dated DS	Pre & post War ALS	War Dated ALS
$43	$	$	$	$	$

Elliott, Stephen, Jr., 1830-66   Confederate Brigadier General

Colonel in Holcombe's Legion, he fought at the Wilderness and was severly wounded at the Battle of the Carter, and near Bentonville.

Signature	Signature with rank	Pre & post War DS	War Dated DS	Pre & post War ALS	War Dated ALS
$90	$165	$	$	$	$

A scarce signature.

Elliott, Washington Lafayette, 1825-88   Union General

A dashing Cavalry General served in the 8th and 3rd Corps. His military career spanned from 1846 in Mexico to 1879 in California.

Signature	Signature with rank	Pre & post War DS	War Dated DS	Pre & post War ALS	War Dated ALS
$25	$	$	$	$	$

Ellsworth, Ephraim Elmer, 1837-61   Union Colonel

11th New York and Martyr; Killed 24 May '61 Marshall House Tavern in Alexandria.

Signature	Signature with rank	Pre War DS	War Dated DS	Pre War ALS	War Dated ALS
$650	$	$1,500	$	$	$

Elmore, E. C., ?-?   Confederate Treasurer

Signature	Signature with rank	Pre & post War DS	War Dated DS	Pre & post War ALS	War Dated ALS
$35	$	$78	$	$	$

(Jones) Elzey, Arnold, 1816-71   Confederate Major General

In 1837 dropped his patronymic for his middle name. WP graduate. Colonal at 1st Manassas, he led   Kirby Smith's Brigade after he was wounded. Genl. Elzey was wounded at the Battle of Seven Days. He led a brigade of infantry under Genl. Ewell, but was later relieved at his own request.

Signature	Signature with rank	Pre & post War DS	War Dated DS	Pre & post War ALS	War Dated ALS
$	$	$	$	$	$

Emory, William Hemsley, 1811-87   Union General

1831 WP graduate, he was a veteran of the Mexican and several Indian wars. He led the 19th Corps and later the Department of W.Va.

Signature	Signature with rank	Pre & post War DS	War Dated DS	Pre & post War ALS	War Dated ALS
$	$65	$	$	$175	$

ALS, (ca. 1863). 1p. Accepting a dinner invitation to dine   with   Colonel   Bvadeau. ML October 1992 $200.

Ericsson, John, 1830-89   Union Naval Designer

Signature	Pre & post War DS	War Dated DS	Pre & post War ALS	War Dated ALS
$85	$	$	$	$

Este, George Peabody, 1829-81 — Union General

At Jonesboro, Ga. he lost over 30% of his men and had his horse killed under him in one of the most daring charges in the war.

Signature	Signature with rank	Pre & post War DS	War Dated DS	Pre & post War ALS	War Dated ALS
$	$45	$	$	$	$

Etheridge, Anna, ?-? — Union Nurse

Known as "Michigan Annie," she was once wounded and had many close calls.

Signature	Pre & post War DS	War Dated DS	Pre & post War ALS	War Dated ALS
$	$	$	$	$

A rare signature.

Evans, Clement Anselm, 1833-1911 — Confederate Brigadier General

Colonel in the 31st Georgia at Fredericksburg, he served under Jackson, Early, and Gordon in 1862. At Petersburg in November of 1864, he succeeded Gordon in command of the Division, and surrender his group at Appomattox.

Signature	Signature with rank	Pre & post War DS	War Dated DS	Pre & post War ALS	War Dated ALS
$86	$178	$	$1,225	$325	$

Evans, George Spafford ?-1883 — Union Brevet General

2nd California Cavalry.

Signature	Signature with rank	Pre & post War DS	War Dated DS	Pre & post War ALS	War Dated ALS
$25	$45	$	$97	$	$

Evans, Nathan George "Shanks", 1824-68   Confederate Brig General
WP graduate. He commanded a Louisiana Battalion of Zouaves. On December 18, 1861, he was assigned to command the 3rd District of South Carolina; he was commissioned B.G. as of this date, for his victory at Ball's Bluff. He was called back to North Carolina in Nov. 1862.

Signature	Signature with rank	Pre & post War DS	War Dated DS	Pre & post War ALS	War Dated ALS
$145	$225	$	$1,378	$850	$2,050

ALS, 1866. 4pp. Marion, SC. To his wife discussing hard times during reconstruction era. GH July 1992 $ 675

Eustis, Henry Lawrence, 1819-85   Union General
1842 WP Graduate, Harvard 1838, top in his class. Served briefly in the 6th Corps and when it became apparent he was physically unfit for duty, he resigned. A learned person.

Signature	Signature with rank	Pre & post War DS	War Dated DS	Pre & post War ALS	War Dated ALS
$25	$38	$	$	$87	$

Ewell, Richard Stoddert, 1817-72   Confederate Lieutenant General
WP graduate. A division commander with the Army of Northern Virginia, he lost his leg at Groveton. He fought with distinction at 1st Winchester, Cross Keys, and was in command of the defenses of Richmond until the evacuation. Captured and POW at Fort Warren. LOC Papers, 1838-96. ca. 200 items.

Signature	Signature with rank	Pre & post War DS	War Dated DS	Pre & post War ALS	War Dated ALS
$375	$	$625	$1,850	$1,125	$

Ewing, Andrew, 1813-64   Confederate Congressman
Judge of General Braggs Mil. Ct.

Signature	Signature with rank	Pre War DS	War Dated DS	Pre War ALS	War Dated ALS
$40	$	$	$	$	$

Ewing, Charles, 1835-83 — Union General

A foster brother to W.T. Sherman. He served at Vicksburg and Atlanta with Sherman.
LOC Family papers, 1769-1950. ca. 9,000 items.

Signature	Signature with rank	Pre & post War DS	War Dated DS	Pre & post War ALS	War Dated ALS
$25	$38	$	$	$67	$

Ewing, George Washington, 1808-88 — Confederate Congressman

Signature	Signature with rank	Pre & post War DS	War Dated DS	Pre & post War ALS	War Dated ALS
$45	$	$	$	$	$

Ewing, Hugh Boyle, 1826-1905 — Union General

Attended WP, he led divisions of the 15th, 16th and 23rd Corps.

Signature	Signature with rank	Pre & post War DS	War Dated DS	Pre & post War ALS	War Dated ALS
$25	$35	$	$	$	$

Ewing, Thomas, Jr., 1829-96 — Union General

Secretary to President Zachary Taylor. He was engaged in Missouri.

Signature	Signature with rank	Pre & post War DS	War Dated DS	Pre & post War ALS	War Dated ALS
$35	$48	$	$	$105	$

F

Fagan, James Fleming, 1828-93 — Confederate Major General

Colonel 1st Arkansas Inf., he fought in the Battle of Shiloh, Helena, Shreveport, Mansfield, Pleasant Hill, and repulsed the Union Army in the campaign against Camden, Ark. He captured over 200 wagons & inflicted some 1,600 casualties.

Signature	Signature with rank	Pre & post War DS	War Dated DS	Pre & post War ALS	War Dated ALS
$80	$	$	$	$	$

136

Misc.
P, CDV, 2/3 standing view in his CSA Maj. coat, which he wears open. B/M Anthony of N.Y., bottom of card slightly trimmed. LR Oct. 1993 $350.

Fairbank, Calvin, ?-?   Runner of the underground railroad

He engaged in running fugitive slaves over the Ohio River to 'freedom.' Caught and convicted for this, he was imprisoned for 17 years, and received 3000 stripes (or whippings) on his back. He was released by Lincoln in 1864.

Signature	Pre & post War DS	War Dated DS	Pre & post War ALS	War Dated ALS
$100	$	$	$	$

ANS, 1888, providing his signature. SR Nov. 1993 $150.

Fairchild, Lucius, 1831-96   Union General

Signature	Signature with rank	Pre & post War DS	War Dated DS	Pre & post War ALS	War Dated ALS
$25	$48	$	$	$67	$

Fargo, William George, 1818-81   Owner & Founder of Wells Fargo Co.

Signature	Pre & post War DS	War Dated DS	Pre & post War ALS	War Dated ALS
$175	$564	$892	$950	$

DS, 1868 Dec. 26. 1p 12x9.5", NY. Stock certificate for 15 shares issued to J.W. Cronkhite. Framed. HD June 1992 $400.
--, Stock Certificate, signed. ALE August 1992 $375.

Farnsworth, Elon John, 1837-63   Union Brigadier General

Killed 3 July 1863 at Gettysburg, Pa. Rare.

Signature	Signature with rank	Pre War DS	War Dated DS	Pre War ALS	War Dated ALS
$165	$	$	$	$	$

Farnsworth, John Franklin, 1820-97   Union General

Signature	Signature with rank	Pre & post War DS	War Dated DS	Pre & post War ALS	War Dated ALS
$20	$38	$	$	$135	$

ALS, Sept. 4, 1866. pert. to a promotion. BG Nov. 1993 $110.
P, CDV, signed on verso "Compliments of the original / Genl. Fransworth." Bust view in civilian dress. AL August 1992 $375.

Farragut, David Glasgow, 1801-70   Union Naval Vice Admiral
Though a Southerner, he moved to New York in support of the Northern cause.

Signature	Signature with rank	Pre & post War DS	War Dated DS	Pre & post War ALS	War Dated ALS
$150	$250	$265	$	$850	$

DS, 1844 September 27. 1p., 3x7.5", partly printed document, Norfolk, Va.. Naval discharge for Lewis F. Linde 1st C Music. CB Aug. 1992 $250.
ES, March 9, 1869. 1pp. 7.75x9.75", on the verso of a letter directed to President Grant by Commodore T.A. Jenkins, "I beg leave to refer this application of a son of Commodore Jenkins for an appointment to the Naval Academy to the Hon. Secretary of the Navy, with an earnest recommendation for a favorable consideration on account of the zeal, energy and fidelity with which his father performed his duties during the war whilst under my command, D.G. Farragut Admiral U.S. Navy." UA Sept. 1993 $1,300.
S, Clip signature. BG Nov. 1993 $155.
-, Large and bold signature on a card, with rank. SK March 1994 $275.

Farrow, James, 1827-92   Member Confederate Congress
In Congress he was an excellent example of South Carolina moderation. Except for his dislike of habeas corpus suspension, he sanctioned all the basic programs designed to strengthen the central government. He war elected to the US Congress in 1865

Signature	Signature with rank	Pre & post War DS	War Dated DS	Pre & post War ALS	War Dated ALS
$42	$	$	$	$	$

Faulkner, Charles James, ?-1928   VMI Cadet; Battle of New Market

Signature	Signature with rank	Pre & post War DS	War Dated DS	Pre & post War ALS	War Dated ALS
$28	$	$50	$	$	$

S, Signature on a card. SK March 1994 $35

Fearn, Thomas, 1789-63   Member Confederate Congress

Signature	Signature with rank	Pre & post War DS	War Dated DS	Pre & post War ALS	War Dated ALS
$80	$	$225	$	$	$

Feathertson, Winfield Scott, 1820-91   Confederate Brigadier General
Colonel of the 17th Mississippi Infantry, he led his brigade on the Peninsula and at Bull Run. He was severely wounded on June 30, 1862 at White Oak Swamp.

Signature	Signature with rank	Pre & post War DS	War Dated DS	Pre & post War ALS	War Dated ALS
$90	$178	$225	$	$	$

Fendall, James R. Y., 1839-?   Confederate Marine Officer

Signature	Signature with rank	Pre & post War DS	War Dated DS	Pre & post War ALS	War Dated ALS
$	$128	$	$	$	$

Ferguson, Samuel Wragg, 1834-1917   Confederate Brigadier General
WP graduate, he commanded a cavalry brigade in Polk's Corps in the Atlanta Campaign.

Signature	Signature with rank	Pre & post War DS	War Dated DS	Pre & post War ALS	War Dated ALS
$165	$245	$350	$478	$950	$

Ferrero, Edward, 1831-99   Union General

Signature	Signature with rank	Pre & post War DS	War Dated DS	Pre & post War ALS	War Dated ALS
$40	$68	$	$	$225	$

Ferry, Orris Sanford, 1823-75   Union General
Led a Brigade of the 10th Corps on several South Carolina Sea Islands.

Signature	Signature with rank	Pre & post War DS	War Dated DS	Pre & post War ALS	War Dated ALS
$35	$50	$	$78	$76	$

S, Clip signature. JH Feb. 1994 $35.

Fessenden, Francis, 1839-1906   Union General
Lost his right leg at Monett's Bluff, also wounded at Shiloh.

Signature	Signature with rank	Pre & post War DS	War Dated DS	Pre & post War ALS	War Dated ALS
$50	$75	$85	$165	$198	$

S, Clip signature. JH Feb. 1994 $50.

Fessenden, James Deering, 1833-82   Union General

Signature	Signature with rank	Pre & post War DS	War Dated DS	Pre & post War ALS	War Dated ALS
$	$	$	$	$	$

Field, Charles William, 1823-92   Confederate Major General
WP graduate. He served at Gaine's Mill, 2nd Bull Run, the Wilderness, Spotsylvania, and in the campaign around Petersburg. He was in command of Field's Division of the 1st Army Crops.

Signature	Signature with rank	Pre & post War DS	War Dated DS	Pre & post War ALS	War Dated ALS
$90	$	$	$	$387	$

Finegan, Joseph, 1814-85   Confederate Brigadier General
At Olustee, Florida, he sharply defeated the Union Army on Feb. 20, 1864. He led his forces at Cold Harbor and in the siege of Petersburg.

Signature	Signature with rank	Pre & post War DS	War Dated DS	Pre & post War ALS	War Dated ALS
$125	$	$	$	$	$

Finley, Jesse Johnson, 1812-1904   Confederate Brigadier General
Entered as a Private in the 6th Florida, with Kirby Smith's Campaign. He commanded a regiment at Chickamauga. Wounded in the Atlanta Campaign.

Signature	Signature with rank	Pre & post War DS	War Dated DS	Pre & post War ALS	War Dated ALS
$85	$	$	$	$	$

Fisk, Clinton Bowen, 1828-90   Union General

Signature	Signature with rank	Pre & post War DS	War Dated DS	Pre & post War ALS	War Dated ALS
$30	$	$78	$	$	$

Flanagin, Harris, 1817-74   Confederate Governor of Arkansas
From 1862 to-64.

Signature	Pre & post War DS	War Dated DS	Pre & post War ALS	War Dated ALS
$45	$	$178	$	$

Fletcher, Thomas, 1817-74   Confederate Governor of Arkansas
During 1862.

Signature	Pre & post War DS	War Dated DS	Pre & post War ALS	War Dated ALS
$40	$	$	$	$

Floyd, John Buchanan, 1806-63   Confederate Brigadier General

Governor of Va, 1849-52; as Buchanan's Secretary of War, 1857-60; bitterly criticized in the North for his transfer of arms to Southern arsenals,. Fought in the 1861 W. Va. campaign & Fort Donelson, where he escaped with his own troops, just prior to the surrender of the Fort He died 11 March 1862 near Abington, Va.

Signature

Secretary of War.

Signature	Signature with rank	Pre War DS	War Dated DS	Pre War ALS	War Dated ALS
$165	$	$	$	$350	$

ALS, 1856 Sept. 6. 3pp., 5x8", Abington, Va., To J. S. Cunningham concerning Fremont. HD June 1992 $200.

Misc.

P, CDV, Bust view in uniform, B/M of Chas. Taber & Co., New Bedford, Mass., corners rounded. LR Sept. 1993 $80.

Foote, Andrew Hull, 1806-63   Union Naval Rear Admiral

Mortally wounded at Fort Donelson on TN River.

Signature	Signature with rank	Pre War DS	War Dated DS	Pre War ALS	War Dated ALS
$	$	$	$	$	$

DS, 1861, Naval doc., also signed by Gideon Welles, assigning Comdr. Breese to the "Mohawk". JH Feb. 1994 $325.

Forbes, Archibald, 1838-1900   Correspodent

Distinguished British war Corespondent.

Signature	Pre & post War DS	War Dated DS	Pre & post War ALS	War Dated ALS
$	$	$	$220	$

ALS, July 18, 1896. 1p., 5x8", n.p., giving high prasie for From Manassas to Appomattox, General James Longstreet's military autobiography. MS Nov. 1993 $200.

Forbes, Edwin, 1839-95   Correspondent and Artist

Signature	Pre & post War DS	War Dated DS	Pre & post War ALS	War Dated ALS
$	$	$	$	$

Misc.

-, Copper plate engravings est. $150 - 350.

Force, Manning Ferguson, 1824-99   Union General

Signature	Signature with rank	Pre & post War DS	War Dated DS	Pre & post War ALS	War Dated ALS
$25	$	$	$	$98	$

Ford, John T., 1829-94   Owner of Ford's Theater, Washington, D.C.

Signature	Pre & post War DS	War Dated DS	Pre & post War ALS	War Dated ALS
$	$	$	$325	$

ALS, 1859 June 12. 2pp., 7.75x10", Baltimore. Theatrical content. HD June 1992 $250.

Ford, Samuel Howard, 1819-1905   Member Confederate Congress

Signature	Signature with rank	Pre & post War DS	War Dated DS	Pre & post War ALS	War Dated ALS
$45	$	$	$	$	$

Forman, Thomas Marsh, 1809-1875   Member Confederate Congress

Signature	Signature with rank	Pre & post War DS	War Dated DS	Pre & post War ALS	War Dated ALS
$65	$	$	$	$	$

Forney, John Horace, 1829-1902   Confederate Major General

WP graduate. Colonel of the 10th Alabama, served under Kirby Smith at 1st Bull Run. He was severely wounded in the arm at Dranesville. He served a year at Mobile before he went to Vicksburg.

Signature	Signature with rank	Pre & post War DS	War Dated DS	Pre & post War ALS	War Dated ALS
$110	$245	$	$	$	$

AES, July 2, 1863. signed with rank. BG Nov. 1993 $395.

Forney, William Henry, 1823-94   Confederate Brigadier General

A noted fighter, wounded at Williamsburg and captured while in the hospital. He was again captured at Gettysburg while Colonel of the 10th Alabama. He was Lee at Appomattox, Va.

Signature	Signature with rank	Pre & post War DS	War Dated DS	Pre & post War ALS	War Dated ALS
$85	$	$	$	$	$

Forrest, French, 1796-1866   Confederate Naval Commander

Signature	Signature with rank	Pre & post War DS	War Dated DS	Pre & post War ALS	War Dated ALS
$100	$150	$	$500	$	$

A scarce signature.

Forrest, Nathan Bedford, 1821-77   Confederate Lieutenant General

His exploits are legendary, one of the most brilliant cavalry generals that ever lived.

Signature	Signature with rank	Pre & post War DS	War Dated DS	Pre & post War ALS	War Dated ALS
$550	$785	$1,895	$8,750	$	$17,500

DS, May 19, 1864. 2pp., 4to., HQ Forrest Cav. Tupelo, Miss. pert. to deserters in 5th Miss. Cav. joining local militia units. With bold ink AES with ranks of Col. Robert McCulloch & Genl. James R. Chalmers. BG Nov. 1993 $9,000.
--, Full bond, signed twice. SK Feb. 1994 $1,550.
--, Half bond, signed. KO Sept. 1993 $850.
--, Half bond, signed. Framed. SK Sept. 1992 $450.
S, Clipped Sig. BG Nov. 1993 $750.
-, Clipped Sig. from a letter. KO Sept. 1993 $525.
-, Clipped Sig. from post-war railroad bond. AL August 1992 $525.
Misc.
-, ALS, 13 July 1862. .5p, 4to, on blue paper, with original envelop addressed by Forrest bearing a hurried pencil drawing which may depict the Murfreesboro battlefield in schematic form. To Lt. Col. John G. Parkhurst. "I must demand an unconditional surrender of your force as prisoner of war or I will have every man put to the sword You are aware of the overpowering force I have at my command & demand is made to

prevent the effusion of blood..." **Text & signature in the hand of** his **Assistant Adjutant General Major J. P. Strange.** C May 1992 $7,700.

-, 1909 UCV Letter opener. GY August 1992 $145.

P, CDV, Bust view in CSA uniform. Wears double breasted coat with rank on collar. B/M of the Monumental Photograph Co., Baltimore, Md., card trimmed at top and at left edge. LR Oct. 1993 $300.

Forsyth, James William, 1835-1906 — Union General

Signature	Signature with rank	Pre & post War DS	War Dated DS	Pre & post War ALS	War Dated ALS
$45	$	$95	$	$	$

Misc.

B, *Report of an expedition up the Yellowstone...*Wash 1875. 17 map 5pls [Howes 272 a] $150.

Foster, John Gray, 1823-74 — Union General

Signature	Signature with rank	Pre & post War DS	War Dated DS	Pre & post War ALS	War Dated ALS
$22	$45	$35	$	$50	$

Foster, Robert Sanford, 1834-1903 — Union General

Signature	Signature with rank	Pre & post War DS	War Dated DS	Pre & post War ALS	War Dated ALS
$25	$	$48	$	$	$

Foster, Thomas Jefferson, 1809-87 — Member Confederate Congress

Signature	Signature with rank	Pre & post War DS	War Dated DS	Pre & post War ALS	War Dated ALS
$30	$	$	$	$	$

Fowler, John D., 1831-62 — Confederate Marine Officer

Signature	Signature with rank	Pre & post War DS	War Dated DS	Pre & post War ALS	War Dated ALS
$	$135	$	$387	$	$

Franklin, William Buell, 1823-1903 — Union General

Signature	Signature with rank	Pre & post War DS	War Dated DS	Pre & post War ALS	War Dated ALS
$65	$115	$135	$	$185	$

S, Clip signature. JH Feb. 1994 $75.
P, CDV, signed " For Miss Sophie T. Cowen / from W. B. Franklin / Maj. Gen. U.S. Vols. Phila.: in uniform. AL August 1992 $395.

Frazer, John Wesley, 1827-1906   Confederate Brigadier General

WP graduate. Colonel of the 28th Alabama, he served with Genl. Bragg at Corinth. He surrendered at Cumberland Gap to Burnside without firing a shot.

Signature	Signature with rank	Pre & post War DS	War Dated DS	Pre & post War ALS	War Dated ALS
$165	$250	$	$	$395	$

Freeman, Thomas W., 1824-65   Member Confederate Congress

Signature	Signature with rank	Pre & post War DS	War Dated DS	Pre & post War ALS	War Dated ALS
$75	$	$	$	$	$

Fremont, John Charles, 1813-90   Union General

Explorer and statesman.

Signature	Signature with rank	Pre & post War DS	War Dated DS	Pre & post War ALS	War Dated ALS
$210	$	$	$875	$823	$

ALS, Aug. 22, n.y., 1p 8vo., "my dear Colonel, I thank you for the letters. Tomorrow I am going to Long Branch on appointment for business purposes." JB Dec. 1993 $475.
---, Aug. 1, (1861). 1p. 8to. HQ Western Dept., St. Louis. pert. to a doctor being attached to his staff & procuring ambulances in N.Y. for his command. BG Nov. 1993 $1,750.
S, Nov. 13, 1878. Clip as Territorial Gov. of Arizona. BG Nov. 1993 $375.
-, Clip sig./rank. NLM Nov. 1992 $95.

French, Samuel Gibbs, 1818-1910   Confederate Brigadier General

WP graduate, he commanded the Department of Southern Virginia and No. Carolina in 1863; served in the Atlanta Campaign, and with Genl. Hood in Franklin and Nashville Campaigns.

Signature	Signature with rank	Pre & post War DS	War Dated DS	Pre & post War ALS	War Dated ALS
$145	$	$295	$	$345	$

French, William Henry, 1815-81   Union General

Signature	Signature with rank	Pre & post War DS	War Dated DS	Pre & post War ALS	War Dated ALS
$45	$	$98	$	$178	$

Frost, Daniel Marsh, 1823-1900   Confederate Brigadier General

WP graduate, he served at Camp Jackson, where he was in command and saw the first blood to be spilled in Missouri. Surrounded by Union troops, he surrendered his command of 689 troops. He led a Missouri State Brigade at Pea Ridge. He was dropped from C.S. rolls in Dec. 1863.

Signature	Signature with rank	Pre & post War DS	War Dated DS	Pre & post War ALS	War Dated ALS
$125	$275	$	$	$	$

S, Clip war time, with rank. BG Nov. 1993 $300.

Fry, Birkett Davenport, 1822-91   Confederate Brigadier General
Dismissed from WP for failing math. He led a brigade in Pickett's Charge, was wounded at Gettysburg, and again at Seven Pines. His arm was shattered at Antietam. He was once more wounded at Chancellorsville, after succeeding to command of Archer's Brigade.

Signature	Signature with rank	Pre & post War DS	War Dated DS	Pre & post War ALS	War Dated ALS
$125	$	$250	$	$	$

Fry, James Barnet, 1827-94   Union General

Signature	Signature with rank	Pre & post War DS	War Dated DS	Pre & post War ALS	War Dated ALS
$35	$	$	$	$	$

Fry, Speed Smith, 1817-92   Union General

Signature	Signature with rank	Pre & post War DS	War Dated DS	Pre & post War ALS	War Dated ALS
$20	$	$56	$	$	$

Fuller, John Wallace, 1827-91   Union General

Signature	Signature with rank	Pre & post War DS	War Dated DS	Pre & post War ALS	War Dated ALS
$35	$65	$152	$	$245	$

Fuller, Thomas Charles, 1832-1901   Member Confederate Congress

Signature	Signature with rank	Pre & post War DS	War Dated DS	Pre & post War ALS	War Dated ALS
$	$	$	$	$	$

Fulton, Robert, 1765-1815   Inventor

Signature	DS	ALS
$675	$1,275	$2,897

S, On 3x1.25" sheet, "Robert Fulton". HD June 1992 $500.

Funsten, David, 1819-66 — Member Confederate Congress

Signature	Signature with rank	Pre & post War DS	War Dated DS	Pre & post War ALS	War Dated ALS
$45	$90	$	$198	$	$

G

Gaither, Burgess Sidney, 1807-92 — Member Confederate Congress

Signature	Signature with rank	Pre & post War DS	War Dated DS	Pre & post War ALS	War Dated ALS
$45	$75	$87	$	$	$

Gamble, William, 1818-66 — Union General

Signature	Signature with rank	Pre & post War DS	War Dated DS	Pre & post War ALS	War Dated ALS
$125	$	$	$	$	$

Gano, Richard Montgomery, 1830-1913 — Conf. Brig General/ Physician

He commanded two companies of Texas Cavalry under General Morgan, and accompanied Kirby Smith's invasion of Kentucky in August, 1862. Later he was transferred to the Trans-Mississippi Department.

Signature	Signature with rank	Pre & post War DS	War Dated DS	Pre & post War ALS	War Dated ALS
$	$	$	$	$	$

Gardenhire, Erasmus Lee, 1815-99 — Member Confederate Congress

Signature	Signature with rank	Pre & post War DS	War Dated DS	Pre & post War ALS	War Dated ALS
$45	$	$	$	$	$

Gardner, Alexander, ?-?   Civil War Photographer

Signature	Pre & post War DS	War Dated DS	Pre & post War ALS	War Dated ALS
$	$	$	$	$

Misc.

-, Albumen photograph, 6.75x8.75", Quaker Guns, Centerville, VA., Plate #6 of Alexander Garder's sketch book. LR Oct. 1993 $250.

-, Albumen photograph, 6.75x8.75", Chesterfield Bridge, North Anna, Va., Plate #66 of Alexander Garder's sketch book. LR Oct. 1993 $300.

-, Albumen photograph, 6.75x8.75", The Pulpit, Fort Fisher, N.C., Plate #79 of Alexander Garder's sketch book. LR Oct. 1993 $300.

-, Albumen photograph, 6.75x8.75", Ruin's of Gaines' Mill, Va., Plate #93, of Alexander Garder's sketch book. LR Oct. 1993 $250.

The following Albumen prints sell between $450 & $750:

-, Albumen print, 6.5 x 8.5" Company "E" 4th U.S. Colored Infantry, Fort Lincoln, Va.

-, Albumen print, 3.5 x 4.5" Lincoln and McClellan.

-, Albumen print, 6.5 x 8" Officers of Signal Corps, Headquarters Army of Potomac, Warrentown, Va.

-, Albumen print, 6.75 x 9" Slaughter Pen, Foot of Round Top, Day after the Battle of Gettysburg.

-, Albumen print, 7 x 9" Appomattox Court-House.

-, Albumen print, 6.5 x 7.5" General Frank P. Blair & Staff.

-, Albumen print, 7 x 9" Residence, Quartermaster Third Army Corps.

Gardner, Joseph M.(or V.) ? - ?   Confederate Naval Officer

Signature	Signature with rank	Pre & post War DS	War Dated DS	Pre & post War ALS	War Dated ALS
$	$145	$	$387	$	$

Gardner, Franklin, 1823-73   Confederate Major General

WP graduate. He entered C.S. service as a Lt. Col. of C.S. Infantry, and served in TN & Mississippi. He commanded a brigade of cavalry at Shiloh. He led a brigade in Polk's Corps after the Kentucky Campaign. In command of Port Hudson from the end of 1862 until the surrender in July 1863.

Signature	Signature with rank	Pre & post War DS	War Dated DS	Pre & post War ALS	War Dated ALS
$300	$	$	$	$895	$

S, Clip, with sentiment. BG Nov. 1993 $285.

Gardner, William Montgomery, 1824-1901   Confederate Brig General

WP graduate. Lt. Col. of Barton's 8th Georgia, he was seriously wounded in the leg at 1st Bull Run. The injury was thought to be fatal, but upon recovery he was unable to resume field service. On July 26, 1864, he was named to command all military prisons in the states east of the Mississippi, excluding Georgia and Alabama.

Signature	Signature with rank	Pre & post War DS	War Dated DS	Pre & post War ALS	War Dated ALS
$95	$	$287	$	$581	$

Garfield, James Abram, 1831-81   Union General & 20th President

Signature	Signature with rank	Pre & post War DS	War Dated DS	Pre & post War ALS	War Dated ALS
$275	$	$865	$	$1,123	$

Garland, Augustus Hill, 1832-99   Member Confederate Congress

Signature	Signature with rank	Pre & post War DS	War Dated DS	Pre & post War ALS	War Dated ALS
$	$65	$87	$	$	$

Garland, Rufus King, 1830-86   Confederate Congressman

Signature	Signature with rank	Pre & post War DS	War Dated DS	Pre & post War ALS	War Dated ALS
$	$	$	$	$	$

Garland, Samuel Jr., 1830-62 — Confederate Brigadier General

V.M.I. graduate. A colonel at Bull Run in D.R. Jones' Brigade. After the Battle of Williamsburg, he was placed in command of Early's troops, due to the wounding of Genl. Early. He was killed Sept. 17 at South Mountain, Md., by Genl. McClellan's advance.

Signature	Signature with rank	Pre & post War DS	War Dated DS	Pre & post War ALS	War Dated ALS
$500	$	$	$	$	$

Garnett, Algernon S., ? - ? — Confederate Naval Officer & Surgeon

Signature	Signature with rank	Pre & post War DS	War Dated DS	Pre & post War ALS	War Dated ALS
$	$	$	$495	$	$

Garnett, Muscoe Russell Hunter, 1821-64 — Confederate Congressman

Signature	Signature with rank	Pre War DS	War Dated DS	Pre War ALS	War Dated ALS
$54	$	$	$	$	$

Garnett, Richard Brooke, 1817-63 — Confederate Brigadier General

WP graduate. He was commissioned a Major of Artillery. Commanded a brigade at 1st Bull Run, sent to Winchester to take Jackson's old Brigade. He saw action at Seven Days, 2nd Bull Run, Fredericksburg, Antietam, and Chancellorsville. He was killed instantly during Pickett's Charge July 3, 1863 at Gettysburg, Pa.

Signature	Signature with rank	Pre War DS	War Dated DS	Pre War ALS	War Dated ALS
$650	$	$	$	$	$

An extremely rare signature.

Garnett, Robert Seldom, 1819-61   Confederate Brigadier General
WP graduate. He was a Colonel and Adjutant at Lee's Headquarters. Opposed Generals
McClellan and Rosecrans at Rich Mountain, where he was killed 13 July 1861 at
Carricks Ford, Va.

Signature	Signature with rank	Pre & post War DS	War Dated DS	Pre & post War ALS	War Dated ALS
$375	$	$	$	$	$

An extremely rare signature.

Garrard, Kenner, 1827-79   Union General

Signature	Signature with rank	Pre & post War DS	War Dated DS	Pre & post War ALS	War Dated ALS
$30	$48	$74	$	$120	$

Garrard, Theophilus Toulmin, 1812-1902   Union General

Signature	Signature with rank	Pre & post War DS	War Dated DS	Pre & post War ALS	War Dated ALS
$25	$	$65	$	$97	$

Garrett, Thomas, 1789-1871   Abolitionist
Often referred to as "Superintendent of the Underground Railroad." More slaves owed
their 'freedom' to him than any other, an incredible total of up to 3,000.

Signature	Pre & post War DS	War Dated DS	Pre & post War ALS	War Dated ALS
$65	$	$	$425	$

ALS, 1853, requesting that his cousin search the county land records to determine
whether there are any liens or mortgages on a piece of property. SR Nov. 1993 $395.

Garrott, Isham Warren, 1816-63   Confederate Brigadier General

Colonel in the 20th Alabama Infantry, stationed in Mobile 1861-62. With Genl. Tracy at Port Gibson, Miss. He was killed 17 June 1863 at Vicksburg, Miss.

Signature	Signature with rank	Pre War DS	War Dated DS	Pre War ALS	War Dated ALS
$250	$475	$	$	$	$

S, Clip with rank, Col. 20th Ala. Vols. BG Nov. 1993 $450.
A rare signature.

Gartrell, Lucius Jeremiah, 1821-91   Confederate Brigadier General

Colonel of the 7th Georgia Infantry at 1st Bull Run, where his 16 year-old son was killed. Member of the C.S. Congress in 1862. As Brig. Genl., he commanded his brigade of Georgia Reserves in South Carolina, and was wounded near Coosawhatchie.

Signature	Signature with rank	Pre & post War DS	War Dated DS	Pre & post War ALS	War Dated ALS
$90	$	$285	$	$	$

Gary, Martin Witherspoon, 1831-81   Confederate Brigadier General

Harvard graduate, he commanded Hamton's Legion at 1st Manassas. He fought with distinction at Chickamauga, Knoxville, Fort Harrison, and Fredericksburg. He was the last General Officer to leave Richmond.

Signature	Signature with rank	Pre & post War DS	War Dated DS	Pre & post War ALS	War Dated ALS
$150	$235	$287	$	$	$

Gatlin, Richard Caswell, 1809-96   Confederate Brigadier General

WP graduate. Colonel in the C.S. Army. He commanded the coastal Defense of the Southern Department. Resigned Sept. 8, 1862. Served as NC Adjutant and I.G.

Signature	Signature with rank	Pre & post War DS	War Dated DS	Pre & post War ALS	War Dated ALS
$85	$	$215	$	$	$

Geary, John White, 1819-73   Union General

Wounded at Harpers Ferry, captured at Leesburg, seriously wounded at Cedar Mountain, also fought at Chancellorsville, Gettysburg, Lookout Mt., Missionary Ridge, the March to the Sea & Carolinas campaign.

Signature	Signature with rank	Pre & post War DS	War Dated DS	Pre & post War ALS	War Dated ALS
$35	$50	$78	$108	$	$

Misc.

P, CDV, Chest up view in uniform of Maj. Gen., b/m Chas. A. Saylor. LR Oct. 1993 $75.

Getty, George Washington, 1819-1901   Union General

Signature	Signature with rank	Pre & post War DS	War Dated DS	Pre & post War ALS	War Dated ALS
$25	$36	$48	$89	$	$

Gholson, Samuel Jameson, 1808-83   Confederate Brigadier General

Enlisted as a Private. He saw service at Fort Donelson and Corinth. In 1864, while in command of a brigade near Egypt, Miss., he was severely wounded and lost his arm.

Signature	Signature with rank	Pre & post War DS	War Dated DS	Pre & post War ALS	War Dated ALS
$87	$	$235	$	$387	$

Gibbon, John, 1827-96   Union General

Commander of Union forces at Gainesville, 2nd Bull Run, and Antietam, seriously wounded at both Fredericksburg and Gettysburg, he saw action from Wilderness through Petersburg and was Appomattox for the surrender.

Signature	Signature with rank	Pre & post War DS	War Dated DS	Pre & post War ALS	War Dated ALS
$50	$110	$145	$	$	$650

ALS, Feb. 13, 1864, Philadelphia, "I have examined with great interest the isometrical map of the battle of Gettysburg by Col. John B. Bachelder." RAS Oct. 1993 $660.

Gibbs, Alfred, 1823-68   Union General

Signature	Signature with rank	Pre & post War DS	War Dated DS	Pre & post War ALS	War Dated ALS
$25	$	$58	$	$87	$

Gibbs, George C., ?-?   Confederate Prison Commander

Signature	Signature with rank	Pre & post War DS	War Dated DS	Pre & post War ALS	War Dated ALS
$	$	$	$	$	$

Gibson, Randell Lee, 1832-92   Confederate General

Colonel 13th Louisiana Inf., he fought at Shiloh, Perryville, Stone River, Chickmauga, Chattanooga, Atlanta campaign, & at Spanish Fort, Mobile.

R. L. Gibson

Signature	Signature with rank	Pre & post War DS	War Dated DS	Pre & post War ALS	War Dated ALS
$80	$175	$	$	$	$1,875

S, Clip signature, "R.L.Gibson, La." LR Oct. 1993 $75.

Gilbert, Charles Champion, 1822-1903   Union General

Signature	Signature with rank	Pre & post War DS	War Dated DS	Pre & post War ALS	War Dated ALS
$27	$	$65	$	$	$

Gilbert, James Isham, 1823-84 — Union General

Signature	Signature with rank	Pre & post War DS	War Dated DS	Pre & post War ALS	War Dated ALS
$30	$	$	$82	$97	$

Gillem, Alvan Cullen, 1830-75 — Union General

Signature	Signature with rank	Pre & post War DS	War Dated DS	Pre & post War ALS	War Dated ALS
$32	$	$	$87	$	$

Gilliss, James Melville, 1811-65 — US Naval Captain

Signature	Signature with rank	Pre & post War DS	War Dated DS	Pre & post War ALS	War Dated ALS
$	$87	$	$	$	$

Gillmore, Quincy Adams, 1825-88 — Union General

Served at Port Royal, S.C., Fort Pulaski, comm. Dept. of the South during the 1863 Charleston Campaign, Bermuda Hundred, Drewy's Bluff, & the 184 Shenandoah Valley Campaign.

Signature	Signature with rank	Pre & post War DS	War Dated DS	Pre & post War ALS	War Dated ALS
$32	$55	$87	$127	$148	$

S, Large signature, in ink, "Q. A. Gillmore, Bvt. Maj. Genl." LR Oct. 1993 $50.

Gilmer, Jeremy Francis, 1818-83 — Confederate Major General

WP graduate. He was Albert S. Johnston's Chief Engineer. Took command of the Confederate Engineer Bureau.

Signature	Signature with rank	Pre & post War DS	War Dated DS	Pre & post War ALS	War Dated ALS
$110	$	$	$	$	$

Gilmore, Harry, 1838-83 — Confederate Major/Partisan Ranger

Signature	Signature with rank	Pre & post War DS	War Dated DS	Pre & post War ALS	War Dated ALS
$45	$	$	$	$	$

Gilson, Helen Louise, 1835-68 — Sanitary Commission/Hospital Worker

Signature	Signature with rank	Pre & post War DS	War Dated DS	Pre & post War ALS	War Dated ALS
$	$	$	$	$225	$

Girardey, Victor Jean Baptiste, 1837-64 Confederate Brigadier General

An Adjutant on the staffs of Generals Wright and Mahone. For outstanding performance at the Battle of the Crater, he was promoted to Brig. Genl. Only sixteen days later he was killed 16 Aug. 1864 at Deep Bottom, Va.

Signature	Signature with rank	Pre War DS	War Dated DS	Pre War ALS	War Dated ALS
$375	$	$	$	$	$

An extremely rare signature.

Gist, States Rights, 1831-64 Confederate Brigadier General

Harvard graduate. Designated by Genl. Beauregard to act as Colonel to the men who scattered at 1st Bull Run. He commanded Walker's Division at Chickamauga and Missionary Ridge. On Nov. 30, 1864, while leading his brigade on foot after his horse had been shot in the Battle of Franklin he was killed 30 Nov. 1864.

Signature	Signature with rank	Pre War DS	War Dated DS	Pre War ALS	War Dated ALS
$450	$	$895	$	$1,285	$

ALS, Pre war, pert. to a legal matters. SK June 1993 $1,000.
A rare signature.

Gladden, Adley Hogan, 1810-62   Confederate Brigadier General

Colonel of the 1st Louisiana. He later led his troops at Shiloh. On the first day of battle he was shot in the arm and had it amputated. He then died April 11, 1862 of wounds rec'd at Shiloh, TN.

Signature	Signature with rank	Pre & post War DS	War Dated DS	Pre & post War ALS	War Dated ALS
$450	$	$987	$	$	$

An extremely rare signature.

Godon, Sylvanus W., ?-?   Union Naval Commander

Signature	Signature with rank	Pre & post War DS	War Dated DS	Pre & post War ALS	War Dated ALS
$45	$67	$86	$148	$	$

Godwin, Archibald Campbell, 1831-64   Confederate Brigadier General

Assistant Provost Marshal of Libby Prison, Richmond, Va. He led the 57th North Carolina Infantry at Fredericksburg and fought at Gettysburg. He was killed 19 Sept. 1864 at Winchester, Va. by a shell fragment.

Signature	Signature with rank	Pre & post War DS	War Dated DS	Pre & post War ALS	War Dated ALS
$150	$350	$786	$1,250	$	$

A scarce signature.

Goggin, James Monore, 1820-89   Confederate Brigadier General
He was first a Major in the 32nd Virginia, and served Genl. Magruder during the Peninsula Campaign. Commanded Genl. Conner's Brigade at Cedar Creek. Captured with Genl. Kershaw at Sayler's Creek in April, 1865.

Signature	Signature with rank	Pre & post War DS	War Dated DS	Pre & post War ALS	War Dated ALS
$225	$	$	$	$	$

Goldsborough, Louis Malesherbes, 1805-77   Union Naval Rear Admiral

Signature	Signature with rank	Pre & post War DS	War Dated DS	Pre & post War ALS	War Dated ALS
$	$78	$	$	$	$

Gonzalez, Samuel Zacharias, 1763-?   Confederate Marine Officer

Signature	Signature with rank	Pre & post War DS	War Dated DS	Pre & post War ALS	War Dated ALS
$	$145	$	$	$	$

Gordon, George Henry, 1823-86   Union General

Signature	Signature with rank	Pre & post War DS	War Dated DS	Pre & post War ALS	War Dated ALS
$25	$	$65	$	$95	$

Gordon, George Washington, 1836-1911   Confederate Brig General
He fought under Bragg at Stones River, where he was first wounded. He commanded a regiment at Chickamauga and Missionary Ridge. He was wounded again, and captured at Franklin.

Signature	Signature with rank	Pre & post War DS	War Dated DS	Pre & post War ALS	War Dated ALS
$210	$	$345	$	$450	$

160

Gordon, James Byron, 1822-64   Confederate Brigadier General
On July 3, at Gettysburg, his regiment fought valiantly. On Sept. 28, 1863, he was
promoted to brigadier general. Died 18 May 1864 of wounds rec'd 11 May at Yellow
Tavern, Va.

Signature	Signature with rank	Pre War DS	War Dated DS	Pre War ALS	War Dated ALS
$350	$	$	$	$	$

Gordon, John Brown, 1832-1904   Confederate Major General
During the Chancellorsville and Gettysburg campaigns he handled his brigade
reasonably well. Confirmed Jan. 25, 1864, to rank from May 7, 1863. At the Wilderness
on May 6 he delivered a crushing blow to the right flank of Grant's line.

Signature	Signature with rank	Pre & post War DS	War Dated DS	Pre & post War ALS	War Dated ALS
$178	$325	$	$1,125	$350	$

ALS, May 29, 1889. 1p 4to. State of Ga., Exec. Dept., Atlanta, to Va. artist John Elder
pert. to photographs sent Gordon. BG Nov. 1993 $325.
---, 1887 April 19. From the Executive Department., Atlanta, Ga., while he was Gov.
[n.d.]. DZ Feb. 1992 $350.
S, Clip sig. with state, mounting residue on verso. BG Nov. 1993 $175.

Gorgas, Josiah, 1818-83   Confederate Brigadier General
Recognized the need for manufacturing capabilities, work with Richmond's Tredegar
Iron Works to make it an important manufacturer of cannon and projectiles. To rank
Nov. 10, 1864.

Signature	Signature with rank	Pre & post War DS	War Dated DS	Pre & post War ALS	War Dated ALS
$178	$	$325	$	$	$

DS, May 7, 1849. 1p., 4to., Watervliet Arsenal (N.Y.) pert. to supplies. BG Nov. 1993 $295.

Gorman, Willis Arnold, 1816-76   Union General

Signature	Signature with rank	Pre & post War DS	War Dated DS	Pre & post War ALS	War Dated ALS
$25	$	$75	$	$	$

Govan, Daniel Chevilette, 1829-1911   Confederate Brigadier General

To rank from Dec. 29, 1863 and assigned command of the Arkansas brigade, which he had led at Chickamauga, Missionary Ridge, and Ringgold Gap. POW at Jonesborough exchanged three weeks later. Fought at Franklin and was wounded at Nashville.

Signature	Signature with rank	Pre & post War DS	War Dated DS	Pre & post War ALS	War Dated ALS
$75	$	$	$	$287	$

Gracie, Archibald , Jr., 1832-64   Confederate Brigadier General

WP graduate. Colonel in the 43rd Alabama, he served under Kirby Smith in eastern TN. Under Preston at Chickamauga, he was wounded at Bean's Station. He was killed Dec. 2, 1864 at Petersburg, Va. by the explosion of a Union shell.

Signature	Signature with rank	Pre War DS	War Dated DS	Pre War ALS	War Dated ALS
$250	$450	$	$	$	$

S, Clip, sign as Brig. General (war date), in brown ink. KO #113 1992 $175.
An extremely scarce signature.

Graham, Charles Kinnaird, 1824-89   Union General

Signature	Signature with rank	Pre & post War DS	War Dated DS	Pre & post War ALS	War Dated ALS
$35	$	$	$	$	$

162

Graham, Lawrence Pike, 1815-1905   Union General

Signature	Signature with rank	Pre & post War DS	War Dated DS	Pre & post War ALS	War Dated ALS
$20	$	$50	$78	$	$

Granbury, Hiram Bronson, 1831-64   Confederate Brig General

Captured at Ft. Donelson, exchanged, and promoted to Col. of the 7th Texas. He fought with Genl. Greeg in northern Mississippi. Led the Texas Brigade at Ringgold Gap. Killed Nov. 30, 1864 at the battle of Franklin, TN

Signature	Signature with rank	Pre War DS	War Dated DS	Pre War ALS	War Dated ALS
$350	$	$	$	$	$

A rare signature.

Granger, Gordon, 1822-76   Union General

Signature	Signature with rank	Pre & post War DS	War Dated DS	Pre & post War ALS	War Dated ALS
$35	$	$87	$	$	$

Granger, Robert Seaman, 1816-94   Union General

Signature	Signature with rank	Pre & post War DS	War Dated DS	Pre & post War ALS	War Dated ALS
$40	$	$	$	$	$

Grant, Julia Dent, 1862-1902   First Lady; wife of Ulysess S. Grant

Signature	Pre & post War DS	War Dated DS	Pre & post War ALS	War Dated ALS
$275	$	$	$650	$

Grant, Lewis Addison, 1828-1918   Union General

Signature	Signature with rank	Pre & post War DS	War Dated DS	Pre & post War ALS	War Dated ALS
$25	$	$	$68	$	$

Grant, Ulysses Simpson, 1822-85   Union General & 18th US President

He succesfully assisted in splitting the Confederacy by taking Forts Henry & Donalson, and finally Vicksburg. From the Spring of 1864 until the end of the War, he drove the Army of the Potomac relentlessly, and saw massive casualties. His later inadequacies as President barely dim the light of one of the major figures of the War Between the States.

Signature	Signature with rank	Pre & post War DS	War Dated DS	Pre & post War ALS	War Dated ALS
$650	$875	$1,287	$	$1,450	$

ALS, April 11, 1863, 2pp., To General Stephen A. Hurlbut, "The movements spoken of previously in your dispatches and now in your letter of the 7th brought by Genl. Lee, you may make so as to effectively co-operate with Rosecrans and without reference to movements here..." SAG Feb. 1994 $16,000.

---, May 13, 1867, 1p. to Gen. Fritz-John Porter pert. to an undefined matter concerning a "Mr. Richard of Flda." HC Feb. 1994 $2,500.

---, Feb. 16, 1867, 2pgs 8vo. regarding the gift of a pipe. HD June 1992 $800.

---, April 27, 1880, 1.5pp, 5x8" Gelena, Ill., To Phillip F. Brennan, Pres. War Vet. Ass. 14th Regt. N.Y.S.M., Brooklyn, N. Y. invitation. HD June 1992 $950.

ANS, Undated. Pencil note re: Commissions. Signed "U.S.G.". ALE August 1992 $395.

LS, Oct., 1871, 1pp. 5 X 8" Executive Mansion, Washington, D.C. "the bearer, Mr. Browning...is entitled to kind consideration from all U.S. Officials abroad." UA July 1993 $1,400.

--, Dec. 6, 1881, 1pp. 4to., 8.3x10.8", New York, transmits a signed release and discusses his responsibility to pay taxes on a property he had previously sold. UA Sept. 1993 $1,500.

--, June, 1865, 4p, Quarto, no place, "Head Quarter Army of the US" lt. HD., details reorganization of the Union's military divisions into fifteen geographical departments. PIH 1992 $12,500.

--, March 25, 1871. 1p, 16x13", Washington, D.C.. Appoints William R. Smith of Iowa as receiver of public money... HD June 1992 $900.

DS, Oct. 28, 1870, 1p., folio, signed as President, appointing Consul of the U.S. to Ghent. MCS Feb. 1994 $1,500.

--, Feb. 13, 1866, Check signed, with CDV and cabinet card, framed. UA Feb. 1994 $1,800.

--, August 28, 1865, 1p., folio, Galena, IL., ornate certificate of Jo Davies Soldiers Monument Association signed by its president U.S. Grant. NS Nov. 1993 $1,500.

--, Oct. 7, 1872. 1p., 4to., Washington, a warrant for the pardon of Charles Brown, reinforced on verso at folds. NS Nov. 1993 $900.

--, Aug. 28, 1865. 1p. 12.25x15.35" Galena, IL. blank Soldiers Moument Association document, signed "U.S. Grant." UA Sept. 1993 $1,000.

Franking Signature, "U.S. Grant" as President, 6x3.5"envelope addressed to "Hon. A.E. Borie/ No. 10-25 Spuce Street / Philadelphia / Pa.". HD June 1992 $800.

PS, Engraving, 5.5x9", signed "U.S. Grant". UA Feb. 1994 $2,000.

--, Post war, Cabinet card, signed "U.S. Grant" in another hand is written "This picture was presented to Corinne Snowden Sanders, by Gen. Grant himself." UA Feb. 1994 $4,000.

S, "U.S. Grant/ Maj. Gen. U.S.A." on card. JB Dec. 1993 $550.

-, Large bold signature on a card. SK Dec. 1993 $675.

-, A large dark signature on a card. SR Nov. 1993 $550.

-, "U.S. Grant/ Lt. General U.S.A.". KO Sept. 1993 $475.

-, Clip with rank, Lt. General on portion of printed letterhead HQ, Armies of the U.S., City Point, Va., Nov. 24, 1864. BG Fall 1993 $750.

-, Signed wardate card as, Lt. Gen. U.S. Volunteers. GH July 1992 $450.

CAUTION - CLIPS OF HIS SON, U.S. Grant, Jr. HAVE RECENTLY BEEN NOTED ON THE MARKET. BEWARE OF ANY CLOSELY CLIPPED AT THE 'T' SIGNATURES, WITH THE "JR." REMOVED.

Misc.

P, CDV, Chest up view as Brig. Gen. early war image shows Grant w/his beard very long while wearing Hardee hat with brim pinned up. B/M sticker from Earles Galleries, Philadelphia. LR Oct. 1993 $150.

Gray, Henry, 1816-92   Confederate General

Colonel in the 28th Louisiana, he fought under Genl. Taylor during the siege at Vicksburg. He was wounded at Bayou Teche. In the Red River Campaign, he led a brigade in Genl. Mouton's Division.

Signature	Signature with rank	Pre & post War DS	War Dated DS	Pre & post War ALS	War Dated ALS
$85	$	$210	$	$	$

Gray, Peter W., 1819-74   Member Confederate Congress

Signature	Signature with rank	Pre & post War DS	War Dated DS	Pre & post War ALS	War Dated ALS
$35	$	$	$	$	$

Grayson, John Breckinridge, 1806-61   Confederate General

WP graduate. He was appointed Brig. Genl in 1861 to command the Department of Middle and Eastern Florida. He died of natural causes Oct. 21, 1861.

Signature	Signature with rank	Pre War DS	War Dated DS	Pre War ALS	War Dated ALS
$150	$	$350	$	$	$

A rare signature.

Graves, Henry Lea, 1842-92   Confederate Marine Officer

Signature	Signature with rank	Pre & post War DS	War Dated DS	Pre & post War ALS	War Dated ALS
$	$	$	$387	$	$

Greely, Horace, 1811-72   Editor, politician and writer

Signature	Pre & post War DS	War Dated DS	Pre & post War ALS	War Dated ALS
$50	$	$	$225	$

ALS, Nov. 29, 1864, 1p., 8vo., Ltrhd. of the Office of the Tribune, NY, to O.J. Coxe of Hartford. "I thank you for yours of Friday which indicates that something is being done..." HMS Feb. 1994 $150.

PS, CDV, casually posed, signed "Horace Greeley". UA Feb. 1994 $1,000.

Green, Martin Edwin, 1815-63   Confederate General

Served under Genl. Price at Lexington, and led his militia at Pea Ridge. As Brig. Genl., he lcd the 3rd Brigade of Price's Army at Corinth, Hatchie Bridge, and Port Gibson. Wounded June 25, 1863 while in command of the 2nd Brigade at Vicksburg. Two days later, on June 27th, Genl. Green was killed June 27, 1863 at Vicksburg, Miss.

Signature	Signature with rank	Pre War DS	War Dated DS	Pre War ALS	War Dated ALS
$225	$	$	$	$	$

A rare signature.

Green, Thomas, 1814-64   Confederate Brigadier General

Colonel of the 5th Texas Mounted Rifles, he served under Sibley in the New Mexico operations. With Genl. Richard Taylor at Camp Bisland, and was given Sibley's Brigade. He was killed April 12, 1864 at Mansfield, La., by a mortar round fired from a Federal gunboat at Blair's Landing.

Signature	Signature with rank	Pre War DS	War Dated DS	Pre War ALS	War Dated ALS
$90	$167	$	$	$225	$

DS, 1857. [partial doc.]., signed as clerk of court of Texas Supreme Court. JH August 1992 $125.

--, 1859. 16p. legal document, concerning the lease of a slave. JH Nov. 1992 $200.

A scarce signature.

Greene, Colton, ?-?   Confederate Brigadier General

Brig. Genl. designated May 24, 1864., Trans-Mississippi.

Signature	Signature with rank	Pre & post War DS	War Dated DS	Pre & post War ALS	War Dated ALS
$80	$	$265	$	$	$

Greene, George Sears, 1801-99   Union General

Worked as an engineer before and after the war.

Signature	Signature with rank	Pre & post War DS	War Dated DS	Pre & post War ALS	War Dated ALS
$35	$	$65	$	$	$

Greene, Israel C., 1824-1909   Confederate Marine Officer

Signature	Signature with rank	Pre & post War DS	War Dated DS	Pre & post War ALS	War Dated ALS
$	$145	$	$	$	$

Greene, Oliver Duff, 1833-1904   MoH, Union Adj. Gen.

Signature	Signature with rank	Pre & post War DS	War Dated DS	Pre & post War ALS	War Dated ALS
$25	$38	$	$145	$	$

DS, 1862 March 3. 1p, 7.5 by 6.5", Special Order No. 58, signed. HOH Oct. 1992 $125.

Greer, Elkanah Brackin, 1825-77   Confederate Brigadier General

Colonel of the 3rd Texas Cavalry, he fought at Wilson's Creek and Pea Ridge before resigning on June 1, 1862. On October 8, 1862, he was recalled and appointed Brig, Genl. and named Chief of the Bureau of Conscription in the Trans-Mississippi Department. Farmer and merchant before the war.

Signature	Signature with rank	Pre & post War DS	War Dated DS	Pre & post War ALS	War Dated ALS
$225	$	$	$	$	$

Gregg, David McMurtie, 1833-1916   Union General

Graduated from West Point 1855, Served in the Army before the war, farmer after.

Signature	Signature with rank	Pre & post War DS	War Dated DS	Pre & post War ALS	War Dated ALS
$40	$98	$85	$187	$	$

Gregg, John, 1828-64   Confederate Brigadier General

Colonel of the 7th Texas, he was captured and exchanged at Fort Donelson. Under Genl. J.R. Anderson, defending the R.F. & P Railroad south of the Rappahannock. He was wounded at Chichamauga and fought at the Battle of the Wilderness. He was killed Oct. 7, 1864 at Darbytown Road, Va.

Signature	Signature with rank	Pre War DS	War Dated DS	Pre War ALS	War Dated ALS
$	$	$	$	$	$

A rare signature.

Gregg, Maxey, 1814-62   Confederate Brig General

He was at Charleston during the firing on Ft. Sumter, he fought with distinction during the Peninsular Campaign, Harpers Ferry, and at Sharpsburg. He was surprised by Federal troops during the Battle of Fredericksburg and was mortally wounded Dec. 13, 1862 and died Dec. 15, 1862.

Signature	Signature with rank	Pre War DS	War Dated DS	Pre War ALS	War Dated ALS
$350	$500	$589	$	$	$

A rare signature.

Gregory, Francis H., ?-?   Union Naval Captain

Signature	Signature with rank	Pre & post War DS	War Dated DS	Pre & post War ALS	War Dated ALS
$	$50	$	$	$87	$

Gresham, Walter Quintin, 1832-95   Union General

Signature	Signature with rank	Pre & post War DS	War Dated DS	Pre & post War ALS	War Dated ALS
$28	$	$65	$	$	$

Grierson, Benjamin Henry, 1826-1911   Union General

Signature	Signature with rank	Pre & post War DS	War Dated DS	Pre & post War ALS	War Dated ALS
$	$120	$	$	$	$650

Griffin, Charles, 1825-67   Union General

Signature	Signature with rank	Pre & post War DS	War Dated DS	Pre & post War ALS	War Dated ALS
$30	$	$87	$	$	$

Griffin, Simon Goodell, 1824-1902   Union General

Signature	Signature with rank	Pre & post War DS	War Dated DS	Pre & post War ALS	War Dated ALS
$25	$	$	$	$85	$

Griffith, Richard, 1814-62   Confederate Brigadier General
He commanded reserve troops at Seven Pines, and fought with distinction at Seven Days. Genl Griffith was mortally wounded during the Battle of Savage's Station , June 29, 1862 and died 30 June 1862.

Signature	Signature with rank	Pre War DS	War Dated DS	Pre War ALS	War Dated ALS
$250	$	$	$	$	$

A rare signature.

Grimball, John, 1840-1922   Confed. Gun Capt., CSN Shenandoah
Fired the last shot of the War between the States.

Signature	Signature with rank	Pre & post War DS	War Dated DS	Pre & post War ALS	War Dated ALS
$50	$98	$145	$	$	$

Grimes, Bryan, 1828-80   Confederate Major General
He was a fearless fighter with the Army of Northern Virginia at the Wilderness, Seven Pines, and Gettysburg. He was the last officer to be made a Major Genl. in the Army of Northern Virginia. He fought at Appomattox the morning of the surrender.

Signature	Signature with rank	Pre & post War DS	War Dated DS	Pre & post War ALS	War Dated ALS
$250	$	$	$	$	$

An extremely scarce signature.

Griswold, John A. 1818-72   Builder of the Monitor
American manufacturer. In 1861, with C.S. Bushnell and John F. Winslow, contacted to build Ericsson's Monitor. He was largely responsible for its completion in the hundred days allowed by the Federal government.

Signature	Pre & post War DS	War Dated DS	Pre & post War ALS	War Dated ALS
$178	$	$	$	$

S, Bold signature on a card. JB Dec. 1993 $150.

Grose, William, 1812-1900   Union General

Signature	Signature with rank	Pre & post War DS	War Dated DS	Pre & post War ALS	War Dated ALS
$35	$48	$	$145	$	$

Grover, Cuvier, 1828-85   Union General

Signature	Signature with rank	Pre & post War DS	War Dated DS	Pre & post War ALS	War Dated ALS
$25	$	$65	$	$	$

Gunther, Charles F. 18?-1920   Civil War Collector
Collection acquired by the Chicago Historical Society.

Signature	DS	ALS
$	$	$165

Gwynn, Thomas Peter, 1836-65+   Confederate Marine Officer

Signature	Signature with rank	Pre & post War DS	War Dated DS	Pre & post War ALS	War Dated ALS
$	$145	$	$	$	$

H

Hackleman, Pleasant Adam, 1814-62   Union General
Killed 3 Oct. 1862 at Corinth, Miss.

Signature	Signature with rank	Pre War DS	War Dated DS	Pre War ALS	War Dated ALS
$50	$178	$98	$	$	$

Hagood, Johnson, 1829-98   Confederate General

Citadel graduate. He was a S.C. Militia officer at 1st Bull Run. Ordered from James Island, Charleston, S.C. to Richmond in April 1864. He saw service at Petersburg, 2nd Cold Harbor and at Globe Tavern.

Signature	Signature with rank	Pre & post War DS	War Dated DS	Pre & post War ALS	War Dated ALS
$98	$185	$275	$	$398	$

Hagner, Peter V., 1815-93   Commander Watervliet Arsenal

Signature	Signature with rank	Pre & post War DS	War Dated DS	Pre & post War ALS	War Dated ALS
$	$	$	$75	$	$

DS, 1864. Orders, sgnd. ML October 1992 $65.

Hale, Stephen Fowler, 1816-62   Member Confederate Congress

Signature	Signature with rank	Pre War DS	War Dated DS	Pre War ALS	War Dated ALS
$50	$	$165	$	$	$

Haley, Alex ?-199?   Author

Wrote Malcolm X, Roots, and Search for Roots.

Signature	DS	ALS
$40	$128	$245

Kimball M. Sterling, Inc. Oct. 1,2,3, 1992 Johnson city, TN. Estate Action:
Manuscript, The Autobiography of Malcolm X, hand edited in red ink by Malcolm X. Re-edited in green ink by A.H. Accompanying letter to Dennis Sherman stating that the red ink editing was done by Malcolm X. $100,000.
DS, File containing initial contracts for autobiography of Malcolm X. & Roots. Signed by both A.H. & Malcolm X with working correspondence. $7,000.
Misc.
Group, All material found relating to ROOTS and Search for Roots. To include: extensive character development work on Kunta Kinte, 1750-1804; Chicken George research work; cockfighting; Extensive notes on the Lea family; Many hand written notes on slavery, Civil War, etc.; Complete correspondence files with Gambian officials; Family charts and research, Kunta Kinte family; Advanced editing manuscripts of Roots... $65,000.

B, Roots by Alex Haley. Number 31 of a limited edition of 500 copies, leather bound. Autographed. Boxed. $550.

Hall, Hiram Seymour, 1835-1908   Union Brevet General; MOH

Signature	Signature with rank	Pre & post War DS	War Dated DS	Pre & post War ALS	War Dated ALS
$	$	$	$125	$	$

DS, December 1863. restock of gloves sufficient large to supply the entire command. ML May 1992 $100.

Halleck, Henry Wager, 1815-72   Union Major General
Commanded Dept. of Mo., saw action at Corinth, became military advisor of President Lincoln & General-in Chief of the Union. He was often called "Old Brains."

Signature	Signature with rank	Pre & post War DS	War Dated DS	Pre & post War ALS	War Dated ALS
$100	$165	$250	$	$	$650

ALS, Jan. 2, 1862. 1p. To General Lorenzo Thomas, in part, " I have the honor to request that Capt. N.H.McLean may be assigned to Duty as Asst. Adj. Genl of this Dept. The duties of this office are so onerous that an additional Asst. Adj. Genl is very necessary..." SAG Feb. 1994 $660.
DS, 1860, 3x7" imprinted check, signed in ink, "H. W. Halleck" LR Sept. 1993 $200.
Misc.
P, CDV, 2/3 standing view in uniform of Maj. Genl., B/M Anthony, NY LR Oct. 1993 $50.

Hamblin, Joseph Eldridge, 1828-70   Union General

Signature	Signature with rank	Pre & post War DS	War Dated DS	Pre & post War ALS	War Dated ALS
$30	$	$	$	$	$

Hamilton, Charles Smith, 1822-91   Union General

Signature	Signature with rank	Pre & post War DS	War Dated DS	Pre & post War ALS	War Dated ALS
$25	$35	$	$	$	$

Hamilton, Schuyler, 1822-1903   Union General

Signature	Signature with rank	Pre & post War DS	War Dated DS	Pre & post War ALS	War Dated ALS
$	$55	$	$	$	$

P, CDV, Signed "Schuyler Hamilton / Maj. Genl. Vols. U.S.A." b/m Brady. AL August 1992 $ 395

Hamlin, Cyrus, 1839-67   Union General

Signature	Signature with rank	Pre & post War DS	War Dated DS	Pre & post War ALS	War Dated ALS
$	$65	$	$	$	$

Hamlin, Hannibal, 1809-91   Statesman, Lincoln's Vice President

Signature	Signature with rank	Pre & post War DS	War Dated DS	Pre & post War ALS	War Dated ALS
$75	$	$165	$	$250	$

S, Clip, Maine. NAL July 1992 $ 100

Hammond, William Alexander, 1828-1900   Union General

Signature	Signature with rank	Pre & post War DS	War Dated DS	Pre & post War ALS	War Dated ALS
$	$45	$	$	$	$

Hampton, Wade, 1818-1902   Confederate Lieutenant. General

He gave himself and his resources unstintingly to the support of the Confederacy. He raised and commanded "Hampton Legion"; was wounded three times and advanced to the rank of lieutenant general. After the war he was involved in state politics. One of the Confederacy's most popular cavalry generals.

Signature	Signature with rank	Pre & post War DS	War Dated DS	Pre & post War ALS	War Dated ALS
$225	$450	$550	$1,850	$950	$7,500

ALS, Jan. 5, 1867, Columbia, 1pp. 5x8", to Mr. Baker "Will you do me the kindness to investigate the matter to which the enclosed letter relates..." UA Sept. 1993 $1,050.
---, Oct. 19, 1900, Columbia, 2pp. 5x8", to George Kershaw, he explains that he is unable to attend a veterans reunion. UA Sept. 1993 $750.
---, May 18th [1864], 2 pages, in pencil, verso light, "Tony House 10.15 A.M./ Colonel [Lt. Col. Taylor]/ I have passed from Rhodes left along my line to this point & their army as yet no instruction. My pickets are at Ny Ri[iver] Bridge with vendettas[2] to Todd's Tavern I placed a battery in rear of his wing's right but Gen. Rhodes did not wish it to open unless he war Attacked This is the best position I can find to obtain an infilading fire on anything that attacks him. so I am putting four guns here. A prisoner just taken by my men says that his Brigade of his 6th corps were marched up to this

---

[2] . Single pickets.

point last night getting here by daylight with them came 3000 heavy arty who all broke when our guns opened. He says that al their troops were in motion last night but that he does not know where they were going to. That he heard they were going to Guinea Sta[tion] .... have been moved up here. think they were called up by the attack last night, & that their movement here is either a demonstration or preparation to meet any attack from us. I shall use every exertion to give you accountable information. I am Very Respectfully/ Wade Hampton/ Maj. Gen'l." SK Jan. 1994 $5,000.

---, May 21, 1886, Senate blue lined letterhead, 2pp., to Col. John B. Bachelder, I will if possible join you at Gettysburg... I would suggest that you have an invitation to all the Cav officers of the South to attend... reach all who take an interest in the matter... I will try to send some money... Jaj T G Barker, Charleston, was my Adj. Gen. Capt. Rankin Lowndes was my A.D.C. Col. Thos Lipscomb, Columbia, S.C., was in command of 2nd S.C. Regt. Genl Lawrence, then Col. 1st N.C., is alive..." J 1993 $1,350.

S, Clip sig. with closing sentimates of letter, 6 lines, mounted on card. BG Nov. 1993 $375.

-, Clip sig. with state, mounting residue on verso & traces of aging. BG Nov. 1993 $300.

-, Clip sig./ "So. Ca." NLM, Nov. 1992 $175

Misc.

P, CDV Waist up view, wearing a double breasted CSA uniform coat. Stars on collar 7 shoulder bars are visible. B/M Anthony, N.Y. LR Dec. 1993 $200.

Hancock, Winfield Scott, 1824-86   Union General

Democratic candidate for president. Fought at Antietam, Fredericksburg, Chancellorsville, commanded the II Corps at Gettysburg where he was severly wounded, Wilderness, Spotsylvania, Cold Harbor & Petersburg.

Signature	Signature with rank	Pre & post War DS	War Dated DS	Pre & post War ALS	War Dated ALS
$150	$225	$	$	$	$

ALS, 1884. 2pp, 5.5 by8.5", To General W.B. Franklin, friendly content. HOH Oct. 1992 $150

LS, Sept. 1, 1879, 2p. 8vo, Governors' Island, To General T.T.Locke turning down an invitation to join in the excursion of the George Washington Post. JB Dec. 1993 $175.

S, Clip sig., with rank & date 1874. BG Nov. 1993 $165.

--, Clip sig., in ink, "Yours very truely, Winf. S. Hancock." LR Sept. 1993 $125.

--, Clip sig. with rank. SK July 1992 $125.

PS, CDV, signed "Winfd. S. Hancock / Mg. Genl. U.S. Cols./ Comdg. 2d corps." Also inscribed on verso, "For Miss Jane Anderson / with compliments of / Winfd. S. Hancock/ Major Genl. / U.S. Vols." AL August 1992 $675.

Misc.

P, CDV, Seated view, wearing a double breasted frock coat of Maj. Gen. & poses with one hand on his waist. B/M showing the Capitol, of Alexander Gardner. LR Dec. 1993 $250.

Hanly, Thomas Burton, 1812-80   Member Confederate Congress

Signature	Signature with rank	Pre & post War DS	War Dated DS	Pre & post War ALS	War Dated ALS
$	$35	$	$	$	$

Hanson, Roger Weightman, 1827-63   Confederate Brigadier General
He held the Confederate right at Fort Donelson for part of the siege, and was captured on February 16, 1862. He served with Forrest at Nashville. on Genl Morgan's Expedition against Hartville, he captured over two thousand Union Troops, losing 68 of his own men. He led the 4th Brigade under Genl. Hardee at Stones River, where he was killed January 2, 1863.

Signature	Signature with rank	Pre War DS	War Dated DS	Pre War ALS	War Dated ALS
$250	$	$545	$	$	$

A rare signature.

Harbin, Thomas H. ? - ?   Confederate Secret Service Agent
Envolved with John W. Booth's escape. A.K.A. Thomas A. Wilson.

Signature	Pre & post War DS	War Dated DS	Pre & post War ALS	War Dated ALS
$	$	$	$	$

Hardee, William Joseph, 1815-73   Confederate Lieutenant. General
He wrote the manual used by the infantry of both North & South, was commandant of West Point. Fought in the Seminole War and Mexican War. He led his corps at Shiloh, Perryville, Stone River, Missionary Ridge, and the Atlanta campaign.

Signature	Signature with rank	Pre & post War DS	War Dated DS	Pre & post War ALS	War Dated ALS
$185	$295	$675	$	$885	$

S, "W.J. Hardee/Lieut Genl." set in a mat with engraved portrait. TP Nov. 1993 $275.
-, Bold Sig. with rank. BG Nov. 1993 $285.
Misc.

P, CDV, Bust view in uniform with eppaulettes, B/M C.D.Fredericks & Co., N.Y., Habana & Paris. LR Oct. 1993 $125.

Hardeman, William Polk, "Gotch", 1816-98   Confederate General
Captain 4th Texas Mounted Volunteers, he fought under Sibley in New Mexico and was promoted Colonel in the latter part of 1862. He succeeded Green as Brigade Commander and led his regiment in the Red River Campaign of 1864.

Signature	Signature with rank	Pre & post War DS	War Dated DS	Pre & post War ALS	War Dated ALS
$90	$	$	$	$	$

Hardie, James Allen, 1823-76   Union General

Signature	Signature with rank	Pre & post War DS	War Dated DS	Pre & post War ALS	War Dated ALS
$55	$78	$	$145	$	$

DS, May 18, 1863. 1p. 7.45x12", pert. to the appointment of a cadet. MS Nov. 1993 $115.
S, Clip signature. NLM Nov. 1992 $65

Hardin, Martin Davis, 1837-1923   Union General

Signature	Signature with rank	Pre & post War DS	War Dated DS	Pre & post War ALS	War Dated ALS
$35	$	$	$	$	$

Harding, Abner Clark, 1807-74   Union General

Signature	Signature with rank	Pre & post War DS	War Dated DS	Pre & post War ALS	War Dated ALS
$	$	$	$	$	$

Harker, Charles Garrison, 1835-64   Union General
Killed 27 June 1864 at Kenesaw Mountain, Ga.

Signature	Signature with rank	Pre War DS	War Dated DS	Pre War ALS	War Dated ALS
$45	$	$95	$	$	$

Harlan, James, ?-?   Lincoln's Secretary of the Interior

Signature	Signature with rank	Pre & post War DS	War Dated DS	Pre & post War ALS	War Dated ALS
$35	$	$85	$	$	$

Harland, Edward, 1832-1915   Union General

Signature	Signature with rank	Pre & post War DS	War Dated DS	Pre & post War ALS	War Dated ALS
$25	$	$	$	$	$

Harney, William Selby, 1800-89   Union General

Signature	Signature with rank	Pre & post War DS	War Dated DS	Pre & post War ALS	War Dated ALS
$	$45	$	$	$	$

Harris, Nathaniel Harrison, 1834-1900   Confederate General

Colonel with the 19th Mississsippi Infantry, Harris fought with distinction at Williamsburg, Chancellorsville, Gettysburg, Cold Harbor, and was appointed Brig. Genl. to take Genl. Carnot Posey's place.

Signature	Signature with rank	Pre & post War DS	War Dated DS	Pre & post War ALS	War Dated ALS
$90	$185	$	$	$	$

Harris, Thomas Alexander, 1826-95   Member Confederate Congress

Signature	Signature with rank	Pre & post War DS	War Dated DS	Pre & post War ALS	War Dated ALS
$40	$	$78	$	$	$

Harris, Thomas Maley, 1817-1906   Union General

Signature	Signature with rank	Pre & post War DS	War Dated DS	Pre & post War ALS	War Dated ALS
$30	$	$75	$	$	$

178

Harris, Wiley Pope, 1818-91   Member Confederate Congress

Signature	Signature with rank	Pre & post War DS	War Dated DS	Pre & post War ALS	War Dated ALS
$40	$	$	$	$	$

Harrison, Benjamin, 1833-1901   Union Officer & US President

Signature	Signature with rank	Pre & post War DS	War Dated DS	Pre & post War ALS	War Dated ALS
$300	$	$550	$	$950	$1,450

Harrison, Burton N. ?-?   Private Secretary to Pres. J. Davis

Signature	Signature with rank	Pre & post War DS	War Dated DS	Pre & post War ALS	War Dated ALS
$	$	$	$250	$	$

Harrison, George Paul, 1841-1922   Confederate General

Wright says he was appointed B.G., May 16, 1865, by Kirby Smith in the Trans-Miss. (?)

Signature	Signature with rank	Pre & post War DS	War Dated DS	Pre & post War ALS	War Dated ALS
$80	$	$	$200	$	$

Harrison, James Edward, 1815-75   Confederate General

Lt. Col. in the 15th Texas, he was engaged in scouting and skirmishing until Sept. 29, 1863, when he led a brigade under Genl. Taylor in Louisiana. Appointed Brig. Genl. Dec. 22, 1864.

Signature	Signature with rank	Pre & post War DS	War Dated DS	Pre & post War ALS	War Dated ALS
$100	$	$287	$	$	$

Harrison, Thomas, 1823-91   Confederate General

Captain of the 8th Texas Cavalry, he was a Major at Shiloh. He led his regiment at Stones River, and led Wharton's Brigade at Chickamauga, and fought under Wheeler to thwart McCook's Brigade at Chickamauga. He saw service with Genl. Hood in TN.

Signature	Signature with rank	Pre & post War DS	War Dated DS	Pre & post War ALS	War Dated ALS
$90	$165	$187	$	$250	$

Harrison, Thomas James, 1811-79   Member Confederate Congress

Signature	Signature with rank	Pre & post War DS	War Dated DS	Pre & post War ALS	War Dated ALS
$	$50	$	$	$	$

Harrow, William, 1822-72   Union General

Signature	Signature with rank	Pre & post War DS	War Dated DS	Pre & post War ALS	War Dated ALS
$30	$55	$	$	$	$

Hartranft, John Frederick, 1830-89   Union General

Signature	Signature with rank	Pre & post War DS	War Dated DS	Pre & post War ALS	War Dated ALS
$	$	$	$	$78	$

Hartridge, Julian, 1829-79   Member Confederate Congress

Signature	Signature with rank	Pre & post War DS	War Dated DS	Pre & post War ALS	War Dated ALS
$45	$	$	$	$	$

Hartsuff, George Lucas, 1830-74   Union General

Signature	Signature with rank	Pre & post War DS	War Dated DS	Pre & post War ALS	War Dated ALS
$	$75	$	$	$	$

Hartwell, Alfred Stedman, 1836-1912 — Union Brevet General

Signature	Signature with rank	Pre & post War DS	War Dated DS	Pre & post War ALS	War Dated ALS
$25	$	$75	$	$97	$

Hartwell, Charles Atherton, 1841-76 — Union Brevet General

Signature	Signature with rank	Pre & post War DS	War Dated DS	Pre & post War ALS	War Dated ALS
$20	$	$	$	$	$

Hascall, Milo Smith, 1829-1904 — Union General

Signature	Signature with rank	Pre & post War DS	War Dated DS	Pre & post War ALS	War Dated ALS
$	$35	$	$	$	$

Haskell, Llewellyn Frost, 1842-1929 — Union Brevet General

Signature	Signature with rank	Pre & post War DS	War Dated DS	Pre & post War ALS	War Dated ALS
$	$	$	$	$	$

Haskin, Joseph Abel, 1818-74 — Union General

Signature	Signature with rank	Pre & post War DS	War Dated DS	Pre & post War ALS	War Dated ALS
$30	$45	$	$	$87	$

Haswell, Charles Haynes, 1809-? — Union Naval Architect

Signature	Signature with rank	Pre & post War DS	War Dated DS	Pre & post War ALS	War Dated ALS
$	$	$	$125	$	$

Hatch, Edward, 1832-89 — Union General

Signature	Signature with rank	Pre & post War DS	War Dated DS	Pre & post War ALS	War Dated ALS
$	$45	$	$	$	$

Hatch, John Porter, 1822-1901   Union General

Signature	Signature with rank	Pre & post War DS	War Dated DS	Pre & post War ALS	War Dated ALS
$	$35	$	$	$	$

Hatcher, Robert Anthony, 1819-86   Member Confederate Congress

Signature	Signature with rank	Pre & post War DS	War Dated DS	Pre & post War ALS	War Dated ALS
$	$55	$	$	$	$

Hatton, Robert Hopkins, 1826-62   Confederate General

Colonel of the 7th TN. Infantry. He saw service under Loring in the Cheat Mountain operation, and with Stonewall Jackson in the Valley. Appointed Brig. Genl. on May 23, 1862, he was killed 1 June 1862 at Fair Oaks, Va.

Signature	Signature with rank	Pre War DS	War Dated DS	Pre War ALS	War Dated ALS
$285	$	$	$	$	$

A very scarce signature.

Haupt, Herman, 1817-1905   Union General

Signature	Signature with rank	Pre & post War DS	War Dated DS	Pre & post War ALS	War Dated ALS
$25	$	$	$	$	$

182

Hawes, James Morrison, 1824-89   Confederate General

WP graduate.   He was appointed Brig. Genl. to command   cavalry in Western
Department under A.S.Johnston.   After Shiloh, he asked to be relieved of the entire
cavalry command to lead a brigade in Breckinridge's Division.   In October 1862, he led
a Texas Brigade near Little Rock, and in 1863 led a brigade during the siege of
Vicksburg.

Signature	Signature with rank	Pre & post War DS	War Dated DS	Pre & post War ALS	War Dated ALS
$90	$	$	$	$	$

Hawkins, Isaac Roberts, 1818-80   Union Brevet General

Signature	Signature with rank	Pre & post War DS	War Dated DS	Pre & post War ALS	War Dated ALS
$20	$	$	$	$	$90

Hawkins, John Parker, 1830-1914   Union General

Signature	Signature with rank	Pre & post War DS	War Dated DS	Pre & post War ALS	War Dated ALS
$	$35	$	$	$	$

Hawley, Joseph Roswell, 1826-1905   Union General, Gov. of Ct.

Signature	Signature with rank	Pre & post War DS	War Dated DS	Pre & post War ALS	War Dated ALS
$	$	$65	$	$	$

Hawthorn, Alexander Travis, 1825-99 — Confederate General

Lt. Col. in the 6th Arkansas in 1861, he led the regiment at Shiloh. During the Vicksburg Campaign. He fought with distinction at Helena under Genl. Holmes, and later at Fort Hindman. As a Brig. Genl. He led a brigade at Jenkins Ferry, Ark.

Signature	Signature with rank	Pre & post War DS	War Dated DS	Pre & post War ALS	War Dated ALS
$150	$	$378	$	$695	$

Hay, John, 1838-1905 — Secretary to Lincoln

Signature	Pre & post War DS	War Dated DS	Pre & post War ALS	War Dated ALS
$45	$165	$265	$197	$

Hayes, Joseph, 1835-1912 — Union General

Signature	Signature with rank	Pre & post War DS	War Dated DS	Pre & post War ALS	War Dated ALS
$50	$	$87	$	$	$

Hayes, Landon Carter, 1816-75 — Member Confederate Congress

Signature	Signature with rank	Pre & post War DS	War Dated DS	Pre & post War ALS	War Dated ALS
$50	$	$	$	$	$

Hayes, Rutherford Birchard, 1822-93 — Union General & US President

Signature	Signature with rank	Pre & post War DS	War Dated DS	Pre & post War ALS	War Dated ALS
$300	$	$568	$	$1,050	$

S, Signature "R.B.Hayes" on white card. JB Dec. 1993 $285.

Haynie, Isham Nicholas, 1824-68 — Union General

Signature	Signature with rank	Pre & post War DS	War Dated DS	Pre & post War ALS	War Dated ALS
$30	$	$76	$	$	$

Hays, Alexander, 1819-64　　　　　　　　Union Brigadier General
Killed 5 May 1864 at the Wilderness, Va.

Signature	Signature with rank	Pre War DS	War Dated DS	Pre War ALS	War Dated ALS
$50	$	$145	$	$	$

Hays, Andrew Jackson, ?-1896　　　　　Confederate Marine Officer

Signature	Signature with rank	Pre & post War DS	War Dated DS	Pre & post War ALS	War Dated ALS
$	$105	$	$	$	$

Hays, Harry Thompson, 1820-76　　　　Confederate General
He served under Genl. Jubal Early as Col. of the 7th Louisiana at 1st Bull Run. He was with Genl. Jackson at the last Chancellorsville. He was wounded at Bloody Angle. He then served in the Trans-Mississippi Department.

Signature	Signature with rank	Pre & post War DS	War Dated DS	Pre & post War ALS	War Dated ALS
$175	$265	$	$1,150	$	$

Hays, William, 1819-75　　　　　　　　Union General

Signature	Signature with rank	Pre & post War DS	War Dated DS	Pre & post War ALS	War Dated ALS
$34	$65	$76	$	$138	$

Hazen, William Babcock, 1830-87　　　　Union General

Signature	Signature with rank	Pre & post War DS	War Dated DS	Pre & post War ALS	War Dated ALS
$30	$	$	$105	$	$

Hebert, Louis, 1820-1901   Confederate General

WP graduate. He entered C.S. service as a Col. in the 3rd Louisiana Infantry. He fought with distinction at Wilson's Creek, and was captured at the Battle of Elkhorn. As Brig. Genl., he saw service at Corinth and Vicksburg.

Signature	Signature with rank	Pre & post War DS	War Dated DS	Pre & post War ALS	War Dated ALS
$85	$155	$235	$468	$	$

Hebert, Paul Octave, 1818-80   Confederate General

WP graduate. As Brig. Genl., he took over the Department of Texas and the defenses of Galveston. At Vicksburg campaign, he was in command of the Sub-district of the Northern Louisiana, and fought with distinction at Milliken's Bend.

Signature	Signature with rank	Pre & post War DS	War Dated DS	Pre & post War ALS	War Dated ALS
$90	$178	$475	$	$650	$

Heckman, Charles Adam, 1822-96   Union General

Signature	Signature with rank	Pre & post War DS	War Dated DS	Pre & post War ALS	War Dated ALS
$25	$43	$75	$	$	$

Heintzelman, Samuel Peter, 1805-80   Union General

BG USV 1861, captured Alexandria, Va. May 17, 1861, led 3rd Corps Army of the Potomac in Penisula Campaign, MG USV 1862, headed Wash. Mil. District 1862-63.

Signature	Signature with rank	Pre & post War DS	War Dated DS	Pre & post War ALS	War Dated ALS
$28	$38	$	$110	$100	$187

ALS, Dec. 20, 1868, 1.5pps, sep. leaves pert. to intercession with the President for a position. EB Dec. 1993 $90.

186

Heiskell, Joseph Brown, 1823-1913   Member Confederate Congress

Signature	Signature with rank	Pre & post War DS	War Dated DS	Pre & post War ALS	War Dated ALS
$	$50	$	$	$	$

Helm, Benjamin Hardin, 1830-63   Confederate Brigadier General
WP graduate. He organized the 1st KY Cavalry, and was appointed Col. in 1861. He commanded a brigade under Beckinridge at Vicksburg. In Jan. 1863, he took over Hanson's Brigade and led it in the Tullahoma Campaign. He was killed 20 Sept 1863 at Chickamauga, Ga.

Signature	Signature with rank	Pre War DS	War Dated DS	Pre War ALS	War Dated ALS
$250	$	$	$	$	$

Hemphill, John, 1803-62   Member Confederate Congress

Signature	Signature with rank	Pre War DS	War Dated DS	Pre War ALS	War Dated ALS
$125	$	$	$	$	$

Henderson, David English, 1832-87   Artist
Oil on canvas, 25x30" *Departure from Fredericksburg before the Bombardment*, 1865 (GNPS). Oil on canvas, 23x30" *The Return to Fredericksburg after the Battle*, 1865 (GNPS).

Signature	Pre & post War DS	War Dated DS	Pre & post War ALS	War Dated ALS
$	$	$	$145	$

Henderson, Richard Henry, 1831-80   Confederate Marine Officer

Signature	Signature with rank	Pre & post War DS	War Dated DS	Pre & post War ALS	War Dated ALS
$	$115	$	$458	$	$

Henry, Gustavous Adolphus, 1804-80   Member Confederate Congress

Signature	Signature with rank	Pre & post War DS	War Dated DS	Pre & post War ALS	War Dated ALS
$35	$	$	$	$	$

Herbert, Caleb Claiborne, 1814-67   Member Confederate Congress

Signature	Signature with rank	Pre & post War DS	War Dated DS	Pre & post War ALS	War Dated ALS
$50	$	$	$	$	$

Herron, Francis Jay, 1837-1902   Union General

Signature	Signature with rank	Pre & post War DS	War Dated DS	Pre & post War ALS	War Dated ALS
$20	$35	$65	$	$97	$

Heth, Henry, 1825-99   Confederate General

Fought in the Ky. campaign, Chancellorsville, & it was Heth's troops that started the battle of Gettysburg on July 1st. He was severly wounded in the battle. He surrendered at Appomattox.

Signature	Signature with rank	Pre & post War DS	War Dated DS	Pre & post War ALS	War Dated ALS
$125	$265	$278	$	$587	$

Misc.
P, CDV, Bust view in CSA uniform, with his large checkered tie. B/M Anthony, N.Y., card shows minor toning. LR Sept. 1993 $350.

Hicks, Thomas, 1823-90   Artist

Oil on Canvas. A. Lincoln. Chicago Historical Society.

Signature	Pre & post War DS	War Dated DS	Pre & post War ALS	War Dated ALS
$	$	$	$138	$

Hicks, T. H., 1798-1865   Maryland CW Governor

Signature	Signature with rank	Pre & post War DS	War Dated DS	Pre & post War ALS	War Dated ALS
$20	$35	$45	$	$	$

Higgins, Edward, 1821-75   Confederate General
Captain of the 1st Louisina Artillery, he was aide-de-camp to Twiggs at New Orleans. He commanded Forts Jackson and St. Philip when Farragut attacked New Orleans. As a Col., he led the 22nd Louisiana Artillery at Snyder's Mill. In 1863 he command the Artillery river batteries at Vicksburg. As Brig. Genl., he was in command of the post at Mobile.

Signature	Signature with rank	Pre & post War DS	War Dated DS	Pre & post War ALS	War Dated ALS
$95	$	$248	$	$356	$

Higginson, Thomas Wentworth, 1823-1911   Author, Antislavery

Signature	Signature with rank	Pre & post War DS	War Dated DS	Pre & post War ALS	War Dated ALS
$35	$	$	$	$175	$

Hill, Ambrose Powell, 1825-65   Confederate Lieutenant. General
Fought at Sharpsburg, Fredericksburg, wounded at Chancellorsville, Comm. II Corps A.N.V. at Gettysburg, & killed April 2, 1865, at Petersburg, Va.

Signature	Signature with rank	Pre War DS	War Dated DS	Pre War ALS	War Dated ALS
$1,800	$2,675	$3,500	$7,500	$	$

DS, Jan. 24, 1865. 2pp., 4to., HQ 3rd Corps, A.N.V. pert to leave request 48th N.C.T., endorsements incl. Genl. John R. Cooke, AES w/rank, Genl. Henry Heth (twice) & Cols. Taylor & Venable of Lee's staff. Hill signature light. BG Nov. 1993 $7,000.
--, February 19, 1861. Check signed. GH July 1992 $3,750.
Misc.

P, CDV, bust pose wearing a CSA uniform with 3 stars on collar & Checkered shirt. LR Oct. 1993 $175.

-, CDV, Chest up view in CSA uniform coat w/checkered shirt visible. B/M Anthony N.Y. LR Dec. 1993 $150.

A rare and desirable signature.

Hill, Benjamin Harvey, 1823-82   Member Confederate Congress

Signature	Signature with rank	Pre & post War DS	War Dated DS	Pre & post War ALS	War Dated ALS
$45	$	$95	$	$	$

Hill, Benjamin Jefferson, 1825-80   Confederate General

Colonel of the 35th TN. Vol. Inf. He fought with distinction at Shiloh, Chickamauga, and Chattanooga.

Signature	Signature with rank	Pre & post War DS	War Dated DS	Pre & post War ALS	War Dated ALS
$90	$150	$187	$	$357	$

Hill, Daniel Harvey, 1821-89   Confederate General

WP graduate. Col. of the 1st North Carolina Infantry, he won the first major battle of the war, at Big Bethel, June 10, 1861. Promoted Brig. Genl. that July. As Major Genl., he had a division and later a Corps, in the Army of Northern Virginia, and fought through the Peninsula Campaign. He fought with distinction at South Mountain and Antietam.

Signature	Signature with rank	Pre & post War DS	War Dated DS	Pre & post War ALS	War Dated ALS
$325	$575	$495	$	$650	$

Hilliard, Henry Wahington, 1808-92   Confederate Commissioner to TN

Signature	Signature with rank	Pre & post War DS	War Dated DS	Pre & post War ALS	War Dated ALS
$30	$	$	$	$	$

Hilton, Robert Benjamin, 1821-94   Member Confederate Congress

Signature	Signature with rank	Pre & post War DS	War Dated DS	Pre & post War ALS	War Dated ALS
$35	$	$78	$	$	$

Hincks, Edward Winslow, 1830-94   Union General

Signature	Signature with rank	Pre & post War DS	War Dated DS	Pre & post War ALS	War Dated ALS
$50	$	$	$	$	$

Hindman, Thomas Carmichael, 1818-68   Confederate General

Colonel 2nd Arkansas Inf., he fought at Prairie Grove, Chickamauga, Chattanooga & was so severely wounded in the Atlanta campaign to make him unfit for any further field service.

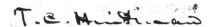

Signature	Signature with rank	Pre & post War DS	War Dated DS	Pre & post War ALS	War Dated ALS
$300	$485	$	$	$	$

S, Clip with tips of rank showing and P.A.C.S., mounted. BG Nov. 1993 $290.
Misc.
P, CDV, Chest up view in CSA uniform. B/M Anthony, N.Y. LR Oct. 1993 $175.

Hitchcock, Ethan Allen, 1798-1870   Union General

Signature	Signature with rank	Pre & post War DS	War Dated DS	Pre & post War ALS	War Dated ALS
$	$50	$	$	$	$

Hobson, Edward Henry, 1825-1901   Union General

Signature	Signature with rank	Pre & post War DS	War Dated DS	Pre & post War ALS	War Dated ALS
$35	$	$86	$	$	$

Hodge, George Baird, 1828-92   Confederate General

Annapolis graduate. He entered C.S. service as a Private but was soon elected to the C.S. Congress. He served on the staff of Genl. Breckinridge, and commanded a brigade under Wheeler. Appointed Brig. Genl. by Davis twice, but was never confirmed by the Senate.

Signature	Signature with rank	Pre & post War DS	War Dated DS	Pre & post War ALS	War Dated ALS
$90	$135	$	$	$365	$

Hoke, Robert Frederick, 1837-1912   Confederate General

Served as Colonel of both the 21st and 33rd N.C. Inf. Regts. He saw action at Big Bethal, New Berne, the Peninsula camign, 2d Manassas, the Sharpsburg campaign, Fredericksburg & was seriously wounded at Chancellorsville.

Signature	Signature with rank	Pre & post War DS	War Dated DS	Pre & post War ALS	War Dated ALS
$100	$150.	$	$	$325	$

ALS, Feb. 19, 1898. 1p. 4to., Raleigh, N.C., pert. to an autograph request. With cover. BG Nov. 1993 $295.
S, Card signed with rank: Large ink autograph, "R.F. Hoke, Maj. Genl., C.S.A." LR Sept. 1993 $125.

Hogg, Joseph Lewis, 1806-62   Union General

Signature	Signature with rank	Pre War DS	War Dated DS	Pre War ALS	War Dated ALS
$50	$175	$	$	$	$

Holabird, Samuel Beckley, 1826-1907   Union General

Signature	Signature with rank	Pre & post War DS	War Dated DS	Pre & post War ALS	War Dated ALS
$20	$35	$	$65	$	$

Holcombe, James Philemon, 1820-73   Member Confederate Congress

Signature	Signature with rank	Pre & post War DS	War Dated DS	Pre & post War ALS	War Dated ALS
$45	$	$	$	$135	$

Holder, William Dunbar, 1824-1900   Member Confederate Congress

Signature	Signature with rank	Pre & post War DS	War Dated DS	Pre & post War ALS	War Dated ALS
$32	$	$	$	$	$

Holliday, Frederick William Mackey, 1828-99   Mem. Confed. Cong.

Signature	Signature with rank	Pre & post War DS	War Dated DS	Pre & post War ALS	War Dated ALS
$	$50	$75	$	$	$

Hollins, George Nichols, 1799-1878   Commodore, Confederate Navy

He captured the St. Nicholas in June '61 on the Potomac River, commanded the defenses of the James River, commanded the naval station at New Orleans, defeated the Union blockade on the Mississsppi River, & assisted in defense of the works at Columbia, Ky.

Signature	Signature with rank	Pre & post War DS	War Dated DS	Pre & post War ALS	War Dated ALS
$	$325	$	$578	$	$

Misc.

-, CDV- bust view in double breasted CSA uniform w/shoulder bars visible. B/M C.D. Fredricks & Co., N.Y. LR Dec. 1993 $125.

Holmes, George, 1825-?   Confederate Marine Officer

Signature	Signature with rank	Pre & post War DS	War Dated DS	Pre & post War ALS	War Dated ALS
$	$108	$	$	$	$

Holmes, Theophilus Hunter, 1804-80   Confederate General

WP graduate. He commanded a brigade at 1st Manassas, and a division at the Battle of Seven Days.

Signature	Signature with rank	Pre & post War DS	War Dated DS	Pre & post War ALS	War Dated ALS
$100	$165	$275	$	$	$

Holt, Hines, 1805-65   Member Confederate Congress

Signature	Signature with rank	Pre & post War DS	War Dated DS	Pre & post War ALS	War Dated ALS
$80	$	$	$	$	$

Holt, Joseph, 1807-94   Union General & Abe's Judge Advocate

Signature	Signature with rank	Pre & post War DS	War Dated DS	Pre & post War ALS	War Dated ALS
$50	$	$	$	$278	$

Holtzclaw, James Thadeus, 1833-93   Confederate General

Major in the 18th Alabama during the Battle of Shiloh, he was thought mortally wounded, but recovered 90 days later. He led the 18th Alabama at Chickamauga and commanded Clayton's Brigade at Lookout Mountain.

Signature	Signature with rank	Pre & post War DS	War Dated DS	Pre & post War ALS	War Dated ALS
$85	$153	$210	$	$	$

S, Clipped signature with rank. SK Feb. 1994 $150.

Hood, John Bell, 1831-79   Confederate General

In April 1861, Hood resigned his commission, joined the Confederate army, and was placed in chage of the cavaly under Magruder. He was rapidly promoted to briadier-general and took command of the "Texas Brigade," and won raves for their success at Gaines Mill, 2nd Manassas and Antietam. Promoted major-general, he was given a division of Longstreet's corps. Wounded at Gettysburg, he rejoined his troops at Chickamauga where he again distinguished himself, but lost his right leg.

Signature	Signature with rank	Pre & post War DS	War Dated DS	Pre & post War ALS	War Dated ALS
$850	$1,500	$	$	$	$

S, Clip sig. with sentiment, mounting traces verso. BG Nov. 1993 $950.
-, 3.5x2.25", "I am sir ... Respectfully Your obt Srvt J B Hood Major Genl." UA Sept. 1993 $1,600.

Hooker, Joseph M, 1814-79   Union General

"Fighting Joe," saw action at Yorktown, Williamsburg, Second Bull Run, Antietam where he was wounded, Fredericksburg, commanded the Army of the Potomac at Chancellorsville.

Signature	Signature with rank	Pre & post War DS	War Dated DS	Pre & post War ALS	War Dated ALS
$165	$250	$389	$575	$478	$

ALS, 1871 September 1p 4.5x7.5", friendly content. Matted w/steel engraving. HOH October 1992 $375.
AES, Jan. 18, 1864. 2pp., 4to., HQ 12th Corps on ALS headed Lookout Valley, Tenn. pert. to recruiting for 15th Ill. Cav., denied by order of Genl. Thomas. BG Nov. 1993 $495.
S, Clip signature with rank. BG Nov. 1993 $175.
PS, CDV, signed "J. Hooker / Maj. Genl." b/m E. & H.T. Anthony. A bust view. AL August 1992 $250.
Misc.
P, CDV, Bust view as Brig. Gen. B/M C.D. Fredicks & Co., NY. LR Dec. 1993 $45.

Homer, Winslow, 1836-1910   Artist

Signature	Pre & post War DS	War Dated DS	Pre & post War ALS	War Dated ALS
$300	$500	$	$1,250	$

Orginial Sketches

-, 1863. N.p., (two) Pencil on paper; 7.5x4.5" each. One signed "Homer," the other "W.H. 1863". These are studies of a soldier being shot, sketched linework depicting motion w/ some erasure. Matted and framed. AL August 1992 $5,500.

Wood engravings: Price averaged are for unframed & unmatted material in very good condition no tears, stains or holes.

	Averages
Expulsion of Negroes and Abolitionists from Tremont Temple, Boston, Massachusetts, on December 3, 1860 December 15, 1860; p. 788; .5page	$55
The Seceding South Carolina Delegation December 22, 1860; p. 801	$35
A Bivouac Fire on the Potomac December 21, 1861; p. 808-809	$45
Seeing the Old Year Out January 5, 1861; pp. 8-9	$25
The Seceding Mississippi Delegation in Congress February 2, 1861; p. 65	$35
The late Rev. Dr. Murray February 23, 1861; p. 117; .25page	$35
The Inauguarl Procession at Washington Passing the Gate of the Capitol Grounds Mar. 16, 1861; p. 161; .5page	$45
President Buchanan and Lincoln Entering the Senate Chamber Before the Inauguration. Mar. 16, 1861; p. 165; .33page	$35 - 55
The Inaugaration of Abraham Lincoln as President of the U.S. at the Capitol, Wash., March 4, 1861 Mar. 16, 1861; p. 168-169; double page	$65 - 75
General Thomas Swearing in the Volunteers Called into the service of the US at Washinton, D.C. April 27, 1861; p. 257; .5page	$35 -45
General Beauregard April 27, 1861; p. 269; .25page	$75 - 95
Colonel Wilson, of Wilson's Brigade May 11, 1861; p. 289; .25page	$15 - 25

The Seventy-Ninth Regiment (Highlanders),
N.Y. State Militia $45 - 55
May 25, 1861; p. 329

The War-Making Havelocks for the Volunteers $35 - 50
June 29, 1861; p. 401

Crew of the United States Stream-Sloop "Colorado"
Shipped at Boston, June 1861 $35 - 4 5
July 13, 1861; p. 439

Filling Cartridges at the U.S. Arsenal, at Watertown, MA. $25 - 45
July 20, 1861; p. 449

Flag-Officers Stringham $25 - 35
September 14, 1861; p. 577; 1/6 page

The Songs of the WAR $25 - 35
September 2 1861; p. 744-745; double page

A Bivouac Fire on the Potomac $35 - 65
December 21, 1861; pp. 808-809; double page

Christmas Boxes in Camp - Christmas, 1861 $40
January 4, 1862; p. 1

The Skating Season $35
January 18, 1862; p. 44

Our Army before Yorktown, Virginia $35 - 45
May 3, 1862; pp. 280-281

News from the War $40 - 50
June 14, 1862; pp. 376-77

The War for the Union,1862 - A Cavalry Charge $50 - 65
July 5, 1862; pp. 424-425

The Surgeon at Work at the rear during an Engagement $65 - 95
July 12, 1862; p.

The War for the Union,1862 - A Bayonet Charge $55 - 75
July 12, 1862; pp. 440-441

Our Women and the War $35 - 45
September 6, 1862; pp. 568-569 double page

The Army of the Potomac - A Sharp-Shooter Nov. 15, 1862; p. 724	$99 - 245
Pay-Day in the Army of the Potomac February 28, 1863; pp. 136-137	$45 - 55
Shell in the Rebel Trenches January 17, 1863	$50 - 75
The Nooning August 16, 1873	$75 - 125
Snap the Whip September 20, 1873	$265 - 350

Hovey, Alvin Peterson, 1821-91 — Union General

Signature	Signature with rank	Pre & post War DS	War Dated DS	Pre & post War ALS	War Dated ALS
$25	$35	$	$87	$	$

Hovey, Charles Edward, 1827-97 — Union General

Signature	Signature with rank	Pre & post War DS	War Dated DS	Pre & post War ALS	War Dated ALS
$	$38	$	$	$	$

Howard, Oliver Otis, 1830-1909 — Union General

Signature	Signature with rank	Pre & post War DS	War Dated DS	Pre & post War ALS	War Dated ALS
$85	$135	$110	$	$225	$325

ALS, 1864 April 25. 1p. 8x5",Dept of the Cumberland, Clearland, TN., re request for autograph and photograph sent thru Genl (Henry) Prince. EB August 1992 $295.
DS, 1900. Check from the Christain Endeavor-Boston endorsed on reverse. ML May 1992 $90.
S, Large signature on card w/ rank. SK Nov. 1993 $100.
-, Clip w/ rank. SK April 1993 $65.

Howe, Albion Paris, 1818-97 — Union General

Signature	Signature with rank	Pre & post War DS	War Dated DS	Pre & post War ALS	War Dated ALS
$20	$30	$	$78	$	$

Howe, Julia Ward, 1819-1910   Writer; Battle Hymn of the Republic

Signature	Pre & post War DS	War Dated DS	Pre & post War ALS	War Dated ALS
$75	$185	$	$300	$

ANS, 1p. 4.5x3.5" "Please convey my thanks to the ladies whose names are joined with yours in the gift of the valued work and believe me, Yours sincerely, Julia Ward Howe." HD Oct. 1993 $110.

Howell, Becket Kemple, 1840-82   Confederate Marine Officer
On the CSS Sumter.

Signature	Signature with rank	Pre & post War DS	War Dated DS	Pre & post War ALS	War Dated ALS
$	$125	$	$385	$	$

Howell, Joshua Blackwood, 1806-64   Union General

Signature	Signature with rank	Pre War DS	War Dated DS	Pre War ALS	War Dated ALS
$	$65	$	$	$	$

Huger, Benjamin, 1805-77   Confederate General
WP graduate. He was in command of the garrison at Norfolk. He saw service at the Seven Days, and was later sent to South Carolina as Inspector of Artillery and Ordnance. In 1863, he was transferred to the Trans-Mississippi Department.

Signature	Signature with rank	Pre & post War DS	War Dated DS	Pre & post War ALS	War Dated ALS
$85	$167	$278	$750	$	$

AES, Sept. 25, 1861. 1.5pp., 4to., Norfolk, Va., on secretarily signed ltr. from Genl. J.H. Winder pert. to POW's & Flag of Truce, signed as B. Genl. BG Nov. 1993 $600.

Humes, William Young Conn, 1830-82   Confederate General

V.M.I. graduate. He was Lt.of Artillery when the war began, and appointed Captain in June 1861. He was captured during the Battle of Island 10. Commanded his own division during the Battle of Atlanta.

Signature	Signature with rank	Pre & post War DS	War Dated DS	Pre & post War ALS	War Dated ALS
$90	$145	$	$378	$575	$

Humphreys, Andrews Atkinson, 1810-83   Union General

Signature	Signature with rank	Pre & post War DS	War Dated DS	Pre & post War ALS	War Dated ALS
$45	$78	$	$	$300	$

Humphreys, Benjamin Grubb, 1808-82   Confederate General

Colonel of the 21st Mississippi, Barksdale's Brigade, McLaw's Division. He fought at Fredericksburg, Chancellorsville, Gettysburg, Chickamauga, and was wounde at Berryville.

Signature	Signature with rank	Pre & post War DS	War Dated DS	Pre & post War ALS	War Dated ALS
$78	$150	$	$	$	$

Hunt, Henry Jackson, 1819-89   Union General

Signature	Signature with rank	Pre & post War DS	War Dated DS	Pre & post War ALS	War Dated ALS
$35	$55	$67	$127	$97	$

Hunt, Lewis Cass, 1824-86   Union General

Signature	Signature with rank	Pre & post War DS	War Dated DS	Pre & post War ALS	War Dated ALS
$30	$	$	$	$86	$

Hunter, David O., 1802-86   Union Major General

Signature	Signature with rank	Pre & post War DS	War Dated DS	Pre & post War ALS	War Dated ALS
$50	$78	$165	$217	$175	$245

ALS, 1862 January 16. Dept of Kansas, Ft Leavenworth, To Adjutant Genl, US Army, Washington, requests Brig Genl Benham be ordered to duty in his Department, sgd as Major General Commanding. EB August 1992 $295.

Hunter, Robert Mercer Taliaferro, 1809-87   Confederate. Sec of State

Signature	Signature with rank	Pre & post War DS	War Dated DS	Pre & post War ALS	War Dated ALS
$95	$	$	$	$210	$356

S, Clip. JH Aug. 1993 $75.
-, Clip. JH Nov. 1992 $50.

Hunter, Thomas T., (?-?)   Commander Confederate Navy

Signature	Signature with rank	Pre & post War DS	War Dated DS	Pre & post War ALS	War Dated ALS
$	$165	$145	$	$	$

Hunter, William, (?-?)   Flag Officer Confederate Navy

Signature	Signature with rank	Pre & post War DS	War Dated DS	Pre & post War ALS	War Dated ALS
$	$178	$	$	$	$

Hunton, Eppa, 1822-1908   Confederate General

Col. of the 8th Virginia. He fought with great distinction at 1st Bull Run, South Mountain, and was wounded during Pickett's Charge at Gettysburg. Captured at Sayler's Creek.

Signature	Signature with rank	Pre & post War DS	War Dated DS	Pre & post War ALS	War Dated ALS
$85	$178	$175	$	$278	$

ALS, 1853. Legal matter. SK Nov. 1993 $250.
DS, 1855. Manuscript check. JH Nov. 1992 $150.

Hurlbut, Stephen Augustus, 1815-82   Union General

Signature	Signature with rank	Pre & post War DS	War Dated DS	Pre & post War ALS	War Dated ALS
$	$53	$	$	$	$

Hyams, Isaac Smith, 1837-?   Confederate Marine Officer

Signature	Signature with rank	Pre & post War DS	War Dated DS	Pre & post War ALS	War Dated ALS
$	$	$	$378	$	$

I

Imboden, John Daniel, 1823-95   Confederate Brig. General

Served with Stonewall Jackson. Saved the Confederate wagon trains when they retreated from Gettysburg.

Signature	Signature with rank	Pre & post War DS	War Dated DS	Pre & post War ALS	War Dated ALS
$135	$278	$425	$786	$	$

S, Clip signature from a document. BG Nov. 1993 $145.
-, Clip signature. KO Sept. 1992 $65.

Ingalls, Rufus, 1818-93   Union General & Explorer

Signature	Signature with rank	Pre & post War DS	War Dated DS	Pre & post War ALS	War Dated ALS
$35	$48	$65	$	$138	$

Ingraham, Duncan Nathaniel,(?-?)   Captain Confederate Navy

Signature	Signature with rank	Pre & post War DS	War Dated DS	Pre & post War ALS	War Dated ALS
$	$147	$	$	$	$

202

Ingraham, Henry Laurens, 1837-78   Confederate Marine Officer

Signature	Signature with rank	Pre & post War DS	War Dated DS	Pre & post War ALS	War Dated ALS
$	$	$	$387	$	$

Ingram, Porter, 1810-1893   Member Confederate Congress

Signature	Signature with rank	Pre & post War DS	War Dated DS	Pre & post War ALS	War Dated ALS
$40	$	$78	$	$	$

Iverson, Alfred Jr., 1829-1911   Confederate General
Commanded at Gettysburg,, wounded at Seven Days Battle, captured Gen. Stoneman and his men.

Signature	Signature with rank	Pre & post War DS	War Dated DS	Pre & post War ALS	War Dated ALS
$125	$238	$297	$	$	$

S, Clip signature. KO Sept. 1993 $95.

J

Jackman, Sidney D., (?-?)   Confederate General
Trans-Mississippi Brig. Genl. designated, B.G. on May 16, 1865.

Signature	Signature with rank	Pre & post War DS	War Dated DS	Pre & post War ALS	War Dated ALS
$80	$178	$	$	$	$

Jackson, Alfred EuGenerale, 1807-89   Confederate General

He served as Genl. Zollicoffer's Chief Quartermaster, and was under Genl. Kirby Smith in the Department of Eastern TN. He commanded a brigade under Donelson, and fought with distinction at Greenville, TN.

Signature	Signature with rank	Pre & post War DS	War Dated DS	Pre & post War ALS	War Dated ALS
$110	$187	$	$1,150	$	$

Jackson, Clairborne Fox, 1807-62   War Gov. of Missouri

Died Dec. 6, 1862.

Signature	Signature with rank	Pre War DS	War Dated DS	Pre War ALS	War Dated ALS
$	$	$167	$	$	$

Jackson, Conrad Feger, 1813-62   Union Brigadier General

Killed 13 Dec 1862 at Fredericksburg, Va.

Signature	Signature with rank	Pre War DS	War Dated DS	Pre War ALS	War Dated ALS
$150	$250	$300	$450	$	$

Jackson, Henry Rootes, 1820-98   Confederate General

Yale graduate. He entered C.S. service as a Brig. Genl., but resigned. Then the Gov. of GA made him a Major Genl. in command of States troops. He was again appointed Brig. Genl. in the C.S.Army, and given a brigade in the Armt of TN. He was taken prisoner at the Battle of Nashville.

Signature	Signature with rank	Pre & post War DS	War Dated DS	Pre & post War ALS	War Dated ALS
$80	$	$189	$	$	$

Jackson, James Streshly, 1823-62   Union Brigadier General
Killed 8 Oct 1862 at Perryville, Ky. Rare.

Signature	Signature with rank	Pre War DS	War Dated DS	Pre War ALS	War Dated ALS
$125	$200	$	$	$	$

Jackson, James T. ?-1861   Confederate sympathizer
Killed Col. Elmer E. Ellsworth at the Marshell House, Alexandria, Va.

Signature	DS	ALS
$	$	$

Jackson, John King, 1828-66   Confederate General
Colonel of the 5th Georgia, he commanded the post at Pensacola. He commanded his own brigade at Shiloh and Stone River. He saw service under Genl. Polk at Chickamauga, and under Hardee at Missionary Ridge. He was in Walker's Division during the Atlanta campaign.

Signature	Signature with rank	Pre & post War DS	War Dated DS	Pre & post War ALS	War Dated ALS
$	$	$	$	$	$

A scarce signature

Jackson, Nathaniel James, 1818-92   Union General

Signature	Signature with rank	Pre & post War DS	War Dated DS	Pre & post War ALS	War Dated ALS
$26	$	$	$	$75	$

Jackson, Richard Henry, 1830-92   Union General

Signature	Signature with rank	Pre & post War DS	War Dated DS	Pre & post War ALS	War Dated ALS
$28	$	$	$	$	$

Jackson, Samuel McCartney, 1833-1907   Union Brevet General

Signature	Signature with rank	Pre & post War DS	War Dated DS	Pre & post War ALS	War Dated ALS
$22	$35	$	$78	$	$

DS, 1864. 1p. Muster roll. 11th Pa. SK Nov. 1992 $55.

Jackson, Thomas Jonathan,"Stonewall," 1824-63   CSA Lt. General
Considered Lee's right arm, he played a major role in the early Confederate victories. Died 10 May 1863 of wounds recd. at Chancellorsville, Va.

Signature	Signature with rank	Pre War DS	War Dated DS	Pre War ALS	War Dated ALS
$2,950	$3,850	$7,500	$14,500	$12,500	$28,500

ALS, Jan. 7, 1849, 1.5pp. 7.8x9.8", 4to., Fort Hamilton, he writes to Laura, "Again I am permitted by an indulgent Providnce to say that I am still among the living, and continue able to correspond with our endeared and only sister. My health, I believe is still improving; my strength certainly is ... I can sympathise with you in such treatments as you speak of Uncle Cummins is in Califorina...Your brother, T.J. Jackson." UA Sept. 1993 $12,000.

---, Aug. 18th, 1848, 1pp. 7.8x9.8" Fort Columbus, New York Harbour. to General George Gibson, "I have the honor to send herewith my bond filled by Ast. Surgeon J.M. Steiner and Lt. L.S. More of the Second Infantry each of whom told me that he was worth the amount mentioned in the bond. The responsibilities of the sureties has not been able to find a person knowing the pecuniary circumstance of both...T.J. Jackson." UA Sept. 1993 $14,500.

---, A collection of four pre-war ALS's, SK spring 1993 $30,000.
Misc.
--, Text book used my a student in his class he taught at VMI. SK Nov. 1993 $750.

Jackson, William Hicks "Red", 1835-1903   Confederate General
WP graduate. He was commissioned Captain in the C.S.A. He was wounded at Belmont, Miss., and named Col. of the 7th TN upon his recovery. After the Battle of Holly Springs, he was appointed Brig. Genl. due to Van Dorn's death. He was placed in command of the cavalry in Mississippi under Pemberton and Johnson.

Signature	Signature with rank	Pre & post War DS	War Dated DS	Pre & post War ALS	War Dated ALS
$80	$	$245	$587	$	$

Jackson, William Lowther "Mudwall", 1825-90   Confederate General

Enlisted as a Private, but was soon elected Lt. Col. of the Virginia Volunteers. In the Western Virginia operations, he served as aide-de-camp to Stonewall Jackson, his cousin. He was commissioned Colonel of the 19th Virginia Cavalry. He fought with distinction at Winchester, Cedar Creek, and Fisher's Hill. He refused to surrender.

Signature	Signature with rank	Pre & post War DS	War Dated DS	Pre & post War ALS	War Dated ALS
$110	$265	$375	$1,585	$	$

Jameson, Charles Davis, 1827-62   Union General

Signature	Signature with rank	Pre War DS	War Dated DS	Pre War ALS	War Dated ALS
$30	$48	$	$	$	$

Jefferson, Thomas,

Signature	DS	ALS
$	$6,675	$

DS, Oct. 14, 1805, 41x52 cm, Ships papers in four lanuages, countersigned by James Madison, inscribed for Ship Mary of Newburyport, Jefferson signature bold and clear, some fading to Madison. S Nov. 1993 $7,700.

--, July 19, 1801 Mediterranean Passport signed, 46x30 cm. scalloped parchment engraved with single panel of an American ship at anchor before a lighthouse. S Nov. 1993 $4,950.

Jemison, Robert, Jr., 1802-71   Member Confederate Congress

Signature	Signature with rank	Pre & post War DS	War Dated DS	Pre & post War ALS	War Dated ALS
$35	$	$87	$	$	$

Jenkins, Albert Gallatin, 1830-64   Confederate General

Havard graduate. Lt. Col. of the 8th Virginia. His independent cavalry forces made many daring raids in the West Virginia mountains. During an engagement at Cloyd's Mt., he was severly wounded, and died in a Union hospital on May 21, 1864.

Signature	Signature with rank	Pre War DS	War Dated DS	Pre War ALS	War Dated ALS
$185	$	$	$	$	$

An extremely scarce signature.

Jenkins, Micah, 1835-64   Confederate General

S.C. Military Academy. Colonel of the 5th S.C. and fought with distinction at 1st Bull Run. He was severly wounded at 2nd Bull Run. He went with Longstreet to TN. While on reconnaissance patrol of Federal Lines he was shot by a Confederate soldier. Killed 6 May 1864 at the Wilderness, Va.

Signature	Signature with rank	Pre War DS	War Dated DS	Pre War ALS	War Dated ALS
$225	$	$	$	$	$

An extremely rare signature.

Jenkins, Thornton Alexander, 1811-?   Union Naval Captain

Signature	Signature with rank	Pre & post War DS	War Dated DS	Pre & post War ALS	War Dated ALS
$	$58	$87	$	$	$

Jett, William S., ? - ?   Pvt. CSA
Aided John W. Booth in his escape.

Signature	Signature with rank	Pre War DS	War Dated DS	Pre War ALS	War Dated ALS
$	$	$	$	$	$

Johnson, Adam Rankin, "Stovepipe," 1834-1922   Confederate General
He entered the war as a scout for Genl. Forrest. He was with John H. Morgan in Indiana
and Ohio. He was accidentally shot in the face by his own men while at Grubbs
Crossroads and was blinded.

Signature	Signature with rank	Pre & post War DS	War Dated DS	Pre & post War ALS	War Dated ALS
$165	$	$278	$	$	$

A scarce signature.

Johnson, Andrew, 1808-75   Union Gen., Mil.Gov.TN; 17th U.S.Pres.
Succeeded to the presidency upon death of Lincoln.

Signature	Signature with rank	Pre & post War DS	War Dated DS	Pre & post War ALS	War Dated ALS
$375	$475	$875	$	$3,890	$

DS, April 20, 1865. 1p., folio, City of Washington. Ornate miltiary appointment of
Duncan S. Walker, A.A.G., with rank of major. Countersigned by Edwin M. Stanton as
Secretary of War. Signed on the fifth day of his term. NS Nov. 1993 $2,750.
*NOTE: Johnson rarely signed military appointments, a stamped signature was more
commonly used.*
S, Signature in pencil "Andrew Johnson/ Greenville, Tenn." on white card. JB Dec.
1993 $325.

Johnson, Bradley Tyler, 1829-1903   Confederate General

Johnson fought at 1st Bull Run, Gaines Mill, 2d Bull Run, Antietam and Wilderness achieving the rank of brigadier-general in the Confederate army. It was Johnson who executed Early's orders to burn Chambersburg, Pa. He was caommandate of prisons at Salibury, N.C.

Signature	Signature with rank	Pre & post War DS	War Dated DS	Pre & post War ALS	War Dated ALS
$95	$200	$475	$1,650	$275	$

ALS, Sept. 4, 1868, 1pp. 5.5x8.5", 8vo., to Francis L. Smith, Esq. "Time is passing send us all the notes you & Marby have in pssession at once & the rest as soon as you reduce them... Bradley T. Johnson." UA Sept. 1993 $275.
S, Clip, Matted with engraving. SK Oct. 1992 $85.

Johnson, Bushrod Rust, 1817-80   Confederate General

WP graduate. Colonel of Engineers. As Brig. Genl., he was severly wounded at Shiloh. He had a division in Anderson's Corps and fought with great distinction at Chickamauga, Drewry's Buff, and Petersburg.

Signature	Signature with rank	Pre & post War DS	War Dated DS	Pre & post War ALS	War Dated ALS
$145	$	$225	$	$350	$

ALS, 1834, 2p. JH Aug. 1993 $325.

Johnson, Edward, 1816-73   Confederate General

WP graduate. Colonel of the 12th GA. He was promoted to Brig. Genl., and commanded
Northwest forces directly under Stonewall Jackson in May 1862. He was captured with
his troops at the "Bloody Angle", and after his exchange, was assigned to a division of
the 2nd Corps, Army of the TN. He was again captured during the Battle of Nashville.

Signature	Signature with rank	Pre & post War DS	War Dated DS	Pre & post War ALS	War Dated ALS
$165	$	$448	$	$	$

Johnson, Herschel Vespasian, 1812-80   Member Confederate Congress

Signature	Signature with rank	Pre & post War DS	War Dated DS	Pre & post War ALS	War Dated ALS
$32	$	$98	$	$	$

Johnson, Richard W., 1827-97   Union General

Signature	Signature with rank	Pre & post War DS	War Dated DS	Pre & post War ALS	War Dated ALS
$28	$	$78	$	$	$

Johnson, Robert Ward, 1814-79   Member Confederate Congress

Signature	Signature with rank	Pre & post War DS	War Dated DS	Pre & post War ALS	War Dated ALS
$38	$	$86	$	$	$

Johnson, Thomas, 1812-1906   Member Confederate Congress

Signature	Signature with rank	Pre & post War DS	War Dated DS	Pre & post War ALS	War Dated ALS
$	$	$	$	$165	$

Johnson, Waldo Porter, 1817-85   Member Confederate Congress

Signature	Signature with rank	Pre & post War DS	War Dated DS	Pre & post War ALS	War Dated ALS
$	$	$87	$	$	$

Johnson, Wilbur F., ?-?   Confederate Marine Officer

Signature	Signature with rank	Pre & post War DS	War Dated DS	Pre & post War ALS	War Dated ALS
$	$	$	$432	$	$

Johnston, Albert Sidney, 1803-62   Confederate General

After a few Texans met at Washington-on the-Brazos and declared their independance, Johnston went to Texas and enlisted as a private in the revolutionary army. By August of that year, he war Appointed senior brigadier-general and Adjutant General of the Army of Texas. In that capacity, Johnston had been sent to New Orleans by Sam Houston, who had been elected president of the new Republic of Texas. He was killed 6 Apr 1862 at Shiloh, Tenn.

Signature	Signature with rank	Pre War DS	War Dated DS	Pre War ALS	War Dated ALS
$275	$565	$1,457	$	$3,250	$

DS, Nov. 20, 1836, New Orleans, 1pp. 8.5x4.85", pert. to payment of printing for the Republic of Texas. UA Sept. 1993 $8,000.

Johnston, George Doherty, 1832-1910   Confederate General

Lt. in the 4th Alabama Infantry and fought with distinction at 1st Bull Run. He commanded a regiment at Shiloh, and fought gallanttly at Stones River and Chickamauga. Two days after he was appointed Brig. Genl., he was severly wounded in the leg during the Battle of Ezra Church.

Signature	Signature with rank	Pre & post War DS	War Dated DS	Pre & post War ALS	War Dated ALS
$85	$	$385	$	$	$

Johnston, Joseph Eggleston, 1807-91   Confederate General

Commander of the comined forces at 1st Bull Run. He took command of the Army of Tennessee and in the Atlanta Campaign dropped back skillfully.

Signature	Signature with rank	Pre & post War DS	War Dated DS	Pre & post War ALS	War Dated ALS
$278	$468	$678	$1250	$854	$

ALS, March 26, 1884, Washington, 1pp, 5.5x5.25", Johnston wrote this letter in response to Darwin Pavey: "...Genl. Albert Sydney Johnston and I were distantly related - being of the same Scotch family. Respectfully & Truly Yours, J.E.Johnston." UA Sept. 1993 $1,000.
PS, 4.25x6", sepia toned cabinet engraving of Johnston in uniform. "J.E. Johnston" UA Feb. 1994 $3,000.
S, Clip signature. BG Nov. 1993 $325.

Johnston, Robert, 1818-85   Member Confederate Congress

Signature	Signature with rank	Pre & post War DS	War Dated DS	Pre & post War ALS	War Dated ALS
$35	$	$	$	$	$

Johnston, Robert Daniel, 1837-1919   Confederate General

Captain 23rd North Carolina, saw service during the Peninsular Campaign of 1861 and '62. Johnson was wounded at Seven Pines, and for his gallant service at Gettysburg was appointed Brig. Genl. He was wounded at Spotsylvania, and fought with distinction under Jubal Early in the Valley in 1864.

Signature	Signature with rank	Pre & post War DS	War Dated DS	Pre & post War ALS	War Dated ALS
$67	$	$	$	$215	$

Jones, Catesby ap Roger, 1821-77   Confederate Naval Officer

Signature	Signature with rank	Pre & post War DS	War Dated DS	Pre & post War ALS	War Dated ALS
$78	$	$145	$	$	$

Jones, David Rumph "Neighbor," 1825-63   Confederate General

WP graduate. He was commissioned Major and was Beauregard's Chief of Staff during the Fort Sumter bombardment. Appointed Brig. Genl., he led his command at 1st Bull Run and at the Seven Days Battles. He was in command of a division under Longstreet, and fought with great distinction at 2nd Bull Run. He died of coronary disease on Jan. 15, 1863 in Richmond, Va.

Signature	Signature with rank	Pre War DS	War Dated DS	Pre War ALS	War Dated ALS
$250	$325	$787	$	$	$

A scarce autograph.

Jones, Edward Franc, 1828-1913   Union Brevet General

Signature	Signature with rank	Pre & post War DS	War Dated DS	Pre & post War ALS	War Dated ALS
$40	$67	$87	$167	$	$

Jones, George Washington, 1806-84   Member Confederate Congress

Signature	Signature with rank	Pre & post War DS	War Dated DS	Pre & post War ALS	War Dated ALS
$45	$	$	$	$	$

Jones, Henry Cox, 1821-1913   Member Confederate Congress

Signature	Signature with rank	Pre & post War DS	War Dated DS	Pre & post War ALS	War Dated ALS
$38	$	$	$165	$87	$

Jones, John, B., 1810-66   Clerk, CSA

Author of "A Rebel War Clerk's Diary"

Signature	Signature with rank	Pre & post War DS	War Dated DS	Pre & post War ALS	War Dated ALS
$	$	$	$400	$	$

DS, Oct. 23, 1861. 1p., 7.25x4", CSA War Dept. imprint, Richmond, pert. to a pass to visit Whiting's Brig. at Manassas. BG Nov. 1993 $350.

Jones, John Marshell, 1820-64   Confederate Brigadier General

He was seriously wounded at Gettysburg in the attack on Culp's Hill. Killed 10 May 1864 at Spotsylvania, Va.

Signature	Signature with rank	Pre War DS	War Dated DS	Pre War ALS	War Dated ALS
$275	$950	$	$2,575	$	$

AES, Jan. 20, 1864., an approval for leave, signed as Brig. General. KO Sept. 1993 $1,250.

Jones, John Robert, 1827-1901   Confederate General

Lt Col. of the 33rd Virginia. He led the 2nd Brigade in Jackson's Division at Malvern Hill, and was wounded at Seven Pines. He was with Lee at Antietam, and during the Battle of Chancellorsville he left the battlefield because of an ulcerated leg., he was then cashiered.

Signature	Signature with rank	Pre & post War DS	War Dated DS	Pre & post War ALS	War Dated ALS
$78	$155	$187	$	$	$1,275

Jones, Patrick Henry, 1830-1900   Union General

Signature	Signature with rank	Pre & post War DS	War Dated DS	Pre & post War ALS	War Dated ALS
$35	$	$	$	$78	$

Jones, Robert McDonald, 1808-72   Member Confederate Congress

Signature	Signature with rank	Pre & post War DS	War Dated DS	Pre & post War ALS	War Dated ALS
$45	$	$	$	$	$

Jones, Samuel, 1819-87 — Confederate General

WP graduate. Major of Artillery, and was Beauregard's Chief Artillery officer at 1st Bull Run. He was then appointed Brig. Genl. He headed the Department of S.C., Georgia, and Florida.

Signature	Signature with rank	Pre & post War DS	War Dated DS	Pre & post War ALS	War Dated ALS
$97	$178	$387	$567	$	$

Jones, Thomas A., ? - ? — Confederate Secret Service Agent

Fed & prtected John W. Booth from 16 April - 21 April 1865, during his escape.

Signature	Pre & post War DS	War Dated DS	Pre & post War ALS	War Dated ALS
$	$	$	$	$

Jones, Thomas McKissick, 1816-92 — Member Confederate Congress

Signature	Signature with rank	Pre & post War DS	War Dated DS	Pre & post War ALS	War Dated ALS
$37	$	$78	$	$	$

Jones William Edmondson, 1824-64 — Confederate Brigadier General

WP graduate. Captain of the "Washington Mounted Rifles." He served under Genl. Stuart and fought with distinction at Cedar Mountain and Sharpsburg. He was killed June 5, 1864 at Piedmont, West Va.

Signature	Signature with rank	Pre War DS	War Dated DS	Pre War ALS	War Dated ALS
$125	$	$225	$1,875	$	$

DS, 1853. Texas. JH Aug. 1993 $150.

--, June 30, 1853. 1p. folio, Ft. Ewell, Tex. abstract for whiskey rations, file folds. BG Nov. 1993 $175.

--, Oct. 1, 1852, 1p., 8x12.5", Fort Merrill, Tx., Abstract of Extra issues to troops. MS Nov. 1993 $250.

Jordon, Thomas, 1819-95   Confederate General

WP graduate. He served as Staff Officer under Genl. Beauregard at 1st Bull Run, and was Asst. Adjutant Genl. under Johnston at Shiloh.

Signature	Signature with rank	Pre & post War DS	War Dated DS	Pre & post War ALS	War Dated ALS
$67	$125	$	$300	$	$389

Josselyn, Robert, ?-?   Private Secretary of Jefferson Davis

Signature	Signature with rank	Pre & post War DS	War Dated DS	Pre & post War ALS	War Dated ALS
$55	$	$	$	$	$

Judah, Henry Moses, 1821-66   Union General

Signature	Signature with rank	Pre & post War DS	War Dated DS	Pre & post War ALS	War Dated ALS
$35	$55	$87	$	$	$

Julio, Everett, 18? - ?   Painter

Signature	Pre & post War DS	War Dated DS	Pre & post War ALS	War Dated ALS
$78	$	$	$	$

Misc.

-, 1869. 14' high orginial frame, The Last Meeting of Lee and Jackson, oil painting. Robert Hicklin, Jr., S.C. 1992 $1,500,000.
On Display at the Confederate Museum, Richmond, Va.

K

Kane, Thomas Leiper, 1822-83   Union General

Signature	Signature with rank	Pre & post War DS	War Dated DS	Pre & post War ALS	War Dated ALS
$35	$52	$80	$127	$	$

Kautz, August Valentine, 1828-95   Union General
LOC. papers, 1846-99. ca. 500 items.

Signature	Signature with rank	Pre & post War DS	War Dated DS	Pre & post War ALS	War Dated ALS
$22	$36	$48	$	$	$

Kearny, Philip, 1815-62   Union Major General
Killed 1 Sept 1862 at Chantilly, Va. LOC. papers, 1861-62. 72 items.

Signature	Signature with rank	Pre War DS	War Dated DS	Pre War ALS	War Dated ALS
$175	$267	$	$	$625	$

Keeble, Edwin Augustus, 1807-68   Member Confederate Congress

Signature	Signature with rank	Pre & post War DS	War Dated DS	Pre & post War ALS	War Dated ALS
$40	$	$	$	$	$267

Keifer, Joseph Warren, 1836-1932   Union Brevet General
LOC. papers, 1861-65. ca. 1,100 items.

Signature	Signature with rank	Pre & post War DS	War Dated DS	Pre & post War ALS	War Dated ALS
$20	$38	$	$	$85	$

Keitt, Lawrence Massillon, 1824-64   Member Conf. Cong. & Colonel

Signature	Signature with rank	Pre War DS	War Dated DS	Pre War ALS	War Dated ALS
$38	$	$	$145	$	$

Keim, William High, 1813-62   Union General
Died of `camp fever' 18 May 1862. LOC. papers 1861-1910. ca. 75 items.

Signature	Signature with rank	Pre War DS	War Dated DS	Pre War ALS	War Dated ALS
$185	$325	$	$	$	$

Kelly, John Herbert, 1840-64   Confederate General

2nd Lt. of Artillery. He commanded the 9th Arkansas during the Battle of Shiloh. He led a brigade under Genl. Buckner at Chickamauga. As Brig. Genl., he led a brigade in Wheeler's Corps during the Battle of Atlanta. Wounded September 2, 1864 and died September 4, 1864 near Franklin, Tn.

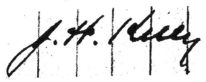

Signature	Signature with rank	Pre War DS	War Dated DS	Pre War ALS	War Dated ALS
$550	$	$978	$	$	$

Perhaps the hardest of Confederate signature to obtain.

Kemper, James Lawson, 1823-95   Confederate General

Colonel of the 7th Virginia Infantry. He was under Genl. Early during 1st Bull Run, South Mountain, and Antietam. He was severly wounded during Pickett's Charge at Gettysburg. He was captured and later exchanged.

Signature	Signature with rank	Pre & post War DS	War Dated DS	Pre & post War ALS	War Dated ALS
$125	$350	$278	$	$386	$

Kenan, Augustus Holmes, 1805-65   Member Confederate Congress

Signature	Signature with rank	Pre & post War DS	War Dated DS	Pre & post War ALS	War Dated ALS
$35	$	$	$	$	$

Kenan, Owen Rand, 1804-87   Member Confederate Congress

Signature	Signature with rank	Pre & post War DS	War Dated DS	Pre & post War ALS	War Dated ALS
$38	$	$	$	$	$

Kenly, John Reese, 1818-91 — Union General

Signature	Signature with rank	Pre & post War DS	War Dated DS	Pre & post War ALS	War Dated ALS
$20	$	$56	$	$	$

Kennedy, Charles H., ?-? — Confederate Naval Officer

Signature	Signature with rank	Pre & post War DS	War Dated DS	Pre & post War ALS	War Dated ALS
$	$78	$	$	$	$

Kennedy, John Doby, 1840-96 — Confederate General

Captain 2nd S.C. Infantry. He fought with distinction at Savage Station, and was wounded at Antietam. Appointed Brig. Genl. Dec. 22, 1864; he led his brigade against Genl. Sherman at Bentonville.

Signature	Signature with rank	Pre & post War DS	War Dated DS	Pre & post War ALS	War Dated ALS
$90	$176	$325	$	$	$

Kenner, Duncan Farrar, 1813-87 — Member Confederate Congress

LOC. collection, 1882-99. 3 items.

Signature	Signature with rank	Pre & post War DS	War Dated DS	Pre & post War ALS	War Dated ALS
$43	$	$	$	$110	$

Kershaw, Joseph Brevard, 1822-94   Confederate Major General

Senior Col. of the 2nd South Carolina, and fought with much distinction at 1st Bull Run. Appointed Brig. Genl. in Feb. 1862, saw continous fighting at Seven Days, 2nd Bull Run, Antietam, Fredericksburg, Chickamauga, and Gettysburg. He was captured at Sayler's Creek and imprisoned at Fort Warren until July 24, 1865.

Signature	Signature with rank	Pre & post War DS	War Dated DS	Pre & post War ALS	War Dated ALS
$175	$345	$890	$	$1,674	$

Ketcham, John Henry, 1832-1906   Union General

Signature	Signature with rank	Pre & post War DS	War Dated DS	Pre & post War ALS	War Dated ALS
$35	$145	$58	$258	$	$

Ketchum, William Scott, 1813-71   Union General

Signature	Signature with rank	Pre & post War DS	War Dated DS	Pre & post War ALS	War Dated ALS
$32	$	$83	$	$	$

Keyes, Erasmus Darwin, 1810-95   Union General

Signature	Signature with rank	Pre & post War DS	War Dated DS	Pre & post War ALS	War Dated ALS
$42	$65	$	$245	$	$

Kiermmnan, James Lawlor, 1837-69   Union General

Signature	Signature with rank	Pre & post War DS	War Dated DS	Pre & post War ALS	War Dated ALS
$32	$	$48	$	$	$

Kilpatrick, Hugh Judson, 1836-81   Union General

Signature	Signature with rank	Pre & post War DS	War Dated DS	Pre & post War ALS	War Dated ALS
$78	$187	$211	$567	$325	$

Kimball, Nathan, 1823-98 — Union General

Signature	Signature with rank	Pre & post War DS	War Dated DS	Pre & post War ALS	War Dated ALS
$20	$	$58	$	$97	$

Kimberly, Robert Lewis, 1836-1913 — Union Brevet General

Signature	Signature with rank	Pre & post War DS	War Dated DS	Pre & post War ALS	War Dated ALS
$20	$	$38	$	$78	$

Misc.
B, The Forty-first Ohio veteran Vol. Inf., in the War of the Rebellion, 1897 ed. $250.

King, Adam Eckfeldt, 1837-1910 — Union Brevet General

Signature	Signature with rank	Pre & post War DS	War Dated DS	Pre & post War ALS	War Dated ALS
$25	$	$	$	$87	$

King, Charles, 1844-? — Soldier & Author

Signature	Signature with rank	Pre & post War DS	War Dated DS	Pre & post War ALS	War Dated ALS
$35	$	$	$	$	$

King, John Haskell, 1820-88 — Union General

Signature	Signature with rank	Pre & post War DS	War Dated DS	Pre & post War ALS	War Dated ALS
$22	$38	$	$156	$	$

King Rufus, 1814-76 — Union General

Signature	Signature with rank	Pre & post War DS	War Dated DS	Pre & post War ALS	War Dated ALS
$25	$	$89	$	$	$

222

King, William Hill, 1839-1910   Confederate General
Brig. Genl. designated B.G. on May 11, 1864. Trans-Mississippi Department.

Signature	Signature with rank	Pre & post War DS	War Dated DS	Pre & post War ALS	War Dated ALS
$80	$	$276	$324	$	$425

Kirby, Edmund, 1840-63   Union Brig General
Died 28 May 1863 of wounds recd at Chancellorsville, Va. Rare.

Signature	Signature with rank	Pre War DS	War Dated DS	Pre War ALS	War Dated ALS
$	$	$	$	$	$

Kirk, Edward Needles, 1828-63   Union Brigadier General
Died July 29, 1863 of wounds recd at Stone River Tn. Rare.

Signature	Signature with rank	Pre War DS	War Dated DS	Pre War ALS	War Dated ALS
$	$	$	$	$	$

Kirkland, Richard Rowland, 1843-63   Confederate LT.,2 S.C. Inf.
Known as the Angel of Marye's Heights. KIA Sept. 20, 1863 at Chickamauga, Ga. Rare.

Signature	Signature with rank	Pre War DS	War Dated DS	Pre War ALS	War Dated ALS
$	$	$	$	$	$

Kirkland, William Whedbee, 1833-1915   Confederate General
1st Lt. in the GA Infantry, and later elected Colonel of the 21st North Carolina Infantry. He led his regiment at 1st Bull Run. He was severly wounded during the Battle of Winchester. He saw service with Genl. Longstreet around Richmond.

Signature	Signature with rank	Pre & post War DS	War Dated DS	Pre & post War ALS	War Dated ALS
$90	$245	$178	$	$	$

Kirkham, Ralph Wilson, 1821-1893 — Brevetted Union General

Signature	Signature with rank	Pre & post War DS	War Dated DS	Pre & post War ALS	War Dated ALS
$20	$	$	$	$	$

Knipe, Joseph Farmer, 1823-1901 — Union General

Signature	Signature with rank	Pre & post War DS	War Dated DS	Pre & post War ALS	War Dated ALS
$25	$35	$48	$125	$	$

Krzyzanowski, Wladimir, 1824-87 — Union General

Signature	Signature with rank	Pre & post War DS	War Dated DS	Pre & post War ALS	War Dated ALS
$20	$38	$	$	$	$

Kurz, Louis (?-1921) — Artist

Signature	DS	ALS
$150	$	$

Kurz & Allison Large folio prints

Battle of Bull Run	$ 385
Battle of Chancellorsville	$ 265
Battle of Fredericksburg	$ 265
Battle of Kenesaw Mountain	$ 265
Battle of Lookout Mountain	$ 235
Battle of Williamsburg	$ 265

L

Laird, John, 1805-74 — Built the CSS Alabama

Signature	Pre & post War DS	War Dated DS	Pre & post War ALS	War Dated ALS
$68	$	$	$278	$

ALS, [n.d.] 3pp. Naval content. JH Nov. 1992 $100.

224

Lamkin, John Tillman, 1811-70 — Member Confederate Congress

Signature	Signature with rank	Pre & post War DS	War Dated DS	Pre & post War ALS	War Dated ALS
$35	$	$	$	$	$

Lane, James Henry, 1833-1907 — Confederate Brigadier General

VMI graduate. Major 1st NC. Col. of the 28th NC and fought under Genl. Branch at Ashland. He was twice wounded during the Peninsula Campaign, and led his brigade at Fredericksburg, Gettysburg, and the Wilderness.

Signature	Signature with rank	Pre & post War DS	War Dated DS	Pre & post War ALS	War Dated ALS
$80	$156	$	$457	$278	$

Lane, Walter Paye, 1817-92 — Confederate Brigadier General

Lt. Col. of the 3rd Texas Cavalry, fought with distinction at Wilson's Creek and Pea Ridge. He was wounded during the Battle of Mansfield. Confirmed as Brig. Genl. on March 17, 1865.

Signature	Signature with rank	Pre & post War DS	War Dated DS	Pre & post War ALS	War Dated ALS
$75	$	$238	$	$	$

Lander, William, 1817-68 — Member Confederate Congress

Signature	Signature with rank	Pre & post War DS	War Dated DS	Pre & post War ALS	War Dated ALS
$	$	$	$	$	$

Lardner, Frederick West, 1821-62 — Union General

Signature	Signature with rank	Pre War DS	War Dated DS	Pre War ALS	War Dated ALS
$65	$	$	$	$	$

Lardner, James L., 1802-81   Union Naval Commodore

Signature	Signature with rank	Pre & post War DS	War Dated DS	Pre & post War ALS	War Dated ALS
$	$48	$87	$147	$	$

Lauman, Jacob Gartner, 1813-67   Union General

Signature	Signature with rank	Pre & post War DS	War Dated DS	Pre & post War ALS	War Dated ALS
$25	$	$74	$	$	$

Law, Evander McIvor, 1836-1920   Confederate Brigadier General

Lt. Col. of the 4th Alabama which he led at Manassas. He fought at South Mountain, Sharpsburg and Gettysburg, where he led Hood's Division after Hood was wounded in action. He was severly wounded at Cold Harbor, and was relieved. He later commanded a cavalry force under Johnston in the Carolina campaign.

Signature	Signature with rank	Pre & post War DS	War Dated DS	Pre & post War ALS	War Dated ALS
$90	$	$245	$	$423	$

Lawler, Michael Kelly, 1814-82   Union General

Signature	Signature with rank	Pre & post War DS	War Dated DS	Pre & post War ALS	War Dated ALS
$25	$	$76	$	$	$

Lawton, Alexander Robert, 1818-96   Confederate Brigadier General

WP & Havard graduate. He was appointed Brig. Genl. on April 13, 1861. He fought with great distinction at Cedar Mountain, 2nd Manassas, and was severly wounded at Dunkard Church, during the Battle of Sharpsburg. He was appointed Quartermaster Genl. in 1863.

Signature	Signature with rank	Pre & post War DS	War Dated DS	Pre & post War ALS	War Dated ALS
$100	$175	$345	$645	$	$

LS, Nov. 18, 1864. 2pp., 4to., QM Gen'l office, Richmond, pert. to failing to deliver officer for court martial. BG Nov. 1993 $575.

Leach, James Madison, 1815-91   Member Confederate Congress

Signature	Signature with rank	Pre & post War DS	War Dated DS	Pre & post War ALS	War Dated ALS
$	$40	$	$87	$	$

Leadbetter, Danville, 1811-66   Confederate Brigadier General

WP graduate,He worked on the defeces of Mobile, and was on Bragg's staff in the Army of TN. He accompanied Genl. Longstreet to Nashville and Knoxville. An engineering officer.

Signature	Signature with rank	Pre & post War DS	War Dated DS	Pre & post War ALS	War Dated ALS
$125	$185	$325	$575	$	$

Ledlie, James Hewett, 1832-82   Union General

Signature	Signature with rank	Pre & post War DS	War Dated DS	Pre & post War ALS	War Dated ALS
$30	$	$58	$	$	$

LeDuc, William Gates, 1823-1917 — Brevet Brigadier General

Capt., AQM, Staff of Brig. Gen. Napoleon J. T. Dana, Lt. Col., Chief Quartermaster, 11th Army Corps and later the 20th, Bvt. Brig. Gen., USV, March 13, 1865.

Signature	Signature with rank	Pre & post War DS	War Dated DS	Pre & post War ALS	War Dated ALS
$25	$	$	$	$78	$

Lee, Albert Lindley, 1834-1907 — Union General

Signature	Signature with rank	Pre & post War DS	War Dated DS	Pre & post War ALS	War Dated ALS
$25	$38	$	$75	$87	$

Lee, Edward Merwin, 1835-1913 — Union Brevet General

Lt. Col., 5th Mich. Cavalry, Bvt. Brig. Gen., USV, March 13, 1865.

Signature	Signature with rank	Pre & post War DS	War Dated DS	Pre & post War ALS	War Dated ALS
$20	$38	$65	$	$	$

Lee, Edwin Gray, 1836-70 — Confederate Brigadier General

2nd Lt. in the 2nd Virginia. For one month, he was Stonewall Jackson's aide-de-camp, and served with the 33rd VA during the Valley Campaign. Appointed Brig. Genl. in Sept. 1864.

Signature	Signature with rank	Pre & post War DS	War Dated DS	Pre & post War ALS	War Dated ALS
$225	$	$485	$	$	$

A scarce signature.

Lee, Fitzhugh, 1835-1905   Confederate Major General

WP graduate and newphew of Robert E. Lee. As Capt., Lee was Adjt. Genl. in Ewell's Brigade. Appointed Brig. Genl. in July 1862, and Major Genl. on Aug. 1863. He had both a brigade and a division of cavalry in the Army of Northern Virginia through all its campaigns. He was wounded at the Battle of the Winchester.

Signature	Signature with rank	Pre & post War DS	War Dated DS	Pre & post War ALS	War Dated ALS
$150	$210	$	$	$325	$

ALS, Dec. 11, 1884. 2pp., 4to., Richmond, Va. to his son in the 12th Cav., USA Manila, Philippines, with cover. BG Nov. 1993 $250.

---, April 1, 1884, 1p. 4to., Alexandria, Va., to Va. artist, John Elder, pert. to supplying background sketch for artist's "Last Council of War of A.N.V." BG Nov. 1993 $295.

---, [n.d.] 3pp. re: Capt. Greenleaf. GH July 1992 $450.

---, [n.d.] as governor of Virginia, (no description of content). ALE August 1992 $225.

S, Clip with rank as Maj. Genl., U.S. Vols. BG Nov. 1993 $195.

-, Clip. NLM Nov. 1992 $125.

-, Clip. JH August 1992 $125.

Lee, George Washington Custis, 1832-1913   Confederate Major General

Robert E. Lee's eldest son. Help construct the fortifications around Richmond. He was Col. on the staff of Pres. Davis, and was appointed Brig. Genl. in June of 1863, and Major Genl. in Feb. 1865. He saw no field service until he cammanded a division in Ewell's Corps during the retreat from Richmond.

Signature	Signature with rank	Pre & post War DS	War Dated DS	Pre & post War ALS	War Dated ALS
$140	$250	$650	$	$345	$

ALS, 1905. 3p, indicating that he does not have any of his father's autographs to give away. GH July 1992 $300.

DS, 1p., folio, partly-printed Washington & Lee Univ. diploma signed as President. BG Nov. 1993 $700.

--, 1880. Washington and Lee diploma. GH July 1992 $500.

S, Clip. JH August 1992 $100.

Lee, Henry, 1756-1818   Cavalry Officer, Father of Robert E. Lee
"Light Horse Harry" Cavalry Comdr. in Am. Rev. War, covered Green's retreat across
No. Car. & Virginia in 1781, mbr of Contl Congress 1785-88, Va. Governor 1792-95,
put down 1797 Whiskey Rebellion in Penn., Us Rep. 1799-1801, wrote Washington's
eulogy "First in war, first in peace."

Signature	Signature with rank	Pre & post War DS	War Dated DS Rev. War	Pre & post War ALS	War Dated ALS Rev.W.
$285	$	$675	$1,498	$1,245	$5,450

S, Clip signature, from a DS. EB Dec. 1993 $195.

Lee, Horace Clark, 1822-84   Union Brevet General
Colonel 27th Mass. Inf., Provost Marshal General, Dept. of Va. and NC, Bvt. Brig.
Gen., USV, March 13, 1865.

Signature	Signature with rank	Pre & post War DS	War Dated DS	Pre & post War ALS	War Dated ALS
$25	$	$	$87	$	$

Lee, John Calvin, 1828-91   Union Brevet General
Colonel 55th Ohio Infantry, Colonel 164th Ohio Infantry.

Signature	Signature with rank	Pre & post War DS	War Dated DS	Pre & post War ALS	War Dated ALS
$	$38	$	$78	$	$

Lee, Mary Custis, 1806-73   Robert E. Lee's wife

Signature	Pre & post War DS	War Dated DS	Pre & post War ALS	War Dated ALS
$150	$650	$	$775	$

ALS, n.d. 1p., 16mo., pert. to family pictures left at Alexandria. AL Dec. 1993 $725.
---, n.d. 1p., pert. to a mistake in applying the wrong postage stamp. KO Sept. 1993
$225.
PS, CDV, profile of Mrs. Lee, signed on the verso, 'Mary Custis Lee," B/M A.M. Hall
of Alexandria, VA. UA Feb. 1994 $1,000.

Lee, Mary W., ?-?   Sanitary Commission worker

Signature	Pre & post War DS	War Dated DS	Pre & post War ALS	War Dated ALS
$	$	$	$123	$

Lee, Robert, 1793-1877   Obstetric physician
Lectured on midwifery, diseases of women.

Signature	Pre & post War DS	War Dated DS	Pre & post War ALS	War Dated ALS
$	$	$	$125	$

Lee, Robert Edward, 1807-70   Confederate General
In the Mexican War (1846), he was Chief Engineer of the Central Army in Mexico. From 1852 to 1855, commanded the US Military Academy and greatly improved efficiency. Served as Cavalry officer on the Texan border (1855-58). At the John Brown raid he was ordered to Harper's Ferry to capture the insurgents. Recalled to Washington in March 1861 when seven states formed the Southern Confederacy. Virginia seceded on April 17, and Lee, believing his allegiance was due to his state, resigned from the US Army. Within two days he was made Commander-In-Chief of the forces of Virginia and of the forces around Richmond. His masterly strategy in the seven day's battles around Richmond defeated General McClellan's purpose; his battles and strategy in opposing General Pope, his invasion of Maryland and Pennsylvania, and other were cardinal to the history of the war. On April 9, 1865, Lee surrendered his army of 28,231 men to General Grant at Appomattox Courthouse, VA, and the war practically ended. Lee frankly accepted the result and although deprived of his former property at Arlington on the Potomac and the White House on the Pamunky, he declined offers of pecuniary aid, and accepted the Presidency of Washington University at Lexington, VA (1865-70).

Signature	Signature with rank	Pre & post War DS	War Dated DS	Pre & post War ALS	War Dated ALS
$3050	$3850	$5995	$12,788	$9435	$26725

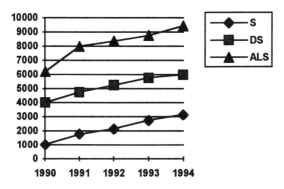

Graph of non war date material for past five years.

ALS August 8, 1857, 1p. San Antonio, Texas, to Capt. N.G. Shanks Evans, U.S. 2nd Cavalry, Camp Cooper, Texas," pert. to care of his mare and reported robberies along the head of the Guadeloupe. GH Nov. 1993 $12,500.

---, Dec. 7, 1860, 1.25pp., 4to, San Antonio, to Major Earl Van Dorn, alluding to Lee's pre-war recognition of the inevitablility of seccession. S May 1993 $34,500.

---, March 10, 1858, 1p. + address leaf, to Edward C. Turner of Fauqier Co., Va., Lee expresses thanks and sends a $100 check for some oxen. AL Dec. 1993 $8,750.

---, Nov. 24, 1861, 1.5pp., 4to, Coosawhatchie, to Mrs. Rhett, discussing the organization of the Confederate Army and including the quote: "Our invaders have everything their own way; it will not be always and our turn will come some day." SG June 1993 $39,600.

---, July 23, 1862, 1p, 24.5x19 cm, silken, laid down, HQ, to Colonel Thomas R. R. Cobb, I am very much obliged to you for your kind attention to my request. I hope that this unpleasant matter will be properly decided. But however decided to by proper authority, I trust it will be approved by all citizens. Skinner's Auction, Boston, MA., Nov. 1993 $19,800.

---, Feb. 18, 1870, Lexington, Va., 2p., pert the Battle of Second Manassas, Lee writes in defense of Union Gen. Fitz John Porter who had been court marshaled and drummed out of the service when he failed to attack Stonewall Jackson's forces on the first day of the battle. GH Nov. 1993 $37,500.

ANS, Feb. 10, 1834, 1p., Ft. Monroe, 'Dear Captain I arrived this morning & will be happy to receive your orders. Present me in the the kindest manner to Mrs. J. Mrs. H, Taylor & the Misses I.H. & T Yours truly & in Haste RE Lee." SAG Feb. 1994 $4,750.

LS, March 1, 1863, 1p., Hd Qrs Army No Va, to Honorable John J. Petus, 'Sir, Private Henry Taylor Co. F. 16th, Miss Regt., a native and citizen of your state has been found guilty of 'Theft' by a court Marshal sitting in this army and sentenced 'to be sent to Mississippi Penitentiary provided the Governor of Mississippi will receive him and there to be confined for two years.' Will you do me the favor to inform me whether you will receive him. I am Resply Yr Obt Servt RE Lee Genl." SAG Feb. 1994 $11,000.

--. Aug. 19, 1846, 2p., Fort Hamilton, 'I did not think when I wrote, that I should so soon have to recall the request I then so earnestly made to my beautiful Matie to visit us this Summer; & should she have seriously thought of complying, it will add to the regret I now feel at leaving here. I rec'd orders last night to Mexico & join the Army. So soon as the officer arrives to relieve me of the charge of my present works, I will take the District in my route to Sant Antonio De Bexar... RE Lee." SAG Feb. 1994 $17,000.

--, Oct. 31, 1836, 1p., Washington, DC, pert. to Engineer Department, signed, "By Order - R.E. Lee - Lt. Asst. Adjutant." GH Nov. 1993 $6,750.

--, Aug. 12, 1864, 1p., HQ Army Northern Virginia, (Petersburg, Va.) to Wade Hampton, "assignment of certain members of your present staff to you for duty in the staff of the Cavalry Corps has been received. GH Nov. 1993 $17,500.

--, Sept. 17, 1836, 1p., Washington, DC, 1p. 8vo. 7.35x8.5", Lee responds to an earlier letter from Captain Eliason requesting technical information about the duties of an Officer of Engineers. UA Sept. 1993 $8,750.

DS, [1838] Portion of a Partly Printed Document Signed, 7.5x2", St. Louis. 'I certify that the articles charged in the within account, have been recived, were necessary for, and have been or will applied, for the objects within stated, to the Improvement of the Harbor of St. Louis. RE Lee Lt. Engrs." SAG Feb. 1994 $2,800.

--, June 28, 1838. 2pp., receipt for the "Improvement of the Harbor of St. Louis, Mo. to Peter Powell & Co. for hinges and locks, for the doors of Shantee." GH Nov. 1993 $4,250.

---, Aug. 31, 1844. 2pp., 4to., U.S. imprint voucher for Corps of Engineers expenses at Ft. Hamilton, N.Y. BG Nov. 1993 $3,500.

---, 1852, 1p, large signature as Captain in the U.S. Engineers. GH Nov. 1993 $3,000.

---, May 10, 1864, 1p., 5x4", in pencil, Field Order, signed "R.E. Lee/ Genl." On the first day of the Battle of Spotsylvania, Lee here orders Ewell to reestablish his "whole line tonight. Set the officers to ... collect & refresh their men and have everything ready for the renewal of the conflict at daylight tomorrow. I wish gen Rodes to rectify his line and improve its defenses, especially that part which seemed so easily overcome this afternoon. If no Flanking arrangements, a ditch had better be dug on the outside & an abatis made in front. Perhaps Grant will make a night attack as it was a favorite amusement of his at Vicksburg." AL Dec. 1993 $26,500.

---, April 10, 1865, 1p., Filo, General Order No. 9: a contemporary souvenir copy, personally signed "R.E. Lee/ Gen'l" while in the field. H.Q., Army of Northern, Va., with a supporting letter of Capt. Edward Graham's Co., Va. Horse Artillery, "Next day he sent a copy of his last order to Gen. Bushrod Johnson's headquarters...I made a copy...asking for his signature & sent it to him... Gen. Lee signed it & Col. Walter Taylor, Lee's aide, sent word by the courier: 'You must not brother the general." AL Dec. 1993 $85,000.

---, June 28, 1866, 1p. 8vo., Printed Reported Card, signed "R E Lee / Pres." Washington College, Lexington ,Va. LA Dec. 1993 $4,650.

Free Frank, April 21, 1837 "R E Lee / Lt." on folded cover addressed in another hand to Capt. W.A. Eliason, Corps of Engineers, Ft. Calhoun, Old Point Comfort, Va. AL Dec. 1993 $4,250.

S, Clipped signature, "Your Obit Servt/ R. E. Lee/ Genl." Professionally framed and matted. SK Feb. 1994 $4,000.

-, Clipped signature, "R.E. Lee." AL Dec. 1993 $3,650.

-, Clipped signature, from an ALS, framed and double matted with engraving of a seated Lee. EB Dec. 1993 $2,995.

-, Clipped signature, "R.E. Lee." SK Aug. 1993 $2,000.

-, Clipped signature, "R.E. Lee/ Genl." KO Sept. 1993 $3,150.

BS, Memoirs of the War of the Southern Department of the United States, by Henry Lee, 1869, New York. Laid into the book is an ADS 1p., n.d. by Henry Lee, pert. to a claim by W.A. Washington, which had been assigned to him. Signature of R.E. Lee, also "Oct 5/89, Presented to him by Gen GWC Lee." J 1993 $13,250.

PS, CDV. of Lee, signed 'RE Lee," B/M M.B. Brady & CO's ...Washington, D.C. UA Feb. 1994 $8,500.

--, CDV, of Lee, vignette bust, in civilian clothing, at foot "M B. Brady & Co. 1865 copyright notice, B/M Brady, signed on face "R.E. Lee." AL Dec. 1993 $8,250.

---, CDV, of Lee, bust, in uniform (c.1862) B/M Minnis & Cowell, Richmond., signed "R. E. Lee" GH Nov. 1993 $8,500.

---, CDV, of Lee seated casually. B/M J.H. Young & Co. of Baltimore, signed on the verso with dark clear signature. NS Nov. 1993 $6,000.

---, CDV, of Lee in uniform. No B/M but with inscription stating this CDV was given to a friend in 1868. KO Sept. 1993 $4,950.

---, CDV, of Lee in uniform. B/M Vannerson, Richmond, signed on the verso with bold signature. SK July 1993 $4,500.

Misc.

P, CDV, of Lee, Bust view in CSA uniformn "A Memorial picture of Genl. R.E. Lee made in the 3rd year of the war retouched by Mary Custis lee for her kind friend Mr. Davis." UA Feb. 1994 $1,250.

-, CDV, of Lee, Bust view in CSA uniform, with 3 stars on collar, B/M C.D. Federicks & Co., N.Y. LR Dec. 1993 $200.

-, CDV, of Lee, full standing with Presentation Sword, C. 1863, B/M Walter's Photograph Gallery - Norfolk, Va. GH Nov. 1993 $1,250.

-, Large oval albumen photograph, taken in 1864 , by J.W. Davies (Meredith p.54-57) GH Nov. 1993 $950.

-, Large oval albumen photograph, 10"h., taken in 1864, by J. Vannerson, (Meredith, pg. 49) GH Nov. 1993 $3,500.

-, Large oval albumen photograph, 12"h., taken in May 1869 by Mathew Brady. GH Nov. 1993 $2,500.

-, Large oval albumen photograph, taken by M. Miley in Lexington, Va., ca. 1870, (Meredith p. 86) GH Nov. 1993 $1,500.

General Order #9 - Norman Bell's copy of the farewell order from General Lee to the Army of Northern Virginia April 10, 1865. The Bell copy is on display at Straford Hall, Lee's birthplace in Westmoreland Co., Va. Drafted the night before the surrender at Appomattox and edited the next day, the document was transcribed by Norman Bell, a clerk at General Lee's Headquarters. Bell wrote 12 copies one for each of Lee's Corps Commanders, and then one extra copy for himself, no. 13. Having all 13 copies signed by General Lee.

A WARNING -- the Steven's copy generally offered is a fake, a mere photographic copy of the original. There is also has been a handful of fake R. E. Lee clips on the market., know who your buying from.

Lee, Samuel Pillips, 1812-97 — Union Naval Rear Admiral
Cousin of Genl R.E. Lee.

Signature	Signature with rank	Pre & post War DS	War Dated DS	Pre & post War ALS	War Dated ALS
$65	$175	$278	$1,785	$	$

AES, Ca. 1862, 1p., double folio 12x24", endorsed mechanical drawing of, "Fire rafts, infernal machines prepared for the Rebels in England. Care of the Senior Officers in the Sounds of North Carolina. - S.P. Lee, Acting Rear Admiral." GH Dec. 1993 $2,500.

Lee, Sidney Smith, ?-? — Union Naval Comdr.
He resigned in 1861 and joined the Commander Confederate Navy.

Signature	Signature with rank	Pre & post War DS	War Dated DS	Pre & post War ALS	War Dated ALS
$	$178	$	$	$	$

234

Lee, Stephen Dill, 1833-1908   Confederate Lieutenant General
WP graduate and nephew to Robert E. Lee. As Capt., Lee was Adjt. Genl. in Ewell's
Brigade. Appointed Brig. Genl. in July 1862, and Major Genl. in August 1863. Genl.
Lee had both a brigade and a division of cavalry in the Amry of Northern Virginia
through all its campaigns. He was wounded during the Battle of Winchester.

Signature	Signature with rank	Pre & post War DS	War Dated DS	Pre & post War ALS	War Dated ALS
$118	$256	$	$1,895	$265	$

Lee, William Henry Fitzhugh, 1837-91   Confederate Major General
The second son of R.E. Lee, he entered Harvard in 1854, but left school when Genl.
Scott gave him a commission in 1857. In command of the 9th Virginia Cavalry, he saw
service with Genl. Stuart on his "ride" around McClellan. He was severly wounded in
the leg at Brandy Station. He was second in command of the Cavalry Corps of the
ANV.

Signature	Signature with rank	Pre & post War DS	War Dated DS	Pre & post War ALS	War Dated ALS
$165	$278	$	$	$	$

S, Clip. JH August 1992 $225.

Lee, William Raymond, 1807-91   Brevet Brigadier General
Colonel, 20th Mass. Infantry, Bvt. Brig. Gen., USV, March 13, 1865, for distinguished
conduct at the battle of Antietam, Md.

Signature	Signature with rank	Pre & post War DS	War Dated DS	Pre & post War ALS	War Dated ALS
$24	$	$	$	$	$

Leech, William Albert, 1832-70   Brevet Brigadier General
Major, 17th Pa. Infantry, Lt. Col., 90th Pa. Infantry, Bvt. Brig. Gen., USV, March 13,
1865.

Signature	Signature with rank	Pre & post War DS	War Dated DS	Pre & post War ALS	War Dated ALS
$20	$32	$43	$52	$	$

Leggett, Mortimer Dormer, 1821-96 — Union General

Signature	Signature with rank	Pre & post War DS	War Dated DS	Pre & post War ALS	War Dated ALS
$20	$38	$	$	$55	$

S, Clip signature, with rank.. KS Feb. 1994 $35.

LeRoy, William E., ?-? — Confederate Naval Commander

Signature	Signature with rank	Pre & post War DS	War Dated DS	Pre & post War ALS	War Dated ALS
$	$89	$	$	$	$

Leslie, Frank, 1821-80 — American engraver and publisher

Frank Leslie's Illustrated Newspaper was particularly effective in its coverage of the Civil War.

Signature	Pre & post War DS	War Dated DS	Pre & post War ALS	War Dated ALS
$75	$	$	$	$

S, Bold signature, "Faithfully yours, Frank Leslie" on card. JB Dec. 1993 $65.

Lester, George Nelson, 1824-92 — Member Confederate Congress

Signature	Signature with rank	Pre & post War DS	War Dated DS	Pre & post War ALS	War Dated ALS
$45	$	$	$	$	$

Letcher, John, 1813-84 — Confederate Governor of Virginia

Gov. 1860-64, member of 1861 Peace Convention. Active supporter of the Confederate Secret Service.

Signature	Signature with rank	Pre & post War DS	War Dated DS	Pre & post War ALS	War Dated ALS
$70	$125	$	$325	$175	$465

DS, May 17, 1861, Richmond, Va., 1p., 7.75x9.5" appointment of Edward R. Archer 1st Lt. of Light Inf. 8th Battalion of Vols., 2nd Brigade, 4th Division of the Va. Militia, signed as Gov. EB Dec. 1993 $275.
S, Clip signature. BG Nov. 1993 $65.
-, Clip signature. KS Feb. 1994 $80.

Letcher, Samuel Houston, 1828-68 — CSA, Colonel

Brother of Virginia's war governor, at. Washington College, Lexington lawyer. Capt., Co., B, 5th Va. Apr. 1861. Lt. Col., 58th Virginia, Oct. 1861 & Col. May 1, 1862. Gov. Letcher demanded a court of inquiry concerning his experiences at Gain's' Mill & resigned Sept. 21, 1862.

Signature	Signature with rank	Pre & post War DS	War Dated DS	Pre & post War ALS	War Dated ALS
$	$	$	$115	$	$

Letterman, Jonathan, 1824-72 — Union Surgeon

Signature	Signature with rank	Pre & post War DS	War Dated DS	Pre & post War ALS	War Dated ALS
$75	$150	$	$225	$	$378

AES, June 1863. An forwarding a medical record and it's approval. KS Aug. 1993 $300.
Misc.
B, Medical recollections of the Army of the Potomac, 1866 ed. $ 150.

Leventhrope, Collett, 1815-89 — Confederate Brigadier General

Col. in the 34th NC. Severly wounded during the retreat from Gettysburg. He was captured and released nine months later. He declined his appointment to Brig. genl., on March 6, 1865.

Signature	Signature with rank	Pre & post War DS	War Dated DS	Pre & post War ALS	War Dated ALS
$75	$110	$145	$	$	$

Lewis, David Peter, 1820-84 — Member Conf. Congress; Gov. AL 72-74

Signature	Signature with rank	Pre & post War DS	War Dated DS	Pre & post War ALS	War Dated ALS
$40	$	$67	$	$98	$

Lewis, David William, 1815-85 — Member Confederate Congress

Signature	Signature with rank	Pre & post War DS	War Dated DS	Pre & post War ALS	War Dated ALS
$35	$	$76	$	$	$

Lewis, Joseph Horace, 1824-1904   Confederate Brigadier General
Col. of the 6th KY Infantry. He fought at Shiloh and Murfreesboro. He led his Brigade
at Chattanooga and in the Battle of Atlanta.

Signature	Signature with rank	Pre & post War DS	War Dated DS	Pre & post War ALS	War Dated ALS
$80	$	$148	$	$	$

Lewis, Levin M., 1832-87   Confederate Brigadier General
Trans-Mississippi - Attended Maryland Military Academy 1848-9; Wesleyan University
1850-1, Lawyer, minister, principal, after the war served as a minister.

Signature	Signature with rank	Pre & post War DS	War Dated DS	Pre & post War ALS	War Dated ALS
$78	$	$145	$	$	$

Lewis, William Gaston, 1835-1901   Confederate Brigadier General
Major 33rd NC during the Battle of New Bern, he fought with distinction at Malvern
Hill, Gettysburg, and Plymouth. He saw service in the Valley against Sheridan and then
around Petersburg. He was wounded and captured at Farmville, VA, April 7, 1865.

Signature	Signature with rank	Pre & post War DS	War Dated DS	Pre & post War ALS	War Dated ALS
$83	$145	$	$675	$	$

Lewis, John Wood, 1801-65   Member Confederate Congress

Signature	Signature with rank	Pre & post War DS	War Dated DS	Pre & post War ALS	War Dated ALS
$45	$	$98	$	$	$

238

Lilley, Robert Doak, 1836-86   Confederate Brigadier General

He formed the "Augusta Lee Guards" and saw service at 2nd Manassas and Sharpsburg. Appointed Brig. Genl. in May 1864, he was given command of Early's 2nd Corps. He lost his arm during the Battle of Winchester.

Signature	Signature with rank	Pre & post War DS	War Dated DS	Pre & post War ALS	War Dated ALS
$83	$143	$380	$567	$	$

Liddell, St. John Richardson, 1815-70   Confederate Brigadier General

Col. on the staff of Genl. Hardee and a special courier for Genl. A.S.Johnston. He commanded a brigade during the Battle of Corinth. He saw service under Genl. Taylor during the Red River Campaign. He was murdered by a former Confederate Colonel on Feb. 14, 1870.

Signature	Signature with rank	Pre & post War DS	War Dated DS	Pre & post War ALS	War Dated ALS
$80	$	$	$	$	$

Lightburn, Joseph Andrew Jackson, 1824-1901   Union General

Signature	Signature with rank	Pre & post War DS	War Dated DS	Pre & post War ALS	War Dated ALS
$35	$50	$72	$	$	$

Lightburn, Joseph Andrew Jackson

Lincoln, Abraham, 1809-65   Union Commander-in-Chief

Signature	Signature with rank	Pre War DS	War Dated DS	Pre War ALS	War Dated ALS
$3,150	$3,650	$4,875	$7250	$9,225	$12,787

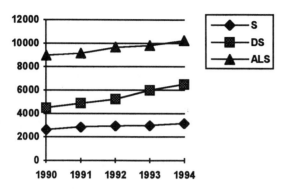

Graph of war dated material sold over the last five years.

Two identical Brady photographs of Lincoln, both signed A. Lincoln. The one on the left bears a forgery; that on the right bears a genuine signature.

240

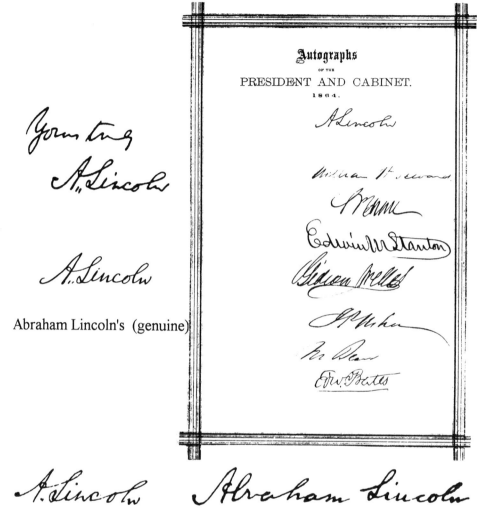

Abraham Lincoln's (genuine)

Forgery (Joseph Cosey)   Forgery (Eugene Feild II)

Forgeries (Perpetrator unknown)

ALS, June 11, 1845, Menard County, Petersburg, Ill., 1p., legal plea. GH Dec. 1993 $7,500.

---, Dec. 28, 1861. 1p 8vo. Directed to Montgomery Meigs., "It is a necessity that Capt. Eddy should not be retained in service at Springfield, Illinois. In This, I am neither deciding, nor saying anything against Capt. Eddy". SG #195 May 1992 $22,000.

---, July 27, 1863. 1p 8vo. Executive Mansion stationary. Reads "Today, my friend Jackson Grimshaw, and asks that his brother, Arthur H. Grimshaw, Col. of the 4th Delaware Vols. may be a Brig. General. A. Lincoln.". SG #197 May 1992 $9,900.

---, July 18, 1863. 1p., written on an envelope, 8.75x3.75". To Attorney General [Edward Bates], "Atty. Genl, please send me a Commission for Judge Brochus, according to the within. A. Lincoln." CB Aug. 1992 $7,000.

---, Aug. 6, 1861. 1p., 13x17," on vellum, Washington, DC. Appoints Augustus V. Barriger as Commissary of Subsistence of Volunteers with the rank of Captain. HD June 1992 $6,000.

---, July 1, 1864. 1p, 16x20" on vellum, Washington, DC. Appoints Edward J. Whitney as Surgeon of Volunteers., countersigned by E.M. Stanton as Secretary of War. HD June 1992 $3,750.

DS, Jan. 12, 1865, 1p., folio, appointing Stoddard B. Colby the Register of the U.S. Treasury. HCS Feb. 1994 $8,500.

--, April 1, 1862, 1p., folio appointment for 2nd Lt. George Heisler, US Marine Corps. GH Dec. 1993 $10,500.

--, July 26, 1861, signed appointment for C.C./ Hewitt, Chief Justice of Supreme Court. S Nov. 1993 $6,600.

--, August 26, 1862, signed appointment for John Sargent, Collector of Taxes, 18x43 cm., bold & clear signature. S Nov. 1993 $4,950.

--, April 18, 1862, 1p., folio on vellum, mil. commission Wash. DC, for Capt. John G. Farnsworth as Asst. QM. BG Nov. 1993 $6,250.

--, July 20, 1861. 1p. folio 18x15" appointment to post of Customs Collector, Newburyport, Mass. BG Nov. 1993 $6,500.

--, July 26, 1861. 1p. folio appointment for Christopher C. Hewitt, Chief Justice Supreme Court of the United States, signature bold. Skinner Nov. 1993 $6,600.

--, August 26, 1862. 1p. 18x43 cm., for John Sargent, Collector of Taxes, signature bold. Skinner Nov. 1993 $4,950.

--, March 11, 1862, City of Washington, 1p 14x18", appointment of Lewis Richmond as Assistant General of Volunteers with the rank of Captain. UA Sept. 1993 $6,500.

--, March 11, 1863, City of Washington, 1p 22.3x18", appointment of Alfred Fox Consul of the US at Falmouth. UA Sept. 1993 $8,900.

--, June 13, 1864, Washington,, 1p. 15.75x19.2", appointing George R. Martin an Assistant Paymaster in the Navy. UA Sept. 1993 $3,850.

--, Aug. 15, 1864, Washington, 1p. 8x9.75", Lincoln congratulated Atanasio Cruz Aguirre on elevation to the presidency of Oriental Republic of Uruguay. UA Sept. 1993 $8,750.

Military commissions have seen a leveling off in price increases in the past two years. Averaging about $5,750.

LS, July 2, 1860. 1p. 5x7.75" Dear Sir, Herewith I send you my autograph, which you requested, Yours Truely, A. Lincoln." UA Feb. 1994 $5,750.

ANS, 'Let this man take the oath of Dec. 8, 1864 and be discharged. A. Lincoln Aug. 13, 1864." HC Feb. 1994 $6,250.

---, Oct. 14, 1862, "Wife of Hon. A.S. Diven - submitted to Secretary of War. - A. Lincoln." GH Dec. 1993 $6,750.

---, Feb. 17, 1865, Allow these men to take the oath of Dec. 8, 1863 & be discharged/ A. Lincoln." J 1993 $6,800.

---, Nov. 2, 1861, "White House Card" requesting the Secretary of War to see Col. McNeil of Missouri. GH Dec. 1993 $7,750.

---, March 9, 1865, "Let this man take the oath of December 8, 1863, and be discharged. - A. Lincoln," a northern citizen drafted into the Confederate Army and now a Prisoner of War on Ship Island, Miss. GH Dec. 1993 $8,500.

AES, Nov. 27, 1863, 1p. 5x8", On the reverse of a letter written to him, Lincoln wrote an endorsement in pencil, "I know nothing of the propriety of this appointment but would be very glad for Mr. Scovel to be obliged. A Lincoln." UA Sept. 1993 $6,000.

S, Cut signature, from the collection of C. Jay French, 1870's military mail supert. KO Sept. 1993 $2,350.

Misc.

P, CDV, bust view image which is mounted inside oval with ornate raised vignettes featuring a spread winged eagle & shield, B/M Salisbury, Bro. & Co., Providence, R.I. LR Dec. 1993 $95.

-, CDV, seated view, Ostendorf #71, B/M Alexander Gardener, Aug. 9, 1863. RS Dec. 1993 $600.

-, CDV, 2.3 standing view, B/M Brady/ Anthony, it was taken by Matthew Brady on Jan. 8, 1864 & affectionately became titled, "Like some solitary pine." LR Dec. 1993 $875.

-, CDV, "President Lincoln and his son Thaddeus - the last photograph the President sat for." B/M G.F. Bouve Boston. GH Dec. 1993 $950.

-, 10.5" x 7.5," Invitation to NATIONAL INAUGURATION BALL, MARCH 4th, 1865." with original envelope. EC August 1993 $1,600.
Other examples seen offered at $1,200 - 1,400. without an envelop.

-, General Order # 67, 8vo, 1p., War Dept., A.G.O., Washington, April 16, 1865..."it is hereby announced to the Armies of the United States, that on Saturday, the 15th day of April, 1865, by reason of the death of Abraham Lincoln, the office of President United States devolved upon Andrew Johnson...". LS Oct. 1992 $895.

-, Funeral card, 3.5x5" deep black border with raised white tombstone "In memory of/ of Abraham Lincoln/ President of the United States/ Born February 12, 1809. Departed this life April 15th, 1865/ "Yet speaketh"/ "For thou art Freedom's now, and Fame's..." LS Nov. 1993 $595.

-, "The New York Times," Monday, April 17, 1865 issue, reporting the assassination of President Lincoln, 8pp, 15x20". Black-bordered on front and back pages plus inside pages. generally, good shape. HD June 1992 $110.

> **Care should be used to insure that similar issues are not later editions on wood pulp paper, which are worth very little and have no value on the collective market.**

Lincoln, Mary Todd 1818-82   Wife of Abraham Lincoln

Signature	Pre & post War DS	War Dated DS	Pre & post War ALS	War Dated ALS
$350	$895	$	$	$

PS   CDV, "Verly truely yours" signed and dated 1865. S May 1993 $6,900.
Misc.
P, CDV, Seated pose wearing black morning dress and dark colored veil, card has been trimmed on all sides. LR Dec. 1993 $170.

Lincoln, Robert Todd, 1843-1926   Union Officer
Son of Abraham Lincoln.

Signature	Signature with rank	Pre & post War DS	War Dated DS	Pre & post War ALS	War Dated ALS
$85	$145	$	$	$245	$

ALS, n.d.. 2.5pp, 7x4.5. personal letter head, regarding his connections with the Red Cross Society. EB August 1992 $225.
TLS, 1916 Oct. 20. 1p, 7x9", Manchester, Vt., To the manager Neale Publishing Company, receipt of General Wilson's" Life of Rawlins". HD June 1992 $110.

Little, Lewis Henry, "Henry," 1817-62   Confederate Brigadier General
One of the rarest of the CSA General, he was promoted after the battle of Elkhorn to Brig. General. He was killed 19 Sept. 1862 at Iuka, Miss. while on his horse talking with Gen. Price.

Signature	Signature with rank	Pre War DS	War Dated DS	Pre War ALS	War Dated ALS
$500	$650	$750	$	$	$

AES, May 1, 1855. 1p 7.5x2.5" pert to QM supplies. BG Nov. 1993 $595.
S, Clip signature from a letter. KO Sept. 1993 $425.

Littlefield, Milton Smith, 1830-99   Union Brevet General
Capt. 14th Ill. Infantry, Capt., Provost Marshal, Staff of Major Gen. Stephen A. Hurlbut, Colonel 21st USCT, Superintendent, Vol. Recruiting Service, Dept. of the South.

Signature	Signature with rank	Pre & post War DS	War Dated DS	Pre & post War ALS	War Dated ALS
$	$38	$	$	$	$

Littlejohn, DeWitt Clinton, 1818-92   Union Brevet General
Colonel 110th NY Inf., Bvt. Brig. Gen., USV, March 13, 1865.

Signature	Signature with rank	Pre & post War DS	War Dated DS	Pre & post War ALS	War Dated ALS
$30	$45	$78	$	$98	$

Lockwood, Henry Hayes, 1814-99   Union General

Signature	Signature with rank	Pre & post War DS	War Dated DS	Pre & post War ALS	War Dated ALS
$20	$35	$68	$	$	$

Logan, George Washington, 1815-89   Member Confederate Congress

Signature	Signature with rank	Pre & post War DS	War Dated DS	Pre & post War ALS	War Dated ALS
$65	$	$	$	$	$

Logan, George W.

Logan, John Alexander, 1826-86   Union General

Fought in the Mexican War and then served in the state legislature and U.S. Congress. He was wounded leading his regiment at Fort Donelson and commissioned B.G. USV March 21, 1862. He commanded, in the Army of the Tenn.

Signature	Signature with rank	Pre & post War DS	War Dated DS	Pre & post War ALS	War Dated ALS
$65	$87	$78	$	$225	$1,250

ALS, April 1, 1864. 4to, 2pp., to his mother pert. personal matters, that he was quite sick, expects another campaign. (Atlanta Campaign) LS Dec. 1993 $1,500.
DS, Per war, Cover addressed entirely in his hand to his wife. LS Dec. 1993 $48.50
S, Clip 2x4.5" signed as Major Genl. EB Dec. 1993 $65.
Misc.
-, G.A.R. card 4x5.5" from his estate. LS Dec. 1993 $95.
B, The Volunteer Soldier of America, 1887.

Logan, Thomas Muldrup, 1840-1914   Confederate Brigadier General

Led S.C. Cav., Hampton Legion wounded during the Seven Days Battles. He fought at Sharpsburg. At the end of the War he commanded Butler's Brigade against Genl. Sherman.

Signature	Signature with rank	Pre & post War DS	War Dated DS	Pre & post War ALS	War Dated ALS
$70	$	$225	$	$278	$

LS, 1879, Va., pert. to politics. JH Aug. 1993 $200.

Lomax, Lunsfrod Lindsay, 1835-1913   Confederate Major General

An 1856 WP Graduate, Col of the 11th Virginia Cavalry at Gettysburg, PA. Led a brigade under Fitzhugh Lee during the Wilderness Campaign. He was given command of the valley District.

Signature	Signature with rank	Pre & post War DS	War Dated DS	Pre & post War ALS	War Dated ALS
$90	$175	$180	$	$275	$

Long, Armistead Lindsay, 1825-91   Confederate Brigadier General
An 1850 WP Graduate, during his ten years in the U.S. Army he was a noted Indian fighter. He severed on Lee's Staff.

Signature	Signature with rank	Pre & post War DS	War Dated DS	Pre & post War ALS	War Dated ALS
$75	$	$87	$	$	$

Long, Eli, 1837-1903   Union General

Signature	Signature with rank	Pre & post War DS	War Dated DS	Pre & post War ALS	War Dated ALS
$30	$	$	$	$78	$

Longstreet, James "Old Pete", 1821-1904   Confederate Lt. General
Graduated from West Point 1842. The U.S. Minister to Turkey after the war.

Signature	Signature with rank	Pre & post War DS	War Dated DS	Pre & post War ALS	War Dated ALS
$400	$765	$478	$	$1,050	$6,435

ALS, July 2, 1852, Camp Johnston, Texas, 1p. 8x10", to Colonel H.K. Craig, Chief of Ordnance, pert. to ordnance stores. Signed with rank, "1st Lt., 8th Inf., Bvt. Maj., Com. Comp. G." LR Dec. 1993 $950.
ANS, Note giving the address of W. F. H. Lee as care of the Internal Revenue Service, Washington, DC SK August 1993 $525.
S, On a limited edition book plate one of 150. JH Nov. 1993 $350.
-, Large clip signature, 1884. BG Nov. 1993 $350.
Misc.
P, CDV, mid chest up view in double breasted, CSA uniform coat, 1862 imprint, E & Anthony, NY LR Dec. 1993 $200.

Loomis, Gustavus, 1789-1872   Union Brevet General

Signature	Signature with rank	Pre & post War DS	War Dated DS	Pre & post War ALS	War Dated ALS
$25	$	$65	$	$	$

Loring, William Wing, 1818-86   Confederate Major General
Lawyer and served in the army before the war. He lost his arm at the Battle of
Chapultepec. He entered C.S. service as a Brig. Genl. in command of the Army of the
Northwest. He commanded divisions during the Battles of Atlanta, Franklin, and
Nashville. Served in Egyptian army following the war.

Signature	Signature with rank	Pre & post War DS	War Dated DS	Pre & post War ALS	War Dated ALS
$90	$175	$267	$	$	$

Lovell, Charles Swain, 1811-71   Union Brevet General

Signature	Signature with rank	Pre & post War DS	War Dated DS	Pre & post War ALS	War Dated ALS
$18	$	$45	$	$	$

Lovell, Frederick Solon, 1813-78   Union Brevet General

Signature	Signature with rank	Pre & post War DS	War Dated DS	Pre & post War ALS	War Dated ALS
$20	$	$	$	$	$

Lovell, Mansfield, 1822-84   Confederate Major General
Graduated from West Point 1842. Served in the regular army before the war, engineer
and Street Commissioner after. He was placed in command of New Orleans, surrendered
the city on April 25, 1862. After Corinth, he was relieved of command.

Signature	Signature with rank	Pre & post War DS	War Dated DS	Pre & post War ALS	War Dated ALS
$85	$178	$	$575	$	$678

Lowe, Thaddeus S. C., 1832-1913   Union Aeronaut/Balloonist

Signature	Signature with rank	Pre & post War DS	War Dated DS	Pre & post War ALS	War Dated ALS
$	$250	$	$	$485	$

248

Lowe, William Warren, 1831-98 — Union Brevet General

Signature	Signature with rank	Pre & post War DS	War Dated DS	Pre & post War ALS	War Dated ALS
$	$	$56	$	$	$

Lowell, Charles Russell, 1835-64 — Union General

Graduated from Harvard at the head of his class of 1854. Served on General George B. McClellan staff. During the battles of Antietam and Winchester, Va., he displayed gallantry and had twelve horses shot from under him. At Cedar Creek he was wounded and died the next day, Oct. 20, 1864. Rare.

Signature	Signature with rank	Pre War DS	War Dated DS	Pre War ALS	War Dated ALS
$	$	$	$	$	$

Lowrey, Mark Perrin, 1828-85 — Confederate Brigadier General

Col. of the 32nd Mississippi Infantry. He was wounded at Perryville, fought at the Battle of Chickamauga. As Brig. Genl., he led a brigade in Hardee's Corps during the Atlanta campaign.

Signature	Signature with rank	Pre & post War DS	War Dated DS	Pre & post War ALS	War Dated ALS
$90	$143	$210	$	$	$

Lowry, Robert, 1830-90 — Confederate Brigadier General

A Private in the 'Rankin Grays," but soon appointed Major of the 6th Mississippi Infantry. He was wounded at Shiloh, and fought with distinction at Vicksburg. He took over Genl. Adams' Brigade during Hood's invasion of TN.

Signature	Signature with rank	Pre & post War DS	War Dated DS	Pre & post War ALS	War Dated ALS
$90	$	$185	$	$	$

Lubbock, Francis Richard, 1815-1905   Conf. Gov. of TX (61-63)

Signature	Signature with rank	Pre & post War DS	War Dated DS	Pre & post War ALS	War Dated ALS
$	$	$	$	$	$

S, Clip. "F.R. Lubbock". Nat July 1992 $100.

Lucas, Thomas John, 1826-1908   Union General

A watchmaker by trade, entered the Mexican War as a 2nd Lt. Commanded the 16th Indiana, lost 200 men at Richmond, KY. At Vicksburg he was wounded three times. Promoted brigadier general Nov. 10, 1864.

Signature	Signature with rank	Pre & post War DS	War Dated DS	Pre & post War ALS	War Dated ALS
$	$	$	$	$110	$

Ludlington, Marshell Independence, 1839-1919   Union Brevet General

Signature	Signature with rank	Pre & post War DS	War Dated DS	Pre & post War ALS	War Dated ALS
$20	$	$	$	$	$

Lyon, Francis Strother, 1800-82   Member Confederate Congress

Signature	Signature with rank	Pre & post War DS	War Dated DS	Pre & post War ALS	War Dated ALS
$38	$	$	$	$	$

Lyon, Hylan Benton, 1836-1907   Confederate Brigadier General

WP graduate, he entered C.S. service as a Capt. of Artillery in Cobb's Battery. He was captured at Fort Donelson and exchanged seven months later. He commanded a brigade of cavalry under Genl. Forrest, and fought with much distinction during the Battle of Chattanooga.

Signature	Signature with rank	Pre & post War DS	War Dated DS	Pre & post War ALS	War Dated ALS
$78	$	$	$	$245	$

Lyon, Nathaniel, 1818-61   Union Brigadier General
Killed 10 August 1861 at Wilson Creek, Va. Rare.

Signature	Signature with rank	Pre War DS	War Dated DS	Pre War ALS	War Dated ALS
$125	$185	$	$	$1,650	$

Lyons, James, 1801-82   Member Confederate Congress

Signature	Signature with rank	Pre & post War DS	War Dated DS	Pre & post War ALS	War Dated ALS
$40	$	$	$	$	$

Lytle, William Haines, 1826-63   Union General
Died 20 September 1863 of wounds rec'd. at Chickamauga, Ga. Rare.

Signature	Signature with rank	Pre War DS	War Dated DS	Pre War ALS	War Dated ALS
$	$	$	$	$	$

Mc and Mac.

Mac Allister, Robert, 1813-1891   Union Brevet General

Signature	Signature with rank	Pre & post War DS	War Dated DS	Pre & post War ALS	War Dated ALS
$	$45	$	$	$	$

Mc Arthur, John, 1826-1906   Union General

Signature	Signature with rank	Pre & post War DS	War Dated DS	Pre & post War ALS	War Dated ALS
$	$38	$58	$	$	$

Mc Arthur, William Miltimore, 1832-1917   Union Brevet General

Signature	Signature with rank	Pre & post War DS	War Dated DS	Pre & post War ALS	War Dated ALS
$18	$	$45	$	$	$

Mc Blair, William, ?-?   Commander Confederate Navy

Signature	Signature with rank	Pre & post War DS	War Dated DS	Pre & post War ALS	War Dated ALS
$	$178	$	$387	$	$

Mc Bride, James Douglas, 1842-1932   Union Brevet General

Signature	Signature with rank	Pre & post War DS	War Dated DS	Pre & post War ALS	War Dated ALS
$15	$	$43	$58	$72	$

Mc Call, George Archibald, 1802-68   Union General

Signature	Signature with rank	Pre & post War DS	War Dated DS	Pre & post War ALS	War Dated ALS
$20	$	$	$	$	$

Mc Call, William Henry Harrison, 1841-83   Union Brevet General

Signature	Signature with rank	Pre & post War DS	War Dated DS	Pre & post War ALS	War Dated ALS
$25	$	$58	$	$	$

Mc Callum, Daniel Craig, 1815-78   Union Brevet General

Signature	Signature with rank	Pre & post War DS	War Dated DS	Pre & post War ALS	War Dated ALS
$15	$	$	$67	$	$

Mc Callum, James, 1806-89   Member Confederate Congress

Signature	Signature with rank	Pre & post War DS	War Dated DS	Pre & post War ALS	War Dated ALS
$	$65	$	$	$	$

Mc Causland, John 1836-1927   Confederate Brigadier General

A VMI grad., first in his class. He was commissioned Col. of the 36th Virginia in 1861. He was with A.S. Johnston in Kentucky and took over Genl. Jenkins' command after he was killed in action at Cloyd's Mountain. He fought with distinction in the Valley, at Petersburg, and during the Battle of Five Forks.

Signature	Signature with rank	Pre & post War DS	War Dated DS	Pre & post War ALS	War Dated ALS
$225	$335	$378	$478	$	$

S, On a book cover, 1871 Blackwood magazine. JH Aug. 1993 $200.

Mc Clellan, George Brinton, 1826-85   Union General

Commander of the Army of the Potomac, known as "the young Napoleon'; Democratic presidential candidate in 1864; governor of New Jersey.

Signature	Signature with rank	Pre & post War DS	War Dated DS	Pre & post War ALS	War Dated ALS
$225	$325	$	$	$475	$2,235

S, Clip. "Very Truely Yours George B. McClellan". Nat July 1992 $200
PS, Oct. 6, 1873. [Bradley & Rulofson}, 4.25x6.5", "With kind regards of Geo. B. McClellan" and dated. MS Nov. 1993 $600.

Mc Clernand, John Alexander, 1812-1900   Lawyer & Union General

Signature	Signature with rank	Pre & post War DS	War Dated DS	Pre & post War ALS	War Dated ALS
$	$65	$87	$135	$	$

Mc Comb, William, 1828-1918   Confederate Brigadier General

He entered C.S. service as a Private in the 14th TN Infantry. He fought with gallantry at Cheat Mountain, and was with Genl. Jackson in the Valley Campaign. Promoted to Col., he led his regiment at Chancellorsville and Sharpsburg, being severely wounded during both battles. He was paroled at Appomattox Court House.

Signature	Signature with rank	Pre & post War DS	War Dated DS	Pre & post War ALS	War Dated ALS
$90	$	$245	$	$	$

Mc Cook, Alexander McDowell, 1831-1903   Union Brevet General

Signature	Signature with rank	Pre & post War DS	War Dated DS	Pre & post War ALS	War Dated ALS
$25	$	$68	$	$87	$

Mc Cook, Daniel Jr., 1834-64   Union Brigadier General

Died 17 July 1864 of wounds rec'd. at Keneasaw Mountain, Ga. Rare.

Signature	Signature with rank	Pre War DS	War Dated DS	Pre War ALS	War Dated ALS
$	$	$	$	$	$

Mc Cook, Edward Moody, 1833-1909   Union General

Signature	Signature with rank	Pre & post War DS	War Dated DS	Pre & post War ALS	War Dated ALS
$25	$	$	$	$	$

Mc Cook, Edwin Stanton, 1837-73   Union Brevet General

Signature	Signature with rank	Pre & post War DS	War Dated DS	Pre & post War ALS	War Dated ALS
$25	$	$	$	$	$

Mc Cook, Robert Latimer, 1827-62   Union Brigadier General

Died. Aug. 6, 1862 of wounds recd by Conf. rangers en route to Decherd, TN. Rare.

Signature	Signature with rank	Pre War DS	War Dated DS	Pre War ALS	War Dated ALS
$	$165	$	$	$	$

254

Mc Cown, John Porter, 1815-79   Confederate Major General

He first took charge of the artillery in the Prov. Army, State of TN. As Brig Genl. he commanded a division in Polk's Army during the Battle of Belmont.   Placed in Command of the Department of East Tennessee, He subsequently commanded a division of the Army of Kentucky during the Battle at Stones River. He was charged with conduct at Murfreesboro prejudicial to good order and military discipline by Genl. Bragg censoring him for the remainder of the war.

Signature	Signature with rank	Pre & post War DS	War Dated DS	Pre & post War ALS	War Dated ALS
$85	$	$290	$	$	$

Mc Culloch, Ben, 1811-62   Confederate Brigadier General

He war An scout and Indian fighter, he followed Davy Crockett to Texas, and distinguished himself in the Battle of San Jacinto. As Brig. Gen., he fought with much gallantry and won the Battle of Wilson's Creek. Under Genl. Van Dorn he was killed 7 March 1862 at Elkhorn Tavern, Pea Ridge, Ark., by a Yankee sharpshooter.

Signature	Signature with rank	Pre War DS	War Dated DS	Pre War ALS	War Dated ALS
$165	$350	$450	$	$	$

Mc Culloch, Henry Eustance, 1816-95   Confederate Brigadier General

Brother of Genl. Ben McCullough, he entered C.S. service as Col. of the 1st Teas Mounted Rifles. He commanded the District of San Antonio, and as Brig. Genl. he led a brigade under Genl. Walker during the Vicksburg campaign. Brother of Genl. Ben McCullough.

Signature	Signature with rank	Pre & post War DS	War Dated DS	Pre & post War ALS	War Dated ALS
$110	$187	$378	$	$	$

McCulluch, Hugh, 1808-95 — Union Sec. of the Treasury

Lincoln appointed him Sec. in 1865.

Signature	Signature with rank	Pre & post War DS	War Dated DS	Pre & post War ALS	War Dated ALS
$48	$	$78	$	$	$

PS, CDV, Brady - Washington, signed "Hugh McCulluch," B/M Brady's No. 352 Pennsylvania Av., Washington, DC & Broadway & Tenth St. RS Jan. 1994 $200.

Mc Dowell, Irvin, 1818-85 — Union General

Signature	Signature with rank	Pre & post War DS	War Dated DS	Pre & post War ALS	War Dated ALS
$65	$115	$145	$	$	$

Mc Dowell, Thomas David Smith, 1823-98 — Confederate Congressman

Signature	Signature with rank	Pre & post War DS	War Dated DS	Pre & post War ALS	War Dated ALS
$45	$	$	$	$	$

Mc Ginnis, George Francis, 1826-1910 — Union General

Signature	Signature with rank	Pre & post War DS	War Dated DS	Pre & post War ALS	War Dated ALS
$20	$	$	$	$67	$

Mc Gowan, Samuel, 1819-97 — Confederate Brigadier General

He commanded a brigade during the bombardment of Fort Sumter. He was wounded no less than four times during the war, and fought with great distinction at Cedar Mountain, 2nd Manassass, and Fredericksburg.

Signature	Signature with rank	Pre & post War DS	War Dated DS	Pre & post War ALS	War Dated ALS
$80	$178	$	$	$	$

Mc Intosh, James McQueen, 1828-62   Confederate Brigadier General

WP graduate, he was first appointed Captain in the C.S. Cavalry, but soon became Col. of the 2nd Arkansas Mounted Rifles. While commanding his cavalry during the Battle of Elkhorn Tavern, McIntosh was killed 7 March 1862 at Pea Ridge, Ark.

Signature	Signature with rank	Pre War DS	War Dated DS	Pre War ALS	War Dated ALS
$250	$	$478	$	$	$

An extremely rare signature.

Mc Intosh, John Baillie, 1829-88   Union Major General

Signature	Signature with rank	Pre & post War DS	War Dated DS	Pre & post War ALS	War Dated ALS
$20	$	$35	$	$48	$

Mac Kall, William Whann, 1817-91   Confederate Brigadier General

WP graduate, he was commissioned Lt. Col., C.S.A., and became A.S. Johnston's Adjt. Genl. Captured at the Battle of Island 10, he war Appointed Bragg's Chief of Staff following his exchange. He was relieved of duty request following the Battle of Chickamauga. He saw little action after the Atlanta campaign.

Signature	Signature with rank	Pre & post War DS	War Dated DS	Pre & post War ALS	War Dated ALS
$90	$	$278	$	$	$

AES, 21 Dec. 1839. 4to. Plaserburg, NY, relating to ordinance, signed as 1 Lt. Art. LS Oct. 1992 $75.

Mc Kay, Charlotte, ?-?   Union Nurse

Signature	Pre & post War DS	War Dated DS	Pre & post War ALS	War Dated ALS
$	$	$	$156	$

Mc Kean, Thomas Jefferson, 1810-70 — Union General

Signature	Signature with rank	Pre & post War DS	War Dated DS	Pre & post War ALS	War Dated ALS
$20	$	$	$	$	$

Mac Kenzie, Ranald Slidell, 1840-89 — Union General

Signature	Signature with rank	Pre & post War DS	War Dated DS	Pre & post War ALS	War Dated ALS
$	$35	$	$	$	$

Mc Kinstry, Justus, 1814-97 — Union General

Signature	Signature with rank	Pre & post War DS	War Dated DS	Pre & post War ALS	War Dated ALS
$25	$	$45	$	$	$

Mc Laws, Lafayette, 1821-97 — Confederate Major General

WP graduate, he entered the Confederate Army as a Col. in the 10th Georgia Infantry. He fought with distinction at the Seven Days and 2nd Manassas. In September 1863 he went west with Longstreet and fought at Chickamauga and Knoxville. In May 1864, McLaws was sent to Georgia and South Carolina, and commanded a division in Hardee's Corps. After the war he was Postmaster of Savannah.

Signature	Signature with rank	Pre & post War DS	War Dated DS	Pre & post War ALS	War Dated ALS
$150	$275	$287	$	$365	$

Mac Lay, Robert Plunket, 1820-1903   Confederate Brig General

Brig. Genl. Designated B.G. on April 30, 1864, by Genl. Kirby Smith, Trans-Mississippi Department.

Signature	Signature with rank	Pre & post War DS	War Dated DS	Pre & post War ALS	War Dated ALS
$65	$	$	$	$178	$

Mc Lean, James Robert, 1823-70   Conf. Officer & Confed. Congress

Signature	Signature with rank	Pre & post War DS	War Dated DS	Pre & post War ALS	War Dated ALS
$48	$	$	$	$	$145

ALS, Nov. 29, 1864. 1p. 8vo.: Camp Stoker, To W.G. Trotter C.S.C. Greensboro, NC, deals with a legal matter. Signed J. R. Mc Lean, Major Commanding. JSA Sept. 1992 $95.

Mc Lean, Nathaniel Collins, 1815-1905   Union General

Signature	Signature with rank	Pre & post War DS	War Dated DS	Pre & post War ALS	War Dated ALS
$50	$	$	$	$	$

Mc Millan, James Winning, 1825-1903   Union General

Signature	Signature with rank	Pre & post War DS	War Dated DS	Pre & post War ALS	War Dated ALS
$20	$	$48	$	$	$

Mc Mullen, LaFayette, 1805-80   Member Confederate Congress

Signature	Signature with rank	Pre & post War DS	War Dated DS	Pre & post War ALS	War Dated ALS
$	$	$	$	$	$

Mc Nair, Evander, 1820-1902   Confederate Brigadier General

He supplied the 4th Arkansas Infantry, of which he was elected Col. He fought with Genl. McCulloch at Wilson's Creek and Elkhorn. Genl . McNair led his brigade at Stones River, and was to join Genl. Johnston during the Vicksburg campaign. He was wounded at Chickamauga, and was later transferred to the Trans-Mississippi Department.

Signature	Signature with rank	Pre & post War DS	War Dated DS	Pre & post War ALS	War Dated ALS
$80	$	$	$	$256	$

Mc Neil, John, 1813-1891   Union General

Signature	Signature with rank	Pre & post War DS	War Dated DS	Pre & post War ALS	War Dated ALS
$20	$	$	$	$	$

Mac Pherson, James Birdseye, 1828-64   Union General

He was killed in action July 22, 1864, near Atlanta, Ga.

Signature	Signature with rank	Pre War DS	War Dated DS	Pre War ALS	War Dated ALS
$350	$650	$	$	$	$

S, Oct. 5, 1863. Vicksburg, Mississippi, a fragment signed as Major General. SAG Feb. 1994 $650.

-, Signature cut from a document, closely trimmed. Richly framed with engraved portrait. JB Dec. 1993 $750.

Mc Quade, James, 1829-85   Union Brevet General

Signature	Signature with rank	Pre & post War DS	War Dated DS	Pre & post War ALS	War Dated ALS
$20	$35	$67	$76	$	$

Mc Queen, John, 1804-67   Member Confederate Congress

Signature	Signature with rank	Pre & post War DS	War Dated DS	Pre & post War ALS	War Dated ALS
$	$	$	$	$	$

Mc Rae, Colin John, 1812-77   Member Confederate Congress

Signature	Signature with rank	Pre & post War DS	War Dated DS	Pre & post War ALS	War Dated ALS
$35	$	$	$	$	$176

Mc Rae, Dandridge K., 1829-99   Confederate Brigadier General

He entered C.S. service as a Major in the 3rd Battalion of Arkansas Infantry. He fought with distinction at Wilson's Creek, Elkhorn, Helena, Mark's Mills, and Jenkins Ferry. He resigned his commission in 1864 and returned to Searcy, Ark. to practice law.

Signature	Signature with rank	Pre & post War DS	War Dated DS	Pre & post War ALS	War Dated ALS
$80	$115	$	$225	$	$

Mc Rae, John Jones, 1815-68   Member Confederate Congress
Gov. of Mississippi.

Signature	Signature with rank	Pre & post War DS	War Dated DS	Pre & post War ALS	War Dated ALS
$45	$	$76	$	$185	$

Mac Rae, William, 1834-82 Confederate Brigadier General

He entered the Confederate Army as a Private in the Monroe Light Infantry, but was soon elected Capt. of the 15th North Carolina. He fought with much distinction at 2nd Manassas, Sharpsburg, and Fredericksburg. After the war, he was engaged in railroading.

Signature	Signature with rank	Pre & post War DS	War Dated DS	Pre & post War ALS	War Dated ALS
$90	$	$245	$	$	$

Mac Willie, Marcus H., ?-? Member Confederate Congress

Signature	Signature with rank	Pre & post War DS	War Dated DS	Pre & post War ALS	War Dated ALS
$	$	$	$	$	$

M

Maffit, John Newland, 1819-86 Captain Confederate Navy

Confederate Cruiser, CSS FLORIDA 1862-63.

Signature	Signature with rank	Pre & post War DS	War Dated DS	Pre & post War ALS	War Dated ALS
$	$175	$	$	$	$

Magrath, Andrew Gordon, 1813-93 South Carolina's CSA Gov.

Signature	Signature with rank	Pre & post War DS	War Dated DS	Pre & post War ALS	War Dated ALS
$30	$	$58	$	$78	$

Magruder, John Bankhead, 1807-71   Confederate Major General

WP graduate, he was appointed Col. in charge of the artillery in and around Richmond. He repelled the attack of Genl. Butler at Big Bethel. Appointed Brig. Genl. on June 17, 1861. He kept McClellan's army in check in Yorktown. He was appointed to the Trans-Mississippi Department. He recaptured Galveston and kept the port open.

Signature	Signature with rank	Pre & post War DS	War Dated DS	Pre & post War ALS	War Dated ALS
$278	$475	$387	$	$567	$

Mahone, William, 1826-95   Confederate Major General

V.M.I. graduate. He fought at Seven Pines, Malvern Hill, 2nd Manassas where he was wounded, Fredericksburg, Chancellorsville, Gettysburg, Wilderness, Spotsylvania, & received an on the spot, battle field promotion by Gen. Lee, to Maj. Gen., for his action at the Battle of the Crater at Petersburg.

Signature	Signature with rank	Pre & post War DS	War Dated DS	Pre & post War ALS	War Dated ALS
$110	$195	$300	$	$	$

LS, 1889, imprinted letter sheet, Republican State Exec. Com., Petersburg, Va., in ink, to M.L. Robinson, Alexandria, Va., "to get places for our colored people whom I have urgently pressed..." LR Sept. 1993 $300.

S, Signature dated 1888 on the verso of his personal calling card. SR Nov. 1993 $95.

Misc.

P, Cabinet card, half view pose with arms crossed upon his chest. Stars & wreath insignia on collar & star on chest. Card has 1876 embossed seal. LR Sept. 1993 $250.

Major, James Patrick, 1836-77   Confederate Brigadier General

WP graduate, he entered C.S. service as a Staff Officer to Genl. Van Dorn. He was chief of Artillery during the siege at Vicksburg. Appointed Brig. Genl. July 21, 1863 and fought during the Red River Camaign.

Signature	Signature with rank	Pre & post War DS	War Dated DS	Pre & post War ALS	War Dated ALS
$	$	$	$	$	$

Mallory, Stephen Russell, 1813-73   Secretary of the CSN

Signature	Signature with rank	Pre & post War DS	War Dated DS	Pre & post War ALS	War Dated ALS
$	$	$	$	$	$

ALS, 1854 February 8. to Hon. W. A. Forward regarding a petition which has not been acted upon. EB August 1992 $150
S, Ornate large clip signature with state. BG Nov. 1993 $125.

Maltby, Jasper Adalmorn, 1826-67   Union General

Signature	Signature with rank	Pre & post War DS	War Dated DS	Pre & post War ALS	War Dated ALS
$	$	$	$	$	$

Maney, George Earl, 1826-1901   Confederate Brigadier General

Capt. in the 11th TN. With R.E. Lee at Cheat Mountain and Stonewall Jackson at Romney. After Shiloh, he was promoted to Brig. Genl. on April 16, 1862. He was wounded at Chattanooga, and was in command of a division during the Atlanta Campaign.

Signature	Signature with rank	Pre & post War DS	War Dated DS	Pre & post War ALS	War Dated ALS
$	$	$	$	$	$

Manigault, Arthur Middleton, 1824-86   Confederate Brigadier General
He was commissioned Captain of the North Santee Mounted Rifles, and was aide-de-camp to Beauregard in April 1861. Transferred to the Army of TN., and fought with this Army from Corinth to Nashville, where he was severly wounded in the head and saw no further action.

Signature	Signature with rank	Pre & post War DS	War Dated DS	Pre & post War ALS	War Dated ALS
$90	$	$265	$	$	$

Manning, Stephen Hart, ?-?   Union Brevet General

Signature	Signature with rank	Pre & post War DS	War Dated DS	Pre & post War ALS	War Dated ALS
$25	$	$57	$65	$	$

Mansfield, Joseph King Fenno, 1803-62   Union Major General
He died Sept. 18, 1862, of wounds rec'd. at Antietam, Md.

Signature	Signature with rank	Pre & post War DS	War Dated DS	Pre & post War ALS	War Dated ALS
$125	$185	$287	$	$425	$

Mansion, Mahlon Dickerson, 1820-95   Union General

Signature	Signature with rank	Pre & post War DS	War Dated DS	Pre & post War ALS	War Dated ALS
$20	$	$52	$	$	$

Marcy, Randolph Barnes, 1812-87   Union General

Signature	Signature with rank	Pre & post War DS	War Dated DS	Pre & post War ALS	War Dated ALS
$25	$	$	$67	$	$

Marmaduke, John Sappington, 1833-87   Confederate Major General
WP graduate, he entered C.S. service as a Col. in the Missouri Militia, and later Col. in the 3rd C.S. Infantry. For his gallant conduct during the battles of Shiloh and Prairie Grove, he was promoted to Brig. Genl. He was a cavalry commander under Price, and fought with great distinction during the Red River Campaign. He was captured at Mine Creek, KS, on October 25, 1864, and appointed Major General while still in prison.

Signature	Signature with rank	Pre & post War DS	War Dated DS	Pre & post War ALS	War Dated ALS
$90	$165	$278	$	$	$

Marshall, Humphrey, 1812-72   Confederate Brigadier General
WP graduate, he was commissioned Brig. Genl. Oct. 30, 1861. He commanded the Army of Eastern KY, which was a small force of about 1,500 men. Their chief action was at Pound Gap, March 16, 1862. He resigned his commission in June 1863.

Signature	Signature with rank	Pre & post War DS	War Dated DS	Pre & post War ALS	War Dated ALS
$95	$265	$	$457	$	$

Marshell, Charles, ?-?,   Confed. Lt. Col. A.A.G. under R.E. Lee
Drafted G.O. No. 9 for Lee to sign for his staff.

Signature	Signature with rank	Pre & post War DS	War Dated DS	Pre & post War ALS	War Dated ALS
$78	$167	$	$485	$	$

Marshell, Henry, 1805-64   Member Confederate Congress

Signature	Signature with rank	Pre War DS	War Dated DS	Pre War ALS	War Dated ALS
$45	$65	$	$	$	$

Marston, Gilman, 1811-90   Legislator & Union General

Signature	Signature with rank	Pre & post War DS	War Dated DS	Pre & post War ALS	War Dated ALS
$28	$36	$76	$	$	$

Martin, James Green, 1819-78   Confederate Brigadier General
WP graduate, he lost his right arm during the Mexican War. He fought with great distinction during the Petersburg operations. He surrendered at Waynesville, May 10, 1865.

Signature	Signature with rank	Pre & post War DS	War Dated DS	Pre & post War ALS	War Dated ALS
$95	$175	$275	$387	$	$

Martin, John Marshall, 1832-1910   Member Confederate Congress

Signature	Signature with rank	Pre & post War DS	War Dated DS	Pre & post War ALS	War Dated ALS
$40	$	$	$	$	$

Martin, William Thompson, 1823-1910   Confederate Major General
He was an Lt. Col. in the Jeff Davis Legion. He was ordered to take 250 of this command and report to Genl. Stuart for his famous " Ride around McClellan." He was Genl. Lee's aide-de-camp during the Battle of Sharpsburg, He commanded a Division of Wheeler's Corps duri ng the Atlanta Campaign.

Signature	Signature with rank	Pre & post War DS	War Dated DS	Pre & post War ALS	War Dated ALS
$90	$165	$	$	$225	$450

Martindale, John Henry, 1815-81   Union General

Signature	Signature with rank	Pre & post War DS	War Dated DS	Pre & post War ALS	War Dated ALS
$20	$	$38	$	$	$

Mason, James Murray, 1798-1871 — Conf. Commissioner to England

Signature	Signature with rank	Pre & post War DS	War Dated DS	Pre & post War ALS	War Dated ALS
$40	$68	$78	$188	$	$245

Free Frank, 1858. Addressed envelop in his hand. BG Nov. 1993 $65.

Mason, John M., 1798-1871 — Confederate diplomat

Sent by his government on a diplomatic mission to Great Britain, he was seized on the high seas by the USS Trent.

Signature	Signature with rank	Pre & post War DS	War Dated DS	Pre & post War ALS	War Dated ALS
$45	$	$	$	$167	$

ALS, Dec. 11, 1847, To Va. Congressmen Blaine and Rives pert. to copies of the Congressional Globe. SR Nov. 1993 $120.

Mason, John Sanford, 1824-97 — Union General

Signature	Signature with rank	Pre & post War DS	War Dated DS	Pre & post War ALS	War Dated ALS
$25	$	$	$	$	$

Matthies, Charles (Karl) Leopold, 1824-68 — Union General

Signature	Signature with rank	Pre & post War DS	War Dated DS	Pre & post War ALS	War Dated ALS
$	$38	$	$86	$	$

Maury, Dabney Herndon, 1822-1900 — Confederate Major General

WP graduate. He entered C.S. service as a Capt. in the C.S. Cavalry. After his gallant service at Pea Ridge, he was promoted to Brig. Genl. on March 18, 1862. He led a division , as Major Genl., with Pemberton's forces in the battle with Sherman at Chickasaw Bayou, Dec. 26, 1862. He commanded the Department of the Gulf, surrendering at Maridian, Miss., May 11, 1865.

Signature	Signature with rank	Pre & post War DS	War Dated DS	Pre & post War ALS	War Dated ALS
$72	$115	$	$267	$378	$

AES, March 14, 1864. HQ Dept. of Gulf, Mobile, Ala., signed Maj. Genl. Comdg. BG Nov 1993 $325.

Maury, Matthew Fontaine, 1806-73 Hydrographer & CSN Commander

Signature	Signature with rank	Pre & post War DS	War Dated DS	Pre & post War ALS	War Dated ALS
$78	$167	$287	$	$	$

DS, 1860. 1p. U.S. Naval Observatory, Washington, document. SK Dec. 1992 $250.
Book Signed, Astronomical Observations made During the Years 1849 & 1850 at the U.S. Naval Observatory, Washington. By M. F. Maury., U.S.N. Vol 5 Washington 1859. Signed with compliments. SK Nov. 1992 $850.

Maury, William Lewis, ?-? Confederate Naval Commander
Confederate Cruiser, CSS GEORGIA 1863.

Signature	Signature with rank	Pre & post War DS	War Dated DS	Pre & post War ALS	War Dated ALS
$	$	$	$378	$	$

Maxey, Samuel Bell, 1825-95 Confederate Major General
WP graduate. Colonel of the 9th Texas Infantry. Promoted Brig. Genl. in 1862 and fought at Port Hudson and Vicksburg. After Poison Springs, Arkansas, he was appointed Major Genl., by Genl. Kirby Smith, thou not confirmed by Davis.

Signature	Signature with rank	Pre & post War DS	War Dated DS	Pre & post War ALS	War Dated ALS
$120	$210	$198	$	$267	$

S, Clip signature with address. BG Nov. 1993 $100.

Maxwell, Augustus Emmett, 1820-1902 Member Confederate Congress

Signature	Signature with rank	Pre & post War DS	War Dated DS	Pre & post War ALS	War Dated ALS
$40	$	$87	$	$	$

Mayer, John F., 1840-1919   Confederate Clerk & autograph collector

Signature	Signature with rank	Pre & post War DS	War Dated DS	Pre & post War ALS	War Dated ALS
$	$	$	$	$	$

Meade, George Gordon, 1815-72   Union General

Signature	Signature with rank	Pre & post War DS	War Dated DS	Pre & post War ALS	War Dated ALS
$425	$650	$	$900	$	$1,225

DS, War dated Imprinted transmital form used for forwarding a presidential signed commission, signed with rank. SK April 1993 $850.
S, Large bold signature on a card. SK Dec. 1993 $675.
-, Clip signature with rank. BG Nov. 1993 $325.
-, Clip Signature with rank. SK August 1993 $400.

Meade, George, Jr. 1843-97   Author
Genl Meade's son, who wrote several books on his father.

Signature	Post War DS	Post War ALS
$	$	$

ALS, March 27, 1886 - July 9, 1888, 32pages, 5x8", Philadelphia, Pa., to Historian Isaac R. Pennypacker, pert. to General Meade and defending his actions at Gettysburg. MS Nov. 1993 $950.

Meager, Thomas Francis, 1823-67   Union General; Irish Brigade

Signature	Signature with rank	Pre & post War DS	War Dated DS	Pre & post War ALS	War Dated ALS
$43	$87	$178	$	$	$

Meeker, Edwin J., ?-?   Artist

Signature	Pre & post War DS	War Dated DS	Pre & post War ALS	War Dated ALS
$	$	$	$135	$

Meigs, Montgomery Cunningham, 1816-92   Union General

Signature	Signature with rank	Pre & post War DS	War Dated DS	Pre & post War ALS	War Dated ALS
$25	$38	$97	$250	$135	$

LS, Oct. 21, 1864. 1p. to E. L. Baker. SAG Feb. 1994 $230.

270

Memminger, Christopher Gustavus, 1803-88   Conf. Sec. of Treasury

Signature	Signature with rank	Pre & post War DS	War Dated DS	Pre & post War ALS	War Dated ALS
$78	$150	$167	$378	$346	$569

DS, Oct. 23, 1863. 1p. pert. to the employment of J.L. Jackson. SAG Feb. 1994 $400.

Menees, Thomas, 1823-1905   Member Confederate Congress

Signature	Signature with rank	Pre & post War DS	War Dated DS	Pre & post War ALS	War Dated ALS
$30	$	$	$	$	$

Mercer, Hugh Weedon, 1808-77   Confederate Brigadier General
WP graduate, he entered C.S. service as Col. of the 1st GA but soon promoted Brig. Genl. on Oct. 29, 1861. He was in command of Savannah for most of the war, but later commanded a brigade under Genl. Hardee during the Atlanta Campaign. Due to poor health, he saw no further action after the Battle of Jonesboro.

Signature	Signature with rank	Pre & post War DS	War Dated DS	Pre & post War ALS	War Dated ALS
$90	$187	$145	$	$	$

S, Clip as Brig Genl. Comdg. BG Nov. 1993 $185.

Meredith, Solomon, 1810-75   Union General

Signature	Signature with rank	Pre & post War DS	War Dated DS	Pre & post War ALS	War Dated ALS
$25	$	$	$	$	$

Merritt, Wesley, 1834-1910   Union General & Indian Fighter
Commanded the first Philippine expedition (1898).

Signature	Signature with rank	Pre & post War DS	War Dated DS	Pre & post War ALS	War Dated ALS
$85	$98	$	$178	$	$

ALS, Feb. 13, n.y., Chicago, 2pages, 8vo, Cordial sentiments and best wishes to a Miss Mason. JB Dec. 1993 $75.
S, Clip signature with rank. BG Nov. 1993 $95.

Miles, Nelson Appleton, 1839-1925   Union General & MoH recipient
Custodian of Jefferson Davis at Fortress \monroe, 1865-1866; Indian fighter, 1869-1880;
led successful campaigns against Apache, Sioux, Nez Perce' tribes; captured Geronimo;
occupied Puerto Rico in Spanish-American War.

Signature	Signature with rank	Pre & post War DS	War Dated DS	Pre & post War ALS	War Dated ALS
$45	$86	$150	$	$178	$

S, Clip signature with rank. BG Nov. 1993 $135.
Misc.
Book Authored: *Military Europe*, New York: 1898, $50.

Miles, William Porcher, 1822-99   Member Confederate Congress

Signature	Signature with rank	Pre & post War DS	War Dated DS	Pre & post War ALS	War Dated ALS
$40	$	$	$	$	$

Miller, John Franklin, 1831-86   Union General

Signature	Signature with rank	Pre & post War DS	War Dated DS	Pre & post War ALS	War Dated ALS
$20	$35	$	$135	$	$

DS, June 24, 1864. On pre-printed HQ, U.S. Forces, Nashville, Tenn. granting leave
approval. BG Nov. 1993 $110.

Miller, Samuel, 1816-90   Justice of U.S. Supreme Court
Appointed by Lincoln.

Signature	Signature with rank	Pre & post War DS	War Dated DS	Pre & post War ALS	War Dated ALS
$	$	$	$	$	$

S, Signed card. SR Nov. 1993 $45.

Miller, Samuel Augustine, 1819-90   Member Confederate Congress

Signature	Signature with rank	Pre & post War DS	War Dated DS	Pre & post War ALS	War Dated ALS
$	$40	$	$	$	$

Miller, Stephen, 1816-81   Union General

Signature	Signature with rank	Pre & post War DS	War Dated DS	Pre & post War ALS	War Dated ALS
$	$	$	$	$	$

Miller, William, 1820-1909   Confederate Brigadier General

He entered C.S. service as a Major. He led his 1st FL Infantry during Bragg's KY invasion, and was wounded at Murfreesboro. Appointed Brig. Genl. August 2, 1864, he was in command of the FL Reserve Forces until the end of the war.

Signature	Signature with rank	Pre & post War DS	War Dated DS	Pre & post War ALS	War Dated ALS
$75	$110	$	$	$	$

Milroy, Robert Huston, 1816-90   Union General

Signature	Signature with rank	Pre & post War DS	War Dated DS	Pre & post War ALS	War Dated ALS
$20	$	$67	$	$	$

Minor, Robert Dabney, 1827-91   Lieutenant Confederate Navy

Signature	Signature with rank	Pre & post War DS	War Dated DS	Pre & post War ALS	War Dated ALS
$35	$	$76	$	$	$

Mitchel, Charles Burton , 1815-64   Member Confederate Congress

Signature	Signature with rank	Pre & post War DS	War Dated DS	Pre & post War ALS	War Dated ALS
$45	$65	$	$	$	$

Mitchel, Ormsby MacKnight, 1809-62   Union General

Died of yellow fever at Beaufort, 30 October 1862. Scarce.

Signature	Signature with rank	Pre & post War DS	War Dated DS	Pre & post War ALS	War Dated ALS
$	$	$	$	$	$

Mitchell, John Grant, 1838-94   Union General

Signature	Signature with rank	Pre & post War DS	War Dated DS	Pre & post War ALS	War Dated ALS
$20	$35	$	$	$87	$

Mitchell, John K., ?-?   Commander, Confederate Navy

Signature	Signature with rank	Pre & post War DS	War Dated DS	Pre & post War ALS	War Dated ALS
$	$85	$	$	$	$

Mitchell, Margaret, 1900-49   Wrote `Gone With The Wind`
Married to Mr. John R. Marsh.

Signature	DS	ALS
$450	$1,200	$2,500

TLS, Jan. 7, 1937, 1p, 7X11", Atlanta, Ga., "I have frequently though that the last six months and their happenings might be of some interest to a psychiatrist - not, I hasten to add, with me as a patient!" HD Oct. 1993 $1300.
---, Dec. 18, 1937, 1.5pp, 3.75x5", Atlanta, "Doctor George Zeller has just sent me photographs of the Rock Island Arsenal Confederate Cemetery and the list of Georgians buried there. He told me that he was indebted to you for the information and photographs, and I thank you so much for your kindness. I hope that you have a happy Christmas." HD Oct. 1993 $940.
S, Signature "Margaret Mitchell Marsh" at top of 4x3" sheet cut from letter. HD June 1992 $275.

Mitchell, Ormsby MacKnight, 1809-62   Astronomer & Union General

Signature	Signature with rank	Pre War DS	War Dated DS	Pre War ALS	War Dated ALS
$	$	$	$	$	$

Mitchell, Robert Byington, 1823-82   Union General

Signature	Signature with rank	Pre & post War DS	War Dated DS	Pre & post War ALS	War Dated ALS
$20	$32	$	$74	$	$

Monroe, James, 1758-1831   5th U.S. President
Term of office 1817-1825.

Signature	Signature with rank	DS		ALS
$175	$250	$375		$500

S, Signature, "James Monroe" closely matted with 6.5x9" printed portrait of Monroe. HD Oct. 1993 $200.

Monroe, Thomas Bell, 1791-65   Member Confederate Congress

Signature	Signature with rank	Pre & post War DS	War Dated DS	Pre & post War ALS	War Dated ALS
$	$50	$	$	$	$

Montague, Robert Latane, 1819-80   Member Confederate Congress

Signature	Signature with rank	Pre & post War DS	War Dated DS	Pre & post War ALS	War Dated ALS
$35	$	$57	$	$	$

Montgomery, William Reading, 1801-71   Union General

Signature	Signature with rank	Pre & post War DS	War Dated DS	Pre & post War ALS	War Dated ALS
$35	$47	$63	$	$	$

Moody, Young Marshell, 1822-66   Confederate Brigadier General
He entered C.S. service as Capt. of the 11th Alabama Infantry, and was later elected Lt. Col. of the 43rd AL. He fought at Chickamauga, and was with Beauregard at Petersburg. He was severly wounded in the ankle at Drewry's Bluff, and commanded the 43rd AL after Genl. Gracie was killed. He was appointed Brig. Genl., March 4, 1865.

Signature	Signature with rank	Pre & post War DS	War Dated DS	Pre & post War ALS	War Dated ALS
$135	$210	$	$	$	$

A scarce signature.

Moore, Andrew B., 1806-73   Alabama Confederate Gov.(1857-61)

Signature	Signature with rank	Pre & post War DS	War Dated DS	Pre & post War ALS	War Dated ALS
$35	$	$87	$	$	$

Moore, James William, 1818-77   Member Confederate Congress

Signature	Signature with rank	Pre & post War DS	War Dated DS	Pre & post War ALS	War Dated ALS
$	$52	$	$	$	$

Moore, John Creed, 1824-1910   Confederate Brigadier General

WP graduate. He recruited the 2nd Texas and was elected its Colonel. He fouught with great distinction at Shiloh, and was promoted to Brig. Genl. on May 26, 1862. Captured at Vicksburg, he was exchanged and saw service under Genl. Bragg at Chattanooga. Resigned Feb. 3, 1864.

Signature	Signature with rank	Pre & post War DS	War Dated DS	Pre & post War ALS	War Dated ALS
$67	$110	$97	$	$	$

Moore, Patrick Theodore, 1821-83   Confederate Brigadier General

Colonel of the 1st Virginia, and fought under Genl. Longstreet at 1st Manassas. After being severly wounded at Manassas, he was on the staff of Genl. Johnston, and later on that of Longstreet. He was promoted Sept. 20, 1864.

Signature	Signature with rank	Pre & post War DS	War Dated DS	Pre & post War ALS	War Dated ALS
$80	$	$123	$387	$	$

Morell, George Webb, 1815-83   Union General

Signature	Signature with rank	Pre & post War DS	War Dated DS	Pre & post War ALS	War Dated ALS
$23	$38	$	$93	$65	$

Morgan, Charles Hale, 1834-75 — Union General

Signature	Signature with rank	Pre & post War DS	War Dated DS	Pre & post War ALS	War Dated ALS
$	$	$	$	$	$

Morgan, George Warhington, 1820-93 — Union General

Signature	Signature with rank	Pre & post War DS	War Dated DS	Pre & post War ALS	War Dated ALS
$	$	$	$	$	$

Morgan, James Dada, 1810-96 — Union General

Signature	Signature with rank	Pre & post War DS	War Dated DS	Pre & post War ALS	War Dated ALS
$	$	$	$	$	$

Morgan, John Hunt, 1825-64 — Confederate Brigadier General

He joined the C.S.A. in command of the Lexington Rifles of Kentucky. He was on scouting duty, and as Col. organized three companies of cavalry known as Morgan's Squadron, which operated in TN & KY. He was killed Sept. 4, 1864 at Greenville, TN.

Signature	Signature with rank	Pre War DS	War Dated DS	Pre War ALS	War Dated ALS
$675	$875	$2,250	$2,850	$	$4,750

An extremely rare signature.

Morgan, John Tyler, 1825-1907 — Confederate Brigadier General

Entered C.S. service as a Private in the Cahaba Rifles in 1861. Later he recruited and was appointed Col. of the 51st Alabama Partiasan Rangers. He fought with much distinction at 1st Manassas, Murfreesboro, and Chickamauga.

Signature	Signature with rank	Pre & post War DS	War Dated DS	Pre & post War ALS	War Dated ALS
$76	$167	$138	$	$325	$3,875

ALS, May 23, 1877. 1.5p. , 4to., Selma, Ala. pert. to Chattanooga, Tenn. battles. BG
Nov. 1993 $295.

Morgan, Simson Harris, 1821-64　　　　Member Confederate Congress

Signature	Signature with rank	Pre War DS	War Dated DS	Pre War ALS	War Dated ALS
$40	$	$87	$	$	$245

Morgan, Thomas Jefferson, 1839-1902　　　　Union Brevet General

Signature	Signature with rank	Pre & post War DS	War Dated DS	Pre & post War ALS	War Dated ALS
$	$28	$	$	$56	$

Morris, Charles M., ?-?　　　　Confederate Naval Commander
Confederate Cruiser, CSS FLORIDA 1864.

Signature	Signature with rank	Pre & post War DS	War Dated DS	Pre & post War ALS	War Dated ALS
$78	$	$	$387	$	$

Morris, William Hopkins, 1827-1900　　　　Union General

Signature	Signature with rank	Pre & post War DS	War Dated DS	Pre & post War ALS	War Dated ALS
$35	$47	$	$	$	$

Morris, William Walton, 1801-65　　　　Union General

Signature	Signature with rank	Pre & post War DS	War Dated DS	Pre & post War ALS	War Dated ALS
$30	$	$47	$87	$	$

Morse, Henry Bagg, 1836-74　　　　Union Officer, N.Y. Maj. 114th

Signature	Signature with rank	Pre & post War DS	War Dated DS	Pre & post War ALS	War Dated ALS
$	$	$	$	$	$

Morse, Samuel F.B., 1791-1872   Portrait artist & inventor

Founder and first President of the National Academy of Design. Invented Morse Code for the use with the telegraph.

Signature	Pre & post War DS	War Dated DS	Pre & post War ALS	War Dated ALS
$145	$1,200	$	$985	$

ALS, Feb. 19, 1856, 1p., to Henry Tuckerman, an inventation. SR Nov. 1993 $695.
DS, Jan. 1, 1843, 1p., Partly-printed document signed "Sam'l F.B. Morse" as President of the National Academy of Design. LP Sept. 1993 $1,500.
S, Clip signature and CDV. SR Nov. 1993 $195.

Morton, Jackson, 1794-1874   Member Confederate Congress

Signature	Signature with rank	Pre & post War DS	War Dated DS	Pre & post War ALS	War Dated ALS
$25	$	$	$	$	$

Morton, James St. Clair, 1829-64   Union General

He was killed in action at Petersburg, VA., June 17, 1864.

Signature	Signature with rank	Pre & post War DS	War Dated DS	Pre & post War ALS	War Dated ALS
$75	$124	$175	$278	$	$

Morton, Oliver Perry, 1823-77   Governor of Indianna

Signature	Signature with rank	Pre & post War DS	War Dated DS	Pre & post War ALS	War Dated ALS
$28	$38	$87	$137	$	$

Mosby, John Singleton, 1833-1916   Confederate Officer

Signature	Signature with rank	Pre & post War DS	War Dated DS	Pre & post War ALS	War Dated ALS
$250	$	$410	$	$470	$

ALS, May 26, 1904. 1.5pp., 4to., Selma, Ala. pert. to a fraudulent watch bill & Special Agent Business. BG Nov. 1993 $850.
---, Feb 13, 1906, 1p, "I had not said a word about Gen Lee's capacity as a General-only said that his report was wrong & that if he thought Hooker would stay in VA when he was in PA he was incompetent to command an army." PAC Dec. 1993 $500.
---, Dec. 23, 1905, 1p, w/envelope, "I have at last found what I have been looking for for 10 years - it is Gen Lee's letter book on the Gettysburg Campaign - Gordon McCabe has it. It confirms all that I have written in defense of Stuart." PAC Dec. 1993 $600.
---, Sept. 20, 1880, 1p as US Counsel, "If Hancock elected, I will turn in my resignation ... Brook in Warrenton Speech said all VA for Hancock. PAC Dec. 1993 $3,500.

---, Dec. 19th "a few minutes ago I had a talk (friendly) with col. Kenn____ who was adj. of Lowells Regt. 2nd Mass. He told me that he was at Front Royal and saw our men hung." PAC Dec. 1993 $1,100.

---, Feb. 6, 1906, 1pp, Department of Justice, Washington, D.C. to Captain Sam Chapman, concerning the controversy of the whereabouts of J.E.B. Stuart during the Battle of Gettysburg. GH Nov. 1993 $3,500.

---, March 21, 1910, 2pg, Department of Justice, Washington, D.C., to Captain Sam Chapman attacking A.P.Hill and Heth for wandering into Gettysburg and thus causing the battle. GH Nov. 1993 $3,500.

---, Sept. 14, 1914, The Alamo, Washington, D.C., to Captain Chapman regarding Mosby's college days at the University of Virginia when he war Arrested and placed in jail in Charlottesville. GH Nov. 1993 $2,500.

---, May 26, 1906, Department of Justice, Washington, D.C., to Captain Sam Chapman regarding what it means to be a Rebel. GH Nov. 1993 $2,500.

---, Oct. 16, 1907, Department of Justice, Washington, D.C., to Captain Sam Chapman concerning the controversy of Stuart's whereabouts at the Battle of Gettysburg. GH Nov. 1993 $3,500.

---, June 1, 1906, The Mosby Drug Company, Bedford City, Va., 2pp., to Capt. Sam Chapman, regarding the death of some of Mosby's Rangers. GH Nov. 1993 $1,750.

S, Clip. NLM Nov. 1992 $325.

-, Envelope addressed to Samuel Chapman and signed by Mosby. PAC Dec. 1993 $275 - eight example sold @ $275.

PS, Photograph 3 x 5" signed. JH May 1992. $850.

Misc.

Reunion Ribbon - 4th, Mosby's Men Baltimore, Oct. 14, 1897. PAC Dec. 1993 $800.
Reunion Ribbon - 5th, Mosby's Men Baltimore, Oct. 25, 1898. PAC Dec. 1993 $900.
Reunion photograph - 1896, in poor condition, PAC Dec. 1993 $1,400.

Over three hunderd post war, ALSs, were placed on the market by Pearson Auction Company (PAC), Catlett, VA, during the spring and in Dec. 1993. War dated material continue to be quite rare.

Mosler, Henry, 1841-1920   Artist and War Correspondent

Signature	Pre & post War DS	War Dated DS	Pre & post War ALS	War Dated ALS
$	$	$	$146	$

Mott, Gershom, 1822-84   Union General

Signature	Signature with rank	Pre & post War DS	War Dated DS	Pre & post War ALS	War Dated ALS
$25	$48	$78	$110	$	$

Mott, Samuel Rolla, ?-1899   Union Officer

Signature	Signature with rank	Pre & post War DS	War Dated DS	Pre & post War ALS	War Dated ALS
$	$	$	$	$	$

Mouton, John Jacques Alfred Alexander, 1829-64 Confed. Brig General
WP graduate. He entered C.S.service as Col. of the 18th Louisiana Infantry. He was severly wounded at Shiloh. On April 8, 1864 at Mansfield, La., while leading his Louisiana Brigade he was killed.

Signature	Signature with rank	Pre War DS	War Dated DS	Pre War ALS	War Dated ALS
$275	$	$	$	$	$

An extremely rare signature.

Mower, Joseph Anthony, 1827-70   Union General

Signature	Signature with rank	Pre & post War DS	War Dated DS	Pre & post War ALS	War Dated ALS
$28	$35	$68	$78	$89	$

Munford, Thomas Taylor, 1831-1918   Colonel 2d Virginia Cavalry
He was photographed wreaing a Brigadier General, though often recommended for brigadiership he never got one. (Boatner's The Civil Dictionary states, " Appointed B.G.,
C.S.A. in Nov. '64 he took command of Fitzhugh Lee's division and fought at Five Forks, High Bridge, Sayler's Creek, and Appomattox." He berated Jackson as insane for pursuing Banks instead of Shields

Signature	Signature with rank	Pre & post War DS	War Dated DS	Pre & post War ALS	War Dated ALS
$140	$150	$	$	$	$

Munnerlyn, Charles James, 1822-98   Member Confederate Congress

Signature	Signature with rank	Pre & post War DS	War Dated DS	Pre & post War ALS	War Dated ALS
$38	$	$	$	$	$

Murray, John Porry, 1830-95   Member Confederate Congress

Signature	Signature with rank	Pre & post War DS	War Dated DS	Pre & post War ALS	War Dated ALS
$	$45	$	$	$	$

Muse, W. T., (?-?)   Commander Confederate Navy

Signature	Signature with rank	Pre & post War DS	War Dated DS	Pre & post War ALS	War Dated ALS
$	$	$	$278	$	$

Mudd, Samuel A., 1833-83   Physician, prisoner

Signature	Pre & post War DS	War Dated DS	Pre & post War ALS	War Dated ALS
$350	$	$	$	$

N

Nagle, James, 1822-66   Union General

Signature	Signature with rank	Pre & post War DS	War Dated DS	Pre & post War ALS	War Dated ALS
$26	$38	$65	$98	$	$

Naglee, Henry Morris, 1815-86   Union General

Signature	Signature with rank	Pre & post War DS	War Dated DS	Pre & post War ALS	War Dated ALS
$25	$	$58	$85	$	$

Nast, Thomas, 1840-1902   Artist, Cartoonist Harper's Weekly
Created the symbolic Democratic donkey and Republican elephant, 1874.

Signature	Pre & post War DS	War Dated DS	Pre & post War ALS	War Dated ALS
$125	$185	$	$	$

S, Bold signature "Th. Nast/ March 10, 1873" on small card. JB Dec. 1993 $110.

Negley, James Scott, 1826-1901   Union General

Signature	Signature with rank	Pre & post War DS	War Dated DS	Pre & post War ALS	War Dated ALS
$20	$	$48	$78	$67	$

Neill, Thomas Hewsom, 1826-85   Union General

Signature	Signature with rank	Pre & post War DS	War Dated DS	Pre & post War ALS	War Dated ALS
$	$	$	$76	$	$

Nelson, Allison, 1822-62   Confederate Brigadier General

Col. of the 10th Texas Infantry. He later served under Genl. Hindman in Arkansas, and was appointed Brig. Genl. on Sept. 12, 1862. He died Oct. 7, 1862, near Austin, Arkansas of natural causes.

Signature	Signature with rank	Pre War DS	War Dated DS	Pre War ALS	War Dated ALS
$190	$300	$	$	$	$

A scarce signature.

Nelson, William, 1824-62   Union General

Signature	Signature with rank	Pre War DS	War Dated DS	Pre War ALS	War Dated ALS
$75	$148	$	$	$	$

Newton John, 1822-95   Union General

Signature	Signature with rank	Pre & post War DS	War Dated DS	Pre & post War ALS	War Dated ALS
$22	$38	$43	$	$	$97

Nicholls, Francis Redding Tillou, 1834-1912   Confed. Brig. General
WP graduate. He was a Captain in the "Phoenix Guards." He fought with much distinction at 1st Manassas, and was with Genl. Jackson in the Valley Campaign. He was wounded and captured during the Battle of Winchester. He was again wounded at Chancellorsville.

Signature	Signature with rank	Pre & post War DS	War Dated DS	Pre & post War ALS	War Dated ALS
$67	$97	$127	$	$	$

S, Clip. BG Nov. 1993 $85.

Nickerson, Franklin Stillman, 1826-1917   Union General

Signature	Signature with rank	Pre & post War DS	War Dated DS	Pre & post War ALS	War Dated ALS
$25	$	$48	$	$92	$

Nisbet, EuGeneralius Aristides, 1803-71 Member Confederate Congress

Signature	Signature with rank	Pre & post War DS	War Dated DS	Pre & post War ALS	War Dated ALS
$40	$56	$	$	$	$

Norton, Nimrod Lindsay, 1830-1903   Member Confederate Congress

Signature	Signature with rank	Pre & post War DS	War Dated DS	Pre & post War ALS	War Dated ALS
$35	$	$	$	$87	$

Northrop, Lucius Bellinger, 1811-94   Conf. Brig. General & Physician
WP graduate. He was appointed Commissary General, with the rank of Col., by Pres. Davis. He was appointed Brig. Genl. on Nov. 26, 1864. He was relieved of all duty in Feb. 1865.

Signature	Signature with rank	Pre & post War DS	War Dated DS	Pre & post War ALS	War Dated ALS
$95	$185	$278	$	$	$

O

Ochiltree, William Beck, 1811-67   Member Confederate Congress

Signature	Signature with rank	Pre & post War DS	War Dated DS	Pre & post War ALS	War Dated ALS
$45	$	$76	$	$98	$

Oglesby, Richard James, 1824-99   Union General

Signature	Signature with rank	Pre & post War DS	War Dated DS	Pre & post War ALS	War Dated ALS
$28	$38	$65	$	$87	$

S, Clipped signature, w/ rank. SK Feb. 1994 $40.

Oldham, William Simpson, 1813-68   Member Confederate Congress

Signature	Signature with rank	Pre & post War DS	War Dated DS	Pre & post War ALS	War Dated ALS
$38	$	$	$	$	$

Oliver, John Morrison, 1828-72   Union General

Signature	Signature with rank	Pre & post War DS	War Dated DS	Pre & post War ALS	War Dated ALS
$20	$	$45	$76	$	$

O'Neal, Edward Asbury, 1818-90   Confederate Brigadier General

Elected Major of the 9th Alabama Infantry in 1861. He was wounded at Seven Pines and at Boonsboro. O'neal fought with great distinction at Chancellorsville and Gettysburg. Appointed Brig. Genl. by Genl. Lee, but President Davis cancelled the appointment. Postwar Gov. of Alabama.

Signature	Signature with rank	Pre & post War DS	War Dated DS	Pre & post War ALS	War Dated ALS
$	$	$	$	$	$

O'Sullivan, Timothy, ? - ?   Civil War Photographer

Signature	Pre & post War DS	War Dated DS	Pre & post War ALS	War Dated ALS
$150	$287	$	$	$

Albumen prints range between $250 to $800, depending on subject matter.

Opdycke, Emerson, 1830-84   Union General

Signature	Signature with rank	Pre & post War DS	War Dated DS	Pre & post War ALS	War Dated ALS
$20	$38	$	$85	$87	$

Ord, Edward Otho Cresap, 1818-83   Union General

Signature	Signature with rank	Pre & post War DS	War Dated DS	Pre & post War ALS	War Dated ALS
$28	$35	$	$145	$	$

Orme, William Ward, 1832-66   Union General

Signature	Signature with rank	Pre & post War DS	War Dated DS	Pre & post War ALS	War Dated ALS
$35	$45	$	$	$	$

Orr, James Lawrence, 1822-73   Member Confederate Congress

Signature	Signature with rank	Pre & post War DS	War Dated DS	Pre & post War ALS	War Dated ALS
$	$45	$	$	$	$

Orr, Jehu Amaziah, 1828-1921   Member Confederate Congress

Signature	Signature with rank	Pre & post War DS	War Dated DS	Pre & post War ALS	War Dated ALS
$30	$	$57	$	$	$

Osborn, Thomas Ogden, 1832-1904   Union General

Signature	Signature with rank	Pre & post War DS	War Dated DS	Pre & post War ALS	War Dated ALS
$20	$38	$74	$98	$	$

Osterhaus, Peter Joseph, 1823-1905   Union General

Signature	Signature with rank	Pre & post War DS	War Dated DS	Pre & post War ALS	War Dated ALS
$28	$42	$76	$	$	$225

Otis, Elwell Stephan, 1838-1909   Union Brevet General

Signature	Signature with rank	Pre & post War DS	War Dated DS	Pre & post War ALS	War Dated ALS
$20	$	$	$	$	$

Otis, Harrison Gray, 1837-1917   Union Officer

Signature	Signature with rank	Pre & post War DS	War Dated DS	Pre & post War ALS	War Dated ALS
$22	$42	$65	$	$	$

Ould, Robert, 1820-82   Confederate Colonel for POW exchange

Signature	Signature with rank	Pre & post War DS	War Dated DS	Pre & post War ALS	War Dated ALS
$58	$97	$134	$	$	$

S, War period clip. BG Nov. 1993 $60.

Oury, Granville Henderson, 1825-91   Member Confederate Congress

Signature	Signature with rank	Pre & post War DS	War Dated DS	Pre & post War ALS	War Dated ALS
$25	$	$64	$	$	$

Owen, Joshua Thomas, 1821-87   Union General

Signature	Signature with rank	Pre & post War DS	War Dated DS	Pre & post War ALS	War Dated ALS
$20	$37	$	$	$	$

Owen, Robert Dale, 1801-77   Reformer

Signature	Pre & post War DS	War Dated DS	Pre & post War ALS	War Dated ALS
$	$	$	$	$

Owens, James Byeram, 1816-89   Member Confederate Congress

Signature	Signature with rank	Pre & post War DS	War Dated DS	Pre & post War ALS	War Dated ALS
$40	$	$75	$	$	$

P

Paine, Charles Jackson, 1833-1916   Union General

Signature	Signature with rank	Pre & post War DS	War Dated DS	Pre & post War ALS	War Dated ALS
$20	$	$48	$87	$	$

Paine, Eleazer Arthur, 1815-82   Union General

Signature	Signature with rank	Pre & post War DS	War Dated DS	Pre & post War ALS	War Dated ALS
$	$38	$64	$78	$	$

Paine, Halbert Eleazer, 1826-1905   Union General

Signature	Signature with rank	Pre & post War DS	War Dated DS	Pre & post War ALS	War Dated ALS
$	$35	$58	$	$	$167

Palmer, Innis Newton, 1824-1900   Union General

Signature	Signature with rank	Pre & post War DS	War Dated DS	Pre & post War ALS	War Dated ALS
$25	$38	$	$67	$	$

Palmer, John McCauley, 1817-1900   Union General
Illinois governor (1869-73) and senator (1891-97)

Signature	Signature with rank	Pre & post War DS	War Dated DS	Pre & post War ALS	War Dated ALS
$	$	$	$	$	$

DS, Dec. 31, 1866, 1p., 7.5x13.25" a construction deed for the Ill. Central Railroad Company. MS Nov. 1993 $95.

Palmer, Joseph Benjamin, 1825-90   Confederate Brigadier General
Col. of the 18th TN. He was captured at Fort Donelson, and after he was exchanged, fought with great distinction at Murfreesboro. Appointed Brig. Genl. on Nov. 15, 1864, he was wounded five times.

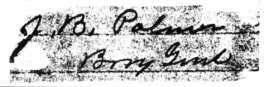

Signature	Signature with rank	Pre & post War DS	War Dated DS	Pre & post War ALS	War Dated ALS
$78	$167	$	$	$238	$

Palmerston, Viscount, 1784-1865   Confederate Prime Minister To G.B.

Signature	Signature with rank	Pre & post War DS	War Dated DS	Pre & post War ALS	War Dated ALS
$45	$	$	$	$	$278

Page, Richard Lucian, 1807-1901   Confederate Brigadier General
He was given the rank of Commander, C.SN. in June 1861. On March 1, 1864, he was appointed Brig. Genl., and was assigned to the defenses at Mobile Bay. He was captured after the fall of Mobile, and not released from Fort Delaware until July 1865.

Signature	Signature with rank	Pre & post War DS	War Dated DS	Pre & post War ALS	War Dated ALS
$85	$143	$178	$	$	$

Page, Thomas J., ?-?   Capt., CSN
Skipper of Iron Clad "Stonewall Jackson"

Signature	Signature with rank	Pre & post War DS	War Dated DS	Pre & post War ALS	War Dated ALS
$78	$145	$167	$	$	$

Parke, John Grubb, 1827-1900   Union General

Signature	Signature with rank	Pre & post War DS	War Dated DS	Pre & post War ALS	War Dated ALS
$28	$42	$	$78	$	$

Parker, Ely Samuel, 1828-95   Union Brevet General

Signature	Signature with rank	Pre & post War DS	War Dated DS	Pre & post War ALS	War Dated ALS
$20	$32	$	$	$145	$

Parker, William Harwar, 1826-96   Lt. Com. Confederate Navy

Signature	Signature with rank	Pre & post War DS	War Dated DS	Pre & post War ALS	War Dated ALS
$67	$	$	$	$	$

Parsons, Lewis Baldwin, 1818-1907   Union General

Signature	Signature with rank	Pre & post War DS	War Dated DS	Pre & post War ALS	War Dated ALS
$25	$40	$75	$98	$	$

Parson, Mosby Monroe, 1822-65   Confederate Major General
Appointed Brig. General on November 5, 1862, he fought with much distinction at Elkhorn and in the Arkansas campaigns. He saw service with Genl. Taylor in the Red River campaign, and was later appointed Major Genl. by Kirby Smith. Never surrendered and went to Mexico, killed by Juaristas, Aug. 15, 1865, near China on the San Juan River.

Signature	Signature with rank	Pre & post War DS	War Dated DS	Pre & post War ALS	War Dated ALS
$150	$245	$	$	$	$

Patrick, Marsena Rudolph, 1811-88   Union General

Known as the police chief of the Army of the Potomac.

Signature	Signature with rank	Pre & post War DS	War Dated DS	Pre & post War ALS	War Dated ALS
$26	$38	$	$73	$78	$110

ALS, May 14, 1869, 1p., 5x7.75", Pawling, N.Y. requests details on an appropriation bill. MS Nov. 1993 $70.

Patterson, Francis Engle, 1821-62   Union General

He was killed while cleaning his pistol, while at Fairfax, VA. He was the son of General Robert Patterson. Rare.

Signature	Signature with rank	Pre & post War DS	War Dated DS	Pre & post War ALS	War Dated ALS
$28	$78	$	$	$	$

Paul, Gabriel Rene, 1813-86   Union General

Signature	Signature with rank	Pre & post War DS	War Dated DS	Pre & post War ALS	War Dated ALS
$25	$	$	$	$	$

Paulding, Hiram, 1797-1878   Union Naval Officer

Signature	Signature with rank	Pre & post War DS	War Dated DS	Pre & post War ALS	War Dated ALS
$	$45	$	$167	$	$

Paxton, Elisha Franklin "Bull", 1828-63   Confederate General

Lt. in the Rocbridge Rifles. He was later a Major on the Staff of Genl. Stonewall Jackson, and appointed Brig. Genl. by Jackson on Nov. 1, 1862. Paxton led his "Stonewall" Brigade in only two battles before he himself was klled 3 May 1863 at Chancellorsville, Va.

Signature	Signature with rank	Pre War DS	War Dated DS	Pre War ALS	War Dated ALS
$350	$487	$1,400	$	$	$

DS, Pre-war legal document signed twice. BS Nov. 1993 $1,200.

An extremely rare signature.

Payne, Eugene Beauharnais, 1835-1910   Union Brevet General
2nd Lt. Chicago Zouaves; Capt. - Bvt. B.G. 37th Ill.

Signature	Signature with rank	Pre & post War DS	War Dated DS	Pre & post War ALS	War Dated ALS
$	$	$	$	$	$

Payne, William Henry Fitzhugh, 1830-1904   Confed. Brig. General
V.M.I. graduate, he enlisted C.S. service as a Private. He was an efficient cavalry commander with the Army of Northern Virginia. During the course of the war, he was wounded and captured a total of three times. The last time he was wounded was at Five Forks, he was later captured in Richmond , while recovering and returned to Johnson's Island.

Signature	Signature with rank	Pre & post War DS	War Dated DS	Pre & post War ALS	War Dated ALS
$80	$165	$145	$378	$	$

Pearce, Nicholas B., 1816-94   Confederate Militia Brigadier General
In May 1861 Ark. State Brig. Genl., he raised troops and fought at Wilson's Creek. He was named Chief Comsy. of the Indian Territory in Dec. of that year, apparently with the CSA rank of Major. He was assigned as a Brig. Genl., by Kirby Smith in the Trans-Miss. Dept. - Listed by Cullum & Wright, however he is not so listed by Wood & C.M.H.

Signature	Signature with rank	Pre & post War DS	War Dated DS	Pre & post War ALS	War Dated ALS
$40	$75	$128	$267	$	$

Peck, John James, 1821-78   Union General
Appointed Brig. Genl. Aug. 9, 1861. In the beginning of the Peninsular campaign he led 3, 1, IV at Yorktown, Williamsburg, and Fair Oaks. He was seriously injured while in command of the VII Dept. of Va. and N.C. at Suffolk, Va.

Signature	Signature with rank	Pre & post War DS	War Dated DS	Pre & post War ALS	War Dated ALS
$	$34	$	$78	$	$

Peck, William Raine, 1818-71   Confederate Brigadier General

A private in the 9th Louisiana Infantry. He served with great distinction in almost every battle with the Army of Northern Virginia. Genl. Peck's appointment to the grade of Brig. Genl. was on Feb. 18, 1865.

Signature	Signature with rank	Pre & post War DS	War Dated DS	Pre & post War ALS	War Dated ALS
$80	$135	$	$	$	$

Pegram, John, 1832-65   Confederate Brigadier General

WP graduate. He enttered C.S. service as a Lt. Col. Captured at Rich Mountain, he was later a Chief Engineer on the Staff of Genl. Beauregard. As Brig. Genl., he fought with great distinction at Murfreesboro and Chickamauga. Genl. Pegram was killed during a skirmish at Hatcher's Run on February 6, 1865.

Signature	Signature with rank	Pre War DS	War Dated DS	Pre War ALS	War Dated ALS
$650	$878	$985	$1,788	$	$

An extremely rare signature.

Pegram, R. B., 1811-94   Captain Confederate Navy

Signature	Signature with rank	Pre & post War DS	War Dated DS	Pre & post War ALS	War Dated ALS
$	$78	$	$168	$	$

Pemberton, John Clifford, 1814-81   Confederate Lt. General

WP graduate. He entered C.S. service as a Major and Cheif of Virginia Artillery. He advanced to the rank of Lt. Genl., and was sent to the Department of Mississippi and East Louisiana, where he took chief command of all the troops therein. He surrendered Vicksburg to Grant on July 4, 1863, and after the exchange, he resigned his commission. In May 1864, with the rank of Lt. Col., he was given command of the artillery defenses att Richmond, where he served until the end of the war. Originator of *Coca Cola*.

Signature	Signature with rank	Pre & post War DS	War Dated DS	Pre & post War ALS	War Dated ALS
$90	$187	$458	$595	$	$

Pender, William Dorsey, 1834-63   Confederate Major General

WP graduate, he entered C.S. service as a Col. in the 6th North Carolina Infantry. He fought with great distinction at Seven Pines, and was promoted to Brig. Genl. on June 3, 1862 for his gallantry in battle. He was wounded three times during Chancellorsville. He died July 18, 1863 of wounds rec'd at Gettysburg, Pa.

Signature	Signature with rank	Pre War DS	War Dated DS	Pre War ALS	War Dated ALS
$500	$900	$1,200	$	$	$

S, 1861 envelope add. by him to Mrs. W. D. Pender, CDS & Paid 5. BG Nov. 1993 $575.

Pendleton, Anzolette E., "Sandie," 1840-64   Confederate staff officer

Who at the age of twenty-two won the confidence, admiration, and affection of Stonewall Jackson. Lt. Colonel Pendleton died Sept. 23, 1864, from a bullet through the abdomen at the Battle of Fisher Hill.

Signature	Signature with rank	Pre War DS	War Dated DS	Pre War ALS	War Dated ALS
$200	$350	$	$1,200	$	$

Pendleton, William Nelson, 1809-83   Confederate Brig. General

WP graduate, he entered C.S. service as a Capt. in the Rockbridge Artillery. He was Genl. J.E. Johnston's Chief of Artillery, and served in the Army of Northern Virgina from 1st Manassas to Appomattox.

W. N. Pendleton

Signature	Signature with rank	Pre & post War DS	War Dated DS	Pre & post War ALS	War Dated ALS
$165	$250	$375	$	$	$

Pennypacker, Galusha, 1844-1916   Union General

Signature	Signature with rank	Pre & post War DS	War Dated DS	Pre & post War ALS	War Dated ALS
$35	$50	$	$	$	$

Penrose, William Henry, 1832-1903   Union General

Signature	Signature with rank	Pre & post War DS	War Dated DS	Pre & post War ALS	War Dated ALS
$20	$	$	$	$	$

Perrin, Abner Monroe, 1827-64   Confederate Brig General

Captain of the 14th South Carolina, he saw service at Seven Days, Cedar Mountain, Harper's Ferry, and Fredericksburg. He led a brigade at Gettysburg, and was promoted to Brigade Genl. Sept. 10, 1863. During the Battle of Spotsylvania he was killed May 12, 1864 at the "Bloody Angle."

Signature	Signature with rank	Pre War DS	War Dated DS	Pre War ALS	War Dated ALS
$325	$500	$	$	$	$

A scarce signature.

Perry, Edward Aylesworth, 1831-89   Confederate Brig. General

He entered the C.S. service as a Captain of the 2nd Florida Infantry. He was severely wounded during the Seven Days Battles and at the Wilderness. At the end of the war he was in command of a reserve force in Alabama.

Signature	Signature with rank	Pre & post War DS	War Dated DS	Pre & post War ALS	War Dated ALS
$85	$	$	$575	$	$

Perry, M. S., 1814-65   Flda Gov. and Colonel of the 7th Florida

Signature	Signature with rank	Pre & post War DS	War Dated DS	Pre & post War ALS	War Dated ALS
$65	$90	$135	$478	$	$

Perry, William Flank, 1823-1901   Confederate Brigadier General

Enlisted as a private in the 44th Alabama, then elected its Major. He fought with great distinction at Sharpsburg, Gettysburg, Chickamauaga, and Spotsylvania. He was not commissioned Brig. Genl. until Feb. 21, 1865.

Signature	Signature with rank	Pre & post War DS	War Dated DS	Pre & post War ALS	War Dated ALS
$75	$118	$	$367	$278	$

Pettigrew, James Johnston, 1828-63   Confederate Brigadier General
He entered C.S. service as an officer in the Hampton Legion. He was wounded at Seven
Pines and taken prisoner.   After his exchange, he saw action at Kinston and
Goldsborough, N.C. He was Senior Brigadier under Heath. He was gravely wounded in
the retreat from Gettysburg and died 17 July 1863 of wounds recd. at Falling Waters,
Md.

Signature	Signature with rank	Pre War DS	War Dated DS	Pre War ALS	War Dated ALS
$150	$375	$487	$	$	$

Pettus, Edmund Winston, 1821-1907   Confederate Brigadier General
He entered C.S. service as a Major in the 20th Alabama. He was captured at Port
Gibson. Mississippi., he managed to escape but was later recaptured at Vicksburg. After
being exchanged, he was promoted to Brig. Genl., Sept. 18, 1863. He fought with great
distinction at Chattanooga and was Genl. Hood in TN.

Signature	Signature with rank	Pre & post War DS	War Dated DS	Pre & post War ALS	War Dated ALS
$95	$175	$	$1,150	$	$3,875

S, Clip signature with list of battles participated in. BG Nov. 1993 $165.

Pettus, John J., 1813-67   Mississippi War Gov

Signature	Signature with rank	Pre & post War DS	War Dated DS	Pre & post War ALS	War Dated ALS
$65	$	$950	$1,578	$	$

Phelps, John Smith, 1814-86   Union General

Signature	Signature with rank	Pre & post War DS	War Dated DS	Pre & post War ALS	War Dated ALS
$20	$	$58	$	$	$

Phelps, John Wolcott, 1813-85   Union General

Signature	Signature with rank	Pre & post War DS	War Dated DS	Pre & post War ALS	War Dated ALS
$22	$32	$	$	$	$

Phillips, Wendell, 1881-84   President of Anti-Slavery Society

Signature	Pre & post War DS	War Dated DS	Pre & post War ALS	War Dated ALS
$30	$48	$	$75	$

Philppoteaux, Paul, 1846-1913   Artist
Painted the Cyclorama of the Battle of Gettysburg, 1884, 25x375 feet, (GNPS).

Signature	DS	ALS
$100	$	$

Piatt, Abram Sanders, 1821-1908   Union General

Signature	Signature with rank	Pre & post War DS	War Dated DS	Pre & post War ALS	War Dated ALS
$22	$38	$	$68	$73	$

Pickett, George Edward, 1825-75   Confederate Major General
WP graduate, he entered C.S. service as a Colonel in charge of the defenses of the lower Rappahannock. He fought with distinction in the Peninsula campaign, and was badly wounded at Gaine's Mill. Commander of the famous Pickett's Charge at Gettysburg, which devasted his Division. He was again defeated at Five Forks, he was relieved of command after the Battle of Sayler's Creek.

Signature	Signature with rank	Pre & post War DS	War Dated DS	Pre & post War ALS	War Dated ALS
$950	$1,500	$1,872	$3,785	$3,115	$

Pickett, John Thomas, 1822-84 Confederate Comm. To Mexico 1861-62
LOC. papers, 1849-84. ca. 4,000items.

Signature	Signature with rank	Pre & post War DS	War Dated DS	Pre & post War ALS	War Dated ALS
$	$	$76	$	$	$

Pierce, Byron Root, 1829-1924   Union General

Signature	Signature with rank	Pre & post War DS	War Dated DS	Pre & post War ALS	War Dated ALS
$30	$45	$	$	$78	$175

Pierce, Franklin, 1804-69   U.S. President
LOC. papers, 1820-69. ca. 2,300 items.

Signature	Signature with rank	Pre & post War DS	War Dated DS	Pre & post War ALS	War Dated ALS
$275	$	$750	$	$1,650	$

Pike, Albert, 1809-91   Confederate Brigadier General
Appionted Brig. Genl. on August 15, 1861, to negotiate a treaty with the Indians of the Five Nations. He was in command of the Department of Indian Territory, and led his Indian Force at Pea Ridge, Ark. He resigned his commission on July 12, 1862, he protest of how the Indians were used in the Confederate cause.

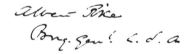

Signature	Signature with rank	Pre & post War DS	War Dated DS	Pre & post War ALS	War Dated ALS
$80	$145	$165	$	$390	$

DS, July 9, 1879. Check signed. BG Nov. 1993 $175.

Pile, William Anderson, 1829-89   Union General

Signature	Signature with rank	Pre & post War DS	War Dated DS	Pre & post War ALS	War Dated ALS
$	$35	$	$	$	$

Pillow, Gideon Johnson, 1806-78, Confederate Brigadier General

Brig. Genl., July 9, 1861. He was second in command at Fort Donelson, and for his inept handling of the surrender was suspended from duty and never given another command.

Signature	Signature with rank	Pre & post War DS	War Dated DS	Pre & post War ALS	War Dated ALS
$90	$135	$	$	$	$

Pinkerton, Allan, 1819-84 Detective, Org. US Secret Service

Signature	Pre & post War DS	War Dated DS	Pre & post War ALS	War Dated ALS
$250	$700	$	$1,250	$

Pitcher, Thomas Gamble, 1824-95 Union General

Signature	Signature with rank	Pre & post War DS	War Dated DS	Pre & post War ALS	War Dated ALS
$	$30	$45	$65	$	$

Pleasonton, Alfred, 1824-97 Union General

Signature	Signature with rank	Pre & post War DS	War Dated DS	Pre & post War ALS	War Dated ALS
$20	$	$	$	$78	$

Plummer, Joseph Bennett, 1816-62 Union General

WP graduate. He was wounded at Wilson Creek and died from this wound nearly a year later.

Signature	Signature with rank	Pre War DS	War Dated DS	Pre War ALS	War Dated ALS
$85	$	$	$	$	$

Poe, Orlando Metcalfe, 1832-95 Union General

Signature	Signature with rank	Pre & post War DS	War Dated DS	Pre & post War ALS	War Dated ALS
$20	$	$	$74	$	$

300

Polignac, Camillus J., 1832-1913 — Confederate Major General

Entered as a Lt. Col. on the Staff of Genl. Beauregard. He was appointed Brig. Genl. Jan. 10, 1863, and Major Genl. April 8, 1864. His service was primarily in Louisiana; he fought with much distinction at Mansfield and Pleasant Hill.

Signature	Signature with rank	Pre & post War DS	War Dated DS	Pre & post War ALS	War Dated ALS
$60	$95	$	$	$185	$

Polk, Leonidas, 1806-1864 — Confederate Lieutenant General

Entered as a Major genl. on June 25, 1861. He was assigned toi the command of the Western Department No. 2, but was replaced by Genl A.S. Johnston. He won the Battle of Belmont, and led the 1st Corps at Shioh. He was killed 14 June 1864 by cannon fire at Kenesaw Mountain, Ga.

Signature	Signature with rank	Pre War DS	War Dated DS	Pre War ALS	War Dated ALS
$300	$450	$	$	$	$2,350

A rare signature.

Polk, Lucius Eu Generale, 1833-92 — Confederate Brigadier General

Entered as a private in the Yell Rifles. He commanded a company at Shiloh, and was severly wounded in the face. He fought with great distinction at Chickamauga, Chattanooga, and during the Atlanta Campaigns. He was wounded four times during the war.

Signature	Signature with rank	Pre & post War DS	War Dated DS	Pre & post War ALS	War Dated ALS
$200	$325	$	$878	$574	$

Pope, John, 1822-92   Union General

Signature	Signature with rank	Pre & post War DS	War Dated DS	Pre & post War ALS	War Dated ALS
$80	$150	$137	$378	$225	$

S, Clip signature. BG Nov. 1993 $125.

Porcher, Francis Peyre, ?-?   Surgeon, P.A.C.S.

Signature	Signature with rank	Pre & post War DS	War Dated DS	Pre & post War ALS	War Dated ALS
$	$	$	$	$	$

Misc.
Books authored:
Resources of the Southern fields and forests, medical, economical and agricultural.
Charleston, S.C., 1863, 601p. [Parrish 6132] $1,700.
_____, Charleston, S.C., 1864 $1,000.
_____, Richmond, Va., 1863, 601p. [Parrish 6133] $1,500.

Porter, Andrew, 1820-72   Union General

Signature	Signature with rank	Pre & post War DS	War Dated DS	Pre & post War ALS	War Dated ALS
$50	$75	$83	$	$125	$

Porter, David Dixon, 1813-91   Union Admiral

Next to Farragut the outstanding Union naval commander. LOC. papers, 1790-1899. ca. 7,000 items.

Signature	Signature with rank	Pre & post War DS	War Dated DS	Pre & post War ALS	War Dated ALS
$95	$165	$173	$	$325	$

David D. Porter signature   **His father David Porter (1780-1843)**
AES, March 26, 1877. 1p., 7.75x9.75", Navy Department letterhead, Washington, D.C., Order to report, signed on verso. MS Nov. 1993 $150.

LS, 1863 September 18. 1p, 8x10", U.S. Mississippi Squadron, Flag Ship Black Hawk off Clair, Ill. To Actg. Master Mate E.C. Williams...The exigencies of the service will not allow me to grant you a leave of absence. HD June 1992 $130.

DS, Sept 18, 1864. 1p. 4to. pert. to discharge of a marine, AES as Rear Admiral. BG Nov. 1993 $225.

S, Signature "David D. Porter/ Admiral/ 1887" on card. JB Dec. 1993 $75.

-, Clip. "David D. Porter / Admiral" NAL July 1992 $100.

Porter, Fitz John, 1822-1901   Union General
LOC. papers, 1830-1949. ca. 13,100 items.

Signature	Signature with rank	Pre & post War DS	War Dated DS	Pre & post War ALS	War Dated ALS
$35	$55	$78	$	$135	$

Porter, Horace, 1837-1921   Union Colonel
LOC. papers, 1854-1921. ca. 1,500 items.

Signature	Signature with rank	Pre & post War DS	War Dated DS	Pre & post War ALS	War Dated ALS
$30	$	$95	$	$	$

Posey, Carnot, 1818-63   Confederate Brigadier General
He was elected Col. of the 16th Mississippi Infantry. He fought at 1st Manassas, Leesburg, Jackson's Valley campaign, Seven Days, and Fredericksburg. Died 13 Nov 1863 of wounds rec'd on Oct. 14, 1863 at Bristoe Station.

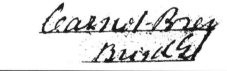

Signature	Signature with rank	Pre War DS	War Dated DS	Pre War ALS	War Dated ALS
$	$	$	$	$	$

A very rare signature.

Potter, Carroll Hagadorn, 1838-1901   Union Brevet General

Signature	Signature with rank	Pre & post War DS	War Dated DS	Pre & post War ALS	War Dated ALS
$18	$	$38	$	$	$

Potter, Edward Elmer, 1823-89 — Union General

Signature	Signature with rank	Pre & post War DS	War Dated DS	Pre & post War ALS	War Dated ALS
$	$45	$76	$	$	$

Potter, Joseph Adams, 1816-88 — Union Brevet General

Signature	Signature with rank	Pre & post War DS	War Dated DS	Pre & post War ALS	War Dated ALS
$16	$	$45	$	$	$

Potter, Joseph Haydn, 1822-92 — Union General

Signature	Signature with rank	Pre & post War DS	War Dated DS	Pre & post War ALS	War Dated ALS
$	$40	$	$	$110	$

Potter, Robert Brown, 1829-87 — Union General

Signature	Signature with rank	Pre & post War DS	War Dated DS	Pre & post War ALS	War Dated ALS
$20	$	$	$83	$	$

Potts, Benjamin Franklin, 1836-87 — Union General

Signature	Signature with rank	Pre & post War DS	War Dated DS	Pre & post War ALS	War Dated ALS
$23	$	$	$87	$	$

Powel, Mary Edith, 1846-1931 — Naval Collector

LOC. collection, 1747 - 1922. ca. 32,000 items.

Signature	Signature with rank	Pre & post War DS	War Dated DS	Pre & post War ALS	War Dated ALS
$	$	$	$	$	$

Powell, Eugene, 1834-1907 — Union Brevet General

Signature	Signature with rank	Pre & post War DS	War Dated DS	Pre & post War ALS	War Dated ALS
$15	$28	$	$	$	$

Powell, William Henry, 1825-1904   Union General

Signature	Signature with rank	Pre & post War DS	War Dated DS	Pre & post War ALS	War Dated ALS
$20	$35	$	$	$	$

Powers, Charles James, 1833-82   Union Brevet General

Signature	Signature with rank	Pre & post War DS	War Dated DS	Pre & post War ALS	War Dated ALS
$20	$	$	$	$	$

Pratt, Calvin Edward, 1828-96   Union General

Signature	Signature with rank	Pre & post War DS	War Dated DS	Pre & post War ALS	War Dated ALS
$	$38	$	$78	$98	$

Preble, George Henry, 1816-85   Union Naval Officer

Signature	Signature with rank	Pre & post War DS	War Dated DS	Pre & post War ALS	War Dated ALS
$	$55	$	$	$95	$

ALS, 1881 July 12. 2p Brookline, Ma, re: his copy of the History of the U.S., Flag. ML October 1992 $85.

Prentiss, Benjamin Mayberry, 1819-1901   Union General

Signature	Signature with rank	Pre & post War DS	War Dated DS	Pre & post War ALS	War Dated ALS
$	$30	$50	$75	$	$

Preston, John Smith, 1809-81   Confederate General

Entered as a Lt. Col. on the Staff of Genl. Beauregard. He was in charge of the Bureau of Conscription, and was appointed Brig. Genl. on June 10, 1864.

Signature	Signature with rank	Pre & post War DS	War Dated DS	Pre & post War ALS	War Dated ALS
$65	$90	$	$245	$	$

305

Preston, William, 1816-87   Confederate Brigadier General
He entered C.S. service as a Colonel on the Staff of Genl. A.S. Johnston. After Johnston's death at Shiloh, he was appointed Brig. Genl., on April 14, 1862. He led his brigades at Corinth, Vicksburg, and Chickamauga. In 1864, he was appointed Foreign Minister to Mexico, and spent the remainder of the war in the Trans-Mississippi Department.

Signature	Signature with rank	Pre & post War DS	War Dated DS	Pre & post War ALS	War Dated ALS
$110	$155	$425	$578	$	$

S, Large Clip. BG Nov. 1993 $125

Preston, William Ballard, ?-?   Confederate Senator from VA
Pre-war Secretary of the Navy.

Signature	Signature with rank	Pre & post War DS	War Dated DS	Pre & post War ALS	War Dated ALS
$30	$	$50	$	$	$

Price, Sterling, 1809-67   Confederate Major General
He officially joined the Confederacy as a Major General March 6, 1862. In 1864, he was sent to the Trans-Mississippi Department and aided Kirby Smith in defeating Genl. Steele in the Camden Expedition.

Signature	Signature with rank	Pre & post War DS	War Dated DS	Pre & post War ALS	War Dated ALS
$250	$378	$365	$	$	$

Prince, Henry, 1811-92   Union General

Signature	Signature with rank	Pre & post War DS	War Dated DS	Pre & post War ALS	War Dated ALS
$25	$35	$55	$	$87	$

306

Pryor, Roger Atkinson, 1828-1919   Confederate Brigadier General
Appointed Brig. Genl. on April 16, 1862, he led his brigades at Seven Days and
Sharpsburg. He resigned his commission on Aug. 18, 1863, and was captured as a
private in 1864.

Signature	Signature with rank	Pre & post War DS	War Dated DS	Pre & post War ALS	War Dated ALS
$105	$167	$275	$	$345	$

S, Clip signature with sentiment. BG Nov. 1993 $80.

Pugh, James Lawrence, 1820-1907   Confederate Congressman

Signature	Signature with rank	Pre & post War DS	War Dated DS	Pre & post War ALS	War Dated ALS
$	$	$65	$	$	$

Puryear, Richard Clauselle, 1801-67   Confederate Congressman

Signature	Signature with rank	Pre & post War DS	War Dated DS	Pre & post War ALS	War Dated ALS
$	$50	$	$	$	$

Q

Quarles, William Andrew, 1825-93   Confederate Brigadier General
Attended Univ. of Virginia. Lawyer and judge before the war. Entered as a a Colonel in
the 42nd TN Infantry. He was captured at Fort Donelson, and after his exchange saw
action at Port Hudson and in the Vicksburg campaign. As a Grig. Genl., he fought with
great distinction in the Atlanta operations; he was again captured at the Battle of
Franklin. After the war he served in TN politics.

Signature	Signature with rank	Pre & post War DS	War Dated DS	Pre & post War ALS	War Dated ALS
$80	$125	$145	$358	$	$

DS, Railroad bond signed as president. BS Aug. 1993 $85.

Quinby, Issac Ferdinand, 1821-91   Union General
Graduated from West Point 1843. College professor befor the war, U.S. Marshel after.

Signature	Signature with rank	Pre & post War DS	War Dated DS	Pre & post War ALS	War Dated ALS
$20	$28	$	$56	$	$

Quincy, Samuel Miller, 1833-87   Union Brevet General

Signature	Signature with rank	Pre & post War DS	War Dated DS	Pre & post War ALS	War Dated ALS
$16	$	$	$	$75	$

R

Radford, William, 1809-90   Union Naval Commander
LOC. papers, 1847-90. 53 items.

Signature	Signature with rank	Pre & post War DS	War Dated DS	Pre & post War ALS	War Dated ALS
$	$65	$	$150	$	$

Rains, Gabriel James, 1803-81   Confederate Brig. Gen'l & Inventor
WP graduate. He was appointed Brig. Genl. on September 23, 1861 and commanded a brigade under Genl. D.H. Hill. Genl. Rains had exceptional knowledge of explosives and invented a new primer for shells - land mines. In Jan. 1863 he was made Chief of the new Bureau of Torpedo.

Signature	Signature with rank	Pre & post War DS	War Dated DS	Pre & post War ALS	War Dated ALS
$90	$185	$	$	$	$

Rains, George Washington, ?-?   Confederate Major
In charge of the Gunpowder Department, C.S.A.

Signature	Signature with rank	Pre & post War DS	War Dated DS	Pre & post War ALS	War Dated ALS
$	$100	$	$178	$	$

Misc.

B, Notes on making saltpeter from the earth of the caves. Augusta, Ga. 1861. 12 p. [Parrish 6135] $400.

-, _____, Richmond, Va. 1862. 15p. [Parrish 6136] $350.

Rains, James Edward, 1833-62   Confederate Brigadier General
Yale graduate. C.S. service as a Private in the 11th TN Infantry. He was killed Dec. 31, 1862 at Stone River, TN.

Signature	Signature with rank	Pre War DS	War Dated DS	Pre War ALS	War Dated ALS
$(200+)	$	$	$	$	$

An extremely rare signature.

Ramsay, George Douglas, 1802-82   Union General

Signature	Signature with rank	Pre & post War DS	War Dated DS	Pre & post War ALS	War Dated ALS
$20	$	$	$74	$	$

Ramsay, James Graham, 1823-1903   Member Confederate Congress

Signature	Signature with rank	Pre & post War DS	War Dated DS	Pre & post War ALS	War Dated ALS
$30	$	$	$	$	$

Ramseur, Stephen Dodson, 1837-64   Confederate Major General
WP graduate. He was a captain in Ellis Light Artillery. He fought with great distinction during the Battle of Seven Days, and was severely wounded at Malvern Hill. He died Oct. 20, 1864, of wounds rec'd at Cedar Creek, Va.

Signature	Signature with rank	Pre War DS	War Dated DS	Pre War ALS	War Dated ALS
$(500+)	$	$	$	$	$

A very rare signature.

Randal, Horace, 1831-64   Confederate Brigadier General
Designated Brig. Genl. on April 14,1864, Trans-Mississippi Department. Killed 30 Apr. 1864 at Jenkins Ferry, Ark.

Horace Randal [signature]

Signature	Signature with rank	Pre War DS	War Dated DS	Pre War ALS	War Dated ALS
$265	$	$	$	$	$

A scarce signature.

Randall, James Garfield, 1881-1953   Lincoln Collector
LOC. papers, 1850-1952. ca. 13,400 items.

Signature	DS	ALS
$	$	$

Randolph, George Wythe, 1818-67   Conf. Brig. Gen'l & Sec. of War
He organized the Richmond Howitzers, and was Genl. Magruder's Chief of Artillery at Big Bethel. Appointed Secretary of War for the Confederacy on March 18, 1862, but resigned in Nov., to take field command. Resigned in Dec. 1864 due to ill health. LOC. letter, 1862. 1 item.

Very truly yours G. W. Randolph [signature]

Signature	Signature with rank	Pre & post War DS	War Dated DS	Pre & post War ALS	War Dated ALS
$250	$	$750	$	$	$

Ransom, Matt Whitaker, 1826-1904   Confederate Brigadier General
Colonel 1st & 35th North Carolina Inf., saw action in Seven Days battles, Sharpsburg, Fredericksburg, Plymouth, Weldon, Suffolk & Petersburg. He was wounded three times during the war & surrendered at Appomattox.

Signature	Signature with rank	Pre & post War DS	War Dated DS	Pre & post War ALS	War Dated ALS
$95	$178	$165	$	$210	$

S, Large clip. BG Nov. 1993 $85.
-, Clipped signature: Large ink autograph, "M.W. Ransom, North Carolina." LR Sept. 1993 $85.

Ransom, Robert, Jr., 1828-92   Confederate Major General
WP graduate. He was a captain in the regular C.S. Army, and was later elected Colonel of the 1st N.C. Cavalry. Appointed Major Genl. on May 26, 1863, he fought with great distinction at Seven Days, Antietam, Fredericksburg, Drewry's Bluff, and commanded Genl. Early's cavalry during the raid on Washington. LOC. letter, 1863. 1 item.

Signature	Signature with rank	Pre & post War DS	War Dated DS	Pre & post War ALS	War Dated ALS
$150	$225	$	$	$	$

Ransom, Thomas Edward, 1834-64   Union General
He was wounded at Charleston, Missouri, Fort Donelson, Shiloh and Sabine Crossroads. He died in an ambulance wagon near Rome, GA., while with the 17th Corps. Rare.

Signature	Signature with rank	Pre War DS	War Dated DS	Pre War ALS	War Dated ALS
$	$75	$	$	$	$

Raum, Green Berry, 1829-1909   Union General

Signature	Signature with rank	Pre & post War DS	War Dated DS	Pre & post War ALS	War Dated ALS
$25	$35	$75	$	$	$

Rawlins, John Aaron, 1831-69   Union General

Signature	Signature with rank	Pre & post War DS	War Dated DS	Pre & post War ALS	War Dated ALS
$70	$135	$	$238	$	$

Read, Charles, ?-?   Confederate Naval Commander
Confederate Cruisers, *CLARENCE & TACONY* 1863

Signature	Signature with rank	Pre & post War DS	War Dated DS	Pre & post War ALS	War Dated ALS
$	$	$	$245	$	$

Read, Henry English, 1824-68   Member Confederate Congress

Signature	Signature with rank	Pre & post War DS	War Dated DS	Pre & post War ALS	War Dated ALS
$	$65	$	$	$	$

Read, Thomas Buchanan, 1822-72   Artist & Poet
LOC. collection, 1864. 3 items

Signature	Pre & post War DS	War Dated DS	Pre & post War ALS	War Dated ALS
$50	$	$	$	$

Reade, Edwin Godwin, 1812-94   Member Confederate Congress

Signature	Signature with rank	Pre & post War DS	War Dated DS	Pre & post War ALS	War Dated ALS
$	$	$	$122	$	$

Reagan, John Henninger, 1818-1905   Postmaster of the Confederacy

Signature	Signature with rank	Pre & post War DS	War Dated DS	Pre & post War ALS	War Dated ALS
$100	$180	$578	$1,450	$	$

ALS, 1904 July 15. 2pp, 8x10", Palestine, Texas., To Dr. W.F. McCaleb," I purposely and willingly joined in the secession movement..." HD June 1992 $225.

Rector, Henry M., 1816-?   Confederate Gov. of Arkansas (1860-62)

Signature	Signature with rank	Pre & post War DS	War Dated DS	Pre & post War ALS	War Dated ALS
$	$35	$	$90	$	$

312

Redwood, Allen Caster, 1834-1922 — Artist

Signature	Pre & post War DS	War Dated DS	Pre & post War ALS	War Dated ALS
$50	$	$	$123	$

Reid, Hugh Thompson, 1811-74 — Union General

Signature	Signature with rank	Pre & post War DS	War Dated DS	Pre & post War ALS	War Dated ALS
$	$	$	$85	$	$

Reilly, James William, 1828-1905 — Union General

Signature	Signature with rank	Pre & post War DS	War Dated DS	Pre & post War ALS	War Dated ALS
$	$35	$	$	$	$

Remington, Frederic, 1861-1909 — Artist

Signature	DS	ALS
$	$	$

ALS, 1890 Jan 13. 1p 7x9", New Rochelle, NY., To Fred B. Schell "I send a double page 'the opening of the Wounded Knee Fight--drawn from description by the men engaged!" HD June 1992 $500.

Reno, Jesse Lee, 1823-62 — Union Major General

Killed 14 Sept. 1862 at Fox's Gap, South Mountain, Md., while leading his men. He war in the Antietam campaign.. Rare.

Signature	Signature with rank	Pre War DS	War Dated DS	Pre War ALS	War Dated ALS
$	$	$	$	$	$

Misc.
P, CDV, Chest up view in double breasted uniform coat of Brig. Gen. B/M J.E. McClees of Phil. LR Sept. 1993 $125.

Revere, Joseph Warren, 1812-80 — Union General

Signature	Signature with rank	Pre & post War DS	War Dated DS	Pre & post War ALS	War Dated ALS
$	$35	$	$74	$	$

Reynolds, Alexander Welch, 1816-76   Confederate Brigadier General
WP graduate. Colonel of the 50th Virginia Infantry. He was captured and exchanged at Vicksburg and appointed Brig. Genl. on Sept. 14, 1863. He commanded a brigade under Genl. Hardee at Chattanooga, and was under Hood during the Battle of Atlanta.

Signature	Signature with rank	Pre & post War DS	War Dated DS	Pre & post War ALS	War Dated ALS
$90	$165	$178	$	$287	$

Reynolds, Daniel Harris, 1832-1902   Confederate Brigadier General
Capt. in the 1st Arkansas Mounted Rifles, and fought with great distinction at Wilson's Creek and Chickamauga. Commissioned Brig. Genl. on March 5, 1864, he fought under Genl. Hood in the Atlanta and TN operations. He had his leg amputated the result of his wounds rec'd at Bentonville.

Signature	Signature with rank	Pre & post War DS	War Dated DS	Pre & post War ALS	War Dated ALS
$75	$115	$	$	$	$

Reynolds, John Fulton, 1820-63   Union Major General
Killed 1 July 1863 at Gettysburg, Pa., while leading the 2nd Corps into battle. During the fighting on he war shot off his house and killed instantly.

Signature	Signature with rank	Pre War DS	War Dated DS	Pre War ALS	War Dated ALS
$550	$1,250	$1,478	$	$	$

Misc.
P, CDV, Bust view in uniform, wearing double breasted uniform. B/M J.E. McClees, at Philad. LR Sept. 1993 $325.

Reynolds, Joseph Jones, 1822-99   Union General

Signature	Signature with rank	Pre & post War DS	War Dated DS	Pre & post War ALS	War Dated ALS
$	$35	$	$	$	$

Rhett (Smith), Robert Barnwell, 1800-76 — Confederate Officer
The "Father of Secession"; C.S. Congressman.

Signature	Signature with rank	Pre & post War DS	War Dated DS	Pre & post War ALS	War Dated ALS
$120	$	$	$	$950	$

Rhodes, James Ford, 1848-1927 — Historian
LOC. manuscripts, 1912. 3 items.

Signature	DS	ALS
$20	$	$98

Rice, Americus Vespucius, 1835- 1904 — Union General

Signature	Signature with rank	Pre & post War DS	War Dated DS	Pre & post War ALS	War Dated ALS
$	$38	$	$67	$	$

Rice, Elliott Warren, 1835-87 — Union General

Signature	Signature with rank	Pre & post War DS	War Dated DS	Pre & post War ALS	War Dated ALS
$	$35	$	$	$	$

Rice, James Clay, 1829-64 — Union General
Killed 10 May 1864 at Spotsylvania, Va.

Signature	Signature with rank	Pre War DS	War Dated DS	Pre War ALS	War Dated ALS
$	$125	$	$278	$	$

DS, 1862. Frameable document promoting a Corporal in the 44th New York (Ellsworth's). JH August 1993 $250.

Rice, Samuel Allen, 1828-64 — Union Brigadier General
Died 6 July 1864 of wounds recd at Jenkins Ferry, Ark. Rare.

Signature	Signature with rank	Pre War DS	War Dated DS	Pre War ALS	War Dated ALS
$70	$145	$	$	$300	$

Richardson, A. D., 1833-69   Union Spy

Signature	Pre & post War DS	War Dated DS	Pre & post War ALS	War Dated ALS
$	$	$	$	$

Richardson, Israel Bush, 1815-1862   Union Major General
Died 3 Nov. 1862 of wounds recd at Antietam, Md. Rare.

Signature	Signature with rank	Pre War DS	War Dated DS	Pre War ALS	War Dated ALS
$	$115	$	$	$	$

Richardson, Robert Vinkler, 1820-70   Confederate Brigadier General
Colonel of the 12th TN Cavalry, and saw service at Shiloh and Corinth. Appointed and confirmed Brig. Genl. on December 3, 1864.

Signature	Signature with rank	Pre & post War DS	War Dated DS	Pre & post War ALS	War Dated ALS
$	$450	$	$	$	$

A scarce signature.

Ricketts, James Brewerton, 1817-87   Union General

Signature	Signature with rank	Pre & post War DS	War Dated DS	Pre & post War ALS	War Dated ALS
$	$32	$	$74	$	$

Ringgold, George Hay, 1814-64   Union Paymaster

Signature	Signature with rank	Pre War DS	War Dated DS	Pre War ALS	War Dated ALS
$	$	$	$65	$	$

Ripley, James Wolfe, 1794-70   Union General

Signature	Signature with rank	Pre & post War DS	War Dated DS	Pre & post War ALS	War Dated ALS
$	$45	$	$	$	$

Ripley, Roswell Sabine, 1823-87   Confederate Brigadier General

WP graduate. He was appointed Brig. Genl. on Aug. 15, 1861, and was in command of South Carolina until 1862. He led a brigade under Genl. D.H. Hill and was severely wounded at Sharpsburg in defense of Genl. Lee's left flank.

Signature	Signature with rank	Pre & post War DS	War Dated DS	Pre & post War ALS	War Dated ALS
$135	$200	$265	$	$	$

A scarce signature.

Roane, John Seldon, 1817-67   Confederate Brigadier General

Appointed Brig. Genl. on March 20, 1862, and fought gallantly at Prairie Grove. He served most of the war in Louisiana and Texas.

Signature	Signature with rank	Pre & post War DS	War Dated DS	Pre & post War ALS	War Dated ALS
$90	$	$	$	$	$

A scarce signature.

Robb, Robert G., ?-?   Commander Confederate Navy

Signature	Signature with rank	Pre & post War DS	War Dated DS	Pre & post War ALS	War Dated ALS
$	$	$	$250	$	$

Roberts, Benjamin Stone, 1810-75   Union General

Signature	Signature with rank	Pre & post War DS	War Dated DS	Pre & post War ALS	War Dated ALS
$	$35	$	$	$	$

Roberts, William Paul, 1841-1910   Confederate Brigadier General

He enlisted as a Private in the 2nd North Carolina. He was promoted through the ranks to Major, and fought with distinction in all the N.C. operations until late 1862. Transferred to the ANV. He was conspicuous at Ream's Station, and was appointed Brig. on Feb. 23, 1865.

Signature	Signature with rank	Pre & post War DS	War Dated DS	Pre & post War ALS	War Dated ALS
$75	$120	$	$	$	$

Robertson, Beverly Holcombe, 1827-1910   Confederate Brig. General

WP graduate. He was appointed Captain in the Adjt. Genl's Department and later appointed Colonel of the 4th Virginia Cavalry. He served with Stonewall and was appointed Brig. Genl. on June 9, 1862. Genl. Robertson served under Longstreet at Knoxville, and surrendered with Johnston on April 26, 1865.

Signature	Signature with rank	Pre & post War DS	War Dated DS	Pre & post War ALS	War Dated ALS
$90	$165	$	$	$278	$

Robertson, Felix Huston, 1839-1928   Confederate Brigadier General

2nd Lt. of Artillery. He commanded a battery at Shiloh, and fought with great distinction at Murfreesboro and Chickamauga. Under Genl. Wheeler, he directed the artillery during the Atlanta Campaign.

Signature	Signature with rank	Pre & post War DS	War Dated DS	Pre & post War ALS	War Dated ALS
$70	$120	$	$	$245	$

Robertson, Jerome Bonaparte, 1815-91   Conf. Brig. General & Phys.
Captain in the 5th Texas Infantry. He was appointed Brig. Genl. on Nov. 1, 1862 and led his Texas Infantry at 2nd Manassass and Gettysburg. Under Longstreet he fought at Chickamauga, and was later transferred to the Trans-Mississippi Department.

Signature	Signature with rank	Pre & post War DS	War Dated DS	Pre & post War ALS	War Dated ALS
$85	$145	$278	$	$	$

Robinson, James Sidney, 1827-92   Union General

Signature	Signature with rank	Pre & post War DS	War Dated DS	Pre & post War ALS	War Dated ALS
$20	$38	$	$	$78	$

Robinson, John Cleveland, 1817-97   Union General
MOH for Laural Hill, Va., Lost his left leg at Spottsylvania, Va.

Signature	Signature with rank	Pre & post War DS	War Dated DS	Pre & post War ALS	War Dated ALS
$45	$70	$	$	$	$

S, Album page signed. JH August 1993 $40.

Roddy, Philip Dale, 1826-97   Confederate Brigadier General
He organized a company of cavalry and was commissioned its Captain. He later organized the 4th Alabama Cavalry and served with distinction under Genls. Forrest and Wheeler.

Signature	Signature with rank	Pre & post War DS	War Dated DS	Pre & post War ALS	War Dated ALS
$90	$170	$350	$	$	$

Rodes, Robert Emmett, 1829-64   Confederate Major General

V.M.I. graduate. Colonel of the 5th Alabama Infantry. For his gallent conduct under Ewell at 1st Manassas, he was promoted to Brig. Genl. on Oct. 21, 1861. He commanded a division at Chancellorsville and Gettysburg in Ewell's 2nd Corps, ANV. He was killed Sept. 19, 1864 at Winchester, Va. while leading a counter-attack.

Signature	Signature with rank	Pre War DS	War Dated DS	Pre War ALS	War Dated ALS
$400	$	$	$	$	$

AES, "Approved" w/ rank & date SK October 1992 $850.
Misc.
-, 1861) June 30. Fairfax Station, Va., envelope addressed by him writing to his wife just after the battle of Manassas. HD July 1992 $250.
A very rare signature.

Rodgers, George W., ?-?   Union Naval Commander

Signature	Signature with rank	Pre & post War DS	War Dated DS	Pre & post War ALS	War Dated ALS
$	$45	$	$	$	$

Rodgers, John, 1812-82   Union Naval Commodore

LOC. papers, 1788-1944. ca. 15,500 items.

Signature	Signature with rank	Pre & post War DS	War Dated DS	Pre & post War ALS	War Dated ALS
$	$85	$	$	$	$325

Rodman, Isaac Peace, 1822-62   Union Brigadier General

Died 30 Sept. 1862 of wounds recd at Antietam, Md.

Signature	Signature with rank	Pre War DS	War Dated DS	Pre War ALS	War Dated ALS
$	$	$	$	$	$

Rogers, William Findlay, ?-1899   Union Brevet General

Signature	Signature with rank	Pre & post War DS	War Dated DS	Pre & post War ALS	War Dated ALS
$20	$	$	$	$	$

320

Rootes, Thomas Read, ?-?   Confederate Naval Commander

Signature	Signature with rank	Pre & post War DS	War Dated DS	Pre & post War ALS	War Dated ALS
$	$	$	$1,250	$	$

Rosecrans, William Starke, 1819-1902   Union General
Commanded the Armies of the Mississippi and the Cumberland.

Signature	Signature with rank	Pre & post War DS	War Dated DS	Pre & post War ALS	War Dated ALS
$65	$128	$	$	$	$1,350

ALS, Jan. 4, 1865. 2pp. to Colonel William Myers request veterinarian's bill be settled. SAG Feb. 1994 $1,600.
S, "W. S. Rosecrans, Maj. Genl." on card. JB Dec. 1993 $125.
-, Ornate signature with rank. BG Nov. 1993 $75.

Ross, Lawrence Sullivan, 1838-98   Confed. Brig. General & Gov. of TX
Colonel in the 6th Texas Cavalry. For his gallant effort in covering Van Dorn's retreat from Corinth he was promoted to Brig. Genl. on Dec. 21, 1863. He was in over 100 battles.

Signature	Signature with rank	Pre & post War DS	War Dated DS	Pre & post War ALS	War Dated ALS
$100	$	$	$	$	$

Ross, Leonard Fulton, 1823-1901   Union General

Signature	Signature with rank	Pre & post War DS	War Dated DS	Pre & post War ALS	War Dated ALS
$	$40	$	$	$	$

Rosser, Thomas Lafayette, 1836-1910   Confederate Major General
WP graduate. 1st Lt. in CSA. He commanded a company of famous New Orleans Washington Artillery at 1st Manassas. He was wounded at Mechanicsville and at Kell's Ford. Promoted to Major Genl. on Nov. 1, 1864. He commanded Early's Cavalry in the Shenandoah Valley operations.

Signature	Signature with rank	Pre & post War DS	War Dated DS	Pre & post War ALS	War Dated ALS
$120	$167	$275	$	$	$

Rousseau, Lovell Harrison, 1818-69   Union General

Signature	Signature with rank	Pre & post War DS	War Dated DS	Pre & post War ALS	War Dated ALS
$	$	$65	$	$	$

Rowan, Stephen Clegg, 1808-90   Union Naval Commodore

Signature	Signature with rank	Pre & post War DS	War Dated DS	Pre & post War ALS	War Dated ALS
$	$	$	$	$	$

Rowley, Thomas Algeo, 1808-92   Union General

Signature	Signature with rank	Pre & post War DS	War Dated DS	Pre & post War ALS	War Dated ALS
$	$37	$	$	$	$

Rucker, Daniel Henry, 1812-1910   Union Brevet General

Signature	Signature with rank	Pre & post War DS	War Dated DS	Pre & post War ALS	War Dated ALS
$	$	$	$58	$	$

Ruff, Charles F., 1817-85   Union Brevet General

Signature	Signature with rank	Pre & post War DS	War Dated DS	Pre & post War ALS	War Dated ALS
$20	$	$	$	$	$

Ruger, Thomas Howard, 1833-1907   Union General
BG USV 1862, led 2nd Div. XII Corps at Gettysburg.

Signature	Signature with rank	Pre & post War DS	War Dated DS	Pre & post War ALS	War Dated ALS
$	$	$	$	$	$

S, Clip, 1.25x4.25" as Bvt MG. EB Dec. 1993 $60.

Ruggles, Daniel, 1810-97   Confederate Brigadier General
WP graduate. He entered C.S. service as a Brig. Genl. on August 9, 1861. He led Bragg's 1st Division at Shiloh, and caused the surprised Union Genl. Prentiss to surrender. He later commanded the Department of East Louisiana at Jackson, Mississippi.

Signature	Signature with rank	Pre & post War DS	War Dated DS	Pre & post War ALS	War Dated ALS
$100	$145	$250	$463	$	$700

ALS, March 1, [1862] to Brigadier General LeRoy P. Walker, in disgust at not getting a more active command. SAG Feb. 1994 $650.
---, March 4, 1864. 1p. 8to. Columbus, Miss., to Genl. J.E. Johnston pert. to accepting command of a brigade. BG Nov. 1993 $550.

Rusling, James Fowler, 1834-1918   Union Brevet General

Signature	Signature with rank	Pre & post War DS	War Dated DS	Pre & post War ALS	War Dated ALS
$	$	$	$	$	$

Russell, Andrew J. 1838-?   Photographer

Signature	Pre & post War DS	War Dated DS	Pre & post War ALS	War Dated ALS
$	$	$	$278	$

S, Album page, large bold signature. SK Feb. 1994 $100.

Russell, David Allen, 1820-64   Union Brigadier General
Killed 19 Sept. 1864 at Winchester, Va. Rare.

Signature	Signature with rank	Pre War DS	War Dated DS	Pre War ALS	War Dated ALS
$	$	$	$	$	$

Russell, Israel, ?-?   Held by John Brown at Harpers Ferry

Signature	Pre & post War DS	War Dated DS	Pre & post War ALS	War Dated ALS
$100	$	$	$	$

Russell, W. H. Sir., ?-?   Correspondent
British war correspondent known as "Bulls Run Russell" for telling the truth about 1st Manassas.

Signature	Pre & post War DS	War Dated DS	Pre & post War ALS	War Dated ALS
$	$	$	$123	$

ALS, 1890 on Army/ Navy letter head, W/E. JH Nov. 1993 $60.

Rust, Albert, 1818-70   Confederate Brigadier General
Colonel in the 3rd Arkansas. He served under R.E. Lee at Cheat Mountain, and under Stonewall Jackson in the Valley Campaign. Appointed Brig. Genl. on March 4, 1862, Genl Rust was transferred to the Trans-Mississippi Department.

Signature	Signature with rank	Pre & post War DS	War Dated DS	Pre & post War ALS	War Dated ALS
$75	$	$	$	$168	$

S

Salomon, Friedrich (Frederick), 1826-97   Union General

Signature	Signature with rank	Pre & post War DS	War Dated DS	Pre & post War ALS	War Dated ALS
$25	$40	$	$	$	$

Sanborn, John Benjamin, 1826-1904   Union General

Signature	Signature with rank	Pre & post War DS	War Dated DS	Pre & post War ALS	War Dated ALS
$	$	$58	$73	$	$

Sanders, Horace Turner, 1820-65   Union Brevet General

Signature	Signature with rank	Pre & post War DS	War Dated DS	Pre & post War ALS	War Dated ALS
$	$28	$	$67	$	$

Sanders, John Caldwell Calhoun, 1840-64   Confederate Brig. General

Captain in the 11th Alabama. He was severely wounded in the leg during the Seven Days Battles, and fought with distinction at Fredericksburg and Gettysburg. For the his gallant assault at the "Mule Shoe", he was then promoted to Brig. Genl., on May 31, 1864. On Aug. 21, 1864 at Weldon Rail Road, Va., he was shot in the leg and bleed to death on the battle field.

Signature	Signature with rank	Pre War DS	War Dated DS	Pre War ALS	War Dated ALS
$	$350	$	$	$	$

An extremely rare signature.

Sanders, William Price, 1833-63   Union Brigadier General

Died 19 Nov. 1863 of wounds recd at Knoxville, TN. Rare.

Signature	Signature with rank	Pre War DS	War Dated DS	Pre War ALS	War Dated ALS
$	$	$	$	$	$

Saxton, Rufus, Jr., 1824-1908   Union General

Signature	Signature with rank	Pre & post War DS	War Dated DS	Pre & post War ALS	War Dated ALS
$40	$65	$	$	$87	$

S, Clip. JH August 1993 $40.

Scales, Alfred Moore, 1827-92   Confederate General

Entered as a Private in 1861. Elected Colonel of the 13th North Carolina, he fought with gallantry at Seven Days and was wounded at Chancellorsville and Gettysburg. Gov. of N.C. 1885-89

Signature	Signature with rank	Pre & post War DS	War Dated DS	Pre & post War ALS	War Dated ALS
$90	$150	$190	$	$	$

DS, Oct. 1, 1886. 1p. folio, with seal, Raleigh, N.C. as Gov. pert. to apt. in Gov. Guards. BG Nov. 1993 $165.

Scammon, Eliakim Parker, 1816-94   Union General

Signature	Signature with rank	Pre & post War DS	War Dated DS	Pre & post War ALS	War Dated ALS
$	$35	$	$	$	$

Schenk, Robert Cumming, 1809-90   Union General

Signature	Signature with rank	Pre & post War DS	War Dated DS	Pre & post War ALS	War Dated ALS
$	$	$	$	$	$

S, Clip. BG Nov. 1993 $45.

Schimmelfennig, Alexander, 1824-65   Union General

Signature	Signature with rank	Pre & post War DS	War Dated DS	Pre & post War ALS	War Dated ALS
$	$	$	$74	$	$

Schoepf, Albin Francisco, 1822-86   Union General

Signature	Signature with rank	Pre & post War DS	War Dated DS	Pre & post War ALS	War Dated ALS
$	$30	$	$	$	$

326

Schofield, John McAllister, 1831-1906   Union Major General

Graduated from West Point 1853 and served in the army before and after the war. BG 1862, MG 1863, with Sherman in Atlanta, defeated Hood at Franklin & Nashville 1864, Secty War 1868-69. LOC. papers, 1837-1906. ca. 30,000 items.

Signature	Signature with rank	Pre & post War DS	War Dated DS	Pre & post War ALS	War Dated ALS
$40	$60	$78	$125	$165	$245

S, Slip 2x5" as MG. EB Dec. 1993 $60.

Schurz, Carl, 1829-1906   Union Major General

Attended Bonn University. 11th Corps Chief; Politics before the war, U.S. Senator after. LOC. papers, 1842-1932. ca. 23,000 items.

Signature	Signature with rank	Pre & post War DS	War Dated DS	Pre & post War ALS	War Dated ALS
$35	$	$98	$	$	$

LS, 1877. Dept. of Interior Stationery. DZ September 1991 $85
S, Clip. JH August 1993 $30

Scott, Robert Kingston, 1826-1900   Union General

Signature	Signature with rank	Pre & post War DS	War Dated DS	Pre & post War ALS	War Dated ALS
$	$32	$	$	$	$

Scott, Thomas Moore, 1829-76   Confederate Brigadier General

Colonel of the 12th Louisiana, and saw duty at island No. 10 and Port Hudson. He accompanied Genl. Polk to Georgia and fought with distinction during the Atlanta campaign. He was severely wounded during the Battle of Franklin. Farmer before and after the war.

Signature	Signature with rank	Pre & post War DS	War Dated DS	Pre & post War ALS	War Dated ALS
$90	$	$	$	$	$

A scarce signature.

Scott, Winfield, 1786-1866 — Union Major General

Attended William and Mary College, then served in the army before the war.

Signature	Signature with rank	Pre & post War DS	War Dated DS	Pre & post War ALS	War Dated ALS
$90	$165	$345	$487	$	$

LS, July 30, 1861. 2pp. "A safeguard is hereby granted to Mrs. Mary Throckmorton, her family, and servants..." SAG Feb. 1994 $525.
S, Clip. "Winfield Scott, 1865" NAT July 1992 $ 100

Scurry, William Read, 1821-64 — Confederate Brigadier General

Served in the army before the war. Lt. Col. of the 4th Texas Cavalry. Appointed Brig. Genl. on Sept. 12, 1862, he fought under Genl. Magruder at Galveston and commanded his own brigade during the Battles of Mansfield and Pleasant Hill. He was killed 30 Apr. 1864 at Jenkins Ferry, Ark.

Signature	Signature with rank	Pre War DS	War Dated DS	Pre War ALS	War Dated ALS
$250	$350	$	$	$	$

A rare signature.

Sears, Claudius Wister, 1817-91 — Confederate Brigadier General

Graduated from West Point 1841. College professor before and after the war. He was commissioned Col. of the 46th Mississippi, and fought with distinction at Chickasaw Bayou and Port Gibson. He was captured at Vicksburg and not exchanged until 1863. Appointed Big. Genl. on March 1, 1864. He was severely wounded at Nashville.

Signature	Signature with rank	Pre & post War DS	War Dated DS	Pre & post War ALS	War Dated ALS
$70	$118	$	$378	$	$

Seddon, James A., 1815-80 — Confederate Secretary of War

Signature	Signature with rank	Pre & post War DS	War Dated DS	Pre & post War ALS	War Dated ALS
$100	$165	$	$650	$	$2,350

LS,   1863 August 26. 1p 8x10.5" Richmond, Va., Notification to Dr. J.W. King that the President has appointed him Surgeon in the Provisional Army in the service of the Confederate States. HD June 1992 $600.

Sedgwick, John, 1813-64   Union Major General

Attended Sharon Academy, then graduated from West Point 1837. Served in the army before the war. Killed 9 May 1864 at Spotsylvania, Va. Rare.

Signature	Signature with rank	Pre War DS	War Dated DS	Pre War ALS	War Dated ALS
$	$	$	$	$	$

Selfridge, Thomas Oliver, 1804-1902   Union Naval Commander

Signature	Signature with rank	Pre & post War DS	War Dated DS	Pre & post War ALS	War Dated ALS
$	$250	$	$	$	$

Semmes, Paul Jones, 1815-63   Confederate Brigadier General

Attended University of Virginia. Farmer and banker before the war. Colonel of the 2nd GA Infantry. Appointed Brig. Genl. on March 11, 1862, he fought with gallantry at Williamsburg, Seven Days, and Sharpsburg. Died 10 July 1863 of wounds rec'd 2 July at the battle of Gettysburg.

Signature	Signature with rank	Pre War DS	War Dated DS	Pre War ALS	War Dated ALS
$900	$1,350	$1,400	$	$	$

ADS, 1861. endorsement, signed at Savannah, Ga. JH Nov. 1993 $1,050.
DS, 1861. Accepting 575 muskets for the formation of the 2nd GA Infantry. JH Nov. 1993 $1,350.
A scarce signature.

Semmes, Raphael, 1809-77   Confederate Naval Admiral

Confederate Cruisers, CSS SUMTER 1861-62; CSS ALABAMA 1862-64.

Signature	Signature with rank	Pre & post War DS	War Dated DS	Pre & post War ALS	War Dated ALS
$325	$450	$	$	$1,750	$

Misc.
---, Cabinet Card. SK May 1993 $295
A scarce signature.

Semmes, Thomas Jenkins, 1824-1899   Member Confederate Congress

Signature	Signature with rank	Pre & post War DS	War Dated DS	Pre & post War ALS	War Dated ALS
$35	$	$	$78	$	$

Seward, William Henry, 1801-1872   Politican, US Secretary of State

A contender for the 1860 Republican presidential nomination, Seward became Lincoln's Secretary of State. He proved extremely capable, arranged the purchase of Alaska from Russian. Later Gov. of N.Y.

Signature	Signature with rank	Pre & post War DS	War Dated DS	Pre & post War ALS	War Dated ALS
$	$50	$	$	$	$

S, A signature as Governor of New York. SR Nov. 1993 $50.

Seward, William Henry Jr., 1839-1920   Union General

Signature	Signature with rank	Pre & post War DS	War Dated DS	Pre & post War ALS	War Dated ALS
$	$65	$175	$375	$	$

Sewell, William J., 1835-1901   Brevetted Union General

Signature	Signature with rank	Pre & post War DS	War Dated DS	Pre & post War ALS	War Dated ALS
$	$32	$	$	$98	$

Sexton, Franklin Barlow, 1828-1900   Member Confederate Congress

Signature	Signature with rank	Pre & post War DS	War Dated DS	Pre & post War ALS	War Dated ALS
$	$45	$	$	$	$

Seymour, Truman, 1824-91   Union General

Signature	Signature with rank	Pre & post War DS	War Dated DS	Pre & post War ALS	War Dated ALS
$20	$	$	$75	$	$

Shackelford, James Murrell, 1827-1909   Union General

Signature	Signature with rank	Pre & post War DS	War Dated DS	Pre & post War ALS	War Dated ALS
$25	$	$65	$	$	$

Shafter, William Rufus, 1835-1906   Brevetted Union General

Signature	Signature with rank	Pre & post War DS	War Dated DS	Pre & post War ALS	War Dated ALS
$	$25	$	$58	$	$

Shaler, Alexander, 1827-1911   Union General

Signature	Signature with rank	Pre & post War DS	War Dated DS	Pre & post War ALS	War Dated ALS
$	$35	$	$98	$	$

Sharp, Jacob Hunter, 1833-1907   Confederate Brigadier General

Univ. of Alabama graduate. He entered C.S. service as a Private in the 1st Mississippi Infantry. He fought with distinction at Shiloh, Murfreesboro, and Chickamauga. He was promoted to Brig. Genl. on July 26, 1864, and saw additional action with Genl. Hood in TN. and the Carolinas.

Signature	Signature with rank	Pre & post War DS	War Dated DS	Pre & post War ALS	War Dated ALS
$80	$135	$167	$	$	$

Shelby, Joseph Orville, 1830-97 Confederate Brigadier General

He led a band of pro-slavery Kentuckians in the Missouri-Kansas "war" of the late 1850's. At the outbreak of C.W. he organized a cavalry co., & was attached to Sterling Price, active in almost every campaign west of the Miss. River. His reputation compared with that of Nathan Bedford Forrest and earned him a contemporary renown of almost equal distinction. When the Confederacy fell, Shelby & his command buried their battle flags in the Rio Grande & escaped into Mexico, refusing to surrender.

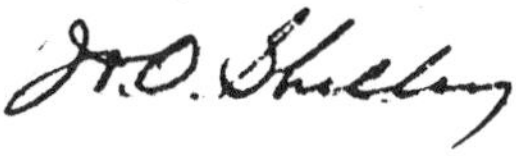

Signature	Signature with rank	Pre & post War DS	War Dated DS	Pre & post War ALS	War Dated ALS
$250	$410	$780	$	$	$

DS, Oct. 26, 1858, folio, legal document, Lafayette Co., Missouri, Signed "Jo. O. Shelby." LR Dec. 1993 $1,150.
--, Oct. 12, 1860. Promissory note in check form. BG Nov. 1993 $750.
PS, Signed on revised. HN Nov. 1993 $1,850.

Shelley, Charles Miller, 1833-1907 Confederate Brigadier General

1st Lt. in the Talladega Artillery, and was on duty at Fort Morgan in 1861. He was captured at Vicksburg and after his exchange was assigned to the Army of TN. He fought at Franklin where he had his horse shot out from under him.

Signature	Signature with rank	Pre & post War DS	War Dated DS	Pre & post War ALS	War Dated ALS
$68	$98	$	$248	$	$

Shepard, Isaac Fitzgerald, 1816-89 Union General

Signature	Signature with rank	Pre & post War DS	War Dated DS	Pre & post War ALS	War Dated ALS
$	$	$	$58	$	$

Shepley, George Foster, 1819-78 Union General

Signature	Signature with rank	Pre & post War DS	War Dated DS	Pre & post War ALS	War Dated ALS
$	$32	$	$	$	$

Sheppard, William Ludlow, 1833-1912   CSA Officer & Artist

Member of the Second Company Richmond Howitzers, VA. Painted News from Home, watercolor on paper, 11x8" and Equipment 61 (n.d.) watercolor on paper 11x8", Museum of the Confederacy, Richmond, Va.

Signature	Signature with rank	Pre & post War DS	War Dated DS	Pre & post War ALS	War Dated ALS
$	$	$	$	$178	$

Sheridan, Phillip Henry, 1831-88   Union General

Nicknamed "Little Phil," he was one of the Union's top soldiers. He led Sheridan's Richmond raid, where Jeb Stuart was killed, and had a string of victories in the Shenandoah Valley campaign. LOC. papers, 1853-88. ca. 18,000 items.

Signature	Signature with rank	Pre & post War DS	War Dated DS	Pre & post War ALS	War Dated ALS
$175	$250	$325	$	$587	$

S, "P.H. Sheridan/ Leut. General, U.S.A." on slip. JB Dec. 1993 $150.

-, Signature with rank, 1870's Mt. Washington, N.H. hotel stationery. BG Nov. 1993 $325.

PS, &.75x10" black and white engraving signed in blue pencil 'P.H. Sheridan Lieut Genl" UA Feb. 1994 $1,000.

--, 8x10" sepia tone photograph. 'Phil. H. Sheridan Mj Genl U.S.A." on verso 'Genl Sheridan - Feby 1865 - sent from the Middle Military Department by Dr. H. O. DuBois Assist. Medical Director." UA Feb. 1994 $2,850.

--, A sepia toned photograph of Sheridan in uniform signed "Phil. H. Sheridan Mj Genl U.S.A." is tipped to heavy stock paper for protection. UA Sept. 1993 $2,850.

Sherman Ellen E., 1823-88   Wife of General William T. Sherman

Signature	Pre & post War DS	War Dated DS	Pre & post War ALS	War Dated ALS
$35	$	$	$145	$

ALS, Nov. 19, 1865. 1.5pp, 5x8" St. Louis, MO, Thanks correspondent for copies of a book. MS Nov. 1993 $115.

Sherman, Francis Trowbridge, 1825-1905   Union General

Signature	Signature with rank	Pre & post War DS	War Dated DS	Pre & post War ALS	War Dated ALS
$20	$32	$	$73	$	$

Sherman, William Tecumseh, 1820-91   Union General

Famous for his capture of Atlanta and subsequent march to the sea.   LOC. papers, 1810-96. ca. 18,000 items. Microfilm, 15 reels.

Signature	Signature with rank	Pre & post War DS	War Dated DS	Pre & post War ALS	War Dated ALS
$265	$350	$378	$1650	$950	$12225

ALS, Dec. 21, 1863. 4p. Hd. Qtrs., Dept. of the Tenn., Nashville., To General John A. Logan, mentioning General Grant, Dodge and Admiral Porter, stating in part: 'I would slay millions on that point I am not only insane but mad. I think I see one or two quick blows that will astonish the natives of the south ... gather forage and supplies and be ready for the next great move. LS Dec. 1993 $47,500.

---, April 27, 1865, 3.5pp., 4to, to Confederate General Jos. E. Johnston, the day after accepting the surrender of Johnston's troops, discussing repatriation of the Coonfederate Army. S May 1993 $40,250.

---, March 20, 1873, 1p. 8vo. Washington, D.C. to C. Edward Lister, pert. to a copy of a book sent to Sherman. UA Sept. 1993 $950.

DS, April 22, 1862, envelope 5.5x3.75", addressed entirely in his hand to his name sake son by Gen. Sherman. LS Dec. 1993 $1,500.

--, Dec. 28 1876. Check signed, to Mrs. General Sherman. BG Nov. 1993 $400.

> NOTE: Appox. 150 post war checks were discovered in the late spring of 1993. Initial price <u>was</u> $250. <u>per in lots of four or more.</u>

PS, CDV, in uniform, waist up. Signed on reverse 'W.T. Sherman/ Lt. Genl". B/M E.R. Gard Photographic Art Gallery of Chicago, w/ two cent rev. stamp. UA Feb. 1994 $2,000.

S, Frank, Signature & addressed. W/CDV. JH Feb. 1994 $475.

-, 'W.T. Sherman/ Lt. Genl." on reverse of his imprinted business card. SK Feb. 1994 $250.

-, "W.T. Sherman/ Lt. Genl." on white card. BJ Dec. 1993 $250.

-, Clip. with rank. BG Nov. 1993 $325.

Misc.

---, Sept. 1, 1845, 4.75x7.65" 1p. 8vo, Augusta, Ga., Arsenal. signed in pencil on the inside frontispiece of the book "Instructions for Field Artillery 1845/ Opposite, on the inside front cover a book plate that reads "Company - [B] Third Regiment of Artillery" and is signed "W. G. Freemont, Asst. Adjutant General". Directly under the bookplate is signed "Capt. JR Vinton's Camp No. 2." UA Sept. 1993 $2,750.

---, Letter. 7 March 1864, 1p. (OFFICIAL COPY) to Adm. D.D. Porter "I do not want the Marine Brigade to have any   thing to do with cotton or trade. It is foreign to their business..." ML January 1993 $100.

P, CDV, Bust view pose in uniform of general. Classic shot of a determined Sherman. Shoulder bar, upraised collar & tie all visible. B/M of A.H. Morse, Photographer, Dept. of the Cumberland, Nashville, TN. LR Sept. 1993 $150.

- CDV, 2/3 view seated view. Sherman wears his double breasted, Maj. Gen. coat open, to expose vest. Also has medal on breast of coat. LR Dec. 1993 $195.

Shewmake, John Troup, 1828-98   Member Confederate Congress

Signature	Signature with rank	Pre & post War DS	War Dated DS	Pre & post War ALS	War Dated ALS
$40	$	$	$	$	$

Shields, James, 1806-79   Union General

Signature	Signature with rank	Pre & post War DS	War Dated DS	Pre & post War ALS	War Dated ALS
$50	$68	$	$	$187	$

ALS, 1852 March 3. 1p, 8x10", Washington, DC., To A. H.H. Stewart, the bearer, Mrs. Ann L. Rogers is the wife of one of your agents who is now in Texas...she assistance. HD June 1992 $150

Shorter, John Gill, 1818-1872   Confederate Governor
Alabama 1861-63. LOC. collection, 1862. 2 items.

Signature	Signature with rank	Pre & post War DS	War Dated DS	Pre & post War ALS	War Dated ALS
$55	$	$	$250	$	$

Shoup, Francis Asbury, 1834-96   Confederate Brigadier General
WP graduate. He entered C.S. service as a 1st Lt. of Artillery. He was Chief of Artillery for Genl. Hardee at Shiloh. As Brig. Genl. he commanded a brigade at Vicksburg, where he was captured. During the Atlanta Campaign, he was Chief of Artillery for Genl. Johnston, and served as Chief of Staff for Genl. Hood in the TN operations.

Signature	Signature with rank	Pre & post War DS	War Dated DS	Pre & post War ALS	War Dated ALS
$75	$115	$	$	$	$

Sibley, Henry Hasting, 1811-91   Union General

Signature	Signature with rank	Pre & post War DS	War Dated DS	Pre & post War ALS	War Dated ALS
$	$	$35	$	$	$

Sibley, Henry Hopkins, 1816-86   Confederate Brigadier General

WP graduate. He entered C.S. service as a Colonel in May 1861. He was appointed Brig. Genl. Shortly thereafter on June 17, 1861. He became Commander of the Army of New Mexico, was repulsed at Glorietta, and driven back to Texas. Relieved of command in December 1862. He invented the Sibly Tent.

Signature	Signature with rank	Pre & post War DS	War Dated DS	Pre & post War ALS	War Dated ALS
$70	$110	$485	$	$875	$

DS, Aug. 8, 1852. 1p. 8to., Ft. Graham, TX. pert. to supplies. BG Sept. 1993 $475.

Sickles, Daniel Edgar, 1819-1914   Union Major General

LOC. papers, 1845-1914. ca. 1,100 items.

Signature	Signature with rank	Pre & post War DS	War Dated DS	Pre & post War ALS	War Dated ALS
$58	$90	$165	$	$	$

TLS, May 19, 1903, 1p. 8x11, New York, NY, Accepts invitation to attend the dedication of an equestrian statue of General Hooker. MS Nov. 1993 $150.

Siegel, Franz, 1824-1902   Union General

He performed well at the capture of Camp Jackson & the battle at Carthage, MO. Sigel contributed greatly to the Union victory at Pea Ridge, Ark., but didn't fare so well at New Market, VA., when he was soundly whipped by the VMI cadets. LOC. collection, 1862-70. 2 items.

Signature	Signature with rank	Pre & post War DS	War Dated DS	Pre & post War ALS	War Dated ALS
$50	$80	$	$	$	$

Misc.
P, CDV, Almost waist up view in double breasted uniform coat with epaulettes. E. Anthony, NY, edges slightly trimmed. LR Dec. 1993 $25.

Sill, Joshua Woodrow, 1831-62   Union General

WP graduate. He was killed in action at Stones River/ Murfreesboro. Rare.

Signature	Signature with rank	Pre War DS	War Dated DS	Pre War ALS	War Dated ALS
$	$	$	$	$	$

336

Simms, James P., 1837-87   Confederate Brigadier General

He entered C.S. service as a Major in the 53rd GA Infantry. He was with Genl. Magruder at Seven Days, and fought with distinction at 2nd Manassas, Sharpsburg, and Salem Church. He was captured at Sayler's Creek on April 6, 1865.

Signature	Signature with rank	Pre & post War DS	War Dated DS	Pre & post War ALS	War Dated ALS
$80	$148	$198	$347	$	$

Simms, John Gill, 1818-72   Member Confederate Congress

Signature	Signature with rank	Pre & post War DS	War Dated DS	Pre & post War ALS	War Dated ALS
$	$45	$78	$	$	$

Simms, William Elliott, 1822-98   Member Confederate Congress

Signature	Signature with rank	Pre & post War DS	War Dated DS	Pre & post War ALS	War Dated ALS
$35	$	$	$	$87	$

Simpson, William Dunlap, 1823-90   Member Confederate Congress

Signature	Signature with rank	Pre & post War DS	War Dated DS	Pre & post War ALS	War Dated ALS
$	$55	$	$	$	$

Singleton, Otho Robards, 1814-89   Member Confederate Congress

Signature	Signature with rank	Pre & post War DS	War Dated DS	Pre & post War ALS	War Dated ALS
$30	$	$	$	$	$

Slack, James Richard, 1818-81   Union General

Signature	Signature with rank	Pre & post War DS	War Dated DS	Pre & post War ALS	War Dated ALS
$	$45	$	$87	$98	$

Slack, William Yarnell, 1816-62   Confederate Brigadier General

Brig. Genl. of the Missouri State Guard by the Gov. of Missouri in 1861. He fought at Carthage, and was wounded during the Battle of Springfield. He was shot at the Battle Elkhorn Tavern, dying March 21, 1862.

Signature	Signature with rank	Pre War DS	War Dated DS	Pre War ALS	War Dated ALS
$300	$450	$	$	$	$

A rare signature.

Slaughter, James Edwin, 1827-1901   Confederate Brigadier General

Resigned from V.M.I. to fight in the Mexican War. Accepted a commission in the Confederate Artillery. He was on Genl. Bragg's Staff at Pensacola, and under Genl. A.S. Johnston at Shiloh. He commanded the last Confederate engagement of the Civil War, at Brownsville, Texas, May 12, 1865.

Signature	Signature with rank	Pre & post War DS	War Dated DS	Pre & post War ALS	War Dated ALS
$75	$125	$	$278	$245	$

Slemmer, Adam Jacoby, 1829-68   Union General

Signature	Signature with rank	Pre & post War DS	War Dated DS	Pre & post War ALS	War Dated ALS
$	$	$	$	$	$

Slidell, John, 1793-1871   Confederate Statesman, Com. to France

Signature	Signature with rank	Pre & post War DS	War Dated DS	Pre & post War ALS	War Dated ALS
$35	$	$105	$	$200	$

ALS, May 19, 1858, 1p., 8to., U.S. Senate, pert. to recommending Beauregard as Supt. of West Point. BG Sept. 1993 $300.

Sloat, John Drake, 1780-1867   Union Naval Officer

Signature	Signature with rank	Pre & post War DS	War Dated DS	Pre & post War ALS	War Dated ALS
$	$45	$	$138	$	$

Slocum, Henry Warner, 1827-94   Union Major General

Severely wounded at 1st Bull Run, also fought at Yotktown, Gaines Mill, Malvern Hill, 2nd Bull Run, Antietam, Chancellorsville, Gettysburg, the March from Atlanta to the Sea & the Carolina campaign.

Signature	Signature with rank	Pre & post War DS	War Dated DS	Pre & post War ALS	War Dated ALS
$50	$78	$	$	$	$

Misc.

P, CDV, half view, seated pose, with one hand inside his Maj. Gen. coat. B/M of J.C. Elord's Gallery, (Louisville, Ky., w/2¢ blue revenue stamp. LR Sept. 1993 $75.

Slough, John Potts, 1829-67   Union General

Signature	Signature with rank	Pre & post War DS	War Dated DS	Pre & post War ALS	War Dated ALS
$	$	$	$	$	$

Smith, Andrew Jackson, 1815-97   Union General

Signature	Signature with rank	Pre & post War DS	War Dated DS	Pre & post War ALS	War Dated ALS
$45	$65	$98	$	$	$

Smith, Charles Ferguson, 1807-62   Union General

LOC. papers, 1825-82. 16 items.

Signature	Signature with rank	Pre War DS	War Dated DS	Pre War ALS	War Dated ALS
$38	$75	$	$178	$	$

Smith, Edmund Kirby, 1824-93   Confederate Major General

WP graduate. He entered Confederate service as Lt. Col. under Genl. Joe Johnston in the Valley operations. He was appointed Brig. Genl. on June 17, 1861, and was severely wounded at 1st Manassas. Chief of all Confederate forces west of the Mississippi. Surrendered on May 26th 1865.

Signature	Signature with rank	Pre & post War DS	War Dated DS	Pre & post War ALS	War Dated ALS
$300	$375	$650	$950	$875	$1,350

ALS, 1893 "I had in Ky. campaign under my command 30,000 veterans for duty. In the Trans-Mississippi Dept., where my command was civil and administrative as well as military, the rolls called for over 50,000." SR Nov. 1993 $695.
ANS, Postwar. 5 lines on verso of a cabinet photo of him. JH Nov. 1993 $425.
DS, May 1865. a Mexican land plat. JH Nov. 1993 $600.
S, Clipped signature with state (Flda.), with engraving. BG Sept. 1993 $295.

Smith, Giles Alexander, 1829-76   Union General

Signature	Signature with rank	Pre & post War DS	War Dated DS	Pre & post War ALS	War Dated ALS
$	$58	$	$	$	$

Smith, Green Clay, 1826-95   Union General

Signature	Signature with rank	Pre & post War DS	War Dated DS	Pre & post War ALS	War Dated ALS
$25	$45	$	$	$	$

Smith, Gustavus Adolphus, 1820-85   Union General

Signature	Signature with rank	Pre & post War DS	War Dated DS	Pre & post War ALS	War Dated ALS
$	$38	$	$78	$	$

Smith, Gustavus Woodson, 1821-96   Confederate Major General

WP graduate. He entered CS service as a Major Genl. He fought at Seven Pines. He was Acting Secy. of War in November 1862. He was later appointed Major Genl. of the Georgia State Militia, fighting with distinction in various battles around Atlanta.

Signature	Signature with rank	Pre & post War DS	War Dated DS	Pre & post War ALS	War Dated ALS
$110	$	$178	$	$350	$475

Smith, James Argyle, 1831-1901   Confederate Brigadier General

WP graduate. He entered C.S. service as Capt. in the Confederate Army, and later was made a Major on the Staff of Genl. Polk. He fought with great distinction and bravery at Shiloh, Perryville, Murfreesbor, and Chickamauga. Commissioned Brig. Genl. on Sept. 30, 1863. He was later in command of Genl. Cleburne's Division.

Signature	Signature with rank	Pre & post War DS	War Dated DS	Pre & post War ALS	War Dated ALS
$80	$120	$187	$	$	$

Smith, James Milton, 1823-90   Member Confederate Congress

Gov. GA. 72-76

Signature	Signature with rank	Pre & post War DS	War Dated DS	Pre & post War ALS	War Dated ALS
$	$	$78	$	$	$

Smith, John Eugene, 1816-97   Union General

Signature	Signature with rank	Pre & post War DS	War Dated DS	Pre & post War ALS	War Dated ALS
$	$35	$	$	$	$

Smith, Martin Luther, 1819-66 — Confederate Major General

WP graduate. He entered C.S. service as a Major in the Corps of Engineers. He was appointed Major Genl. on Nov. 4, 1862. He was captured at Vicksburg; after his exchange, he was appointed Chief Engineer for the Army of Northern Virginia.

Signature	Signature with rank	Pre & post War DS	War Dated DS	Pre & post War ALS	War Dated ALS
$80	$115	$	$	$	$2,578

Smith, Melancthon, ?-1893 — Union General

Signature	Signature with rank	Pre & post War DS	War Dated DS	Pre & post War ALS	War Dated ALS
$	$35	$	$	$	$

Smith, Morgan Lewis, 1821-74 — Union General

Signature	Signature with rank	Pre & post War DS	War Dated DS	Pre & post War ALS	War Dated ALS
$	$	$	$78	$	$

Smith, Preston, 1823-63 — Confederate Brigadier General

He entered C.S. service as a Colonel in the 154th TN. He was wounded while leading this unit at Shiloh, and was in command of a brigade under Kirby Smith during the Kentucky operation. He was killed 19 Sept. 1863 at Chickamauga, GA., on the battlefield.

Signature	Signature with rank	Pre War DS	War Dated DS	Pre War ALS	War Dated ALS
$250	$	$	$	$	$

An extremely rare signature.

Smith, Thomas Church Haskell, 1819-97 — Union General

Signature	Signature with rank	Pre & post War DS	War Dated DS	Pre & post War ALS	War Dated ALS
$	$35	$	$	$	$

Smith, Thomas Benton, 1823-1923 — Confederate Brigadier General

2nd Lt. in the 20th TN and first saw action at Mill Springs and Shiloh. He was severely wounded at the Battle of Murfreesboro, and fought with distinction during the Atlanta operation.

Signature	Signature with rank	Pre & post War DS	War Dated DS	Pre & post War ALS	War Dated ALS
$110	$175	$	$	$1,150	$3,200

Smith, Thomas Kilby, 1820-87 — Union General

Signature	Signature with rank	Pre & post War DS	War Dated DS	Pre & post War ALS	War Dated ALS
$	$35	$	$	$	$

Smith, William, 1797-1887 — Confederate Major General

He entered C.S. service as Colonel of the 49th Virginia Infantry. He first action was at 1st Manassas. He was then elected to the Confederate Congress, he attended sessions between battles, fighting with great distinction at Seven Days, Sharpsburg, and Gettysburg. He was elected Gov. of Va. on Jan. 1, 1864 and saw no further action.

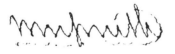

Signature	Signature with rank	Pre & post War DS	War Dated DS	Pre & post War ALS	War Dated ALS
$120	$180	$245	$	$	$2,225

Smith, William Duncan, 1825-62   Confederate Brigadier General

WP graduate. Entered as a Captain and rapidly rose through the ranks, appointed Colonel of the 20th GA in July 1861. Brig. Genl. on March 7, 1862. He was ordered to Charleston, and was instrumental in the Confederate victory at Secessionville, S.C. He died of yellow fever in Charleston.

Signature	Signature with rank	Pre War DS	War Dated DS	Pre War ALS	War Dated ALS
$	$	$	$	$	$

A rare signature.

Smith, William Ephraim, 1829-90   Member Confederate Congress

Signature	Signature with rank	Pre & post War DS	War Dated DS	Pre & post War ALS	War Dated ALS
$40	$	$67	$	$	$

Smith, William Farrar, 1824-1903   Union General

LOC. Letter, 1863. 1 item.

Signature	Signature with rank	Pre & post War DS	War Dated DS	Pre & post War ALS	War Dated ALS
$	$35	$	$	$	$178

Smith, William Nathan Harrell, 1812-89   Member Conf. Congress

Signature	Signature with rank	Pre & post War DS	War Dated DS	Pre & post War ALS	War Dated ALS
$40	$	$	$	$	$

Smith, William Russell, 1815-96   Member Confederate Congress

Signature	Signature with rank	Pre & post War DS	War Dated DS	Pre & post War ALS	War Dated ALS
$35	$	$	$	$	$

Smith, William Sooy, 1830-1916   Union General

Signature	Signature with rank	Pre & post War DS	War Dated DS	Pre & post War ALS	War Dated ALS
$	$25	$	$	$56	$

Smyth, Thomas Alfred, 1832-65   Union Brigadier General

Died of wounds rec'd at Farmville, VA. Rare.

Signature	Signature with rank	Pre & post War DS	War Dated DS	Pre & post War ALS	War Dated ALS
$	$	$	$	$	$

Sorrel, Gilbert Moxley, 1838-1901   Confederate Brigadier General

Aide-de-camp on the Staff of Genl. Longstreet, from 1st Manassas to the Wilderness. He was made Brig. Genl. on Oct. 27, 1864 and was given a GA brigade in Mahone's 3rd Corps. He was severely wounded at Hatcher's Run and saw no further action.

Signature	Signature with rank	Pre & post War DS	War Dated DS	Pre & post War ALS	War Dated ALS
$110	$280	$	$2,250	$	$

Spears, James Gallent, 1816-69   Union General

Signature	Signature with rank	Pre & post War DS	War Dated DS	Pre & post War ALS	War Dated ALS
$	$35	$	$	$	$

Speed, James, 1812-87   Lincoln's Attorney General

Signature	Signature with rank	Pre & post War DS	War Dated DS	Pre & post War ALS	War Dated ALS
$50	$80	$	$278	$	$

Spencer, George Eliphaz, 1836-93   Brevetted Union General

Signature	Signature with rank	Pre & post War DS	War Dated DS	Pre & post War ALS	War Dated ALS
$22	$35	$	$	$	$

Spinola, Francis Barretto, 1821-90   Union General

Signature	Signature with rank	Pre & post War DS	War Dated DS	Pre & post War ALS	War Dated ALS
$	$45	$	$87	$	$

Spinner, F. E.,   Lincoln's Treasurer

Signature	Signature with rank	Pre & post War DS	War Dated DS	Pre & post War ALS	War Dated ALS
$30	$50	$75	$125	$	$

LS, 1861. 1p., signed as Treasure of the U.S. JH Feb. 1994 $75.
S, Cut signature on a printed Treasury envelope. SR Nov. 1993 $25.

Sprague, John Wilson, 1817-93   Union General

Signature	Signature with rank	Pre & post War DS	War Dated DS	Pre & post War ALS	War Dated ALS
$	$45	$	$	$	$

Sprague, William, 1830-1915   Gov. of R.I.
Col. State Militia

Signature	Signature with rank	Pre & post War DS	War Dated DS	Pre & post War ALS	War Dated ALS
$30	$50	$75	$175	$185	$275

Stafford, Leroy Augustus, 1822-64   Confederate Brigadier General
Captain in the Stafford Guards. Appointed Lt. Col. of the 9th Louisiana, he fought with distinction at Seven Days, 2nd Manassas, and Sharpsburg. While commanding the 2nd Louisiana Brigade during the Battle of the Wilderness, he was mortally wounded and died of wnds rec'd at Wilderness.

Signature	Signature with rank	Pre War DS	War Dated DS	Pre War ALS	War Dated ALS
$	$	$	$	$	$

A very rare signature.

Stahel, Julius, 1825-1912   Union General
LOC. papers, 1861-1916. In part, transcripts. Microfilm, 1 reel.

Signature	Signature with rank	Pre & post War DS	War Dated DS	Pre & post War ALS	War Dated ALS
$	$35	$50	$	$	$

Stanley, David Sloane, 1823-1902   Union General

Signature	Signature with rank	Pre & post War DS	War Dated DS	Pre & post War ALS	War Dated ALS
$30	$45	$	$	$	$875

Stannard, George Jerrison, 1820-86   Union General

Signature	Signature with rank	Pre & post War DS	War Dated DS	Pre & post War ALS	War Dated ALS
$	$35	$	$	$	$

Stanton, Edwin McMasters, 1814-69   Sec. of War, Lincoln & Johnson
LOC. papers, 1831-70. ca. 7,600 items.

Signature	Signature with rank	Pre & post War DS	War Dated DS	Pre & post War ALS	War Dated ALS
$50	$85	$137	$195	$210	$465

DS, May 19, 1865 1p, Quarto, Signed Edw. Stanton" as Secretary of War, concerning the appointment of a Captain for distinguished service and heroic courage in action..." LP Sept. 1993 $200.

--, March 24, 1862 1p., 4to., War Dept. To doctor's exam. for appointment to Asst. Surgeon, U.S.A. BG Sept. 1993 $195.

Starke, Peter Burwell, 1815-88   Confederate Brigadier General
Colonel of the 28th Mississippi Cavalry, on Feb. 24, 1862. He saw service under Genl. Johnston in the Vicksburg Campaign, and under Genl. Armstrong in the Atlanta Campaign.

P. B. Starke

Signature	Signature with rank	Pre & post War DS	War Dated DS	Pre & post War ALS	War Dated ALS
$80	$110	$	$278	$	$

S, A large signature on a card. SK Feb. 1994 $85.

Starke, William Edwin, 1814-62   Confederate Brigadier General

Aid-de-camp on the Staff of Genl. Garnett. He fought with gallantry at the Seven Days, he was then appointed Brig. Genl., on August 6, 1862. He commanded a division during Genl. Jackson's Maryland operations, and on the first day of the Battle of Sharpsburg he fell dead, Sept. 17, 1862.

Signature	Signature with rank	Pre War DS	War Dated DS	Pre War ALS	War Dated ALS
$	$	$	$	$	$

An extremely scarce signature.

Starkweather, John Converse, 1830-90   Union General

Signature	Signature with rank	Pre & post War DS	War Dated DS	Pre & post War ALS	War Dated ALS
$	$38	$67	$87	$	$

Steedman, James Blair, 1817-83   Union General

Signature	Signature with rank	Pre & post War DS	War Dated DS	Pre & post War ALS	War Dated ALS
$	$35	$	$	$87	$

Steele, Frederick, 1819-68   Union General

Signature	Signature with rank	Pre & post War DS	War Dated DS	Pre & post War ALS	War Dated ALS
$	$40	$	$	$	$

Steele, William, 1819-85   Confederate Brigadier General

WP graduate. He entered the service as a Col. in the 7th Texas Cavalry. He was appointed Brig. Genl. on Sept. 12, 1862 and fought during the Red River Campaign and in the Battle of Pleasant Hill.

Signature	Signature with rank	Pre & post War DS	War Dated DS	Pre & post War ALS	War Dated ALS
$80	$140	$110	$272	$	$

Stephens, Alexander Hamilton, 1812-83   Confederate Vice President

LOC. papers, 1784-1886. ca. 27,000 items. 57 reels on microfilm.

Signature	Signature with rank	Pre & post War DS	War Dated DS	Pre & post War ALS	War Dated ALS
$120	$250	$285	$485	$378	$675

ANS, 1p. 4.5x5", Crawfordville, GA., pert. to granting a request. BG Sept. 1993 $285.
Franking Signature, Envelope to brother (two Stephens signatures) with blue Columbus, Ga. post marked & "FREE". BG Sept. 1993 $195.
--, [1845] Sept. 27. 6x3.5", address leaf folded to letter size, addressed by him to John L. Stephens Esqr / Hamilton / Ga. HD June 1992 $110.
S, Clip. 1881. Nat July 1992 $200.
B, Annual Report/ of the/ Board of Regents/ of the/ Smithsonian Institution; Washington, James B Steedman, Printer, 1858, 8vo, 438pp.. Signed "From Alexander H. Stephens.", as Congressman. LS October 1992 $595.

Steuart, George Hume "Maryland", 1828-1903   Confed. Brig. General

WP graduate. He entered C.S. service as a Captain in the Confederate Cavalry. He commanded the 1st Maryland Infantry at 1st Manassas, and a brigade under Genl. Ewell during the Valley Campaign. He was seriously wounded at Cross Keys, and was captured at the "Mule Shoe" in 1864.

Signature	Signature with rank	Pre & post War DS	War Dated DS	Pre & post War ALS	War Dated ALS
$78	$148	$115	$	$243	$

Stevens, Clement Hoffman, 1821-64   Confederate Brigadier General

He entered C.S. service as aide-de-camp on the Staff of Genl. Barnard Bee, his brother in-in-law. He was severely wounded at 1st Manassa and Chickamauga, and was appointed Brig. Genl. on Jan. 20, 1864, D. 25 July 1864 of wounds. rec'd 20 July 1864 at Atlanta, Ga.

Signature	Signature with rank	Pre War DS	War Dated DS	Pre War ALS	War Dated ALS
$250	$	$	$	$	$

A rare signature.

Stevens, Isaac Ingalls, 1818-62   Union General

Colonel 79th NY, 'Highlanders' Regt., he fought in the Port Royal Expedition & at Secessionville, S.C. Commanded a division at 2nd Bull Run, and was killed in action Sept. 1, 1862 at Chantilly, Va. Rare.

Signature	Signature with rank	Pre War DS	War Dated DS	Pre War ALS	War Dated ALS
$110	$175	$	$	$	$

Misc.
P, CDV, Mid chest up engraved portrait, B/M Elias Dexter, NY. LR Dec. 1993 $35.

Stevens Thaddeus, 1792-1868   American Statesman

Signature	Pre & post War DS	War Dated DS	Pre & post War ALS	War Dated ALS
$35	$	$	$225	$

Stevens, Walter Husted, 1827-67   Confederate Brigadier General

WP graduate and one of the finest Engineers in the Confederacy produced. He was on the staff of Beauregard at 1st Manassas, and later served as Chief Eng. under R.E. Lee.

Signature	Signature with rank	Pre & post War DS	War Dated DS	Pre & post War ALS	War Dated ALS
$200	$	$	$	$	$

An extremely scarce signature.

Stevenson, Carter Littlepage, 1817-88   Confederate Major General

WP graduate. He entered C.S. service as an officer in the regular Army but soon promoted to Col. of the 53rd Virginia. Appointed Brig. Genl. on Feb. 27, 1862, he fought with great distinction at Cumberland Gap and in the Kentucky Campaign. He was captured and exchanged at Vicksburg, and served gallantly in all battles of the Army of TN, from Missionary Ridge to Bentonville.

Signature	Signature with rank	Pre & post War DS	War Dated DS	Pre & post War ALS	War Dated ALS
$100	$280	$225	$575	$	$

Stevenson, John Dunlop, 1821-97   Union General

Signature	Signature with rank	Pre & post War DS	War Dated DS	Pre & post War ALS	War Dated ALS
$	$35	$	$	$	$

Stevenson, Thomas Greely, 1836-64   Union General

Killed 10 May 1864 at Spottsylvania, Va. Rare.

Signature	Signature with rank	Pre War DS	War Dated DS	Pre War ALS	War Dated ALS
$	$	$	$	$	$

Stewart, Alexander Peter, 1821-1908   Confederate Lt. General

WP graduate. Led the 2nd Brigade at Shiloh; fought in Hardee's Corps at Chattanooga; and was wounded at Mt. Ezra Church, NC.

Signature	Signature with rank	Pre & post War DS	War Dated DS	Pre & post War ALS	War Dated ALS
$150	$250	$	$	$	$

S, Clip signature with rank, Lt. Genl., C.S.A. BG Sept. 1993 $250.
-, Clip from a letter written to General Marcus Wright concerning an appointment for an unknown soldier. TP Nov. 1993 $275.

St. John, Isaac M., 1827-80   Confederate Brigadier General

Yale graduate. He entered as a Private in the Fort Hill Guards. He served as an Engineer under Genl. Magruder in fortifying the Peninsula. In 1862, he was appointed Chief of Mining and Nitre Bureau, and was commissioned Brig. Genl. on Feb. 16, 1864.

Signature	Signature with rank	Pre & post War DS	War Dated DS	Pre & post War ALS	War Dated ALS
$80	$175	$	$	$	$

Stokes, James Hughes, 1815-90   Union General

Signature	Signature with rank	Pre & post War DS	War Dated DS	Pre & post War ALS	War Dated ALS
$	$35	$	$	$	$

Stolbrand, Charles John, 1821-94   Union General

Signature	Signature with rank	Pre & post War DS	War Dated DS	Pre & post War ALS	War Dated ALS
$	$	$	$87	$	$

Stone, Charles Pomeroy, 1824-87   Union General

Signature	Signature with rank	Pre & post War DS	War Dated DS	Pre & post War ALS	War Dated ALS
$	$38	$	$	$	$

Stoneman, George, 1822-94   Union General

Signature	Signature with rank	Pre & post War DS	War Dated DS	Pre & post War ALS	War Dated ALS
$80	$150	$178	$	$257	$

Stoughton, Edwin Henry, 1828-68   Union General

Signature	Signature with rank	Pre & post War DS	War Dated DS	Pre & post War ALS	War Dated ALS
$	$35	$	$	$	$

Stovall, Marcellus Augustus, 1818-95   Confederate Brigadier General
Lt. Col. of the 3rd Georgia Infantry. He fought with great distinction at Murfreesboro
and Chickamauga. He was appointed Brig. Genl. on January 20, 1863, and saw further
service under Genl. Hood in TN operations. He surrendered with Genl. Johnston in NC

Signature	Signature with rank	Pre & post War DS	War Dated DS	Pre & post War ALS	War Dated ALS
$75	$165	$148	$278	$	$

Stowe, Harriet Beecher, 1811-96   Author
Wrote *Uncle Tom's Cabin, etc.*

Signature	Pre & post War DS	War Dated DS	Pre & post War ALS	War Dated ALS
$225	$575	$	$1,150	$

S, Fine cut signature cut from letter, with portrait. JB Dec. 1993 $125.

Strahl, Otho French, 1831-64   Confederate Brigadier General
Captain of the 4th TN Vol. Inf. He fought with distinction at Shiloh, Murfreesboro,
and Perryville, and was appointed Brig. Genl. on July 28, 1863. Killed 30 Nov. 1864 at
Franklin, TN.

Signature	Signature with rank	Pre War DS	War Dated DS	Pre War ALS	War Dated ALS
$250	$	$	$	$	$

An extremely rare signature.

Stringham, Silas Horton, 1798-1876   Union Naval Admiral

Signature	Signature with rank	Pre & post War DS	War Dated DS	Pre & post War ALS	War Dated ALS
$	$67	$	$	$	$

Strong, George Crockett, 1832-63   Union Major General

Died 30 July 1863 of wounds recd at Fort Wagner, S.C.

Signature	Signature with rank	Pre War DS	War Dated DS	Pre War ALS	War Dated ALS
$175	$250	$	$	$	$

Strong, William Kerley, 1805-67   Union General

Signature	Signature with rank	Pre & post War DS	War Dated DS	Pre & post War ALS	War Dated ALS
$	$35	$	$	$	$

Stuart, David, 1816-68   Union General

Signature	Signature with rank	Pre & post War DS	War Dated DS	Pre & post War ALS	War Dated ALS
$	$35	$	$	$	$

Stuart, James Ewell Brown "Jeb", 1833-64   Confederate Major General

WP graduate. He served with R.E. Lee at Harper's Ferry in 1859, when both men were U.S. Army officers. Colonel of the 1st Virginia Cavalry. He was promoted to Brig. Genl. on Sept. 24, 1861, for his gallant cavalry charge on Henry Hill during the Battle of 1st Manassas. He made an incredible attack on Genl. Hooker's flank at Chancellorsville. He fought his greatest cavalry battle, at Brandy Station, June 9, 1863.

Signature	Signature with rank	Pre War DS	War Dated DS	Pre War ALS	War Dated ALS
$3,000	$	$4,750	$	$12,500	$20,000+

ALS, May 17, 1862. 1p. to E. P. Alexander pert. to carbines. BG Dec. 1993 $20,000.

---, [pre-war] 1p., pert. to West Point and military matters. AB Nov. 1993 $14,000.

S, Signs a Young ladies autograph album during his retreat after the battle of Gettysburg. "Yours truly/ JEB Stuart/ Funkstown Md/ July 8 1863." GH Nov. 1993 $12,500.

Misc.

P, 10" albumen in his Confederate Major General's uniform. GH Nov. 1993 $1,750.

354

Stumbaugh, Frederick Shearer, 1817-97 — Union General

Signature	Signature with rank	Pre & post War DS	War Dated DS	Pre & post War ALS	War Dated ALS
$	$	$	$78	$	$

Sturgis, Samuel Davis, 1822-89 — Union General

Signature	Signature with rank	Pre & post War DS	War Dated DS	Pre & post War ALS	War Dated ALS
$	$32	$	$	$	$

Sullivan, Jeremiah Cutler, 1830-90 — Union General

Signature	Signature with rank	Pre & post War DS	War Dated DS	Pre & post War ALS	War Dated ALS
$20	$	$	$	$	$

Sullivan, Peter John, 1821-83 — Brevetted Union General

Signature	Signature with rank	Pre & post War DS	War Dated DS	Pre & post War ALS	War Dated ALS
$	$27	$75	$	$140	$

Sully, Alfred, 1820-79 — Union General

Signature	Signature with rank	Pre & post War DS	War Dated DS	Pre & post War ALS	War Dated ALS
$	$42	$	$	$	$

Sumner, Charles, 1811-74 — Union Statesman
U.S. Senator, Mass. Opponent to slavery.

Signature	Pre & post War DS	War Dated DS	Pre & post War ALS	War Dated ALS
$58	$	$	$164	$

S, Clip. BG Sept. 1993 $ 25.
-, Clip. NS July 1992 $100.

Sumner, Edwin Vose, 1797-1863 — Union Major General

Signature	Signature with rank	Pre War DS	War Dated DS	Pre War ALS	War Dated ALS
$60	$90	$175	$278	$	$

355

Surratt, Mary Eugenia Jenkins, 1820-65   Alleged Lincoln Conspirator
Hung. Very rare.

Signature	Pre & post War DS	War Dated DS	Pre & post War ALS	War Dated ALS
$	$	$	$	$

Swan, William Graham, 1821-69   Member Confederate Congress

Signature	Signature with rank	Pre & post War DS	War Dated DS	Pre & post War ALS	War Dated ALS
$	$45	$	$	$	$

Swayne, Wager, 1834-1902   Union General

Signature	Signature with rank	Pre & post War DS	War Dated DS	Pre & post War ALS	War Dated ALS
$	$35	$64	$	$	$

Sweeney, Thomas William, 1820-92   Union General
He lost his right arm at the Battle of Churubusco, in Mexican War. He fought at Carthage, & Wilson's Creek, Mo., became Col. 52nd Ill. Inf. He saw action at Fort Donelson, Shiloh, & the Atlanta campaign.

Signature	Signature with rank	Pre & post War DS	War Dated DS	Pre & post War ALS	War Dated ALS
$	$40	$	$	$	$

Misc.
P, CDV, Full standing view, as Captain, 2nd U.S. Infantry. He is wearing a single breasted frock coat with captain shoulders bars, holding a kepi with Infantry insignia & the numeral "2". B/M Anthony, NY LR Dec. 1993 $150.

Swift, Frederick William, 1831-1916   Brevetted Union General

Signature	Signature with rank	Pre & post War DS	War Dated DS	Pre & post War ALS	War Dated ALS
$	$50	$98	$	$	$

Sykes, George, 1822-80   Union General

Signature	Signature with rank	Pre & post War DS	War Dated DS	Pre & post War ALS	War Dated ALS
$	$120	$87	$197	$	$

T

Tabor, Walton, ?-1931

Artist

Signature	DS	ALS
$	$	$138

Taliaferro, William Booth, 1822-98   Confederate Brigadier General

Havard graduate. He was appointed Colonel of the 23rd Virginia Infantry, and was with Genl. Garnett at Rich Mountain. Appointed Brig. Genl. on March 4, 1862, he served with Stonewall Jackson in the Valley, and was severly wounded at Groveton. He was appointed Major Genl., on Jan. 1, 1865.

Signature	Signature with rank	Pre & post War DS	War Dated DS	Pre & post War ALS	War Dated ALS
$90	$178	$	$345	$385	$

Tappan, James Camp, 1825-1906   Confederate Brigadier General

Yale graduate. Colonel of the 13th Arkansas. He fought at the Battle of Belmont and at Shiloh. Appointed Brig. Genl. on Nov. 5, 1862. He was transferred to the Trans-Mississippi Department. He was commended for his bravery at Pleasant Hill.

Signature	Signature with rank	Pre & post War DS	War Dated DS	Pre & post War ALS	War Dated ALS
$70	$120	$	$	$210	$

Taylor, George William, 1808-62

Union General

He died September 1, 1862 of wounds recd at Bull Run.. Rare.

Signature	Signature with rank	Pre War DS	War Dated DS	Pre War ALS	War Dated ALS
$125	$	$	$	$	$

Taylor, Joseph Pannell, 1796-1864   Union General

Signature	Signature with rank	Pre War DS	War Dated DS	Pre War ALS	War Dated ALS
$	$65	$	$	$	$

Taylor, Nelson, 1821-94   Union General

Signature	Signature with rank	Pre & post War DS	War Dated DS	Pre & post War ALS	War Dated ALS
$	$35	$	$87	$	$

Taylor, Richard, 1826-79   Confederate Lt. General

Son of President Zachary Taylor, brother-in-law of Jefferson Davis, Colonel 9th Louisiana Inf., fought with Stonewall Jackson in the 1862 Valley campaign, & during the 7 Days battles before Richmond, but his greatest accomplishment was the complete repulse of N.P. Bank's, Red River expedition.

Signature	Signature with rank	Pre & post War DS	War Dated DS	Pre & post War ALS	War Dated ALS
$200	$378	$785	$1,875	$	$

DS, 1860. Promissory note in the amount of $5,000, plus 8% interest, signed " R. Taylor." LR Sept. 1993 $750.

Taylor, Thomas Hart, 1825-1901 Confederate Brigadier General

Lt. Col. in the 1st KY Inf. He saw action under Genl. Kirby Smith in TN, and commanded a brigade at Cumberland Gap. He was appointed Brig. Genl. on Nov. 4, 1862, but Pres. Davis declined to nominate him to the Confederate Senate.

Signature	Signature with rank	Pre & post War DS	War Dated DS	Pre & post War ALS	War Dated ALS
$70	$105	$98	$187	$245	$

Taylor, William Rufus, 1824-62 Union Brigadier General

Killed 8 Oct 1862 at Perryville, Ky. Rare.

Signature	Signature with rank	Pre War DS	War Dated DS	Pre War ALS	War Dated ALS
$	$	$	$	$	$

Terrill, James Barbour, 1838-64 Confederate General

V.M.I. graduate. Major of the 13th Virginia. He was killed in action May 30, 1864 at Bethesda Church, VA.

Signature	Signature with rank	Pre War DS	War Dated DS	Pre War ALS	War Dated ALS
$	$	$	$	$	$

A very rare signature.

Terry, Alfred Howe, 1827-90 Union General

Signature	Signature with rank	Pre & post War DS	War Dated DS	Pre & post War ALS	War Dated ALS
$90	$150	$450	$789	$	$

S, Clip with rank, Maj. Genl./ 1888. BG Nov. 1993 $125.

Terry, Henry Dwight, 1812-69　　　　　Union General

Signature	Signature with rank	Pre & post War DS	War Dated DS	Pre & post War ALS	War Dated ALS
$	$40	$78	$	$125	$

Terry, William H., 1814-88　　　　Confederate Brigadier General
Lt. of the 4th Virginia Infantry. He fought at 1st Manassas, Seven Days, and was wounded during the Battle of 2nd Manassas. As Brig. Genl., he commanded a brigade at Cold Harbor and Petersburg.

Signature	Signature with rank	Pre & post War DS	War Dated DS	Pre & post War ALS	War Dated ALS
$65	$105	$	$	$	$

Terry, William Richard, 1827-97　　　Confederate Brigadier General
V.M.I. graduate. Captain in the Confederate Cavalry. Colonel of the 24th Virginia. Appointed Brig. Genl. on May 31, 1864, Genl. Terry was wounded more than six times during the war, seriously at Dinwiddie Court House on March 31, 1865.

Signature	Signature with rank	Pre & Post War DS	War Dated DS	Pre & post War ALS	War Dated ALS
$87	$180	$	$567	$390	$

Thatcher, Henry K., ?-?　　　　Union Naval Commander

Signature	Signature with rank	Pre & post War DS	War Dated DS	Pre & post War ALS	War Dated ALS
$	$65	$	$	$	$

Thayer, John Milton, 1820-1906　　　　Union General

Signature	Signature with rank	Pre & post War DS	War Dated DS	Pre & post War ALS	War Dated ALS
$	$35	$87	$	$	$

Thomas, Allen, 1830-1907   Confederate Brigadier General

Princeton graduate. Colonel of the 29th Louisiana Infantry. He was captured and exchanged at Vicksburg. He was appointed Brig. Genl. on Feb. 4, 1864, he succeeded in commanding Genl. Polignac's Division.

Signature	Signature with rank	Pre & post War DS	War Dated DS	Pre & post War ALS	War Dated ALS
$	$75	$	$	$	$

Thomas, Bryan Morel, 1836-1905   Confederate Brigadier General

WP graduate. He was assigned as Chief of Artillery on the Staff of Genl. Withers at Shiloh. He was captured at Fort Blakely, on April 9, 1865.

Signature	Signature with rank	Pre & post War DS	War Dated DS	Pre & post War ALS	War Dated ALS
$75	$150	$	$328	$	$

Thomas, Edward Lloyd, 1825-98   Confederate Brigadier General

Colonel in the 35th GA Infantry, and took over Anderson's Brigade at Seven Days. He was wounded at Mechanicsville, and after his recovery saw service at Cedar Mt. and Groveton. He was under Stonewall Jackson at Chancellorsville.

Signature	Signature with rank	Pre & post War DS	War Dated DS	Pre & post War ALS	War Dated ALS
$70	$90	$	$	$	$

Thomas, George Henry, 1818-70   Union Major General

Signature	Signature with rank	Pre & post War DS	War Dated DS	Pre & post War ALS	War Dated ALS
$	$85	$	$	$	$

Thomas, Henry Goddard, 1837-97   Union General

"The Rock of Chickamauga," was one of the ablest Union commanders in the western armies. He fought at Shiloh, Perrryville, Stones River, Chickamauga, Lookout Mountain, Missionary Ridge, Atlanta, Franklin & Nashville.

Signature	Signature with rank	Pre & post War DS	War Dated DS	Pre & post War ALS	War Dated ALS
$	$	$	$	$	$

Misc.
P, CDV, Waist up view, wearing double breasted coat of Maj. Gen. B/M of Morse's Gallery of Cumberland, Nashville, TN. LR Dec. 1993 $135.

Thomas, Lorenzo, 1804-75   Union General

Fought in the Seminole & Mexican Wars. He war Adjutant Genl. of the army from 1861-69. In 1863 he went to Miss. to raise negro regts.

Signature	Signature with rank	Pre & post War DS	War Dated DS	Pre & post War ALS	War Dated ALS
$	$48	$	$150	$	$

DS, Sept. 16, 1864, 1p., 4to., Louisville, Ky., pert. to apt. for Captain in 117th Regt., U.S. Colored Inf., with officer's unsigned 1p., 4to., Louisville, Ky. 10/18/64 ALS, retained copy of acceptance. BG Nov. 1993 $150.
MISC.
P, CDV, full standing view in uniform, w/sword & holding Hardee hat. Card trimmed. LR Sept. 1993 $50.

Thomas, Stephen, 1809-1903   Union General

Signature	Signature with rank	Pre & post War DS	War Dated DS	Pre & post War ALS	War Dated ALS
$	$35	$	$87	$	$

Thompson, Jacob, 1810-85   CS Colonel, Miss. Gov. & Secret Agent

Signature	Signature with rank	Pre & post War DS	War Dated DS	Pre & post War ALS	War Dated ALS
$	$	$350	$	$	$

Thompson, M. Jefferson, 1826-76   Brig Gen. Missouri State Guards

Noted Guerrilla fighter & "Swamp Fox of the Confederacy".

Signature	Signature with rank	Pre & post War DS	War Dated DS	Pre & post War ALS	War Dated ALS
$100	$175	$	$	$	$1,425

ALS, Aug. 13, 1862, 2pp., 4to. Pontichitousles, La., to Genl. Ruggles pert. to military operations & getting inf. into & out of New Orleans. BG Nov. 1993 $1,750.

Thruston, Charles Mynn, 1798-1873 — Union General

Signature	Signature with rank	Pre & post War DS	War Dated DS	Pre & post War ALS	War Dated ALS
$	$45	$78	$	$	$

Thruston, Gates Phillips, 1835-? — Brevetted Union General

Signature	Signature with rank	Pre & post War DS	War Dated DS	Pre & post War ALS	War Dated ALS
$	$25	$	$	$	$

Tibbits, William Badger, 1837-80 — Union General

Signature	Signature with rank	Pre War DS	War Dated DS	Pre War ALS	War Dated ALS
$	$	$76	$	$	$

Tidball, John Caldwell, 1825-1906 — Brevetted Union General

Signature	Signature with rank	Pre & post War DS	War Dated DS	Pre War ALS	War Dated ALS
$20	$50	$	$	$	$

Tilghman, Lloyd, 1816-63 — Confederate Brigadier General

WP graduate. He was appointed Brig. Genl. on Oct. 18, 1862, and was placed in command of Fort Henry. He surrendered to Genl. Grant, and was not exchanged until the Summer of 1862. He was killed 16 May 1863 at Champion Hills, Miss.

Signature	Signature with rank	Pre War DS	War Dated DS	Pre War ALS	War Dated ALS
$115	$240	$	$	$489	$

A scarce signature.

Tillson, Davis, 1830-95 — Union General

Signature	Signature with rank	Pre & post War DS	War Dated DS	Pre & post War ALS	War Dated ALS
$	$45	$	$87	$	$

Todd, John Blair Smith, 1814-72   Union General

Signature	Signature with rank	Pre & post War DS	War Dated DS	Pre & post War ALS	War Dated ALS
$	$38	$76	$	$	$

Toombs, Robert Augustus, 1810-85   Confederate Brigadier General

He was the first Secretary of State. He resigned and was appointed Brig. Genl. on July 19, 1861 and fought with distinction at Sharpsburg. He resigned his commission when he was refused promotion, March 5, 1863.

Signature	Signature with rank	Pre & post War DS	War Dated DS	Pre & post War ALS	War Dated ALS
$110	$190	$	$	$	$

Toon, Thomas Fentress, 1840-1902   Confederate Brigadier General

1st Lt. in the Columbus Guards. This company was later part of the 20th N.C. which he led at Chancellorsville and Gettysburg. He was appointed Brig. Genl. on May 31, 1864. He was wounded seven times.

Signature	Signature with rank	Pre & post War DS	War Dated DS	Pre & post War ALS	War Dated ALS
$70	$165	$	$	$	$

Torbert. Alfred Thomas Archimedes, 1833-80   Union General

Signature	Signature with rank	Pre & post War DS	War Dated DS	Pre & post War ALS	War Dated ALS
$25	$40	$	$	$	$

Totten, Joseph Gilbert, 1788-1864   Union General/Engineer

Signature	Signature with rank	Pre War DS	War Dated DS	Pre & post War ALS	War Dated ALS
$	$35	$	$175	$	$

364

Tower, Zealous Bates, 1819-1900   Union General

Signature	Signature with rank	Pre & post War DS	War Dated DS	Pre & post War ALS	War Dated ALS
$18	$35	$	$	$55	$

Townsend, Edward Davis, 1817-93   Brevetted Union General

Signature	Signature with rank	Pre & post War DS	War Dated DS	Pre & post War ALS	War Dated ALS
$20	$	$47	$	$63	$

Tracy, Benjamin Franklin, 1830-1915   Brevetted Union General

Signature	Signature with rank	Pre & post War DS	War Dated DS	Pre & post War ALS	War Dated ALS
$20	$	$	$	$	$

Tracy, Edward Dorr, 1833-63   Confederate Brigadier General

Captain in the 4th Alabama Infantry. Lt. Col. of the 19th Alabama, and fought with great distinction at Shioh. While leading his regiments, he was killed May 1, 1863, at Port Gibson, Miss.

Signature	Signature with rank	Pre War DS	War Dated DS	Pre War ALS	War Dated ALS
$125	$285	$445	$	$925	$

Trapier, James Heyward, 1815-65   Confederate Brigadier General

WP graduate. Appointed Brig. Genl. on Oct. 21, 1861, he saw field service under Genl. Bragg at Corinth. In 1862, he was placed in command of the District of South Carolina.

Signature	Signature with rank	Pre War DS	War Dated DS	Pre War ALS	War Dated ALS
$105	$	$296	$	$378	$

Trenholm, George Alfred, 1807-76   Confederate Sec. of Treasury

Signature	Signature with rank	Pre & post War DS	War Dated DS	Pre War ALS	War Dated ALS
$90	$155	$	$	$598	$

Trimble, Isaac Ridgeway, 1802-88   Confederate Major General

WP graduate. He was with Genl. Crittenden's Brigade at 1st Manassas. He fought with distinction under Stonewall Jackson at Cross Keys. He lost his leg and was captured at Gettysburg. He was exchanged in Feb. 1865.

Signature	Signature with rank	Pre & post War DS	War Dated DS	Pre & post War ALS	War Dated ALS
$165	$345	$	$	$385	$1,578

Tucker, John Randolph, 1812-83   Commander Confederate Navy

Signature	Signature with rank	Pre & post War DS	War Dated DS	Pre & post War ALS	War Dated ALS
$	$165	$	$	$	$

Tucker, William Feimster, 1827-81   Confederate Brigadier General

Captain in the 11th Mississippi Infantry. He saw action at 1st Manassas. Fought at Murfreesboro, Chickamauga, and Chattanooga, he was commissioned Brig. Genl. on March 1, 1864. He was severely wounded at the battle of Resaca.

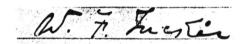

Signature	Signature with rank	Pre & post War DS	War Dated DS	Pre & post War ALS	War Dated ALS
$78	$	$	$	$	$

366

Turchin, John B.(Ivan Vasilovitchv Turchinoff)1822-1901,Union General

Signature	Signature with rank	Pre & Post War DS	War Dated DS	Pre & post War ALS	War Dated ALS
$	$40	$	$850	$	$

Turner, John Wesley, 1833-99 — Union General

Signature	Signature with rank	Pre & post War DS	War Dated DS	Pre & post War ALS	War Dated ALS
$	$100	$	$	$289	$

Tuttle, James Madison, 1823-92 — Union General

Signature	Signature with rank	Pre & post War DS	War Dated DS	Pre & post War ALS	War Dated ALS
$	$45	$78	$	$	$

Twiggs, David Emmanuel, 1790-1862 — Confederate Major General

He was appointed Major Genl. in the Confederate Army. He was in command of the District of Louisiana.

Signature	Signature with rank	Pre War DS	War Dated DS	Pre War ALS	War Dated ALS
$100	$178	$325	$	$1,450	$

DS, June 18, 1837 1p., HQ 2nd Dragoons, Jefferson Barracks, Board of Survey report pert. to equipment. BG Nov. 1993 $300.

Tyler, Daniel, 1799-1882 — Union General

Signature	Signature with rank	Pre & post War DS	War Dated DS	Pre & post War ALS	War Dated ALS
$	$	$74	$	$	$

Tyler, Erastus Barnard, 1822-91 — Union General

Signature	Signature with rank	Pre War DS	War Dated DS	Pre & post War ALS	War Dated ALS
$	$30	$	$	$	$

Tyler, John Jr., 1819-95 — Conf. Major/Acting Chief Bureau of War

Signature	Signature with rank	Pre & post War DS	War Dated DS	Pre & post War ALS	War Dated ALS
$	$75	$	$135	$	$

Tyler, Robert Charles, ?-1865 — Confederate Brigadier General

Private in the 15th TN Infantry. He was appointed Quartermaster, and led this same unit. At Shiloh, he was on the Staff of Genl. Bragg in 1862. He lost a leg during the Battle of Missionary Ridge. He was killed 16 April 1865 at West Point, GA.

R. C. Tyler

Signature	Signature with rank	Pre War DS	War Dated DS	Pre War ALS	War Dated ALS
$	$	$	$	$	$

A rare signature.

Tyler, Robert Ogden, 1831-74 — Union General

Signature	Signature with rank	Pre & post War DS	War Dated DS	Pre & post War ALS	War Dated ALS
$	$	$76	$	$	$

Tyndale, (George) Hector, 1821-80 — Union General

Signature	Signature with rank	Pre & post War DS	War Dated DS	Pre & post War ALS	War Dated ALS
$	$35	$	$90	$	$

368

U

Ullmann, Daniel, 1810-92 Union General

Colonel 78th New York "Highlanders," 2nd Manassas in Augur's division of Bank's corps. Captured & parole in Richmond. Organized five Negro regiments, which formed the nucleus of the "Corps d'Afrique." Served at Port Hudson in 1864.

Signature	Signature with rank	Pre & post War DS	War Dated DS	Pre & post War ALS	War Dated ALS
$	$48	$	$178	$	$

Underwood, Adin Ballou, 1828-88 Union General

Captain 2nd Mass. Inf., took part in the Shenandoah Valley campaign of 1862, Lt. Col. of the 33rd Mass. Colonel at the battle of Chancellorsville. Engaged at Gettysburg, then sent to support troops at Chattanooga. His leg was shattered by a ball on Oct. 29, 1863. Brig. Gen. Nov. 19, 1863.

Signature	Signature with rank	Pre & post War DS	War Dated DS	Pre & post War ALS	War Dated ALS
$	$45	$	$125	$	$

Upton, Emory, 1839-81 Union General

He smashed into the "Bloody Angle" at Spotsylvania and might have overrun the position. He was commissioned brig. gen. May 12 , 1864. He shot himself on March 15, 1881.

Signature	Signature with rank	Pre & post War DS	War Dated DS	Pre & post War ALS	War Dated ALS
$	$32	$54	$	$	$178

V

Valentine, Edward V., 1838-1922 American sculptor

Known for portrait busts of Southern leaders including Robert E. Lee.

Signature	Pre & post War DS	War Dated DS	Pre & post War ALS	War Dated ALS
$75	$	$	$	$

S, Fine signature on card. JB Dec. 1993 $65.

Van Alen, James Henry, 1819-86 — Union General

On April 15, 1865 commissioned brig. gen. Took part in the Peninsular campaign, 2nd Manassas, Chancellorsville, Aquia Creek. He resigned July 14, 1863.

Signature	Signature with rank	Pre & post War DS	War Dated DS	Pre & post War ALS	War Dated ALS
$	$32	$	$85	$	$

Van Buren, D.T., 1826-90 — Union General

Signature	Signature with rank	Pre & post War DS	War Dated DS	Pre & post War ALS	War Dated ALS
$	$45	$	$125	$84	$

Van Cleve, Horatio Phillips, 1809-91 — Union General

Signature	Signature with rank	Pre & post War DS	War Dated DS	Pre & post War ALS	War Dated ALS
$	$32	$	$73	$	$

Van Derveer, Ferdinand, 1823-92 — Union General

Signature	Signature with rank	Pre & post War DS	War Dated DS	Pre & post War ALS	War Dated ALS
$	$35	$	$	$	$

Van Dorn, Earl, 1820-63 — Confederate Major General

WP graduate. He was appointed a C.S. Brig. Genl. on June 5, 1861. He was defeated at Corinth, but in December 1862, in a daring raid on Holly Springs, Miss., he destroyed Genl. Grant's supply depot. He was killed by Dr. Peters after having had a 'liaison' with Mrs. Peters.

Signature	Signature with rank	Pre War DS	War Dated DS	Pre War ALS	War Dated ALS
$225	$350	$	$	$725	$

A rare signature.

370

Van Vliet, Stewart, 1815-1901   Union General

Signature	Signature with rank	Pre & post War DS	War Dated DS	Pre & post War ALS	War Dated ALS
$	$35	$73	$	$	$

Van Wyck, Charles Henry, 1824-95   Union General

Signature	Signature with rank	Pre & post War DS	War Dated DS	Pre & post War ALS	War Dated ALS
$	$32	$76	$128	$98	$

Vance, Robert Brank, 1828-99   Confederate Brigadier General

Capt. of the "Buncombe Life Guards." He was soon Colonel of the 29th N.C. and accompanied Kirby Smith to Ky. He was captured at Crosby Creek, TN., on Jan. 14, 1864, and release March 10, 1865.

Signature	Signature with rank	Pre & post War DS	War Dated DS	Pre & post War ALS	War Dated ALS
$85	$138	$	$	$345	$

S, Large clip. BG Nov. 1993 $80.

Vance, Zebulon Baird, 1830-94   Governor of N.C., 1862-65

Col. 26th N.C.T.

Signature	Signature with rank	Pre & post War DS	War Dated DS	Pre & post War ALS	War Dated ALS
$105	$	$	$350	$	$

DS, Jan. 6, 1863 8pp. folio, with red seal & pink ribbon, State of NC, pert. to Power of Attny. & cert. by Judge W.H. Battle of NC Supreme Court. BG Nov. 1993 $300.
S, Clip w/ state. BG Nov. 1993 $100.

Vandever, William, 1817-93   Union General

Signature	Signature with rank	Pre & post War DS	War Dated DS	Pre & post War ALS	War Dated ALS
$	$35	$64	$127	$	$

Vaughan, Alfred Jefferson, Jr., 1830-99   Confederate Brigadier General
V.M.I. graduate.   Capt. in the Dixie Rifles.   Colonel of the 13th TN, and fought with
great distinction at Belmont, Shiloh, Perryville, and Chickamauga.   He was made Brig
Genl. Nov. 18, 1863. During the Atlanta Campaign he had his leg shot off.

Signature	Signature with rank	Pre & post War DS	War Dated DS	Pre & post War ALS	War Dated ALS
$78	$150	$	$	$278	$

Vaughn, John Crawford, 1824-75   Confederate Brigadier General
Col. of the 3rd TN.   He was with Genl. Johnston at Harper's Ferry and 1st Manassas.
He was captured at Vicksburg and commanded a cavalry brigade in the Shenandoah.

Signature	Signature with rank	Pre & post War DS	War Dated DS	Pre & post War ALS	War Dated ALS
$70	$186	$	$	$	$

Veatch, James Clifford, 1819-95   Union General

Signature	Signature with rank	Pre & post War DS	War Dated DS	Pre & post War ALS	War Dated ALS
$	$35	$	$	$	$

Viele, Egbert Ludovicus, 1825-1902   Union General/Engineer

Signature	Signature with rank	Pre & post War DS	War Dated DS	Pre & post War ALS	War Dated ALS
$	$28	$	$127	$	$

Villepique, John Bordenave, 1830-62   Confederate Brigadier General

WP graduate.   Captain in the regular C.S. Army. As Colonel of the 36th GA, he was temporarily in command of the Army of Mobile. He was severly wounded in defense of Fort McRee, Florida. He died at Port Hudson, LA., 9 Nov 1862.

Signature	Signature with rank	Pre War DS	War Dated DS	Pre War ALS	War Dated ALS
$245	$350	$	$	$	$

A rare signature.

Vincent, Strong, 1837-63   Union General

Died 7 July 1863 of wnds rec'd at Gettysburg, PA. Rare.

Signature	Signature with rank	Pre War DS	War Dated DS	Pre War ALS	War Dated ALS
$	$	$	$	$	$

Vincent, Thomas M., 1832-1909   Brevetted Union General

Signature	Signature with rank	Pre & post War DS	War Dated DS	Pre & post War ALS	War Dated ALS
$20	$38	$	$	$	$

Vinton, Francis Laurens, 1835-79   Union General

Signature	Signature with rank	Pre & post War DS	War Dated DS	Pre & post War ALS	War Dated ALS
$	$30	$	$84	$	$

Vogdes, Isreal, 1816-89   Union General

Signature	Signature with rank	Pre & post War DS	War Dated DS	Pre & post War ALS	War Dated ALS
$	$35	$	$	$	$

Von Steiwehr, Adolph Wilhelm "Baron," 1822-77   Union General

Signature	Signature with rank	Pre & post War DS	War Dated DS	Pre & post War ALS	War Dated ALS
$	$35	$75	$147	$	$

W

Wade, Melancthon Smith, 1802-68   Union General

Signature	Signature with rank	Pre & post War DS	War Dated DS	Pre & post War ALS	War Dated ALS
$	$45	$	$	$	$

Waddell, James Iredell, 1824-86   Commander Confederate Navy

Last Confederate Officer to surrender. Ommanded the CSS SHENANDOAH 1864-65; surrendered her on Nov. 6, 1865 to the British Government.

Signature	Signature with rank	Pre & post War DS	War Dated DS	Pre & post War ALS	War Dated ALS
$85	$200	$	$	$	$

Wadswoth, James Samuel, 1807-64   Union General

Gettysburg hero, killed in action during the Battle of the Wilderness. Rare.

Signature	Signature with rank	Pre War DS	War Dated DS	Pre War ALS	War Dated ALS
$	$85	$	$	$250	$

Wagner, George Day, 1829-69   Union General

Signature	Signature with rank	Pre & post War DS	War Dated DS	Pre & post War ALS	War Dated ALS
$	$	$	$	$	$

Walcutt, Charles Carroll, 1838-98   Union General

Signature	Signature with rank	Pre & post War DS	War Dated DS	Pre & post War ALS	War Dated ALS
$	$35	$	$124	$	$

Walker, Francis Amasa, 1840-97   Brevetted Union General

He rose from a private to brigadier general under Hancock. After the War, he was a noted historian.

Signature	Signature with rank	Pre & post War DS	War Dated DS	Pre & post War ALS	War Dated ALS
$35	$55	$	$	$110	$

S, Cut Signature. SK Nov. 1993 $40.

Walker, Henry Harrsion, 1832-1912   Confederate Brigadier General

WP graduate. Captain in the Regular C.S. Army. Lt. Col. of the 40th Virginia Infantry. He was severly wounded at Gaines's Mill, and later fought with distinction at Bristoe Station and in Mine Run campaign. He was wounded at Spotsylvania.

Signature	Signature with rank	Pre & post War DS	War Dated DS	Pre & post War ALS	War Dated ALS
$90	$178	$	$	$278	$

Walker, James Alexander, 1832-1901   Confederate Brigadier General

Dismissed from V.M.I. by professor T.J. Jackson, he challenged him to a duel which was never fought. He was later recommended by Jackson as a Brig. Gen. He was severly wounded at Spotsyvania Court House.

Signature	Signature with rank	Pre & post War DS	War Dated DS	Pre & post War ALS	War Dated ALS
$	$145	$174	$318	$	$

Walker, John George, 1822-93   Confederate Major General

Major in the C.S. Cavalry. He was appointed Brig. Genl. on Jan. 9, 1862. He fought with the Army of Northern Virginia at Sharpsburg and Harper's Ferry. As Major Genl., he was transferred to the Trasns-Mississippi Department.

Signature	Signature with rank	Pre & post War DS	War Dated DS	Pre & post War ALS	War Dated ALS
$90	$165	$	$	$	$

Walker, Leroy Pope, 1837-84   Conf. Brig. Genl. & Sec. of War

Univ. of Alabama graduate. He entered C.S. service as its first Secretary of War, Feb. 21, 1861. He resigned this office on Sept. 16th of that year and was then appointed Brig. Genl. He saw no battle action and resigned on March 31, 1862.

Signature	Signature with rank	Pre & post War DS	War Dated DS	Pre & post War ALS	War Dated ALS
$120	$245	$187	$398	$	$

Walker, Lucius Marshell, 1829-63   Confederate Brigadier General

WP graduate. Lt. Col. of the 40th TN Infantry. He was appointed Brig. Genl. on March 11, 1862. Transferred to the Trans-Mississippi Department. He was killed in duel with Gen. J.S. Marmaduke at Little Rock, Ark., September 6, 1863.

Signature	Signature with rank	Pre War DS	War Dated DS	Pre War ALS	War Dated ALS
$225	$	$650	$	$	$

Walker, Mary Edwards, 1831-1917   Union Doctor/Nurse

One of the earliest female medical school graduates, and women's rights advocate, she served as a military surgeon during the Civil War for the 52nd Ohio. He was awarded the Congressional Medal of Honor.

Signature	Signature with rank	Pre & post War DS	War Dated DS	Pre & post War ALS	War Dated ALS
$275	$500	$	$1,150	$	$

S, A signed album leaf, 1879. SR Nov. 1993 $250.

Walker, Reuben Lindsay, 1827-90   Confederate Brigadier General
V.M.I. graduate. Captain of an artillery battery at 1st Manassas. Major/ Chief of
Artillery for Genl. A. P. Hill's Division. He fought at 2nd Manassas, Cedar Mountain,
Fredericksburg, and Gettysburg. He commanded artillery in 63 battles and skirmishes.

Signature	Signature with rank	Pre & post War DS	War Dated DS	Pre & post War ALS	War Dated ALS
$	$45	$	$	$	$

Walker, William Henry Talbot, 1816-64   Confederate Major General
WP graduate. He entered C.S. service as Brig. Genl. on May 25, 1861, and commanded
a brigade in the 2nd Corps, Army of Misssissippi. He was at Vicksburg and
commanded the reserves at Chickamauga. He was in Genl. Hardee's Corps during the
Chattanooga and Atlanta campaigns. He was killed by a Union sharpshooter in
Decatur, GA., on July 22, 1864.

Signature	Signature with rank	Pre War DS	War Dated DS	Pre War ALS	War Dated ALS
$140	$180	$345	$	$	$

A scarce signature.

Walker, William Stephen, 1822-99   Confederate Brigadier General
Entered C.S. service as a Captain in the regular army. He commanded his troops at
Pocotaligo, S.C. and was appointed Brig. Genl. on Oct. 30, 1862. He was sent to join
Genl. Beauregard in the defense of Petersburg, and was wounded in the foot.

Signature	Signature with rank	Pre & post War DS	War Dated DS	Pre & post War ALS	War Dated ALS
$78	$150	$	$	$	$

Wallace, Lewis, 1827-1904   Union Major General, wrote "Ben Hur"

Signature	Signature with rank	Pre & post War DS	War Dated DS	Pre & post War ALS	War Dated ALS
$80	$175	$287	$	$	$

Wallace, William Harvey Lamb, 1821-62   Union General
Died 10 April 1862 of wnds recd at Shiloh, TN. Rare.

Signature	Signature with rank	Pre War DS	War Dated DS	Pre War ALS	War Dated ALS
$	$65	$	$	$	$

Wallace, William Henry, 1827-1901   Confederate Brigadier General
S.C. College graduate. Enlisted as a Private. He was named Adjt. of the 18th South
Carolina. He fought at Malvin Hill, 2nd Manassas and South Mountain.

Signature	Signature with rank	Pre & post War DS	War Dated DS	Pre & post War ALS	War Dated ALS
$80	$178	$	$347	$	$

Walthall, Edward Cary, 1831-98   Confederate Major General
Lt. of the 15th Mississippi Infantry. He was appointed Brig. Genl. on Dec. 13, 1862. He
fought at Missionary Ridge. He covered Genl. Hood's retreat at Nashville and prevented
the capture of the Army of TN by Union Genl. Thomas.

Signature	Signature with rank	Pre & post War DS	War Dated DS	Pre & post War ALS	War Dated ALS
$90	$175	$	$965	$378	$

Ward, John Henry Hobart, 1823-1903   Union General

Signature	Signature with rank	Pre & post War DS	War Dated DS	Pre & post War ALS	War Dated ALS
$	$35	$	$	$87	$

Ward, William H., ?-?   Commander Confederate Navy

Signature	Signature with rank	Pre & post War DS	War Dated DS	Pre & post War ALS	War Dated ALS
$	$95-1	$	$278	$	$

Ward, William Thomas, 1808-78   Union General

Signature	Signature with rank	Pre & post War DS	War Dated DS	Pre & post War ALS	War Dated ALS
$	$30	$60	$	$76	$

Warner, James Meech, 1836-97   Union General

Signature	Signature with rank	Pre & post War DS	War Dated DS	Pre & post War ALS	War Dated ALS
$	$35	$	$74	$	$

Warren, Fitz Henry, 1816-78   Union General

Signature	Signature with rank	Pre & post War DS	War Dated DS	Pre & post War ALS	War Dated ALS
$	$32	$	$	$98	$

Warren, Gouvernor Kemble, 1830-82   Union General

Signature	Signature with rank	Pre & post War DS	War Dated DS	Pre & post War ALS	War Dated ALS
$80	$165	$	$489	$325	$

Washburn, Cadwallader Colden, 1818-82   Union General

Signature	Signature with rank	Pre & post War DS	War Dated DS	Pre & post War ALS	War Dated ALS
$	$35	$95	$	$	$

Washington, John A., ?-1861   Confederate Lt. Col.

Gen R.E. Lee's aide de camp & George Washington's Nephew. Killed 13 Sept 1861 at the Battle of Cheat Mtn. Rare.

Signature	Signature with rank	Pre War DS	War Dated DS	Pre War ALS	War Dated ALS
$100	$	$	$	$	$

Waterhouse, Richard, 1832-76   Confederate Brigadier General

Colonel of the 19th Texas Infantry. He saw service under Genl. Holmes in Arkansas, and under Taylor in Louisiana. He fought at Milliken's Bend, Mansfield, Pleasant Hill, and was appointed Brig. Genl. on April 30, 1864.

Signature	Signature with rank	Pre & post War DS	War Dated DS	Pre & post War ALS	War Dated ALS
$140	$	$	$	$	$958

A very scarce signature.

Watkins, Louis Douglas, 1833-68   Union General

Signature	Signature with rank	Pre & post War DS	War Dated DS	Pre & post War ALS	War Dated ALS
$	$34	$	$	$	$

Watie, Stand, 1806-71   Confederate Brigadier General

A Cherokee Indian, he entered C.S. service as Col. of the Cherokee Mounted Rifles. He led his Indian troops at Wilson's Creek and Elkhorn Traven, and was appointed Brig. Genl. in May 6, 1864.

Signature	Signature with rank	Pre & post War DS	War Dated DS	Pre & post War ALS	War Dated ALS
$180	$	$375	$	$	$

A very scarce signature.

Watts, Thomas Hill, 1819-92   Gov. of Alabama

Signature	Signature with rank	Pre & post War DS	War Dated DS	Pre & post War ALS	War Dated ALS
$	$48	$	$248	$	$

Waud, Alfred R., 1828-91   Artist

Signature	Pre & post War DS	War Dated DS	Pre & post War ALS	War Dated ALS
$125	$	$	$250	$

Waul, Thomas Neville, 1813-1903   Confederate Brigadier General

Colonel in Waul's Texas Legion. He was captured and exchanged at Vicksburg, and was appointed Brig. Genl. on Sept. 18, 1863. He fought at Pleasant Hill and Jenkin's Ferry.

Thomas N. Waul

Signature	Signature with rank	Pre & post War DS	War Dated DS	Pre & post War ALS	War Dated ALS
$78	$	$212	$425	$378	$

Wayne, Henry Constantie, 1815-83   Confederate Brigadier General

WP graduate. Appointed Brig. Genl. Dec. 16, 1861, resigned on Jan. 7, 1862. During the remainder of the war, he was Adjt, and Inspector General of the State of GA.

Signature	Signature with rank	Pre & post War DS	War Dated DS	Pre & post War ALS	War Dated ALS
$	$167	$	$248	$	$

Webb, Alexander Stewart, 1835-1911   Union General

Signature	Signature with rank	Pre & post War DS	War Dated DS	Pre & post War ALS	War Dated ALS
$	$125	$74	$238	$	$

Webb, William A., ?--?   Commander Confederate Navy

Signature	Signature with rank	Pre & post War DS	War Dated DS	Pre & post War ALS	War Dated ALS
$	$	$	$435	$	$

Weber, Max, 1824-1901 — Union General

Signature	Signature with rank	Pre & post War DS	War Dated DS	Pre & post War ALS	War Dated ALS
$20	$33	$	$	$	$

Webster, Joseph Dana, 1811-76 — Union General

Signature	Signature with rank	Pre & post War DS	War Dated DS	Pre & post War ALS	War Dated ALS
$	$35	$	$	$	$

Weed, Stephen Hinsdale, 1831-63 — Union Brigadier General

He was killed at Gettysburg, PA., on July 2, 1863. Rare.

Signature	Signature with rank	Pre War DS	War Dated DS	Pre War ALS	War Dated ALS
$	$	$	$	$	$

Weir, Robert, ?--? — Harpers Artists

Signature	Pre & post War DS	War Dated DS	Pre & post War ALS	War Dated ALS
$65	$	$	$145	$

Weisiger, David Addison, 1818-99 — Confederate Brigadier General

Present at John Brown's hanging. Colonel in the 12th Virginia Infantry. He was assigned to Genl. Mahone's Brigade. He was seriously wounded at 2nd Mannassas. He fought at the Battle of the Crater, with great distinction.

Signature	Signature with rank	Pre & post War DS	War Dated DS	Pre & post War ALS	War Dated ALS
$80	$120	$200	$	$	$

Weitzel, Godfrey, 1835-84 — Union General

Signature	Signature with rank	Pre & post War DS	War Dated DS	Pre & post War ALS	War Dated ALS
$	$35	$	$89	$	$

Welles, Gideon, 1802-78   Lincoln's Secretary of the Navy

Signature	Signature with rank	Pre & post War DS	War Dated DS	Pre & post War ALS	War Dated ALS
$50	$90	$250	$650	$385	$987

LS, Dec. 15, 1864. 1p., 4to., Navy Department, Washington, to Lt. Com. G.W. Morris commanding the U.S.S. Shawmut, pert. to a deserter on board. HMS Feb., 1994 $775.

Wells, William, 1837-92   Union General

Signature	Signature with rank	Pre & post War DS	War Dated DS	Pre & post War ALS	War Dated ALS
$	$25	$	$	$	$

Welsh, Thomas, 1824-63   Union General

He died August 14, 1863.

Signature	Signature with rank	Pre War DS	War Dated DS	Pre War ALS	War Dated ALS
$	$75	$	$	$	$

Wessells, Henry Walton, 1809-89   Union General

Signature	Signature with rank	Pre & post War DS	War Dated DS	Pre & post War ALS	War Dated ALS
$	$35	$	$	$	$

West, Joseph Rodman, 1822-98   Union General

Signature	Signature with rank	Pre & post War DS	War Dated DS	Pre & post War ALS	War Dated ALS
$20	$	$65	$	$	$

Wharton, Gabriel Colvin, 1824-1906   Confederate Brigadier General

V.M.I. graduate. Major in the 45th Virginia. He narrowly escaped capture at Fort Donelson. He commanded a brigade at New Market

Signature	Signature with rank	Pre & post War DS	War Dated DS	Pre & post War ALS	War Dated ALS
$65	$100	$	$	$167	$

Wharton, John Austin, 1828-65   Confederate Major General
Capt. in the 8th Texas Cavalry, which he led at Shiloh where he was severly wounded.
He fought with great distinction at Murfreesboro and Chickamauga. He was killed in a
feud with Col. George W. Baylor at Houston, TX, on April 6, 1865.

Signature	Signature with rank	Pre & post War DS	War Dated DS	Pre & post War ALS	War Dated ALS
$	$	$	$	$	$

Wheaton, Frank, 1833-1903   Union General

Signature	Signature with rank	Pre & post War DS	War Dated DS	Pre & post War ALS	War Dated ALS
$	$28	$55	$97	$	$

Wheeler, Joseph, 1836-1906   Confederate Major General
Chief of the Army of Mississippi, and was appointed Brig. Genl. on Oct. 30, WP
graduate. 1st Lt. of Artillery. Genl. Bragg appointed him Cavalry Commander-in 1862.
He had over a dozen horses shot out from under him.

Signature	Signature with rank	Pre & post War DS	War Dated DS	Pre & post War ALS	War Dated ALS
$125	$278	$195	$	$178	$1,278

Whipple, Amiel Weeks, 1816-63   Union General
He died of wounds rec'd at Chancellorsville, VA., on May 7, 1863.

Signature	Signature with rank	Pre War DS	War Dated DS	Pre War ALS	War Dated ALS
$	$75	$	$	$245	$

Whipple, William Denison, 1826-1902   Union General

Signature	Signature with rank	Pre & post War DS	War Dated DS	Pre & post War ALS	War Dated ALS
$	$35	$	$	$	$

Whitaker, Walter Chiles, 1823-87   Union General

Signature	Signature with rank	Pre & post War DS	War Dated DS	Pre & post War ALS	War Dated ALS
$	$28	$	$78	$	$

White, Julius, 1816-90   Union General

Signature	Signature with rank	Pre & post War DS	War Dated DS	Pre & post War ALS	War Dated ALS
$16	$22	$	$	$	$

Whitfield, John Wilkins, 1818-79   Confederate Brigadier
General

Major 4th Texas Cavalry. He fought at Elkhorn Taven and was wounded at the Balle of
Iuka, Miss. He was appointed Brig. Genl. on May 9, 1863 and saw action during the
Vicksburg Campaign.

Signature	Signature with rank	Pre & post War DS	War Dated DS	Pre & post War ALS	War Dated ALS
$78	$	$	$287	$	$

Whiting, William Henry, 1824-65   Confederate Major General

WP graduate. Major of Engineers, he was appointed Brig. Genl. on July 21, 1861. He
served with Stonewall Jackson in the Valley Campaign and at Chancellorsville. At
Drewry's Bluff, he refused to attack - drunk, Genl. Hill took over. He went to Fort
Fisher where he was wounded and captured. He died of his wounds while imprisoned at
Governor's Island, N.Y., March 10, 1865.

Signature	Signature with rank	Pre & post War DS	War Dated DS	Pre & post War ALS	War Dated ALS
$178	$	$	$	$	$

Wickham, Williams Carter, 1820-88   Confederate Brigadier General
Captain of the Hanover Dragoons and fought with distinction at 1st Manassas. He was
wounded at Williamsburg, and served with JEB Stuart in the raid on Calett's Station
and into Maryland. He rsigned Nov. 9, 1864, and took a seat in the Confederate
Congress.

Signature	Signature with rank	Pre & post War DS	War Dated DS	Pre & post War ALS	War Dated ALS
$80	$135	$	$378	$	$

Wigfall, Louis Trezevant, 1816-74   Confederate Brigadier General
He was appointed Brig. Genl. on Oct. 11, 1861. He saw service with Genl. Longstreet.
He resigned on Feb. 20, 1862 and took a seat in the Confederate Congress.

Signature	Signature with rank	Pre & post War DS	War Dated DS	Pre & post War ALS	War Dated ALS
$125	$180	$	$	$	$

Wilcox, Cadmus Marcellus, 1824-90   Confederate Brigadier General
WP graduate. Colonel of the 9th Alabama, which he led at 1st Manassas. He was
appointed Brig. Genl. on Oct. 21, 1861 and served with the Army of Northern Virginia
at Sevn Pines, 2nd Manasas, and Sharpsburg. He was promoted to Major Genl. on
August 3, 1863.

Signature	Signature with rank	Pre & post War DS	War Dated DS	Pre & post War ALS	War Dated ALS
$95	$178	$175	$389	$	$

Wild, Edward Augustus, 1825-91 — Union General

Signature	Signature with rank	Pre & post War DS	War Dated DS	Pre & post War ALS	War Dated ALS
$	$80	$	$157	$183	$

Wilcox, Orlando Bolivar, 1823-1907 — Union General

Signature	Signature with rank	Pre & post War DS	War Dated DS	Pre & post War ALS	War Dated ALS
$	$35	$65	$	$125	$

Wilkes, Charles, 1798-1877 — Union Naval Captain

Signature	Signature with rank	Pre & post War DS	War Dated DS	Pre & post War ALS	War Dated ALS
$	$50	$	$150	$	$

Wilkinson, John, ?-? — Confederate Naval Commander
CSS CICKAMAUGA, 1864. Rare.

Signature	Signature with rank	Pre & post War DS	War Dated DS	Pre & post War ALS	War Dated ALS
$	$90	$	$	$	$

Williams, Alpheus Starkey, 1810-78 — Union General

Signature	Signature with rank	Pre & post War DS	War Dated DS	Pre & post War ALS	War Dated ALS
$	$36	$	$	$	$

Williams, David Henry, 1819-91 — Union General

Signature	Signature with rank	Pre & post War DS	War Dated DS	Pre & post War ALS	War Dated ALS
$	$25	$	$	$	$

Williams, John Stuart, "Cerro Gordo," 1818-98   Conf. Brigadier General
Colonel of the 5th Kentucky, and was appointed Brig. Genl. on April 16, 1862. He
commanded the Department of Eastern TN. He stopped Union Genl. Burnside before
Knoxville.

Signature	Signature with rank	Pre & post War DS	War Dated DS	Pre & post War ALS	War Dated ALS
$80	$115	$	$178	$	$

Williams, Nelson Grosvenor, 1823-97   Union General

Signature	Signature with rank	Pre & post War DS	War Dated DS	Pre & post War ALS	War Dated ALS
$	$28	$48	$	$	$

Williams, Seth, 1822-66   Union General

Signature	Signature with rank	Pre & post War DS	War Dated DS	Pre & post War ALS	War Dated ALS
$	$40	$	$78	$	$

Williams, Thomas, 1815-62   Union General
He was killed August 5, 1862, at Baton Rouge, LA. Rare.

Signature	Signature with rank	Pre War DS	War Dated DS	Pre War ALS	War Dated ALS
$	$250	$	$	$	$

Willoamson, James Alexander, 1829-1902   Union General

Signature	Signature with rank	Pre & post War DS	War Dated DS	Pre & post War ALS	War Dated ALS
$	$25	$	$	$	$

Willoch, August(von), 1810-78   Union General

Signature	Signature with rank	Pre & post War DS	War Dated DS	Pre & post War ALS	War Dated ALS
$	$35	$	$73	$	$

Wilson, Claudius Charles, 1831-63   Confederate Brigadier General

Captain in the 25th GA. He served with Genl. Johnston during the Vicksburg campaign. He commanded a brigade at Chickamauga under Genl. W.H.T. Walker. He died Nov. 27, 1863 of natural causes. He was promoted posthumously.

[signature]

Signature	Signature with rank	Pre War DS	War Dated DS	Pre War ALS	War Dated ALS
$175	$285	$	$	$	$

A rare signature.

Wilson, Henry, 1812-75   Chairman Senate Comm.

Signature	Signature with rank	Pre & post War DS	War Dated DS	Pre & post War ALS	War Dated ALS
$78	$	$	$	$	$

Wilson, William Sydney, 1816-62   Confederate Congressman

Signature	Signature with rank	Pre War DS	War Dated DS	Pre War ALS	War Dated ALS
$65	$145	$138	$	$	$

Winder, Charles Sidney, 1829-62   Confederate Brigadier General

WP graduate. Captain of Artillery at the Charleston Arsenal. Appointed Brig. Genl. March 1, 1862. In Stonewall Jackson's command, he was second only to Jackson as Senior Officer. He was killed in artillery fire at Cedar Mt., August 9, 1862.

[signature]

Signature	Signature with rank	Pre War DS	War Dated DS	Pre War ALS	War Dated ALS
$	$	$	$	$	$

A very rare signature.

Winder, John Henry, 1800-65   Confederate Brigadier General
WP graduate. Provost Marshel in charge of prison camps. He died of natural causes on
Feb. 7, 1865, at Florence, S.C.

Signature	Signature with rank	Pre & post War DS	War Dated DS	Pre & post War ALS	War Dated ALS
$	$125	$	$465	$	$

Winslow, John A., 1811-73   Union Naval Commander
While commanding the U.S. Ship Kearsarge, he sank the celebrated Confederate raider
Alabama, off Cherbourg.

Signature	Signature with rank	Pre & post War DS	War Dated DS	Pre & post War ALS	War Dated ALS
$80	$150	$250	$	$	$

DS, Nov. 22, 1871, 2pps., folio, San Francisco, shipping orders for the U.S. Flag Ship
California. JB Dec. 1993 $225.

Wirz, Henry, 1823-65   Confederate Major
Commandant of Andersonville Prison. He was hung for war crimes, Nov. 1865.

Signature	Signature with rank	Pre & post War DS	War Dated DS	Pre & post War ALS	War Dated ALS
$278	$450	$	$	$	$4,250

Wise, Henry Alexander, 1806-76   Confederate Brigadier General
Brig. Genl. on June 5, 1861. He served with Genl. Lee in West Virginia, and was under
Genl. Holmes at Seven Days. He fought at Petersburg and Sayler's Creek.

Signature	Signature with rank	Pre & post War DS	War Dated DS	Pre & post War ALS	War Dated ALS
$80	$180	$	$	$325	$

ALS, 1874. 2 pages in ink, on his letterhead, To Col. Archer concerning a lady's 1200
acres in Texas. With envelope. JH Nov. 1993 $175.

Wistar, Isaac Jones, 1827-1905   Union General

Signature	Signature with rank	Pre & post War DS	War Dated DS	Pre & post War ALS	War Dated ALS
$	$32	$65	$	$	$

Witcher, John S., 1839-1906   Union Bvt. General

Signature	Signature with rank	Pre & post War DS	War Dated DS	Pre & post War ALS	War Dated ALS
$	$35	$	$	$65	$

Withers, Jones Mitchell, 1814-90   Confederate Major General

WP graduate. Colonel in the 3rd Alabama. He was appointed Brig. Genl. on July 10, 1861, and was promoted Major Genl., after the Battle of Shiloh.

Signature	Signature with rank	Pre & post War DS	War Dated DS	Pre & post War ALS	War Dated ALS
$65	$115	$	$278	$	$

Withers, R. W., 1835-96   Colonel 42nd Va. Inf.

Signature	Signature with rank	Pre & post War DS	War Dated DS	Pre & post War ALS	War Dated ALS
$	$45	$	$75	$	$

Withers, Thomas Jefferson, 1804-65   Confederate Congressman

Signature	Signature with rank	Pre & post War DS	War Dated DS	Pre & post War ALS	War Dated ALS
$	$55	$	$	$	$

Witherspoon, James Hervey, 1810-65   Confederate Congressman

Signature	Signature with rank	Pre & post War DS	War Dated DS	Pre & post War ALS	War Dated ALS
$50	$	$	$	$	$

Wofford, William Tatum, 1824-84   Confederate Brigadier General

Colonel in the 18th GA. He command Hood's Texas Brigade and Cobb's Brigade after he was killed at Fredericksburg, VA. He fought at Chancellorsvile, Chickamauga, the Wilderness, and Spotsylvania Court House.

Signature	Signature with rank	Pre & post War DS	War Dated DS	Pre & post War ALS	War Dated ALS
$80	$178	$176	$367	$	$

Wood, Fernando, 1812-81   NYC's Mayor

A noted Copperhead. He wanted the South turned loose & NYC the trade zone.

Signature	Signature with rank	Pre & post War DS	War Dated DS	Pre & post War ALS	War Dated ALS
$20	$	$	$	$	$

S, Clipped signature. JH Nov. 1993 $15.

Wood, John Taylor, 1830-1904   Commander Confederate Navy

CSS TALLAHASSEE, 1864. Rare.

Signature	Signature with rank	Pre & post War DS	War Dated DS	Pre & post War ALS	War Dated ALS
$	$87	$	$	$350	$

Wood, Sterling Alexander Martin, 1823-91   Confed. Brigadier General

Captain of the Florence Guards, AL. As Brig. Genl., he commanded a brigade at Perryville and was severly wounded. He resigned on October 17, 1863.

Signature	Signature with rank	Pre & post War DS	War Dated DS	Pre & post War ALS	War Dated ALS
$75	$135	$	$378	$	$

Wood, Thomas John, 1823-1906 — Union General

Signature	Signature with rank	Pre & post War DS	War Dated DS	Pre & post War ALS	War Dated ALS
$	$35	$	$78	$	$

Woodbury, Daniel Phineas, 1812-64 — Union General

Signature	Signature with rank	Pre War DS	War Dated DS	Pre War ALS	War Dated ALS
$	$45	$	$	$	$

Woodford, Stewart L., 1835-1913 — Union Beverted General

Led the 103th U.S. Colored Troops on Morris Island, S.C.

Signature	Signature with rank	Pre & post War DS	War Dated DS	Pre & post War ALS	War Dated ALS
$30	$48	$	$	$	$

S, Clip Signature. JH Nov. 1993 $25.

Woods, Charles Robert, 1827-85 — Union General

Signature	Signature with rank	Pre & post War DS	War Dated DS	Pre & post War ALS	War Dated ALS
$	$45	$	$	$	$

Woods, William Burham, 1824-87 — Union General

Signature	Signature with rank	Pre & post War DS	War Dated DS	Pre & post War ALS	War Dated ALS
$	$34	$56	$	$87	$

Woodward, John D., 1846-1922 — Artist

Signature	DS	ALS
$50	$	$

Wool, John Ellis, 1784-69 — Union General

Signature	Signature with rank	Pre & post War DS	War Dated DS	Pre & post War ALS	War Dated ALS
$	$65	$125	$	$	$

Worden, John Lorimer, 1818-97 — Union Naval Captain

Signature	Signature with rank	Pre & post War DS	War Dated DS	Pre & post War ALS	War Dated ALS
$125	$150	$	$	$375	$

Wright, Ambrose Ranson, 1826-72 — Confederate Major General
Colonel of the 3rd GA in May 1861. He served with Huger at Norfolk, and led Blanchard's Brigade at Seven Pines. Major Genl. as of Nov. 26, 1863.

Signature	Signature with rank	Pre & post War DS	War Dated DS	Pre & post War ALS	War Dated ALS
$75	$120	$	$	$	$

Wright, Augustus Romaldus, 1813-91 — Confederate Congressman

Signature	Signature with rank	Pre & post War DS	War Dated DS	Pre & post War ALS	War Dated ALS
$	$35	$65	$	$87	$

Wright, George, 1801-65 — Union General

Signature	Signature with rank	Pre & post War DS	War Dated DS	Pre & post War ALS	War Dated ALS
$	$35	$	$	$	$

Wright, Horatio Gouvernor, 1820-99 — Union General

Signature	Signature with rank	Pre & post War DS	War Dated DS	Pre & post War ALS	War Dated ALS
$	$38	$78	$	$225	$

Wright, John Wright, 1823-1908 — Confederate Congressman

Signature	Signature with rank	Pre & post War DS	War Dated DS	Pre & post War ALS	War Dated ALS
$	$48	$	$	$	$

394

Wright, Marcus Joseph, 1831-1922   Confederate Brigadier General
Lt. Col. of the 154th TN in April, 1861. He was Military Governor of KY in 1862. He was appointed Brig. Genl. on Dec. 13, 1862, and he fought at Chickamuga and Chattanooga.

Signature	Signature with rank	Pre & post War DS	War Dated DS	Pre & post War ALS	War Dated ALS
$90	$178	$	$	$287	$

ALS, 1893. 2 pages in ink, concerning helping getting a CSA Col. get his deafness disability from the Mexican war. JH Nov. 1933 $175.

Wright, William Bacon, 1830-95   Confederate Congressman

Signature	Signature with rank	Pre & post War DS	War Dated DS	Pre & post War ALS	War Dated ALS
$40	$	$76	$	$	$

Y

Yancey, William Lowndes, 1814-63   Confederate Commissioner

Signature	Signature with rank	Pre War DS	War Dated DS	Pre War ALS	War Dated ALS
$	$	$	$	$	$

Yates, Henry, Jr., ?-1871   Union Brevet General

Signature	Signature with rank	Pre & post War DS	War Dated DS	Pre & post War ALS	War Dated ALS
$	$32	$	$	$	$

Young, Pierce Manning B., 1836-96   Confederate Major General

He resigned from WP and was commissioned a 2nd Lt. of Artillery in the Confederate Army. He fought in the Maryland campaign, he was appointed Brig. Genl. on Sept. 28, 1863. He commanded a division under Wade Hampton, to slow Sherman's advance in the Carolinas.

Signature	Signature with rank	Pre & post War DS	War Dated DS	Pre & post War ALS	War Dated ALS
$80	$140	$	$335	$	$

Young, William Hugh, 1838-1901   Confederate Brigadier General

Univ. of Virginia graduate. Captain of the 9th Texas Infantry. He was shot at Murfreesboro and at Vicksburg. He was shot in the chest at Chickamauga, and twice wounded during the Atlanta campaign. Appointed Brig. Genl. on August 15, 1864. He was wounded at Allatoona, GA., where was captured and not released until July 1865.

Signature	Signature with rank	Pre & post War DS	War Dated DS	Pre & post War ALS	War Dated ALS
$70	$165	$	$278	$156	$

Z

Ziegler, George Milton, 1834 - 1912   Union Officer, Bvt. Gen'l

Colonel, 3rd Ohio Cavalry.

Signature	Signature with rank	Pre & post War DS	War Dated DS	Pre & post War ALS	War Dated ALS
$35	$	$	$78	$	$

Zinn, George, 1842 - 76   Union Officer, Bvt. Gen'l

Captain, AAAG, Staff of Brig. Gen. Samuel S. Carroll, Lt. Col., 84th PA. Infantry, Colonel, 57th PA Infantry.

Signature	Signature with rank	Pre & post War DS	War Dated DS	Pre & post War ALS	War Dated ALS
$20	$35	$	$67	$	$

Zollicoffer, Felix Kirk, 1812-62   Confederate Brigadier General

Newspaper editor, fought in Seminole War, U.S. Congressman, and Whig political power in the State of Tenn., was killed 19 January 1862 at Mill Spring, Ky. by a volley of musketry from a Union regiment.

Signature	Signature with rank	Pre War DS	War Dated DS	Pre War ALS	War Dated ALS
$350	$550	$	$1,500	$675	$

ALS, 1845, Comptroller Office, Nashville, Tenn., 1 pg. in ink, 8 x 10, concerns accounting matters of the state, has a beautiful signature, "Very respectfully, F. K. Zollicoffer, Comtr." LR Sept. 1993 $600.

S, Clipped signature, bold. SK Feb. 1994 $350.

-, Return address on a prewar cover. JH Aug. 1993 $300.

Misc.

P, CDV, Full standing view, in uniform. Below image 'Entered according to Act of Congress in the year 1862, by M.B. Brady ..." B/M Brady. SK Jan. 1994 $150.

A Scarce signature.

Zook Samuel Kosciuszko, 1821-63   Union General

Died July 3, 1863 of wounds rec'd at Gettysburg, Pa.

Signature	Signature with rank	Pre War DS	War Dated DS	Pre War ALS	War Dated ALS
$	$	$	$	$	$

A very rare signature.

Zulick, Samuel Morton, 1824 -76   Union Officer, Bvt. Gen'l

Colonel, 29th PA. Infantry, physician.

Signature	Signature with rank	Pre & post War DS	War Dated DS	Pre & post War ALS	War Dated ALS
$20	$	$65	$88	$	$

APPENDIX

Dealers and Auction Houses

The sales individually recorded in this volume are from the auction houses and dealers' catalogs listed below and are designated by code letters.

AL Abraham Lincoln
Book Shop
18 East Chestnut Street
Chicago, Il 60611
Tel: (312) 944-3085

AC Antebellum Covers
P.O. Box 8006
Gaithersburg, MD 20885
Tel: (301) 869-2623

KO Antiques Americana
K. C. Owings, Jr.
P.O. Box 19R
N. Abington, MA 02351

A Antiquities Ltd.
P.O. Box 18659
Atlanta, GA 30326
Tel: (404) 451-2897

CB Catherine Barnes
2031 Walnut Street
Philadelphia, PA 19103
Tel: (215) 854-0175
Fax: (215) 854-0831

RB Robert F. Batcher
1 West Butler Ave.
Ambler, PA 19002
Tel: (215) 643-1430

WRB Walter R. Benjamin
P.O. Box 255
Hunter, N.Y. 12442
Tel: (518) 263-4133

EB Edward N. Bomsey
7317 Farr Street
Annandale, VA 22003
Tel: (703) 642-2040

TC Tom Cardineau
P.O. Box 1255
Sound Beach, NY 11789

C Christie's
502 Park Avenue
New York, NY 10022
Tel: (718) 784-1480

CI Cohasco, Inc.
P.O. Box 821
Yonkers, NY 10702
Tel: (914) 476-8500

HDA Herman Darvick
Autographs Auctions
P.O. Box 467
RockvilleCentre, NY 11571

KHD Kaller Historical Documents
P.O. Box 173
Allenhurst, N.J. 07711
Tel: (908) 774-0222
Fax: (908) 774-9401

BK Brain Katherenes
124 Pickford Avenue
Trenton, NJ 08618
Tel: (609) 530-1350

EC East Coast Books
Merv Slotnick
P.O. Box 849
Wells, ME 04090
Tel: (207) 646-3584

PG Paul & Linda Gibson
P.O. Box 962
Blountville, TN 37617
Tel: (615) 323-2427

JH   Jim Hayes
P.O. Box 12560
James Island, SC 29422
Tel: (803) 795-0732

GH   Gary Hendershott
P.O. Box 22520
Little Rock, AK 72221

HCS   Heritage Collectors'
Society
161 Peddlers Village
Lahaska, PA
Tel: (215) 794-0901

HC   Historical Collections
Mr. John H. Herbert
P.O. Box 31623
Houston, TX 77231-1623
Tel: (713) 723-0296

MBC   McGowan Book Co.
Doug Saunders
P.O. Box 16325
Chapel Hill, N.C. 27516
Tel: (919) 968-1121

DN   F. Don Nidiffer
P.O. Box 8184
Charlottesville, VA 22906
Tel: (804) 296-2067

OCS   Old Colony Shop
Gary D. Eyler, Pres.
222-B South Washington
Alexandria, VA 22314
Tel: (703) 548-8008

PA   Paper Antiquities
P.O. Box 408
Coventry, RI 02816
Tel: (401) 823-8440

BJP   Barb & John Pengelly
502 Madison Avenue
Ft.Washington, PA 19034
Tel: (215) 643-5646

PH   Profiles in History
Mr. Joseph Maddalena
9440 Santa Monica Blvd.
Beverly Hills, CA 90210
Tel: (800) 942-8856

SR   Steven S. Raab
2033 Walnut Street
Philadelphia, PA 19103
Tel: (215) 446-6193
Fax: (215) (72-8150

KWR Kenneth W. Rendell
989-P Madison Ave.
New York, NY 10021
Tel: (212) 717-1776

RWA Remember When Antiquities
P.O. Box 629
Acton, Maine 04001

JR   Joseph Rubinfine
505 South Flagler Drive
W. Palm Beach, FL 33401
Tel: (407) 659-7077

MS   Michael Saks
2 Catalpa
Providence, RI 02906
Tel: (401) 272-6318

SA   Seaport Autographs
6 Brandon Lane
Mystic, CT 06355
Tel: (203) 572-8441

RWS Richard W. Spellman
Old & Rare Historical
Newspapers
610 Monticello Drive
Bricktown, NJ 08723
Tel: (908) 477-2413

RS   Rex Stark
49 Wethersfield Rd.
Bellingham, MA 02019

SR Sergeant Kirkland's
912 Lafayette Blvd.
P.O. Box 7171
Fredericksburg,VA 22401
Tel: (703) 899-5565
Fax: (703) 899-5565

SAR Robert A. Siegel Galleries
Park Ave. Tower, 17th Fl.
65 East 55th Street
New York, N. Y. 10022
Tel: (212) 753-6421
Fax: (212) 753-6429

JS James Smalldon -
Americana
1 Main Street
Jackson, CA 95642
Tel: (209) 223-4023

BS Barry A. Smith
1707 Brookcliff Drive
Greensboro, NC 27408
Tel: (919) 288-4375

RMS R.M. Smythe Auctions
26 Broadway
New York, NY 10004
Tel: (800) 622-1880
Tel: NY (212) 943-1880
Fax: (212) 908-4047

S Sotheby's
1334 York Avenue
New York, NY 10021

SAG Superior Galleries
9478 W. Olympic Blvd.
Beverly Hills, CA 90212

CS Christophe Stickel
167 Central Avenue
Pacific Grove, CA 93950

SG Swann Galleries
104 E. 25th St.
New York, NY 10010
Tel: (212) 254-4710

OP The Old Paperphiles
P.O. Box 135
Tiverton, R.I. 02878
Tel: (401) 624-9420

TP Theme Prints, Ltd.
P.O. Box 123
Bayside, NY 11361
Tel: (718) 225-4067

VCS Vintage Cover Story
P.O. Box 975
Burlington, N.C. 27215
Tel: (910) 570-2810
Fax: (910) 570-2748

UA University Archives
Mr. John Reznikoff
600 Summer Street
Stamford, Ct. 06901
Tel: (800) 237-5692
Fax: (203) 348-3560

W Waverly Auctions
7649 Old Georgetown Rd
Bethesda, MD 20814

DZ David Zullo
18779 B North Frederick Rd.
Gaithersburg, MD 20879

USEFUL REFERENCE BOOKS

The following list of books has been kept brief. There are many fine books on the War Between the States, but few deal with document collecting and preservation. The following books are just a few recommended titles.

Appleton's Cyclopedia of American Biography, 6 Vols., New York, 1886-89.

Boatner, Mark M., **The Civil War Dictionary.**

Callahan, Edward W., **List of Officers of the Navy of the United States and of the Marine Corps from 1775 to 1900.**

Carroll, John M., **Register of Officers of the Confederate States Navy, 1861 - 1865.**

Cox, Richard J., **Archives & Manuscripts Administration, A Basic Annotated Bibliography.**

Crute, Joseph H., **Confederate Staff Officers, 1861 - 1865.**

Davis, William C., **The Confederate General, 6 vols. National Historical Society.**

Hall, Charles B., **Military Record of General Officers of the Confederate States of America.**

Hall, Virginius C., **Portraits in the Collection of the Virginia Historical Society.**

Hamilton, Charles, **American Autographs, 2 vols.**

Hamilton, Charles, **Signatures of America.**

Hamilton, Charles, **Collecting Autographs and Manuscripts.**

Hamilton, Charles, **Great Forgers and Famous Fakes.**

Hayes, Jim, **War Between The States, Autographs & Biographical Sketches.**

Heitman, Francis Bernard, **Historical Register and Dictionary of the U. S. Army 2 vols.**

Hunt, Roger, **Brevet Generals in Blue.**

Hyder, Max, **Matting, Mounting & Framing Art, A Practical Guide for Professional Results.**

Keefe, Laurence E., **The Life of a Photograph.**

Marquis, A. N., **Who was who in America - Historical Volume 1607 - 1896.**

Phillips, David G., **Confederate States of America Stampless Cover Catalog.**

Porter, David D., **Naval History of the Civil War.**

Powell, William H., **Officers of the Army & Navy (Regular) who served in the Civil War.**

Reese, Michael II, **Autographs of the Confederacy.**

Reilly, James M., **Care & Identification of 19th Century Photographic Prints.**

Ritzenthaler, Mary Lynn, **Admin. of Photographic Collections.**

Seagrave, Ronald R., **Civil War Autographs & Manuscripts, Prices Current 1992.**

Sharp & Dunnigan, **The Congressional medal of Honor.**

Spencer, James, **Civil War Generals.**

Vrzalik, Larry F. & Minor, Michael, **From the President's Pen: An Illustrated Guide To Presidential Autographs.**

Wakelyn, John L., **Biographical Dictionary of the Confederacy.**

Warner, Ezra J., **Biographical Register of the Confederate Congress.**

Warner, Ezra J., **Generals in Blue, Lives of the Union Commanders.**

Warner, Ezra J., **Generals in Gray, Lives of the Confederate Commanders .**